Developments in Aquaculture and Fisheries Science, 9

WATER QUALITY MANAGEMENT FOR POND FISH CULTURE

DEVELOPMENTS IN AQUACULTURE AND FISHERIES SCIENCE

Developments in Aquaculture and Fisheries Science, 9

WATER QUALITY MANAGEMENT FOR POND FISH CULTURE

CLAUDE E. BOYD

Department of Fisheries and Allied Aquacultures, Agricultural Experiment Station, Auburn University, Alabama, U.S.A.

ELSEVIER SCIENTIFIC PUBLISHING COMPANY
Amsterdam — Oxford — New York 1982

ELSEVIER SCIENCE PUBLISHERS B.V.
Molenwerf 1
P.O. Box 211, 1000 AE Amsterdam, The Netherlands

Distributors for the United States and Canada:

ELSEVIER SCIENCE PUBLISHING COMPANY INC.
52, Vanderbilt Avenue
New York, NY 10017

First edition 1982
Second impression 1984

Library of Congress Cataloging in Publication Data

Boyd, Claude E.
    Water quality management for pond fish culture.

    (Developments in aquaculture and fisheries science ;
9)
    Includes bibliographical references and indexes.
    1. Fish-culture--Water supply. 2. Fish ponds.
3. Water quality management. I. Title. II. Series.
SH151.B79   639.3'11   81-19442
ISBN 0-444-42054-1   AACR2

ISBN 0-444-42054-1 (Vol. 9)
ISBN 0-444-41709-5 (Series)

Printed in The Netherlands

Emergency aeration of ponds. Upper: paddle wheel aerator. Lower: Crisafulli
pump with sprayer.

PREFACE

My earlier book, "Water Quality in Warmwater Fish Ponds", provides a discussion
of the basic principles of water quality, gives a condensed treatment of water
quality management in ponds, and contains directions for making selected water
quality determinations. It was written as a text for a college course in water
quality for fisheries students and as a practical guide to water quality for
fisheries biologists and for fish farmers. The present book goes beyond "Water
Quality in Warmwater Fish Ponds" in that it is an intensive treatment of water
quality management in pond fish culture written for researchers and graduate
students, and for biologists responsible for linking research to fish farming.
The presentation is as straightforward and simple as possible, but the reader is
presumed to have a basic understanding of limnology and equilibrium chemistry and
to be generally aware of the principles of applied ecology. Nevertheless, much
of the practical information is given in a form that fish farmers can appreciate.

I relied heavily on studies of water quality that were conducted in ponds in
the southeastern United States and especially at the Fisheries Research Unit,
Auburn University. Much of the text deals with water quality problems encountered
either in the production of sunfish and largemouth bass for sport fishing or in
the commercial production of channel catfish. However, the water quality problems
common in these two types of fish culture also occur frequently in other kinds
of fish culture. This approach prevented me from extending beyond my experience,
but it requires the reader to make certain generalizations in applying the information to other fish cultures.

Research on water quality management in fisheries is in its infancy. Most
research has been conducted in the past 10 years, but there is a growing aware-
ness of the importance of water quality management in fish culture. Therefore,
this book deals primarily with the "state of the art"; hence, it raises more
questions than it answers. I hope that the book will provide useful information
for managers and stimulate researchers to delve for better methods of improving
water quality in ponds.

A number of people provided valuable assistance in the preparation of this
book, and I am grateful to them:

Bill Hollerman read the manuscript several times in search of errors; he also
helped prepare the reference lists and indexes.

Marty Armstrong, Jay Shelton, and Mike McGee also searched the manuscript
for errors. Marty Armstrong prepared most of the drawings.

My wife, Glenda, typed the manuscript. The book would not have been possible
without her help.

CONTENTS

Chapter 1

INTRODUCTION

1.1   THE BASIS FOR FISH PRODUCTION

As with all types of animal production, the production of fish originates with solar radiation. Energy in solar radiation is captured as chemical energy in carbohydrate by the photosynthetic reaction of green plants:

$$6 \; CO_2 + 6 \; H_2O \rightarrow C_6H_{12}O_6 + 6 \; O_2$$

Photosynthesis is the source of essentially all organic matter and biologically available energy. Of course, plants require a number of inorganic nutrients in addition to carbon dioxide and water for growth. These include nitrogen, phosphorus, sulfur, potassium, calcium, magnesium, iron, manganese, zinc, copper, and sometimes others. Some of the carbohydrate produced in photosynthesis is used by plants in respiration — a process that is essentially the reverse of photosynthesis. In respiration carbohydrate is oxidized to carbon dioxide and water, with the release of energy that can be used in biochemical reactions to do work. Much of the remaining carbohydrate from photosynthesis is synthesized by plants into an array of organic compounds: starch, cellulose, pectin, lignin, amino acids, proteins, nucleic acids, fats, waxes, pigments, oils, vitamins, etc. These compounds are used to construct plant tissues or for other vital functions.

Plants are the only source of energy and organic matter for animals. The carbonaceous compounds built up by plants are required by animals as energy sources and as essential biochemicals for growth and maintenance. Hence, photosynthesis and biochemical assimilation by plants are linked to animal production. Further, microbial organisms without the capacity for photosynthesis utilize dead plant and animal material for food — disease producing microorganisms may use living tissue for food.

The oxygen evolved in photosynthesis is used in respiration to oxidize organic material fixed in photosynthesis and to release the carbon and energy stored in carbohydrate. In turn, carbon dioxide released in respiration may be used once again as a reactant in photosynthesis. Some of the energy released in respiration is used to do biological work, but ultimately all of the energy that is released in respiration is lost to the environment as heat. All life depends upon the input of energy from the sun and upon the cyclic transformations of carbon and oxygen (Fig. 1.1). The management of these transformations to produce human food is the goal of fish culture and of agriculture in general.

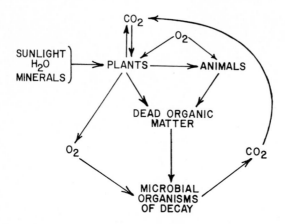

Fig. 1.1. Cyclic transformations of carbon and oxygen in ecological systems.

1.2 TYPES OF FISHERIES

Fisheries may be divided into three broad types. In the first type, fish are simply harvested from natural waters. Certain management procedures may be utilized: regulation of fishing gear, restriction on harvest, stocking of new species, pollution abatement, etc. However, the basic fertility of the environment ultimately regulates production. This type of fishery is not agriculture and is comparable to hunting. As with hunting, the yield of food per unit of surface area is low. In the second type of fishery, selected species are stocked in natural waters or impoundments, and fertilizers are applied to stimulate primary productivity. Greater abundance of fish food organisms resulting from higher levels of primary productivity enhances fish yields. Food webs are simple in the culture of plankton-feeding fish but complex when fish feed upon insects and other fish (Fig. 1.2). This type of fish culture is true agriculture and is similar to the terrestrial practice of fertilizing pastures to favor more forage for greater production of livestock. The third type of fishery involves stocking desirable species and supplying feed to increase fish production above that possible in fertilized ponds. The amount of water required to produce a given quantity of fish is greatly reduced by this method. However, agricultural land is required for the production of the fish feed. This method of fish culture is analogous to the production of livestock in feed lots.

1.3 GOALS OF WATER QUALITY MANAGEMENT

In water quality management, we regulate environmental conditions so that they are within a desirable range for survival and growth of fish. In natural bodies of water, fish occur in relatively low density and often in large expanses of

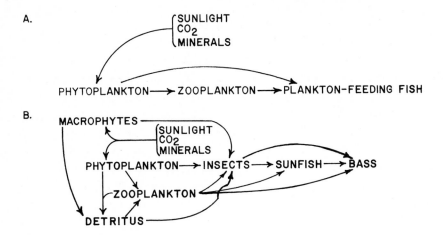

Fig. 1.2. A. Food web for plankton-feeding fish. B. Food web for fish that feed on a variety of organisms.

water. In a natural fishery, it may be necessary to prevent human activities from adversely affecting water quality and fish production. Effluents may cause eutrophication resulting in fish kills or changes in dominant species. Aquatic weed infestations may be disasterous to fisheries. Agricultural runoff may contain chemicals toxic to fish. Recently, acid precipitation resulting from the increasing use of fossil fuels, especially coal, has acidified natural waters and reduced fish production in certain regions. Natural bodies of water normally serve a multitude of purposes and water quality management is usually directed towards improving the entire ecology rather than just improving the fishery.

In waters used for fish culture, production is increased by using either fertilizers, fish feeds, or occasionally both. In waters where fertilizers are used, water quality management usually involves manipulation of nutrient budgets to increase plankton production for greater fish growth. Some waters are too acidic and must be limed before fertilizers are used. Pond waters may be so turbid that light penetration is inadequate for fertilizer nutrients to increase photosynthesis. Water exchange rates may be so high that fertilizer nutrients are flushed from ponds before they can have a favorable influence on plankton production. The proper grade and application rate for fertilizers must be selected. For example, if only phosphorus is needed to stimulate plankton growth, it is wasteful to use a fertilizer containing nitrogen, phosphorus, and potassium. Excessive applications of nutrients in fertilizer encourage over-abundance of plankton and dissolved oxygen problems may occur. Insufficient applications of fertilizer may result in low levels of turbidity, so that light penetrates to the bottom resulting in aquatic weed infestations.

The intensification of fish culture through the use of high stocking and

4

feeding rates can lead to severe water quality problems. Although fish eat most of the feed applied, a great percentage of the dietary intake is excreted into the water as metabolic wastes. These wastes include carbon dioxide, ammonia, phosphorus, and other plant nutrients that stimulate plankton production. Ammonia is directly toxic to fish, and some of the ammonia may serve as a substrate for the production of nitrite that is also highly toxic. Carbon dioxide in high concentration interferes with the utilization of dissolved oxygen. Thus, as the feeding rate increases, the abundance of plankton and the concentrations of certain toxic metabolites increase. Large densities of plankton in ponds cause large imbalances in dissolved oxygen budgets, which may lead to poor growth or even death of fish. Many other water quality problems occasionally occur in intensive fish culture, but excessive production of plankton, low dissolved oxygen, and toxic metabolites are usually the most important. Careful attention to water quality problems is an absolute necessity in intensive fish culture. No matter how much care is taken in constructing ponds, stocking, feeding, and parasite and disease control, all will be to no avail if the large crop of fish dies before harvest because of dissolved oxygen depletion or some other water quality problem.

1.4 RELATIONSHIP TO ECONOMICS

Each management input in fish culture has both an effect and a cost. For example, fertilizers may be used to increase fish yields, but fertilizers are costly. Obviously, the value of the increase in yield resulting from fertilization must exceed the cost of the fertilizer or fertilization is not economically

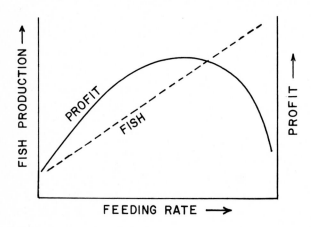

Fig. 1.3. Relationships among feeding rates, fish production, and profits.

feasible. Likewise, feeds may be applied to increase fish production. The increase in yield must have an economic value greater than the feed. In addition feeding results in poorer water quality, so as feeding rates increase, water quality deteriorates and procedures for preventing water quality-related fish kills must be implemented. If water quality is maintained through aeration, water exchange, or some other procedure, extremely high levels of fish production may be achieved. Unfortunately, the cost of maintaining adequate water quality will increase with increasing feeding rates until a point of diminishing returns is reached (Fig. 1.3). Thus, from an economic standpoint maximum production is not necessarily the most favorable level of production.

The cost effectiveness of management procedures must be carefully considered. What is possible in research may not necessarily be feasible or even economically rewarding in practical application. Far too little emphasis has been placed upon the economics of water quality management, and fish farmers often have a poor understanding of monetary benefits of a given management procedure. Likewise, researchers are often so intrigued by the scientific aspects of their endeavors that they do not consider the economic practicality of their findings.

Chapter 2

WATER QUALITY

2.1   INTRODUCTION

In the broadest sense, water quality is determined by a myriad of biological, physical, and chemical variables that affect the desirability of water for any particular use. In fish culture, water quality is usually defined as the suitability of water for the survival and growth of fish, and it is normally governed by only a few variables. Most fish culturists are aware of these variables and are acquainted with relationships between them and fish production. However, a brief review of some salient features of water quality will be helpful to most readers.

2.2   CONSTITUENTS OF POND WATER

Natural waters contain gases, inorganic ions, and organic substances in solution and particulate substances (inorganic and organic, living and dead) in suspension. The distinction between dissolved matter and particulate matter is somewhat arbitrary, being based on whether or not a substance can be removed by filtration. The gases nitrogen, oxygen, and carbon dioxide are the most abundant in natural water, but un-ionized ammonia, hydrogen sulfide, and methane may reach significant concentrations under certain conditions. Un-ionized silicic acid and calcium, magnesium, sodium, potassium, bicarbonate, carbonate, chloride, and sulfate ions contribute most of the weight of inorganic solutes in water (Table 2.1). However, natural waters also contain small concentrations of many other inorganic ions, some of which are listed in Table 2.1. Dissolved organic substances include a wide variety of compounds that were originally synthesized by either the pond biota or the biota of

TABLE 2.1

Concentrations of elements in a water sample from a pond located on soils of the Alabama prairies.

Variable	mg/l	Variable	mg/l	Variable	mg/l
Calcium	20.2	Sulfate	4.3	Iron	0.12
Magnesium	1.5	Chloride	6.8	Manganese	0.01
Potassium	1.5	Silica	10.1	Zinc	0.005
Sodium	4.3	Nitrate	0.15	Copper	0.004
Bicarbonate	61.1	Ammonium	0.21	Boron	0.05
Carbonate	2.0	Phosphate	0.008		

the watershed. Some examples of dissolved organic substances are amino acids, proteins, sugars, fatty acids, vitamins, and tannic acid. Particulate organic matter is comprised of bacteria, phytoplankton, zooplankton, and the decaying remains of organisms; particulate inorganic matter consists of fine, suspended soil particles.

Waters may be categorized according to concentrations of particular groups of constituents defined below:

Total solids: A water sample is evaporated to dryness, and the weight of the residue, usually in milligrams per liter, is termed the total solids concentration. For practical purposes, total solids represent all dissolved and particulate material except gases.

Total volatile solids: This variable is the weight loss upon ignition at 550°C of the residue from the total solids analysis. Total volatile solids are a measure of the dissolved and particulate organic matter.

Dissolved solids: A water sample is filtered, usually with a filter that retains most particles smaller than 0.5-1 μ, and the filtrate is evaporated to dryness. For practical purposes, the weight of the residue represents the concentration of dissolved substances, excluding gases.

Dissolved volatile solids: The residue from the dissolved solid analysis is ignited at 550°C and the weight loss is determined. This measurement indicates the concentration of dissolved organic substances.

Particulate matter: The weight of dry material retained after passing a water sample through a fine filter is the total particulate matter. This variable may also be estimated by subtracting dissolved solids from total solids.

Particulate organic matter: This variable may be determined as the weight loss upon ignition at 550°C of the dry material retained on the filter used in the particulate matter analysis or by subtracting dissolved volatile solids from total volatile solids.

To further elucidate the gross characterization of water, consider the following example. A 100-ml aliquot of a water sample is poured into a tared evaporating dish (50.2025 g) and evaporated to dryness at 102°C. The weight of the dish and residue after cooling is 50.2125 g. The dish and residue are heated at 550°C and after cooling weigh 50.2100 g. A second aliquot of the water sample is passed through a fine glass fiber filter; 100 ml of the resulting filtrate are poured into a second tared evaporating dish (49.7035 g); the filtrate is evaporated at 102°C. After cooling, the weight of the second dish and residue is 49.7115 g. The second dish and residue are heated to 550°C and after cooling weigh 49.7104 g. The appropriate calculations follow:

Total solids (evaporation, first dish)
50.2125 g - 50.2025 g = 0.0100 g or 10 mg/100 ml or 100 mg/l

Total volatile solids (ignition, first dish)
50.2125 g - 50.2100 g = 0.0025 g or 2.5 mg/100 ml or 25 mg/l

Dissolved solids (evaporation, second dish)
49.7115 g - 49.7035 g = 0.0080 g or 8.0 mg/100 ml or 80 mg/l

Dissolved volatile solids (ignition, second dish)
49.7115 g - 49.7104 g = 0.0011 g or 1.1 mg/100 ml or 11 mg/l

Particulate matter (total solids - dissolved solids)
100 mg/l - 80 mg/l = 20 mg/l

Particulate organic matter (total volatile solids - dissolved volatile solids)
25 mg/l - 11 mg/l = 14 mg/l

Thus, the sample contained 100 mg/l of total dissolved and suspended substances
(exclusive of gases), 25 mg/l of which were organic in nature. Dissolved substances accounted for 80 mg/l of the total solids, 11 mg/l of which were or organic
material. The particulate matter accounted for 20 mg/l of the total solids, and
14 mg/l of the particulate matter were organic substances.

The simplicity of the gross analyses is obvious, and the data obtained are often
informative. For example, high values for dissolved solids indicate waters with
large concentrations of solutes. If these waters have low concentrations of volatile dissolved solids, they are highly mineralized. On the other hand, waters
with high concentrations of total solids and low concentrations of total volatile
and dissolved solids contain large amounts of suspended inorganic matter. Waters
from fish ponds will vary in solids concentrations depending upon degree of mineralization, amount of suspended clay, and abundance of plankton. Measurements of
dissolved solids and particulate organic matter, which indicate the total concentration of dissolved ions and the total concentration of suspended organic matter,
respectively, have been more widely used in fish culture than the other analyses
of solids.

2.3   CHEMICAL EQUILIBRIUM

Many chemical reactions in natural water stop before all of the reactants are
converted to products. An equilibrium state is reached in which there is a
definite ratio of reactants and products:

aA + bB → cC + dD + eE.

If the reactants A and B are combined, the products C, D, and E are formed. However, a back reaction occurs in which C, D, and E form A and B. Therefore, at equilibrium there will be a mixture of products and reactants. The coefficients a, b, c, d, and e represent the proportions in which the substances combine. There is a definite mathematical relationship at equilibrium between the concentrations of substances on each side of the equation. The product of the activities (in moles per liter) of the products, each raised to the power indicated by its numerical coefficient, divided by the product of the activities of the reactants, each also raised to the power indicated by its numerical coefficient, equals a constant at a given temperature. For a gas, concentrations are expressed in atmospheres of pressure. A mathematical definition of equilibrium is:

$$\frac{(C)^c (D)^d (E)^e}{(A)^a (B)^b} = K$$

where K = the equilibrium constant and the parentheses denote activities of substances. The addition or removal of any product or reactant will disrupt the equilibrium. However, the reactants and products will undergo rearrangement, and the new concentrations of reactants and products will be such that the value of the equilibrium constant will remain unchanged.

Reactions discussed in the following chapters generally involve inorganic ions. The activities of inorganic ions may be calculated from measured molar concentrations as follows:

$$a = (\gamma)(M)$$

where a = activity in moles per liter; γ = the activity coefficient (unitless); M = measured molar concentration. For dilute solutions, the activity of a single ion may be calculated with the Debye-Huckel equation:

$$-\log \gamma_i = \frac{(A)(z_i)^2 (I)^{\frac{1}{2}}}{1 + (B)(S_i)(I)^{\frac{1}{2}}}$$

where γ_i = the activity coefficient of the ion; A = 0.5085 at 25°C; z_i = charge of the ion; B = 0.3281 at 25°C; S_i = effective size of the ion (Table 2.2); I = ionic strength. The ionic strength of a solution is a measure of the strength of the electrostatic field caused by its ions. Ionic strength varies with the concentrations and charges of the ions and may be calculated from the following expression:

$$I = \frac{\Sigma(M_i)(z_i)^2}{2}$$

where M_i = the measured molar concentration.

TABLE 2.2
Values for ion size (S_i) for use in the Debye-Huckel equation (Hem, 1970).

Ion	S_i
OH^-, HS^-, K^+, Cl^-, NO_2^-, NO_3^-, NH_4^+	3
Na^+, PO_4^{3-}, SO_4^{2-}, HPO_4^{2-}, HCO_3^-, $H_2PO_4^-$	4
CO_3^{2-}	5
Ca^{2+}, Cu^{2+}, Zn^{2+}, Mn^{2+}, Fe^{2+}	6
Mg^{2+}	8
Al^{3+}, Fe^{3+}, H^+	9

The calculation of activities will be demonstrated for a solution with the following composition: HCO_3^- = 63 mg/1, SO_4^{2-} = 4.2 mg/1, Cl^- = 2.6 mg/1, Ca^{2+} = 15 mg/1, Mg^{2+} = 4.3 mg/1, Na^+ = 2.6 mg/1, and K^+ = 1.0 mg/1. First, the concentrations of ions are converted to moles per liter by dividing the concentrations of each ion by its molecular weight. For HCO_3^-, this calculation is:

0.063 g/1 ÷ 61 g/mole = 0.00103 mole/1 (M).

Concentrations of other ions follow: SO_4^{2-} = 0.000044 M, Cl^- = 0.000073 M, Ca^{2+} = 0.00037 M, Mg^{2+} = 0.00018 M, Na^+ = 0.00011 M, and K^+ = 0.000026 M. The ionic strength is:

$$I = \tfrac{1}{2}\Sigma[0.00103(1)^2 + 0.000044(2)^2 + 0.000073(1)^2 + 0.00037(2)^2 + 0.00018(2)^2 + 0.00011(1)^2 + 0.000026(1)^2]$$
$$I = 0.0018 \text{ M}$$

The activity coefficient for HCO_3^- is:

$$-\log\gamma_i = \frac{(0.5085)(1)^2(0.0018)^2}{1 + (0.3281)(4)(0.0018)^{\frac{1}{2}}}$$

$$-\log\gamma_i = \frac{0.0216}{1.0557} = 0.0205$$

$$\gamma_i = 0.954$$

The activity is:

$$a_{HCO_3^-} = (0.954)(0.00103)$$

$$a_{HCO_3^-} = 0.00098 \text{ M}$$

By similar computations, the activities of the other ions are as follows: $a_{SO_4^{2-}} = 0.000036$ M, $a_{Cl^-} = 0.000070$ M, $a_{Ca^{2+}} = 0.00031$ M, $a_{Mg^{2+}} = 0.00015$ M, $a_{Na^+} = 0.00010$ M, and $a_{K^+} = 0.000025$ M.

The calculation of activities of ions is necessary because electrostatic effects between ions reduce their effective concentrations. At infinite dilution, the activity coefficient would be 1.0, and the measured molarity would be equal to the activity. However, at greater solute concentrations, electrostatic interactions increase causing a reduction in the effective concentrations of the ions. For example, 0.0003 M Ca^{2+} has an activity of 0.00026 M in a solution with I = 0.001 M but an activity of only 0.00020 M if I = 0.01 M.

Although the above method is widely used in calculating activities of single ions, a large fraction of the cations and anions are strongly attracted to each other and act as if they are un-ionized. Ions that are strongly attracted in this manner are called ion-pairs. To illustrate, Ca^{2+} and SO_4^{2-} form the ion-pair $CaSO_4^0$, Ca^{2+} and HCO_3^- form $CaHCO_3^+$, and K^+ and SO_4^{2-} form KSO_4^-. The degree to which ions form ion-pairs may be handled as follows:

$$CaHCO_3^+ = Ca^{2+} + HCO_3^-$$

$$\frac{(Ca^{2+})(HCO_3^-)}{(CaHCO_3^+)} = K$$

The activity coefficients of ion-pairs are taken as unity. Equilibrium constants for ion-pairs formed by major ions in natural water are given in Table 2.3.

Analytical methods (specific ion electrodes excluded) do not distinguish between free ions and ion-pairs. Thus, sulfate in solution might be distributed among

SO_4^{2-}, $CaSO_4^0$, $MgSO_4^0$, KSO_4^-, and $NaSO_4^-$. The total sulfate concentration may be

TABLE 2.3
Equilibrium constants at 25°C and zero ionic strength for ion-pairs in natural waters (Adams, 1971).

Reaction	Equilibrium constant (K)
$CaSO_4^0 = Ca^{2+} + SO_4^{2-}$	5.25×10^{-3}
$CaCO_3^0 = Ca^{2+} + CO_3^{2-}$	6.3×10^{-4}
$CaHCO_3^+ = Ca^{2+} + HCO_3^-$	5.5×10^{-2}
$MgSO_4^0 = Mg^{2+} + SO_4^{2-}$	5.88×10^{-3}
$MgCO_3^0 = Mg^{2+} + CO_3^{2-}$	4.0×10^{-4}
$MgHCO_3^+ = Mg^{2+} + HCO_3^-$	6.9×10^{-2}
$NaSO_4^- = Na^+ + SO_4^{2-}$	2.4×10^{-1}
$NaCO_3^- = Na^+ + CO_3^{2-}$	5.35×10^{-2}
$NaHCO_3^0 = Na^+ + HCO_3^-$	1.78
$KSO_4^- = K^+ + SO_4^{2-}$	1.1×10^{-1}

measured; SO_4^{2-} can only be calculated. Since actual ionic concentrations are always less than measured ionic concentrations in solutions containing ion-pairs, ionic activities calculated directly from analytical data — as done above — are not exact. Adams (1971) developed a method for correcting for ion-pairing in the calculation of ionic activities and demonstrated a considerable effect of ion-pairing on ionic strength, ionic concentrations, and ionic activities in soil solutions. The method of correcting for ion-pairing involves: (1) using measured ionic concentrations to calculate ionic strength assuming no ion-pairing, (2) calculating ionic activities assuming no ion-pairing, (3) calculating ion-pair concentrations with respective ion-pair equations, equilibrium constants, and initial estimates of ionic activities, (4) revising ionic concentrations and ionic strength by subtracting the calculated ion-pair concentrations, and (5) repeating steps 2, 3, and 4 until all ionic concentrations and activities remain unchanged with succeeding calculations. Adams (1971, 1974) discusses all aspects of the calculations and gives examples. The iterative procedure is tedious and slow unless it is programmed into a computer.

Boyd (1981) calculated activities of major ions in samples of natural water with analytical data uncorrected for ion-pairing and analytical data corrected for ion-

pairing. Ion-pairing had little effect on ionic activity calculations for weakly
mineralized water (I < 0.002 M). However, for more strongly mineralized waters,
ionic activities corrected for ion-pairing were appreciably smaller than uncorrected ionic activities. As a general rule, if waters contain less than 500 mg/l of
total dissolved ions, ion-pairing may be ignored in calculating ionic activities
unless highly accurate data are required.

The formation of ion-pairs is not restricted to the major ions. Equilibrium
constants for ion-pairs involving aluminum, boron, phosphorus, iron, manganese,
ammonium, and zinc are presented by Adams (1971). Schindler (1967) presented
information on the formation of soluble inorganic complexes (ion-pairs) of iron,
manganese, zinc, and copper with carbonate and hydroxide. A large percentage of
the total iron, manganese, zinc, and copper exists as ion-pairs; concentrations of
free ions are normally less than 5-10% of the total.

2.4   RELATIONSHIPS AMONG IONS

Because of the principle of electrical neutrality, the milliequivalents per liter
of anions in water must equal the milliequivalents per liter of cations. The milliequivalents per liter of major anions and of major cations in water will very nearly
balance (Table 2.4) because other ions are usually present at such low concentration
that they account for little of the total ionic charge. The anion-cation balance
principle is useful to fish culturists because it allows an estimate of the accuracy
of a water analysis. If the anion and cation concentrations in an analysis of the
major ions in a sample do not agree reasonably well, the analysis is in error. To
illustrate, a reference to the literature indicates that a stream serving as the
water supply for a series of fish ponds contains 0 mg/l CO_3^{2-}, 40 mg/l HCO_3^-,
10 mg/l SO_4^{2-}, 12 mg/l Cl^-, 60 mg/l Ca^{2+}, 10 mg/l Mg^{2+}, 80 mg/l K^+, and 12 mg/l Na^+.
The anion-cation balance is as follows:

		Anion (meq/l)	Cation (meq/l)
40 mg/l HCO_3^-	÷ 61 mg/meq	0.66	
10 mg/l SO_4^{2-}	÷ 48 mg/meq	0.21	
12 mg/l Cl^-	÷ 35.5 mg/meq	0.34	
60 mg/l Ca^{2+}	÷ 20 mg/meq		3.00
10 mg/l Mg^{2+}	÷ 12.2 mg/meq		0.82
80 mg/l K^+	÷ 39.1 mg/meq		2.05
12 mg/l Na^+	÷ 23 mg/meq		0.52
		1.21	6.39

The analysis is obviously in error because of the great disparity between the
summations of anion and cation concentrations.

TABLE 2.4

Anion-cation balance of four water samples with different degrees of mineral-ization.[a]

Variable	milliequivalents/liter			
	A	B	C	D
Bicarbonate	1.00	0.23	1.56	2.79
Carbonate	0.0	0.0	0.0	0.0
Sulfate	0.09	0.12	21.25	0.12
Chloride	0.19	0.34	2.54	0.11
Calcium	0.98	0.27	18.3	0.28
Magnesium	0.12	0.14	4.50	0.04
Potassium	0.04	0.19	2.61	2.69
Sodium	0.19	0.03	0.12	0.08
Σ Anions	1.28	0.69	25.35	3.02
Σ Cations	1.33	0.63	25.53	3.09

[a]Sample A: Pond on calcareous soil.
Sample B: Pond filled with runoff from a humid coastal forest.
Sample C: Pond in arid region.
Sample D: Pond filled with naturally softened well water.

Because surface waters are usually dilute solutions of alkaline earth bicar-bonates and carbonates, calcium, magnesium, bicarbonate, and carbonate are usually the dominant ions. However, there are some notable exceptions. In arid regions, carbonates and bicarbonates may precipitate from solution as evaporation increases ionic concentrations. Such waters may have relatively large propor-tions of sodium, sulfate, and chloride. Acidic waters in humid, coastal areas are often low in alkaline earth bicarbonates but comparatively enriched in sodium and chloride. Well waters along coastal plains are often softened by exchange of calcium and magnesium in ground water for sodium in solid materials of the aquifer. Ponds filled from these wells may have relatively large concen-trations of sodium and bicarbonate but little calcium and magnesium. Propor-tions of ions in the four types of water described above are illustrated in Table 2.4. Pie diagrams (Fig. 2.1) illustrate the anion-cation principle; they may also be drawn to illustrate degrees of mineralization of different waters.

Within a given climatic area, the degree of mineralization of surface waters reflects the solubilities of minerals in soils and rocks of the drainage basin. Waters in areas of thin, infertile soils are generally less mineralized than those

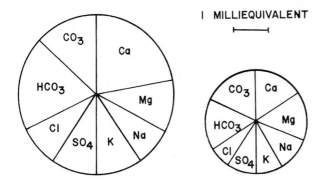

Fig. 2.1. Pie diagrams illustrating the proportions of major ions and the degrees of mineralization for two water samples.

in regions with deep, fertile soils. Waters draining from soils developed from limestone are more highly mineralized than those draining from sandy soils. Data for ponds in Alabama (Arce and Boyd, 1980) demonstrate the influence of surface soils on the mineralization of surface waters (Fig. 2.2). The Limestone Valleys

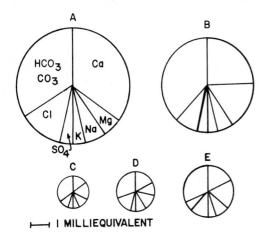

Fig. 2.2. Distribution of major ions and degrees of mineralization in waters from ponds in different soils areas of Alabama: A = Prairies, B = Limestone Valleys and Uplands, C = Piedmont Plateau, D = Coastal Plains, E = Appalachian Plateau. The positioning of the segments representing ionic proportions all correspond to graph A (Arce and Boyd, 1980).

and Uplands and the Prairies contain large areas of soils that developed from weathered limestone. Few soils in the Appalachian Plateau and Coastal Plains, and none in the Piedmont Plateau, developed from limestone. Heavy clay soils are common in the Prairies, but surface soils of the Coastal Plains are frequently sandy. The degree of mineralization increased in the order Piedmont Plateau, Coastal Plains, Appalachian Plateau, Limestone Valleys and Uplands, and Prairies. However, there was remarkably little difference in the proportions of major ions in waters of the different soils areas; all were dilute solutions of alkaline earth carbonates and bicarbonates with low concentrations of sodium, potassium, chloride, and sulfate.

Heavy rainfall in humid climates favors relatively low concentrations of dissolved ions in surface waters. In arid climates, evaporation concentrates ions in surface waters. Waters from wells are usually more concentrated in ions than surface waters because they stand for long periods in close contact with minerals. Total ion concentrations in some representative waters are presented in Table 2.5.

TABLE 2.5

Concentrations of total dissolved ions in samples of water from different sources (Boyd, unpublished).

Source of water	mg/l
River water draining resistant rocks	18
Lakes in region of resistant rocks	20
Pond with watershed of sandy soils	25
Pond with watershed of sandy clay soils	45
Pond with watershed of deep, fertile soils	95
Stream draining calcareous soils	175
Pond with watershed of calcareous soils	127
Pond with deep, clay soils weathered from limestone on watershed	251
Stream in arid region[a]	1,264
Pond in arid region[a]	750
Well water from sand aquifer	75
Well water from limestone aquifer	350

[a]Values for some waters may be much higher.

In general, surface waters in areas of moderate or high rainfall will have total ion concentrations of 20-500 mg/l. In arid regions, total ion concentrations in surface waters often range between 500 and 2,500 mg/l, and even higher values are sometimes encountered. In contrast, sea water contains about 35,000 mg/l of total ions.

The term salinity refers to the total concentration of all dissolved ions in

TABLE 2.6

Equivalent ionic conductance at infinite dilution (ionic strength = 0) and 25°C for selected anions and cations frequently found in natural waters (Sawyer and McCarty, 1967).

Cation	μmho-cm/meq	Anion	μmho-cm/meq
H^+	349.8	OH^-	198.0
Na^+	50.1	HCO_3^-	44.5
K^+	73.5	Cl^-	76.3
Ca^{2+}	59.5	SO_4^{2-}	79.8
Mg^{2+}	53.1		

water. Although it is often impractical to measure concentrations of all ions in water, the ability of water to conduct an electrical current (conductivity) increases as salinity rises. Thus, a conductivity meter may be used to measure conductivity and the conductivity values indicate the relative degrees of salinity. Ions differ in their ability to conduct an electrical current (Table 2.6). Therefore, the relationship between conductivity and salinity depends to some extent upon the proportions of major ions. Specific conductances for fresh waters often range from <25 to >500 μmhos/cm; the dissolved solids content in milligrams per liter can be approximated by multiplying the specific conductance by an empirical factor varying from about 0.55 to 0.9. Sea water has a relatively constant ionic composition and is much more concentrated in ions than fresh water. In estuaries where sea water and fresh water mix, the ionic composition of the water is dominated by the sea water. Conductivity meters can be used in estuaries to estimate salinity directly because these meters often have scales for reading either conductivity or salinity. Fresh waters are more varied in proportions of major ions, so a given conductivity value will usually not corres- pond to a single salinity value. Nevertheless, conductivity provides a useful estimate of salinity in fresh water. Another way of obtaining the approximate salinity is to measure the total dissolved solids concentration. In estuarine water salinity may be estimated from chloride concentration (Swingle, 1969) by the following equation:

Salinity in mg/l = 30 + (1.805)(Chloride in mg/l)

Chloride concentration can be measured by a titrametric procedure or estimated with either a refractometer or a temperature corrected hydrometer.

The osmotic pressure of water increases with increasing salinity. According to McKee and Wolf (1963), the blood of freshwater fishes has an osmotic pressure approximately equal to 6 atmospheres of pressure, or about 7,000 mg/l as sodium chloride; freshwater fish have been able to live well in sea water diluted to this level. For general purposes, McKee and Wolf stated that dissolved solids up to 2,000 mg/l would not harm freshwater fish and other aquatic life. Among inland waters in the United States supporting good mixed fish fauna, about 5% have total dissolved solids concentrations <72 mg/l, about 50% <169 mg/l, and about 95% <400 mg/l. Salinity limits for several species of food fish are presented in Table 2.7.

TABLE 2.7
Highest concentrations of salinity which permit normal survival and growth of some cultured food fish.

Species	Salinity (mg/l)	Reference
Catla catla	Slightly brackish water	Hora and Pillay (1962)
Labeo rohita	Slightly brackish water	Hora and Pillay (1962)
Ctenopharyngodon idella	12,000	Jhingran (1975)
Hypophthalmichthys molitrix	8,000	Jhingran (1975)
Cyprinus carpio	9,000	Clay (1977)
Tilapia aurea	18,900	Clay (1977)
T. nilotica	24,000	Clay (1977)
T. mossambica	30,000	Clay (1977)
Mugil cephanos	14,500	Clay (1977); Fishleson and Popper (1968)
Chanos chanos	32,000	Bardach et al. (1972)
Ictalurus punctatus	11,000	Perry and Avault (1969)

Some species of freshwater fish are sensitive to sudden changes in salinity. Fry might be killed by osmotic imbalance if they were suddenly transferred from 1,000 mg/l salinity to 50 mg/l salinity. Adult fish are usually more tolerant to salinity changes. Sodium chloride may be used to increase salinity in holding facilities and small experimental ponds. It is seldom practical to adjust the salinity of large ponds, except in brackish water ponds where sea water may be introduced by gravity flow or tidal movement.

As a rule, salinity is not normally an important factor in fish culture.

Further, differences in the proportions of major ions do not usually have great effects on pond management. For example, a water with a salinity of 75 mg/l and a predominance of alkaline earth bicarbonates and carbonates can produce just as many fish as a water with a salinity of 500 mg/l that contains an abundant supply of sodium, chloride, and sulfate in addition to alkaline earth carbonates and bicarbonates. Assuming other factors are similar, essentially identical procedures could be used in both ponds to increase fish yields.

2.5   ACID-BASE RELATIONSHIPS
2.5.1   pH

The pH is defined as the negative logarithm of the hydrogen ion activity [1]:

$$pH = -\log (H^+) \tag{2.1}$$

The parentheses in Equation 2.1 denote activity in moles per liter. The concept of pH was developed from the ionization of water:

$$H_2O + H_2O = H_3O^+ + OH^-$$

For simplicity, we will let H^+ represent H_3O^+ and write:

$$H_2O = H^+ + OH^- \tag{2.2}$$

The equilibrium constant for pure water (K_w) at 25°C is 10^{-14}, so:

$$(H^+)(OH^-) = K_w = 10^{-14}$$

From Equation 2.2, each H^+ is balanced by one OH^-, so $(H^+) = (OH^-)$ and by substitution:

$$(H^+)(H^+) = 10^{-14}$$
$$(H^+) = 10^{-7} \text{ or } 0.0000001$$

To prevent having to work with such small numbers, chemists in the early 1900's decided to express the hydrogen ion concentration as the negative logarithm of (H^+). For pure water we obtain:

---

[1] The glass electrodes of pH meters respond to hydrogen ion activity rather than hydrogen ion concentration. Therefore, measured pH values may be converted directly to hydrogen ion activity. Concentrations of hydrogen ions must be converted to activities before calculating pH.

$$pH = - \log(10^{-7}) = 7$$

For any solution, the product $(H^+)(OH^-)$ must equal 10^{-14} at 25°C. Hence, if $(H^+) = 10^{-2}$, we may calculate (OH^-) as follows:

$$(10^{-2})(OH^-) = 10^{-14}$$
$$(OH^-) = 10^{-12}$$

The pH scale is usually shown to extend from 0 to 14, but negative pH values and pH values above 14 are possible. A solution with $(H^+) = 10^1$ has a negative pH:

$$pH = - \log(10^1)$$
$$pH = - 1$$

A solution with $(OH^-) = 10^1$ has a pH above 14:

$$(H^+)(10^1) = 10^{-14}$$
$$(H^+) = 10^{-15}$$
$$pH = - \log(10^{-15})$$
$$pH = 15$$

Although pH 7 is generally taken as the neutral point of water, this convention is not strictly correct except at 25°C where $K_w = 10^{-14}$. Values for K_w at other temperatures (Garrels and Christ, 1964) are presented in Table 2.8. The

TABLE 2.8
Equilibrium constants (K_w) for pure water at different temperatures (Garrels and Christ, 1964).

°C	K_w	°C	K_w
0	0.1139×10^{-14}	20	0.6809×10^{-14}
5	0.1846×10^{-14}	25	1.008×10^{-14}
10	0.2920×10^{-14}	30	1.469×10^{-14}
15	0.4505×10^{-14}	35	2.089×10^{-14}

neutral point of water at 15°C may be calculated as follows:

$$(H^+)(OH^-) = 10^{-14.35}$$

$(H^+)^2 = 10^{-14.35}$
$(H^+) = 10^{-7.175}$
pH = 7.18

Since pH is a negative logarithm, the following procedure must be used to average pH values. Values for pH are converted to hydrogen ion concentrations; hydrogen ion concentrations are averaged; the average hydrogen ion concentration is used to compute the average pH. To illustrate, the average of pH values 7.5, 8.5, 9.0, 9.1, and 10.2 is incorrectly reported as 8.9 when pH values are averaged directly. The correct average pH is:

pH	(H^+)
7.5	3.2 X 10^{-8}
8.5	0.32 X 10^{-8}
9.0	0.1 X 10^{-8}
9.1	0.079 X 10^{-8}
10.2	0.0063 X 10^{-8}
	3.7053 X 10^{-8} ÷ 5 = 0.74 X 10^{-8}

$(H^+) = 7.4$ X 10^{-9}
pH = $- (\log 7.4 + \log 10^{-9}) = - [0.87 + (- 9)]$
pH = 8.13

Most natural waters have pH values of 6.5-9, but there are many exceptions. Factors affecting the pH of pond water will be discussed in the following sections.

The relationship of pH to pond fish culture (Swingle, 1961) is summarized in Fig. 2.3. The acid and alkaline death points for fish are about pH 4 and 11, respectively. However, if waters are more acidic than pH 6.5 or more alkaline than pH 9-9.5 for long periods, reproduction and growth will diminish (Swingle, 1961; Mount, 1973). Problems with pH are not uncommon in fish ponds; in mining areas acid-mine seepage may acidify lakes and streams. Long term acidification of lakes and streams because of acid precipitation is having disastrous effects on fish populations in certain areas of Europe and North America (Beamish et al., 1975).

2.5.2 Carbon dioxide

Although carbon dioxide is highly soluble in water, it is only a minor constituent of the atmosphere and equilibrium concentrations in pure water and

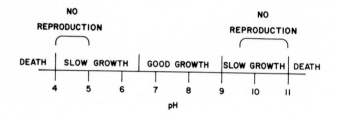

Fig. 2.3. Effect of pH on pond fish (Swingle, 1969).

small (Table 2.9). Carbon dioxide has an acidic reaction in water:

$$H_2O + CO_2 = H_2CO_3$$

$$H_2CO_3 = H^+ + HCO_3^-$$

Less than 1% of the carbon dioxide in water forms carbonic acid and carbonic acid strongly dissociates. Therefore, we may consider carbon dioxide plus carbonic acid as total CO_2 and write:

$$\text{Total } CO_2 + H_2O = H^+ + HCO_3^- \tag{2.3}$$

The equilibrium constant (K_1) for Equation 2.3 at 25°C is $10^{-6.35}$.

TABLE 2.9
Solubility of carbon dioxide in pure water at different temperatures (Hutchinson, 1957).

°C	mg/l[a]	°C	mg/l
0	1.10	20	0.56
5	0.91	25	0.48
10	0.76	30	0.42
15	0.65		

[a]For an atmospheric carbon dioxide content of 0.033%.

Pure water at 25°C has a total carbon dioxide concentration of 0.48 mg/l. The corresponding pH may be calculated using Equation 2.3 as follows:

$(H^+) = (HCO_3^-)$ and $(Total\ CO_2) = 10^{-4.96}\ M$

$$\frac{(H^+)(H^+)}{10^{-4.96}} = 10^{-6.35}$$

$(H^+)^2 = 10^{-11.31}$

$(H^+) = 10^{-5.66}$

pH = 5.66

At greater carbon dioxide concentrations, pH will be less; 30 mg/l carbon dioxide would result in a pH of 4.8. As a general rule, carbon dioxide will not cause pH to fall below 4.5.

Bicarbonate resulting from the dissociation of carbonic acid further dissociates to give carbonate:

$$HCO_3^- = H^+ + CO_3^{2-} \tag{2.4}$$

for which the equilibrium constant (K_2) is $10^{-10.33}$ at 25°C. Because K_2 is small, carbonate concentration is negligible in water containing carbon dioxide. The pH at which carbon dioxide concentration decreases to an analytically undetectable value and carbonate appears in measurable concentration is important for both practical and analytical purposes. At this pH, carbon dioxide and carbonate will be at equally low concentrations, and $(Total\ CO_2) = (CO_3^{2-})$. The pH may be calculated by combining the mass action forms of Equations 2.3 and 2.4:

$$\frac{(H^+)(HCO_3^-)}{(Total\ CO_2)} \times \frac{(H^+)(CO_3^{2-})}{(HCO_3^-)} = 10^{-6.35} \times 10^{-10.33}$$

This expression reduces to:

$$\frac{(H^+)^2(CO_3^{2-})}{(Total\ CO_2)} = 10^{-16.68}$$

Because $(CO_3^{2-}) = (Total\ CO_2)$, we may further reduce the expression:

$(H^+)^2 = 10^{-16.68}$

$(H^+) = 10^{-8.34}$

pH = 8.34

Therefore, for practical purposes, carbon dioxide does not occur above pH 8.3. and carbonate only occurs above this pH.

The distribution of carbon dioxide, bicarbonate, and carbonate at different pH values is given in Fig. 2.4.

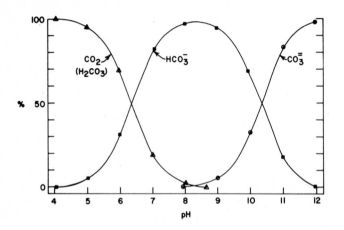

Fig. 2.4. Relationship between mole fractions (%) of CO_2, HCO_3^-, and CO_3^{2-} and pH.

Carbon dioxide is not appreciably toxic to fish; most species will survive for several days in waters containing up to 60 mg/l, provided dissolved oxygen is plentiful (Hart, 1944). When dissolved oxygen concentrations are low, the presence of appreciable carbon dioxide hinders oxygen uptake by fish. Unfortunately, carbon dioxide concentrations are normally quite high when dissolved oxygen concentrations are low (Boyd, 1979a). This results because carbon dioxide is released in respiration and utilized in photosynthesis. When dissolved oxygen is low, photosynthesis is not proceeding rapidly. Therefore, carbon dioxide concentrations rise because carbon dioxide released by respiration is not absorbed by phytoplankton and assimilated into organic matter. Because of the relationship of carbon dioxide to respiration and photosynthesis, carbon dioxide concentrations usually increase during the night and decrease during the day. Particularly high concentrations of carbon dioxide occur in ponds after phytoplankton die-offs, after loss of thermal stratification, and during cloudy weather.

2.5.3 Mineral acidity

Since carbon dioxide cannot make waters more acid than pH 4.5, the occurrence of lower pH values indicates that a stronger acid is present. Some organic acids that occur in water may depress pH below 4.5 (Brosset, 1979). However, mineral acids are usually responsible for excessively low pH. The common mineral acid in natural waters is sulfuric acid which results from the oxidation of iron pyrite (see Chapter 4).

2.5.4   Alkalinity

Natural waters normally contain more bicarbonate than results from the ionization of carbonic acid in waters saturated with carbon dioxide. Carbon dioxide in natural waters reacts with bases in rocks and soils to form bicarbonate as illustrated for calcium carbonate:

$$CaCO_3 + CO_2 + H_2O \ = \ Ca^{2+} + 2 \ HCO_3^-$$

Reactions involving the formation of bicarbonate from carbonate are equilibrium reactions, and a certain amount of carbon dioxide must be present to maintain a given amount of bicarbonate in solution. If the amount of carbon dioxide at equilibrium is increased, more carbonate will dissolve; a decrease in carbon dioxide results in the precipitation of carbonate.

Dilute bicarbonate solutions at equilibrium are weakly alkaline. This results because bicarbonate can act either as a base or as an acid:

$$HCO_3^- + H^+ \ = \ H_2O + CO_2 \tag{2.5}$$

$$HCO_3^- \ = \ H^+ + CO_3^{2-} \tag{2.6}$$

The second reaction (Equation 2.6) cannot proceed any further to the right than the first reaction (Equation 2.5) because any hydrogen ion from the second reaction is used up in the first reaction. Therefore, $(CO_2) = (CO_3^{2-})$ and the pH will be approximately 8.3. To better visualize why a bicarbonate solution at equilibrium is alkaline, consider that it contains both an acid, carbon dioxide, and a base, carbonate, in equal concentrations. Carbonate is a base because it hydrolyzes to give hydroxyl ion:

$$CO_3^{2-} + H_2O \ = \ HCO_3^- + OH^- \tag{2.7}$$

This hydrolysis can be thought of as the removal of hydrogen ion from water. Thus, more water has to dissociate to maintain the K_w, and as a result, the hydroxyl ion concentration will increase relative to the hydrogen ion concentration — pH will rise. More specifically, carbonate is a stronger base

$(K_b = 10^{-3.67})$ than carbon dioxide is an acid $(K_1 = 10^{-6.35})$, and (OH^-) must exceed (H^+) in a bicarbonate solution at equilibrium.

The interdependence of pH, carbon dioxide, bicarbonate, and carbonate has already been illustrated (Fig. 2.4). The primary reason for changes in these variables in fish ponds is changes in carbon dioxide concentrations resulting from photosynthesis and respiration. The effects of changes in carbon dioxide concentrations are readily apparent if Equations 2.5 and 2.6 are combined by addition to yield the following expression:

$$2\ HCO_3^- \ = \ CO_2 + CO_3^{2-} + H_2O; \qquad K = 10^{-3.98}$$

If carbon dioxide is removed, bicarbonate will dissociate to form more carbon dioxide and carbonate. Notice that two bicarbonate ions must dissociate to replace one carbon dioxide molecule and that carbonate will increase. The hydrolysis of carbonate, as illustrated in Equation 2.7, replaces only one bicarbonate ion for each pair of bicarbonate ions that dissociate. This maintains the equilibrium constant as carbon dioxide is removed, but the hydrolysis of carbonate causes pH to rise. Hence, bicarbonate and hydrogen ion must decrease and carbonate and hydroxyl ion must increase as carbon dioxide is removed. Natural waters also contain calcium ions. As the carbonate concentration rises, the solubility product of calcium carbonate may be exceeded, resulting in precipitation:

$$Ca^{2+} + CO_3^{2-} \ = \ CaCO_3; \qquad K = 10^{-8.3}$$

Thus, the precipitation of calcium carbonate will limit the accumulation of carbonate and moderate the rise in pH. For instance, pH will rise much higher in a sodium bicarbonate solution than in a calcium bicarbonate solution during rapid carbon dioxide removal by algae.

Because of the influence of carbon dioxide, the pH of pond waters is lowest near dawn and highest in the afternoon. The diel fluctuation in pH is greatest when phytoplankton growth is rapid. King (1970) noted that early morning pH values gradually increased during the growing season. The conversion of carbon dioxide to organic matter by photosynthesis was greater than the release of carbon dioxide from organic matter by respiration, hence pH increased. Waters with moderate or high bicarbonate concentrations have greater carbon dioxide reserves than waters with low bicarbonate concentrations, so diel pH fluctuations are often less in the former than in the latter.

Changes in carbon dioxide concentrations also result in alterations of the proportions of bicarbonate and carbonate. Waters may contain only bicarbonate in the early morning, but in the afternoon they may contain both carbonate and bicarbonate.

The term total alkalinity refers to the total concentration of bases in water expressed in milligrams per liter of equivalent calcium carbonate. In most waters bicarbonate, carbonate, or both are the predominant bases. The alkalinity determination is carried out in two steps. First, phenolphthalein indicator is added to the sample. If a pink color develops, the pH is above 8.3, and the sample is titrated with standard acid until the pink color is discharged. Next, methyl orange indicator is added, and the sample is titrated with standard acid to the methyl orange end point (pH 4.5). The total amount of acid used in the titration, expressed as equivalent calcium carbonate, represents the total alkalinity. The amount of acid required to titrate to the phenolphthalein end point (pH 8.3), expressed as equivalent calcium carbonate, is the phenolphthalein alkalinity.

Natural waters that contain 40 mg/l or more total alkalinity are considered more productive than waters of lower alkalinity (Moyle, 1945; Mairs, 1966). According to Moyle (1946), the greater productivity of waters of higher alkalinity does not result directly from alkalinity, but rather from phosphorus and other nutrients that increase along with total alkalinity. Relationships between total alkalinity and yields of yellow pikeperch (Stizostedion vitereum) in unfertilized ponds in Minnesota are presented in Table 2.10. Turner (1960) found a relatively

TABLE 2.10
Annual yields of yellow pikeperch (Stizostedion vitereum) in ponds with waters of different total alkalinities (Moyle, 1946).

Total alkalinity (mg/l)	Number of ponds	Average yield (kg/ha)
8-20	7	19
21-40	7	32
41-80	20	71
81-120	15	70
>120	20	54

high positive correlation ($r = 0.67$) between total alkalinity and standing crops of fish in 22 unfertilized farm ponds in Kentucky.

In fertilized fish ponds total alkalinity values in the range of 20-120 mg/l have little effect on fish production (Boyd and Walley, 1975). However, in fertilized ponds containing 0-20 mg/l total alkalinity, fish production tends to increase with increasing alkalinity. Therefore, it is desirable for total alkalinity values to be above 20 mg/l in fertilized ponds.

Ponds with total alkalinities of 200-300 mg/l have been successfully used for fish culture. However, there is sometimes a shortage of carbon dioxide in lakes with high concentrations of calcium carbonate in muds or on watersheds, resulting in low productivity (Wetzel, 1975).

2.5.5   Total hardness

The term total hardness refers to the concentration of divalent metal ions in water, expressed as milligrams per liter of equivalent calcium carbonate. Total hardness is usually related to total alkalinity because the anions of alkalinity and the cations of hardness are normally derived from the solution of carbonate minerals. For example, Arce and Boyd (1980) demonstrated a high positive correlation between total alkalinity and total hardness in waters from ponds in Alabama. In waters of arid regions, concentration of ions by evaporation may result in precipitation of ions responsible for alkalinity, and total hardness may be considerably greater than total alkalinity. Along coastal plains, waters from wells (ground waters) sometimes have high alkalinity and low hardness; waters of ponds filled by the flow from such wells may also have high alkalinity and low hardness. Some selected data on total hardness and total alkalinity in pond waters are presented in Table 2.11.

TABLE 2.11
Total hardness and total alkalinity of waters from some different ponds.

Type of water	Total alkalinity (mg/liter)	Total hardness (mg/liter)
Pond on sandy soil	13.2	12.9
Pond on acidic, clay soil	11.6	12.3
Pond on calcareous soil	51.1	55.5
Pond filled with soft but alkaline well water	93.0	15.1
Pond in arid region	346	708

Many authors incorrectly use the term hard water to refer to water with high alkalinity. Most waters of high alkalinity are hard waters, but this is not always true. The term hard water was first used to describe waters with a high calcium and magnesium content that precipitated soap. In fact, the degree of hardness was originally determined from the amount of soap required to form suds.

Sanitary engineers often assign degrees of hardness (Sawyer and McCarty, 1967) to water as follows: soft, 0-75 mg/l; moderately hard, 75-150 mg/l; hard, 150-300 mg/l; very hard, >300 mg/l. Such a classification has little meaning in fish culture.

Waters are also said to contain carbonate and noncarbonate hardness. The part of the total hardness chemically equivalent to the total alkalinity is termed the carbonate hardness. Thus, if total alkalinity is less than total hardness, the carbonate hardness equals the total alkalinity. When the alkalinity is equal to or greater than the total hardness, the carbonate hardness equals the total hardness.

When the total alkalinity of a water exceeds its total hardness, some of the bicarbonate and carbonate is associated with sodium and potassium rather than calcium and magnesium. Likewise, if the total hardness is greater than the total alkalinity, some of the calcium and magnesium is associated with anions other than bicarbonate and carbonate.

Fish culturists often place undue emphasis on the total hardness of waters. It should be obvious from the preceding discussion that total hardness is not nearly as important as total alkalinity in fish culture. Fortunately, in most waters, total hardness and total alkalinity have similar concentrations, and few mistakes result from the misplaced emphasis. Water for fish culture needs to contain a small amount of calcium and magnesium, but the necessary quantities are apparently present if total hardness is above 20 mg/l. Some waters with high total alkalinity and low total hardness may develop problems with high pH during periods of rapid plant growth.

2.6 NITROGEN, PHOSPHORUS, AND SULFUR

2.6.1 Comments

The inorganic forms of phosphorus in natural water are usually ionization products of orthophosphoric acid:

$$H_3PO_4 \ = \ H^+ + H_2PO_4^-; \qquad K_1 = 10^{-2.13}$$

$$H_2PO_4^- \ = \ H^+ + HPO_4^{2-}; \qquad K_2 = 10^{-7.21}$$

$$HPO_4^{2-} \ = \ H^+ + PO_4^{3-} \ ; \qquad K_3 = 10^{-12.36}$$

In natural waters, $H_2PO_4^-$ and HPO_4^{2-} are usually predominant (Fig. 2.5).

Although a relatively minor constituent, phosphorus is often the most important nutrient relative to productivity in aquatic ecosystems. Thus, phosphorus concentrations in pond waters and muds are of considerable interest. Phosphorus

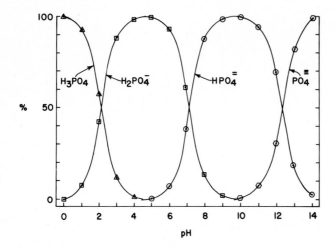

Fig. 2.5. Relationship between mole fraction (%) of orthophosphate species and pH.

fertilizers are widely used in fish culture, and phosphorus originating from metabolic waste is an important factor in ponds that receive applications of feed.

Nitrogen and sulfur are also important as plant nutrients because they are key constituents of protoplasm. Furthermore, nitrogen and sulfur are involved in several important biochemical transformations mediated by microorganisms.

Since it is more convenient, phosphorus and nitrogen will be discussed under pond fertilization (Chapter 3), and most of the discussion of sulfur is under liming (Chapter 4). Here, I will limit the discussion of these three elements to nitrite, ammonia, and hydrogen sulfide — substances potentially toxic to fish.

2.6.2 Ammonia

Ammonia reaches water in fertilizers, in fish excrement, and from microbial decay of nitrogenous compounds. Plants rapidly absorb ammonia, certain bacteria oxidize ammonia to nitrate, and ammonia may be lost through other pathways. However, in ponds where high densities of fish are fed supplemental feeds, ammonia concentration may increase to undesirably high levels.

In water, un-ionized ammonia exists in a pH and temperature dependent equilibrium with ammonium ion:

$$NH_3 + H_2O = NH_4^+ + OH^-; \quad K = 10^{-4.74} \tag{2.8}$$

Un-ionized ammonia is highly toxic to fish, but the ammonium ion is relatively nontoxic. The sum of un-ionized ammonia and ammonium is called total ammonia

nitrogen. The proportion of the total ammonia nitrogen existing as un-ionized
ammonia increases with increasing temperature and pH (Table 2.12). The influence
of pH on un-ionized ammonia concentration is greater than the effect of temperature. Similar tables that included lower temperatures were presented by
Trussell (1972) and Emerson et al. (1975). In order to obtain the un-ionized
ammonia concentration, the percentage un-ionized ammonia value for the appropriate
temperature and pH is multiplied by the total ammonia nitrogen concentration.
For example, a water at pH 7, 26°C, and 2 mg/l total ammonia nitrogen contains
2 mg/l X 0.006 = 0.012 mg/l of un-ionized ammonia. The same water at pH 9
contains 2 X 0.4123 = 0.823 mg/l un-ionized ammonia.

According to Colt and Armstrong (1979), as the ammonia level increases in
water, ammonia excretion by fish decreases and levels of ammonia in blood and
tissue increase. The result is an elevation in blood pH (see Equation 2.8) and
adverse effects on enzyme-catalyzed reactions and membrane stability. High un-
ionized ammonia concentrations in the water affect the permeability of the fish
by water and reduce internal ion concentrations. Ammonia also increases oxygen
consumption by tissues, damages gills, and reduces the ability of blood to transport oxygen. Histological changes occur in the kidneys, spleen, thyroid tissues,
and blood of fish exposed to sublethal concentrations of ammonia. Exposure to
sublethal concentrations of ammonia probably increases susceptibility of fish to
diseases.

The European Inland Fisheries Advisory Commission (1973) stated that toxic
concentrations of ammonia for short-term exposure are between 0.6 and 2 mg/l of
NH_3-N for most species. The 96-h LC50 value of NH_3-N to fish was reported by
Ball (1967) and Colt and Tchobanoglous (1976) to range from 0.4 to 3.1 mg/l.
The 24-h LC50 of NH_3 to channel catfish (Ictalurus punctatus) fingerlings was
2.36 mg/l (Robinette, 1976). Ammonia is more toxic when dissolved oxygen concentration is low (Merkens and Downing, 1957). However, this effect is probably
nullified in fish ponds since carbon dioxide concentrations are usually high
when dissolved oxygen levels are low; Lloyd and Herbert (1960) showed that the
toxicity of ammonia decreases with increasing carbon dioxide concentration.

Tomasso et al. (1980) clearly demonstrated the importance of pH in the
toxicity of ammonia. The 24-h LC50 values for total ammonia nitrogen to catfish
at 21-25°C were 264, 39, and 4.5 mg/l at pH values of 7, 8, and 9. These values
corresponded to 24-h LC50 values for NH_3-N of 1.39, 1.82, and 1.49 mg/l at pH
7, 8, and 9. The toxicity of ammonia to catfish was decreased slightly by high
concentrations of calcium.

Sublethal concentrations of ammonia caused pathological changes in fish organs
and tissues (Smith and Piper, 1975). Histological effects were attributed to
continuous exposure to 0.006-0.34 mg/l of NH_3. Poor growth of fish in culture
tanks has been attributed to the accumulation of ammonia (Smith and Piper, 1975;

TABLE 2.12

Percentage un-ionized ammonia in aqueous solutions of different temperatures and pH values.

pH	Temperature (°C)						
	8	12	16	20	24	28	32
7.0	0.2	0.2	0.3	0.4	0.5	0.7	1.0
8.0	1.6	2.1	2.9	3.8	5.0	6.6	8.8
8.2	2.5	3.3	4.5	5.9	7.7	10.0	13.2
8.4	3.9	5.2	6.9	9.1	11.6	15.0	19.5
8.6	6.0	7.9	10.6	13.7	17.3	21.8	27.7
8.8	9.2	12.0	15.8	20.1	24.9	30.7	37.8
9.0	13.8	17.8	22.9	28.5	34.4	41.2	49.0
9.2	20.4	25.8	32.0	38.7	45.4	52.6	60.4
9.4	30.0	35.5	42.7	50.0	56.9	63.8	70.7
9.6	39.2	46.5	54.1	61.3	67.6	73.6	79.3
9.8	50.5	58.1	65.2	71.5	76.8	81.6	85.8
10.0	61.7	68.5	74.8	79.9	84.0	87.5	90.6
10.2	71.9	77.5	82.4	86.3	89.3	91.8	93.8

Andrews et al., 1971). Robinette (1976) reported that 0.12 mg/l of NH_3 caused reduced growth and gill damage in channel catfish. He did not notice any harmful effects of 0.06 mg/l of NH_3. Colt and Tchobanoglous (1978) found that un-ionized ammonia reduced the growth of juvenile channel catfish during a 31-day test. The effect was linear over the range of 0.058-0.99 mg/l of NH_3-N. A concentration of 0.52 mg/l of NH_3-N caused a 50% reduction in growth, and no growth occurred at 0.97 mg/l. They concluded that any measurable concentration of ammonia would adversely affect growth. This is a misleading statement because there is no practical way of preventing the accumulation of ammonia nitrogen in fish ponds, and relatively high concentrations (1-2 mg/l) are often observed in ponds where fish culture is profitable. Studies with coldwater species also revealed that NH_3-N concentrations as low as 0.05 mg/l reduced growth.

2.6.3   Nitrite

When nitrite is absorbed by fish, it reacts with hemoglobin to form methemoglobin. Since methemoglobin is not effective as an oxygen carrier, continued absorption of nitrite can lead to hypoxia and cyanosis. Blood containing appreciable methemoglobin is brown, so nitrite poisoning in fish is frequently referred to as "brown blood disease".

Sources of excessive nitrite in fish ponds have not been definitely identified. Hollerman and Boyd (1980) suggested that nitrite originates from the reduction of nitrate by bacteria in anaerobic mud or water. However, the common opinion is that an imbalance in the nitrification reaction leads to the accumulation of nitrite. Regardless of the source, ponds occasionally contain nitrite concentrations of 0.5-5 mg/l of NO_2^--N.

Konikoff (1975) reported a 96-h LC50 for NO_2^--N at 21°C of 4.6 mg/l for channel catfish. A 96-h LC50 of 13 mg/l of NO_2^--N for channel catfish was reported by Russo and Thurston (1977). Tomasso et al. (1979) exposed channel catfish fingerlings for 24 h to 1, 2.5, and 5 mg/l of NO_2^- and found methemoglobin levels in blood of 21, 60, and 77%, respectively. Concentrations of NO_2^- as low as 0.5 mg/l were toxic to certain coldwater fish (Crawford and Allen, 1977). Addition of calcium (Wedemeyer and Yasutake, 1978) and chloride (Perrone and Meade, 1977; Tomasso et al., 1979) reduced the toxicity of nitrite to fish.

2.6.4 Hydrogen sulfide

Under anaerobic conditions, certain heterotrophic bacteria can use sulfate and other oxidized sulfur compounds as terminal electron acceptors in metabolism and excrete sulfide as illustrated below:

$$SO_4^{2-} + 8 H^+ \rightarrow S^{2-} + 4 H_2O$$

The sulfide excreted is an ionization product of hydrogen sulfide and participates in the following equilibria:

$$H_2S = HS^- + H^+; \qquad K_1 = 10^{-7.01}$$

$$HS^- = S^{2-} + H^+; \qquad K_2 = 10^{-13.89}$$

The pH obviously regulates the distribution of total reduced sulfur among its species. Un-ionized hydrogen sulfide is toxic to fish, but the ions resulting from its dissociation are not appreciably toxic. Analytical procedures measure total sulfide; values from Table 2.13 may be multiplied by total sulfide concentrations to obtain the concentrations of un-ionized hydrogen sulfide. The proportion of un-ionized hydrogen sulfide decreases with increasing pH.

Adelman and Smith (1970) showed that egg survival and fry development in northern pike (Esox lucius) were limited by 0.006 mg/l of H_2S. Bluegill (Lepomis macrochirus) are also very sensitive to hydrogen sulfide. Smith et al. (1976) gave the 72-h LC50 for bluegill eggs at 22°C as 0.019 mg/l of

TABLE 2.13

Percentage un-ionized hydrogen sulfide in aqueous solutions of 25°C and different pH values.

pH	%	pH	%
5.0	99.0	7.5	24.4
5.5	97.0	8.0	9.3
6.0	91.1	8.5	3.1
6.5	76.4	9.0	1.0
7.0	50.6		

H_2S. They also reported the 96-h LC50 for 35-day-old bluegill fry at 22°C as 0.013 mg/l, for juvenile bluegill at 20°C as 0.048 mg/l, and for adult bluegill at 20°C as 0.045 mg/l. Chronic exposure to 0.002 mg/l of H_2S for up to 826 days did not cause mortality in bluegill, but egg deposition did not occur. Growth of adult bluegills was retarded by 0.011 mg/l of H_2S. However, if exposure was started at the egg stage, 0.003 mg/l adversely affected growth.

The 3-h LC50 for H_2S to channel catfish fry at 25-30°C in water of pH 6.8 was 0.8 mg/l (Bonn and Follis, 1967). At pH 7 the LC50 for H_2S was 1.0 mg/l for channel catfish fingerlings, 1.3 mg/l for advanced fingerlings, and 1.4 mg/l for adults. The duration of channel catfish bioassays was so brief that interpretation of the results is difficult. Nevertheless, in a field study, Bonn and Follis (1967) demonstrated that high concentrations of hydrogen sulfide were responsible for poor growth of channel catfish in acid lakes in northeast Texas.

Bioassays of bluegill and certain other species (Smith et al., 1976) suggest that any detectable concentration of hydrogen sulfide should be considered detrimental to fish production.

2.7 DISSOLVED OXYGEN

2.7.1 Solubility

Dissolved oxygen is a critical factor in intensive fish culture, and success or failure in fish farming often depends upon the ability of the farmer to cope with problems of low dissolved oxygen. The dynamics of dissolved oxygen in ponds is a complex subject and will be treated in Chapter 5. For now, I will only discuss the solubility of oxygen in water and the oxygen requirements of fish.

Oxygen is a major component of air, comprising 20.95%, but it is sparingly soluble in water. The solubility of oxygen in pure water is presented in Table 2.14. Dissolved oxygen concentrations are greatest at 0°C and decrease with increasing temperature. The values in Table 2.14 represent the solubility

TABLE 2.14
Solubility of oxygen in pure water at different temperatures[a].

°C	mg/l	°C	mg/l	°C	mg/l
0	14.16	12	10.43	24	8.25
1	13.77	13	10.20	25	8.11
2	13.40	14	9.98	26	7.99
3	13.05	15	9.76	27	7.86
4	12.70	16	9.56	28	7.75
5	12.37	17	9.37	29	7.64
6	12.06	18	9.18	30	7.53
7	11.76	19	9.01	31	7.42
8	11.47	20	8.84	32	7.32
9	11.19	21	8.68	33	7.22
10	10.92	22	8.53	34	7.13
11	10.67	23	8.38	35	7.04

[a]For an atmosphere saturated with water vapor and at a pressure of 760 mm Hg.

of oxygen from moist air at a pressure of 760 mm of mercury (1 atmosphere of pressure). To correct the solubility of oxygen for another atmospheric pressure, use the following equation:

$$DO_c = DO_t \times \frac{P_o - P_w}{760 - P_w}$$

where DO_c = corrected solubility of oxygen; DO_t = solubility of oxygen at 760 mm of pressure; P_o = observed atmospheric pressure; P_w = vapor pressure of water. The vapor pressure of water at different temperatures may be found in Table 2.15.

The major factor affecting atmospheric pressure is altitude. The approximate decrease in pressure with altitude is as follows: 0-600 m, 4% for each 300 m; 600-1,500 m, 3% for each 300 m; 1,500-3,000 m, 2.5% for each 300 m. Equations for more accurate calculation of atmospheric pressure are presented by Hutchinson (1957), but it is more convenient and accurate to measure pressure with a barometer.

The solubility of oxygen in water decreases with increasing salinity; each 9,000 mg/l increase in salinity reduces the solubility of oxygen by roughly 5% of that in pure water. Thus, the influence of salinity may be ignored in

TABLE 2.15
Vapor pressure of pure water at different temperatures.

°C	mm Hg	°C	mm Hg
0	4.58	20	17.54
5	6.54	25	23.76
10	9.21	30	31.82
15	12.79	35	42.18

freshwaters.

Water containing the amount of dissolved oxygen that it should at equilibrium with the atmosphere is saturated with oxygen; water with less oxygen than it should hold is undersaturated; water having more oxygen than should exist at equilibrium is supersaturated. Oxygen concentration may conveniently be expressed as percentage of saturation. To illustrate, the percentage saturation at 25°C and 760 mm pressure will be computed for waters containing 5.15, 8.11, and 13.25 mg/l of dissolved oxygen. The theoretical solubility from Table 2.14 is 8.11 mg/l, so:

$(5.15/8.11)(100) = 64\%$ (undersaturation)

$(8.11/8.11)(100) = 100\%$ (saturation)

$(13.25/8.11)(100) = 163\%$ (supersaturation)

The solubility of oxygen in water may also be expressed as oxygen tension. The oxygen tension represents the partial pressure of oxygen in the atmosphere required to hold a certain concentration of oxygen in the water. The partial pressure or tension of oxygen in the air at standard pressure is 760 mm X 0.2095 = 159.2 mm. Water containing 4.4 mg/l of dissolved oxygen at 20°C has an oxygen tension of:

$(4.4/8.84)(159.2) = 79.2$ mm

In other words, an oxygen tension of 79.2 mm in the atmosphere would be at equilibrium with 4.4 mg/l of oxygen in water of 20°C. A water at 20°C with 15.2 mg/l dissolved oxygen would have a greater tension:

$(15.2/8.84)(159.2) = 273.7$ mm

Oxygen concentrations may also be reported in milliliters per liter. A water at 0°C and 760 mm pressure contains 14.16 mg/l of dissolved oxygen at saturation. To convert to milliliters per liter consider that 22.4 l of air at 0°C and 760 mm pressure contain 1 mole of oxygen, so the density of oxygen is 32,000 mg/mole ÷ 22,400 ml/mole = 1.43 mg/ml. Converting weight of oxygen to volume, 14.16 mg/l ÷ 1.43 mg/l = 9.90 ml/l. The density of oxygen decreases as the temperature rises and the pressure drops, but the volume occupied by 1 mole of oxygen can be calculated from the general gas law equation:

$$PV = nRT$$

where P = pressure in atmospheres; V = volume in liters; n = number of moles; R = universal gas law constant with the value, 0.082 liter-atmosphere per mole per degree Kelvin; T = °K.

2.7.2 Oxygen requirements of fish

The loading and unloading of hemoglobin with oxygen is governed by oxygen tension. At the gills the tension of oxygen is higher in the water than in the blood, and oxygen is loaded onto hemoglobin. In the tissues oxygen is used rapidly, causing tissues to have lower oxygen tensions than blood. Thus, hemoglobin unloads oxygen to the tissues. The relationship between oxygen tension and the percentage saturation of hemoglobin with oxygen (Fig. 2.6) is called the oxyhemoglobin dissociation curve. Curves are either hyperbolic or sigmoid in shape. Warmwater species typically have sigmoid oxyhemoglobin dissociation

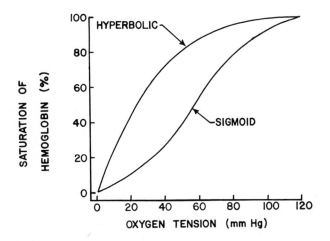

Fig. 2.6. Oxyhemoglobin dissociation curves for warmwater fish (sigmoid) and coldwater fish (hyperbolic).

curves. They can load hemoglobin with oxygen at a lower oxygen tension and unload a greater proportion of oxygen from hemoglobin at the tissues than coldwater species, which usually have hyperbolic oxyhemoglobin dissociation curves.

Carbon dioxide is carried in the blood. It is lost to the water at the gills because its tension is greater in venous blood than in the water. In arterial blood, carbon dioxide tension is low, so the high tension of carbon dioxide in tissue favors its movement into blood. The percentage saturation of hemoglobin with oxygen at a given oxygen tension declines as carbon dioxide tension increases. This phenomenon facilitates unloading of oxygen from hemoglobin at the tissues. However, high concentrations of carbon dioxide in the water are antagonistic to the loading of hemoglobin with oxygen. Therefore, fish require a higher concentration of dissolved oxygen when the carbon dioxide concentration in water is high than when it is low.

Although fish culturists usually think of the oxygen requirements of fish in terms of milligrams per liter, fish respond to oxygen tension. For example, 2 mg/l corresponds to an oxygen tension of 42 mm at 30°C, but only 33 mm at 15°C. The loading of hemoglobin with oxygen would be greater at 30°C than at 15°C in

TABLE 2.16
Oxygen consumption (mg/kg per h) at 17-20°C for several freshwater fish.

Species	Resting[a]	Active[b]
Micropterus salmoides	228	
Ictalurus melas	273	
Pomoxis annularis	205	
Notemigonus crysoleucas	278	
Notropis cornutus	329	
Erimyzon sucetta	449	
Campostoma anomalum	500	
Etheostoma blennioides	261	
Salvelinus fontinalis		329
Catostomus commersoni		306
Cyprinus carpio		888
Carassius auratus		373
Ictalurus nebulosus		266

[a]Clausen (1936)
[b]Basu (1959)

TABLE 2.17

Oxygen consumption for well-fed channel catfish at 26-28°C (Andrews and Matsuda, 1975).

Dissolved oxygen (mg/1)	Weight fish (g)	Oxygen consumption (mg O_2/kg per h)
1	200	90
2	200	190
4	200	390
7	200	690
7	5	1,225
7	10	1,050
7	50	750
7	100	625
7	500	480
7	1,000	340

oxygen-saturated water.

The rates of respiration (oxygen consumption) by fish vary with species, size, activity, temperature, nutritional status, and other factors. The consumption of oxygen at 17-20°C for nine common species of freshwater fish at rest (Table 2.16) ranged from 65 to 210 mg/kg per h (Clausen, 1936). Consumption of oxygen by five species forced to exercise at 20°C (Table 2.16) ranged from 266 to 888 mg/kg per h (Basu, 1959). Shell (1965) found that oxygen consumption by moderately active white catfish (Ictalurus catus) increased from 60 mg/kg per h at 11°C to 276 mg/kg per h at 25°C. The rate of oxygen consumption by Tilapia nilotica at 25°C ranged from 220 mg/kg per h for fish forced to swim at 30 cm/sec to 458 mg/kg per h for fish forced to swim at 60 cm/sec (Farmer and Beamish, 1969).

Oxygen was consumed faster by channel catfish that had recently eaten than by fasted catfish (Andrews and Matsuda, 1975). For example, oxygen consumption values at 28°C in water containing 7 mg/1 of dissolved oxygen were: immediately after feeding, 520 mg/kg per h; 1 h after feeding, 680 mg/kg per h; fasted overnight, 380 mg/kg per h; fasted 3 days, 290 mg/kg per h; fasted 9 days, 290 mg/kg per h. Catfish also consumed more oxygen at high dissolved oxygen concentrations than at low dissolved oxygen concentrations (Table 2.17). At oxygen concentrations of 1 and 2 mg/1, fasted fish consumed as much oxygen as fed fish. Andrews and Matsuda reported Q_{10} values (increases in oxygen consumption resulting from 10°C increases in temperature) of 1.9 and 2.3 for fed and fasted channel catfish, respectively. Small fish consume more oxygen per unit of weight than large fish, as illustrated for channel catfish in Table 2.17. Moss and Scott (1964) reported that lean catfish consumed less oxygen than fat catfish.

Boyd et al. (1978) averaged data on oxygen consumption by fed and fasted channel catfish and subjected them to multiple regression analysis. The resulting equation was:

$$\log O_2 \text{ consumption (mg } O_2/g \text{ of fish per h)} = -0.999 - 0.000957 \, W + 0.0000006 \, W^2$$
$$+ 0.0327 \, T + 0.0000087 \, T^2 + 0.0000003 \, WT \tag{2.9}$$

where W = average fish weight in grams and T = °C. The correlation coefficient was 0.99. Data used in preparing the equation ranged from 2.3 to 1,006 g for fish weight and from 24 to 30°C. This equation obviously has limitations, but it will permit an estimate of oxygen consumption by channel catfish in ponds.

Moss and Scott (1961) reported oxygen consumption rates for resting fish at 26-35°C: 53-195 mg O_2/kg fish per h for bluegill, 100-119 mg/kg per h for largemouth bass (Micropterus salmoides), and 83-171 mg/kg per h for channel catfish. Small bluegill (<15 g) used more oxygen than larger bluegill (30-50 g), but there were no apparent differences in oxygen consumption with size in largemouth bass (5-80 g) and channel catfish (20-105 g). Unfortunately, all largemouth bass and channel catfish were rather small; larger fish would have likely consumed more oxygen. All three species consumed considerably more oxygen at low oxygen concentration than at saturation with dissolved oxygen. Moss and Scott also reported that comparable size fish of all three species used oxygen at about the same rates at 25 and 35°C.

Schroeder (1975) gave a general equation for calculating fish respiration at 20-30°C:

$$Y = 0.001 \, W^{0.82} \tag{2.10}$$

where Y = oxygen consumption per fish in grams per hour and W = weight of fish in grams. Approximate, but useful, estimates of oxygen consumption can be obtained with this equation.

Prolonged exposure to sublethally low concentrations of dissolved oxygen is harmful to fish. Fathead minnows (Pimephales promelas) were exposed to continuously low dissolved oxygen concentrations for 11 months (Brungs, 1971). Fry survival was reduced at dissolved oxygen concentrations of 4 mg/l or less. Growth of fry was reduced by all dissolved oxygen concentrations less than the control value of 7.8 mg/l. Andrews et al. (1973) grew channel catfish in laboratory tanks at three levels of dissolved oxygen: 100, 60, and 36% of saturation. When fed _ad libitum_, weight gain and feed consumption declined with decreasing dissolved oxygen saturation. Feed conversion rates for fish held at 36% of oxygen saturation were lower than rates for fish held at 60% and 100% of air saturation. Channel catfish in ponds also reduce their feed consumption when dissolved oxygen concentrations are low (Tucker et al., 1979). Continuous exposure of largemouth bass to low dissolved oxygen concentrations reduced food intake and growth (Stewart et al., 1967).

Continued exposure to low dissolved oxygen is also considered a precursor to bacterial infection in fish (Snieszko, 1973; Plumb et al., 1976). Under culture conditions, carbon dioxide and ammonia concentrations are often high when dissolved oxygen concentrations are low. Walters and Plumb (1980) showed the triad of environmental stresses to be more effective than low dissolved oxygen concentration alone in causing bacterial infections in fish.

Wide diel fluctuations in dissolved oxygen concentrations typically occur in fish ponds. In channel catfish ponds dissolved oxygen concentrations often exceed 15 mg/l in the afternoon, yet concentrations are frequently below 3 mg/l at dawn (Boyd et al., 1979). Little is known about the effects of diel fluctuations in oxygen on channel catfish growth, except that fish may not feed well on days when dissolved oxygen concentrations fall below 1 mg/l (Tucker et al., 1979). In experiments with carp in Israel, Rappaport et al. (1976) reported that fish growth decreased if dissolved oxygen concentrations in pond waters dropped below 25% of saturation at sunrise.

The minimum concentration of dissolved oxygen tolerated by fish is obviously a function of the exposure time. A fish might survive 0.5 mg/l dissolved oxygen for a few hours but not for several days. Further, the minimum tolerable concentration of dissolved oxygen will vary with species, size, physiological condition, concentrations of solutes, and other factors.

Moore (1942) confined several species of fish in boxes of wire netting lowered to varying depths — and oxygen concentrations — in lakes (Table 2.18). Median values for lethally low oxygen concentrations (24- and 48-h exposure) were 3.1 mg/l in summer and 1.4 mg/l in winter. Lethal concentrations of dissolved oxygen, as determined in laboratory tests, for several species of warmwater pond fish are summarized in Table 2.19. These concentrations are generally lower than those reported by Moore (1942). Coldwater species die at considerably higher concentrations of dissolved oxygen than warmwater species. For example, minimum concentrations of dissolved oxygen tolerated for 84-h by rainbow trout (_Salmo gairdneri_) and perch (_Perca_ sp.) were given by McKee and Wolf (1962) as 1.89-3.00 mg/l and 1.05-1.34 mg/l, respectively.

Ellis et al. (1947) indicated that under average stream conditions, 3.0 mg/l of dissolved oxygen, or less, should be regarded as hazardous for fish, and for

TABLE 2.18

Highest observed concentrations of dissolved oxygen (mg/l) at which fish held in lakes in cages died after 24-h exposure in summer and 48-h exposure in winter (Moore, 1942).

Species	Summer	Winter
Esox lucius	3.1	2.3
Micropterus salmoides	3.1	2.3
Pomoxis nigromaculatus	4.2	1.4
Lepomis cyanellus	3.1	0.8
Perca flavescens	3.1	1.5
Lepomis gibbosus	3.1	0.8
Ictalurus melas	2.9	0.3

TABLE 2.19

Lethal concentrations of dissolved oxygen for several species of pond fish (Doudoroff and Shumway, 1970).

Species	mg/l
Carassius auratus	0.1-2.0
Catla catla	0.7
Cirrhina mrigala	0.7
Ctenopharyngodon idella	0.2-0.6
Cyprinus carpio	0.2-0.8
Hypophthalmichthys molitrix	0.3-1.1
Labeo rohita	0.7
Ictalurus punctatus	0.8-2.0
Lepomis macrochirus	0.5-3.1
Micropterus salmoides	0.9-3.1

a good, varied fish fauna, the oxygen concentration should be 5.0 mg/l or more. McKee and Wolf (1962) felt that the following assessment of dissolved oxygen concentrations in habitats for warmwater fish was logical: "The dissolved oxygen content of warmwater fish habitats shall be not less than 5 mg/l during at least 16 h of any 24-h period. It may be less than 5 mg/l for a period not to exceed 8 h within any 24-h period, but at no time shall the oxygen content be less than 3 mg/l. To sustain a coarse fish population, the dissolved oxygen may be less

than 5 mg/l for a period of not more than 8 h out of any 24-h period, but at no
time shall the concentration be lower than 2 mg/l." Swingle (1969) made a similar
practical assessment of the dissolved oxygen requirements of warmwater pond fish:

Dissolved oxygen	Effects
<1 mg/l	Lethal if exposure lasts longer than a few hours.
1-5 mg/l	Fish survive, but reproduction poor and growth slow if exposure is continuous.
>5 mg/l	Fish reproduce and grow normally.

For coldwater species, critical concentrations of dissolved oxygen cited by McKee
and Wolf (1962) and Swingle (1969) should be increased by 2-3 mg/l.

Davis (1975) reported changes in behavior and blood chemistry that occur long
before dissolved oxygen drops to lethal levels. For example, Moss and Scott
(1961) showed that bluegill and largemouth bass could survive for at least 2
weeks in water containing 0.8-1.0 mg/l of dissolved oxygen. However, Davis (1975)
reported that dissolved oxygen concentrations of 3-4.5 mg/l caused behavioral
changes in these two species.

Supersaturation with atmospheric gases of waters falling over high dams can
cause gas bubble disease and mortality in fish living in streams below (Nebeker
and Brett, 1976). Gas bubble disease can also be induced by suddenly moving
fish from a water of high dissolved oxygen concentration to one of low dissolved
oxygen concentration. When transferred to the low dissolved oxygen concentration,
gas bubbles may form in the blood as equilibrium is established with the low
oxygen concentration. Supersaturation of pond waters is a normal occurrence
during daylight hours because of phytoplankton photosynthesis. McKee and Wolf
(1962) quoted several reports dealing with effects of supersaturation with oxygen
on fish. In ponds, carp exposed to 150% of oxygen saturation had a greater
frequency of disease than carp exposed to 100-125% of oxygen saturation. Fish
died in a pond when oxygen concentration reached 300% of saturation; the lethal
effect was attributed to oxygen bubbles surrounding the gills. Bass (species
not specified) could not tolerate more than 40 mg/l of dissolved oxygen for even
a few hours. Faruqui (1975) observed gas bubble disease and associated mortality
in carp fry in a hatchery pond when dissolved oxygen concentrations reached 20
mg/l during rapid phytoplankton growth.

The occurrence of gas bubble disease in pond fish has not been carefully
studied. However, in ponds with plankton blooms, self-shading by phytoplankton
usually limits light penetration and restricts rapid photosynthesis and supersaturation with dissolved oxygen to surface waters. Therefore, if supersaturation
with oxygen in surface waters reaches harmful levels, fish will move into deeper

waters where oxygen saturation is less. Thus, in most ponds, supersaturation
with oxygen would only threaten eggs or fry restricted to surfaces by lack of
mobility. Of course, supersaturation may occur to greater depths in ponds where
waters are clear and macrophytes abound.

2.8   TURBIDITY

Turbidity caused by plankton is generally desirable in fish ponds. Troublesome underwater weeds are eliminated by plankton turbidity. Plankton blooms
favor greater fish production by stimulating the growth of fish food organisms.
Plankton turbidity also improves fishing because the suspended particles limit
the vision of fish, making them less wary (Swingle, 1945).

Turbidity resulting from high concentrations of humic substances is not directly
harmful to fish, but such waters are usually dystrophic because of acidity, low
nutrient levels, and limited light penetration for photosynthesis.

An extremely undesirable type of turbidity is that resulting from suspended
particles of clay. Wallen (1951) noticed behavioral changes in fish exposed to
clay turbidities greater than 20,000 mg/l, but individuals of 16 species survived
exposure to 100,000 mg/l of clay turbidity for 1 week or longer. Appreciable
mortality occurred at turbidity values above 175,000 mg/l. Turbidities in natural
waters seldom exceed 20,000 mg/l (Irwin, 1945).

Even though turbidity caused by suspended soil particles will seldom have
immediate direct effects on fish, in the long run, it may harm fish populations.
Clay turbidity will restrict light penetration, adversely affecting productivity,
and some of the particles will settle to the bottom and smother fish eggs and
destroy benthic communities. Duchrow and Everhart (1971) pointed out that direct
turbidity measurements are of questionable value for establishing water quality
standards. The main concern with regard to protection of the aquatic fauna is
not the suspended particles (turbidity) per se, but the amount of solids in suspension that can potentially settle out (settleable solids).

Buck (1956) divided a series of Oklahoma farm ponds into three catagories:
clear ponds with average turbidities below 25 mg/l, intermediate ponds with
turbidities from 25 to 100 mg/l, and muddy ponds, with turbidities above 100
mg/l. The average total weights of fish (sunfish and largemouth bass) were:
clear ponds, 181 kg/ha; intermediate ponds, 105 kg/ha; muddy ponds, 33 kg/ha.
Differences were due to faster growth and greater reproduction in the less turbid
ponds. Volumes of net phytoplankton averaged 19.2 µl/l in clear ponds, 2.4 µl/l
in intermediate ponds, and 1.5 µl/l in muddy ponds. Buck felt that light penetration was important in limiting plankton growth. In water having a turbidity
of 25 mg/l, 24.9% of the red light penetrated to a depth of 10 cm, as compared
to 6.3% and 0% at turbidities of 50 mg/l and 150 mg/l, respectively.

Buck (1956) also established different levels of turbidity in hatchery ponds. Total fish production was 153 kg/ha in clear ponds, 105 kg/ha in intermediate ponds, and 110 kg/ha in muddy ponds. Channel catfish were stocked with sunfish and largemouth bass in the hatchery pond experiment. The greater production of fish in muddy hatchery ponds compared to muddy farm ponds was attributed to high survival and good growth of channel catfish.

2.9   ORGANIC MATTER

In waters of fish ponds, organic matter is present as living plankton, suspended particles of decaying organic matter (detritus), and dissolved organic matter. The dynamics of plankton will be discussed in Chapters 3 and 5. In this section, I discuss two variables, biological oxygen demand (BOD) and chemical oxygen demand (COD), frequently mentioned in connection with organic matter in pond water.

The standard BOD determination involves incubation of a water sample with ample nutrients at 20°C, usually for 5 days (American Public Health Association et al., 1975). The amount of dissolved oxygen consumed during the incubation period is considered the amount required to decompose the most reactive organic matter in the sample (stabilize the organic matter). The BOD is useful in water pollution investigations because the amount of oxygen required to stabilize an effluent may be calculated from the BOD and the volume of the effluent.

Standard BOD measurements are not generally meaningful to fish culturists because most of the BOD of a pond water sample results from plankton respiration, rather than from the decomposition of organic waste. Furthermore, fish respond quickly to dissolved oxygen depletion, so the hourly rate of oxygen consumption in pond water is more useful than a standard BOD value. Boyd et al. (1978) recommended that BOD values for fish ponds be determined by simply measuring the decline in dissolved oxygen in a sealed bottle of pond water over a 6- to 24-h period. The 6-h BOD values for ponds waters were closely correlated with phytoplankton density.

The COD of a sample represents the amount of oxygen required to oxidize all of the organic matter to carbon dioxide and water (Maciolek, 1962). The sample is treated with sulfuric acid and potassium dichromate and digested for 2 h. The oxygen equivalent of the potassium dichromate consumed in oxidizing the organic matter is the COD. There is usually a high correlation between the COD and BOD, hence BOD may be calculated from less time consuming COD analyses. Boyd et al. (1978) presented an equation for predicting the hourly rate of dissolved oxygen consumption in pond waters from COD. The equation is:

$$O_2 \text{ consumption in mg/l per h} = -1.006 - 0.00148 \ C - 0.0000125 \ C^2 + 0.0766 \ T - 0.00144 \ T^2 + 0.000253 \ CT \tag{2.11}$$

where C = COD in milligrams per liter and T = °C. The correlation coefficient was 0.92. Data used in preparing the equation ranged from 20 to 140 mg/l for COD and from 20 to 32°C. Boyd (1973) found the COD of pond waters to be closely correlated with chlorophyll a concentrations, suggesting that phytoplankton was a major contributor to COD.

It is also possible to isolate individual organisms from ponds and determine their COD — the amount of oxygen needed to decompose them. The COD of some organisms from fish ponds (Table 2.20) ranged from 0.96 to 1.28 mg O_2/mg dry weight.

Since plankton is a major source of turbidity in many fish ponds, the Secchi disk visibility provides an estimate of plankton density (Almazan and Boyd, 1978). There is also a high correlation between Secchi disk visibility and the COD of pond waters (Boyd et al., 1978). Further, the hourly rate of dissolved oxygen consumption in pond waters may be estimated from Secchi disk visibility by the following equation:

$$O_2 \text{ consumption in mg/l per h} = -1.133 + 0.00381\ S + 0.0000145\ S^2 + 0.0812\ T - 0.000749\ T^2 - 0.000349\ ST \tag{2.12}$$

where S = Secchi disk visibility in centimeters and T = °C. The correlation coefficient was 0.91. Data used in preparing the equation ranged from 20 to 120 cm for Secchi disk visibility and from 20 to 32°C.

2.10 MEASUREMENTS

There are several good manuals on methods of water analysis: American Public Health Association et al. (1975), American Society for Testing and Materials (1976), United States Environmental Protection Agency (1976), and Golterman et al. (1978). These manuals include methods for many variables, only a few of which are usually important in fish culture. The most important variables in fish culture are dissolved oxygen, pH, carbon dioxide, total alkalinity, total hardness, acidity, specific conductance, total ammonia nitrogen, nitrate, nitrite, filterable orthophosphate, total phosphorus, biochemical oxygen demand, chemical oxygen demand, turbidity, and plankton abundance.

Dissolved oxygen may be determined by the traditional Winkler procedure, but polarographic dissolved oxygen meters provide an easier and more rapid means of analysis. Dissolved oxygen meters provide reliable results as shown in Table 2.21 with data from Reynolds (1969). When using dissolved oxygen meters, it is important to occasionally check results against data obtained by the Winkler technique to verify the accuracy of the meter. If means for making Winkler determinations are not available, water of known temperature can be saturated

TABLE 2.20
Chemical oxygen demand (COD) of organisms commonly found in fish ponds (Boyd, 1973).

Material	No. of samples	COD (mg/1)
Fish	7	1.20
Particulate matter[a]	14	0.96
Aquatic angiosperms	9	0.99
Macroscopic algae	4	1.02
Phytoplankton from laboratory cultures	10	1.28

[a]Residue resulting from centrifugation of pond water — contained mostly plankton and organic detritus.

TABLE 2.21
Comparison of the Winkler titration technique and the polarographic oxygen meter for dissolved oxygen analysis (Reynolds, 1969).

Type of water	No. of samples	Dissolved oxygen (mg/1)	
		Oxygen meter	Titration
Dilution water for BOD analysis	19	8.3	8.3
Raw wastewater	100	4.13	4.14
Primary municipal effluent	75	3.17	3.16
Final municipal effluent	150	5.09	5.02
Effluent from soybean refinery	100	3.51	3.39
Effluent from corn refinery	100	4.90	4.84

with dissolved oxygen by stirring and the dissolved oxygen value obtained with the oxygen meter compared with the theoretical solubility of oxygen for the particular temperature. This is only an approximate check because it is difficult to bring a water exactly to saturation by stirring. A dissolved oxygen meter may be fitted with a BOD probe for direct measurement of oxygen in BOD bottles.

The only reliable method for determining pH is the glass electrode (pH meter). Most workers standardize pH meters with a buffer solution of pH 7. This practice can lead to erroneous results. A defective pH meter can often be standardized to pH 7 yet give inaccurate measurements for samples. A better way is to standardize the meter at pH 7 and then verify that the meter will correctly indicate the pH of a buffer solution of some other pH. A pH meter gives more reliable results if it is standardized with a buffer solution of a pH near that of the samples.

The usual procedure for carbon dioxide is titration to the phenolphthalein end point (pH = 8.3) with standard base (sodium hydroxide or sodium carbonate). Total alkalinity is normally determined by titration to the methyl orange end point (pH = 4.5) with standard acid (sulfuric or hydrochloric). Some workers prefer to use a pH electrode rather than an indicator to detect the end point of the total alkalinity titration. Mineral acidity may be determined by titration with a standard base (usually sodium hydroxide) to the methyl orange end point. Total acidity is based on the titration to the phenolphthalein end point of a recently boiled sample.

Total hardness is usually determined by titration with standard ethylenediamine tetracetic acid (EDTA). Eriochrome black-T is commonly used to detect the end point of this titration. Data on calcium and magnesium concentration may be used to calculate total hardness as described by Boyd (1979a).

There are several procedures for determining orthophosphate concentrations in water. However, Boyd and Tucker (1980) demonstrated that ascorbic acid reduction of the complex formed when orthophosphate reacts with ammonium molybdate in presence of sulfuric acid is the best procedure for determining orthophosphate in waters from fish ponds. Most procedures suggest that water be filtered through 0.45-μ membrane filters in preparation for filtrable orthophosphate analysis. Nevertheless, there were no differences in orthophosphate concentrations among filtrates of pond water samples passed through 0.45-μ membrane filters, glass fiber filters, Whatman No. 42 filter papers, and Whatman No. 1 filter papers (Boyd and Tucker, 1980). Samples for total phosphorus determinations may be prepared by digestion with sulfuric acid and ammonium persulfate.

The nesslerization technique has been widely used for the determination of total ammonia nitrogen in water. This procedure is time consuming because distillation is required to separate the ammoniacal nitrogen in pond water samples from substances that interfere with nesslerization. Boyd (1979b) found that the phenate method for total ammonia nitrogen did not require distillation. Ammonia sensitive electrodes may also be used for determining ammoniacal nitrogen on undistilled samples (Cuenco and Stickney, 1980).

Nitrate has often been determined by the phenoldisulfonic method. This procedure is usually not sensitive enough for highly accurate analysis of pond waters because of the low concentrations of nitrate commonly present. The cadmium reduction procedure is highly desirable for nitrate determinations of pond waters (Boyd and Hollerman, 1981). In the cadmium column, nitrate is reduced to nitrite. The nitrite is then determined by the highly sensitive diazotization technique that employs sulfanilamide as a diazotizing reagent and N-(1-naphthyl)-ethylenediamine as a coupling reagent. The diazotization procedure is also widely used for the determination of nitrite in filtrates of pond water.

The determination of BOD was mentioned above. Boyd (1979b) suggested the use of a heat-of-dilution technique for determining the COD of pond waters. This procedure requires less apparatus, is less expensive, and is more rapid than the standard method for COD. The heat-of-dilution technique underestimated the standard COD, but there was a high, positive correlation between values obtained on the same samples by the two techniques.

Plankton abundance may be estimated from total particulate organic matter analyses or from direct enumeration of organisms. In practical applications, Secchi disk visibility often provides a rough estimate of plankton abundance (Almazan and Boyd, 1978).

Phytoplankton may be enumerated, but this procedure often does not provide reliable data on standing crop because of size differences among individuals of different species. Chlorophyll a analysis is indicative of phytoplankton abundance. Primary productivity of phytoplankton communities may be measured by light and dark bottle techniques (American Public Health Association et al., 1975).

Water analysis kits are popular in fisheries because they are comparatively inexpensive, compact, portable, and suitable for field use. The kits permit rapid analyses and require little knowledge of quantitative chemistry. Boyd (1976, 1977, 1980a, 1980b) evaluated the accuracy of kits produced by firms in the United States. The results of some selected comparisons are presented in Table 2.22. In general, concentrations measured with water analysis kits differed somewhat from those obtained with standard analytical procedures. Nevertheless, water analysis kits were sufficiently reliable for use in fisheries management. Some procedures were even reliable enough for use in research, but most researchers will, and rightfully so, prefer to employ standard techniques.

TABLE 2.22

Comparisons between water analysis kits and standard methods of water analysis.[a]
Each entry is based on seven replicate analyses each of three to eight samples
(Boyd, 1980b).

Test kit	pH	Total alkalinity	Dissolved oxygen	Carbon dioxide	Total ammonia nitrogen
Hach DR-EL/2[b]	100	101	108	106	128
Bausch and Lomb[c]		114	112	130	59
LaMotte[d]	100	153	109	93	400
Ecologic[e]	110	118	101	131	
Hellige[b]	107	107	98		367

[a](Kit value ÷ standard value) X 100
[b]Hach Chemical Company, Loveland, Colorado.
[c]Bausch and Lomb, Inc., Rochester, New York.
[d]LaMotte Chemical Products Company, Box 329, Chestertown, Maryland.
[e]Ecologic Instruments, Inc., Bohemia, New York.
[f]Hellige, Inc., Garden City, New York.

REFERENCES

Adams, F., 1971. Ionic concentrations and activities in soil solutions. Soil
    Sci. Soc. Amer. Proc., 35: 420-426.
Adams, F., 1974. Soil solution. In: W. E. Carson (Editor), The Plant Root and
    its Environment. University Press of Virginia, Charlottesville, Virginia,
    pp. 441-481.
Adelman, I. R. and Smith, L. L., Jr., 1970. Effect of hydrogen sulfide on
    northern pike eggs and sac fry. Trans. Amer. Fish. Soc., 99: 501-509.
Almazan, G. and Boyd, C. E., 1978. An evaluation of Secchi disk visibility for
    estimating plankton density in fish ponds. Hydrobiologia, 65: 601-608.
American Public Health Association, American Water Works Association, and Water
    Pollution Control Federation, 1975. Standard Methods for the Examination of
    Water and Wastewater, 14th edition. American Public Health Association,
    Washington, D. C., 1193 pp.
American Society for Testing and Materials, 1976. Annual Book of ASTM Standards,
    Part 31. American Society for Testing and Materials, Philadelphia, 956 pp.
Andrews, J. W. and Matsuda, Y., 1975. The influence of various culture conditions
    on the oxygen consumption of channel catfish. Trans. Amer. Fish. Soc., 104:
    322-327.
Andrews, J. W., Knight, L. H., Page, J. W., Matsuda, Y., and Brown, E. E., 1971.
    Interactions of stocking density and water turnover on growth and food
    conversion of channel catfish reared in intensively stocked tanks. Prog.
    Fish-Cult., 33: 197-203.
Andrews, J. W., Murai, T., and Gibbons, G., 1973. The influence of dissolved
    oxygen on the growth of channel catfish. Trans. Amer. Fish. Soc., 102: 835-838.
Arce, R. G. and Boyd, C. E., 1980. Water chemistry of Alabama ponds. Auburn

University Agricultural Experiment Station, Auburn University, Alabama, Bulletin 522, 35 pp.

Ball, I. R., 1967. The relative susceptibility of some species of freshwater fish to poisons — I. Ammonia. Water Res., 1: 767-775.

Bardach, J. E., Ryther, J. H., and McLearney, W. O., 1971. Aquaculture. Wiley-Interscience, New York, 868 pp.

Basu, S. P., 1959. Active respiration of fish in relation to ambient concentrations of oxygen and carbon dioxide. J. Fish. Res. Bd. Canada, 16: 175-212.

Beamish, R. J., Lockhard, W. L., Van Loon, J. C., and Harvey, H. H., 1975. Long-term acidification of a lake and resulting effects on fishes. Ambio, 4: 98-102.

Bonn, E. W. and Follis, B. J., 1967. Effects of hydrogen sulfide on channel catfish, Ictalurus punctatus. Trans. Amer. Fish. Soc., 96: 31-36.

Boyd, C. E., 1973. The chemical oxygen demand of waters and biological materials from ponds. Trans. Amer. Fish. Soc., 102: 606-611.

Boyd, C. E., 1976. An evaluation of a water analysis kit. Auburn University Agricultural Experiment Station, Auburn, Alabama, Leaflet 92, 4 pp.

Boyd, C. E., 1977. Evaluation of a water analysis kit. J. Environ. Qual., 6: 381-384.

Boyd, C. E., 1979a. Water Quality in Warmwater Fish Ponds. Auburn University Agricultural Experiment Station, Auburn, Alabama, 359 pp.

Boyd, C. E., 1979b. Determination of total ammonia nitrogen and chemical oxygen demand in fish culture systems. Trans. Amer. Fish. Soc., 108: 314-319.

Boyd, C. E., 1980a. Reliability of water analysis kits. Trans. Amer. Fish. Soc., 109: 239-243.

Boyd, C. E., 1980b. Comparisons of water analysis kits. Proc. Annual Conf. Southeast. Assoc. Fish and Wildl. Agencies, 34: in press.

Boyd, C. E., 1981. Effects of ion-pairing on calculations of ionic activities of major ions in freshwater. Hydrobiologia, 80: 91-93.

Boyd, C. E. and Hollerman, W. D., 1981. Determination of nitrate in waters from fish ponds. Auburn University Agricultural Experiment Station, Auburn University, Alabama, Leaflet 99, 4 pp.

Boyd, C. E. and Tucker, L., 1980. Determination of filtrable orthophosphate in water from fish ponds. Trans. Amer. Fish. Soc., 109: 314-318.

Boyd, C. E. and Walley, W. W., 1975. Total alkalinity and hardness of surface waters in Alabama and Mississippi. Auburn University Agricultural Experiment Station, Auburn, Alabama, Bull. 465, 16 pp.

Boyd, C. E., Romaire, R. P., and Johnston, E., 1978. Predicting early morning dissolved oxygen concentrations in channel catfish ponds. Trans. Amer. Fish. Soc., 107: 484-492.

Boyd, C. E., Romaire, R. P., and Johnston, E., 1979. Water quality in channel catfish production ponds. J. Environ. Qual., 8: 423-429.

Brosset, C., 1979. Factors influencing pH in lake water. Water, Air, Soil Pollut., 11: 57-61.

Brungs, W. A., 1971. Chronic effects of low dissolved oxygen concentrations on the fathead minnow (Pimephales promelas). J. Fish. Res. Bd. Canada, 28: 1119-1123.

Buck, D. H., 1956. Effects of turbidity on fish and fishing. Trans. N. Amer. Wildl. Conf., 21: 249-261.

Clausen, R. G., 1936. Oxygen consumption in freshwater fishes. Ecology, 17: 216-226.

Clay, D., 1977. Preliminary observations on salinity tolerance of Clarias lazera from Israel. Bamidgeh, 29: 102-109.

Colt, J. and Armstrong, D., 1979. Nitrogen toxicity to fish, crustaceans and molluscs. Department of Civil Engineering, University of California, Davis, California, 30 pp.

Colt, J. and Tchobanoglous, G., 1976. Evaluation of the short-term toxicity of nitrogenous compounds to channel catfish, Ictalurus punctatus. Aquaculture, 8: 209-224.

Colt, J. and Tchobanoglous, G., 1978. Chronic exposure of channel catfish, Ictalurus punctatus, to ammonia: effects on growth and survival. Aquaculture, 15: 353-372.

52

Crawford, R. E., and Allen, G. H., 1977. Seawater inhibition of nitrite toxicity to chinook salmon. Trans. Amer. Fish. Soc., 106: 105-109.

Cuenco, M. L. and Stickney, R. P., 1980. Reliability of an electrode and a water analysis kit for determination of ammonia in aquaculture systems. Trans. Amer. Fish. Soc., 109: 571-576.

Davis, J. C., 1975. Minimal dissolved oxygen requirements of aquatic life with emphasis on Canadian species: a review. J. Fish. Res. Bd. Canada, 32: 2295-2332.

Doudoroff, P. and Shumway, D. L., 1970. Dissolved oxygen requirements of freshwater fishes. FAO United Nations, Fisheries Technical Paper 86, 291 pp.

Duchrow, R. M. and Everhart, W. H., 1971. Turbidity measurement. Trans. Amer. Fish. Soc., 100: 682-690.

Ellis, M. M., Westfall, B. A., and Ellis, M., 1948. Determination of water quality. U. S. Fish and Wildlife Service, Washington, D. C., Research Report 9, 122 pp.

Emerson, K., Russo, C., Lund, R., and Thurston, R. V., 1975. Aqueous ammonia equilibrium calculations: effects of pH and temperature. J. Fish. Res. Bd. Canada, 32: 2379-2388.

European Inland Fisheries Advisory Commission, 1973. Water quality criteria for European freshwater fish. Report on ammonia and inland fisheries. Water Res., 7: 1011-1022.

Farmer, G. J. and Beamish, F. W. H., 1969. Oxygen consumption of _Tilapia nilotica_ in relation to swimming speed and salinity. J. Fish. Res. Bd. Canada, 26: 2807-2821.

Faruqui, A. M., 1975. Fluctuation in oxygen concentration and occurrence of mortality of carp hatchlings in a hatchery pond at Parta Fish Farm, Bhopal. Broteria Ser. Trimest. Cienc. Nat., 44: 67-79.

Fishleson, L. and Popper, D., 1968. Experiments on rearing fish in salt waters near the Dead Sea, Israel. Proc. World Symposium on Warmwater Pond Fish Culture. FAO United Nations, Fish. Rep. 44, 5: 244-245.

Garrels, R. M. and Christ, C. L., 1964. Solutions, Minerals, and Equilibria. Harper and Row, New York, 450 pp.

Golterman, H. L., Clymo, R. S., and Ohnstad, M. A. M., 1978. Methods for Physical and Chemical Analysis of Fresh Waters. Blackwell Scientific Publications, Oxford, 213 pp.

Hart, J. S., 1944. The circulation and respiratory tolerance of some Florida freshwater fishes. Proc. Fla. Acad. Sci., 7: 221-246.

Hem, J. D., 1970. Study and interpretation of the chemical characteristics of natural water. U. S. Geological Survey Water-Supply Paper 1473. U. S. Government Printing Office, Washington, D. C., 363 pp.

Hollerman, W. D. and Boyd, C. E., 1980. Nightly aeration to increase production of channel catfish. Trans. Amer. Fish. Soc., 109: 446-452.

Hora, S. L. and Pillay, T. V. R., 1962. Handbook on fish culture in the Indo-Pacific region. FAO United Nations, Fisheries Biology Technical Paper No. 14, 204 pp.

Hutchinson, G. E., 1957. A Treatise on Limnology: Vol. I. Geography, Physics, and Chemistry. John Wiley and Sons, New York. 1015 pp.

Irwin, W. H., 1945. Methods of precipitating colloidal soil particles from impounde waters of central Oklahoma. Bull. Oklahoma A. and M. College, Vol. 42, 16 pp.

Jhingran, V. G., 1975. Fish and Fisheries of India. Hindustan Publishing Corporation, New Delhi, India, 954 pp.

King, D. L., 1970. The role of carbon in eutrophicaton. J. Water Pollut. Control Fed., 42: 2035-2051.

Konikoff, M., 1975. Toxicity of nitrite to channel catfish. Prog. Fish-Cult., 37: 96-98.

Lloyd, R. and Herbert, D. W. M., 1960. The influence of carbon dioxide on the toxicity of un-ionized ammonia to rainbow trout (_Salmo gairdnerii_ Richardson). Ann. Appl. Biol., 48: 399-404.

Maciolek, J. A., 1962. Limnological analysis by quantitative dichromate oxidation. U. S. Bureau of Sport Fisheries and Wildlife Research, Washington, D. C., Report 60, 61 pp.

Mairs, D. F., 1966. A total alkalinity atlas for Maine lake waters. Limnol. Oceanogr., 11: 68-72.

McKee, J. E. and Wolf, H. W. (Editors), 1963. Water Quality Criteria, 2nd edition. State of California, State Water Quality Control Board, Sacremento, Publication 3-A, 548 pp.

Merkens, J. C. and Downing, K. M., 1957. The effect of tension of dissolved oxygen on the toxicity of un-ionized ammonia to several species of fish. Ann. Appl. Biol., 45: 521-527.

Moore, W. G., 1942. Field studies on the oxygen requirements of certain fresh-water fishes. Ecology, 23: 319-329.

Moss, D. D. and Scott, D. C., 1961. Dissolved oxygen requirements of three species of fish. Trans. Amer. Fish. Soc., 90: 377-393.

Moss, D. D. and Scott, D. C., 1964. Respiratory metabolism of fat and lean channel catfish. Prog. Fish-Cult., 26: 16-20.

Mount, D. I., 1973. Chronic effect of low pH on fathead minnow survival, growth and reproduction. Water Res., 7: 987-993.

Moyle, J. B., 1945. Some chemical factors influencing the distribution of aquatic plants in Minnesota. Amer. Midl. Natur., 34: 402-420.

Moyle, J. B., 1946. Some indices of lake productivity. Trans. Amer. Fish. Soc., 76: 322-334.

Nebeker, A. V. and Brett, J. R., 1976. Effects of air-supersaturated water on survival of Pacific salmon and steelhead smolts. Trans. Amer. Fish. Soc., 105: 338-342.

Perrone, S. J. and Meade, T. L., 1977. Protective effect of chloride on nitrite toxicity to coho salmon (Oncorhynchus kisutch). J. Fish. Res. Bd. Canada, 34: 486-492.

Perry, W. G., Jr. and Avault, J. W., Jr., 1969. Experiments on the culture blue, channel and white catfish in brackish water ponds. Proc. Annual Conf. Southeast. Assoc. Game and Fish Comm., 23: 592-605.

Plumb, J. A., Grizzle, J. M., and DeFigueriredo, J., 1976. Necrosis and bacterial infection in channel catfish (Ictalurus punctatus) following hypoxia. J. Wildl. Diseases, 12: 247-253.

Rappaport, U., Sarig, S., and Marek, M., 1976. Results of tests of various aeration systems on the oxygen regime in the Genosar experimental ponds and growth of fish there in 1975. Bamidgeh, 28: 35-49.

Reynolds, J. F., 1969. Comparison studies of Winkler vs. oxygen sensor. J. Water Pollut. Control Fed., 41: 2002-2009.

Robinette, H. R., 1976. Effect of selected sublethal levels of ammonia on the growth of channel catfish (Ictalurus punctatus). Prog. Fish-Cult., 38: 26-29.

Russo, R. C. and Thurston, R. V., 1977. The acute toxicity of nitrite to fishes. In: R. A. Tubb (Editor), Recent Advances in Fish Toxicology. U. S. Government Printing Office, Washington, D. C., 203 pp.

Sawyer, C. N. and McCarty, P. L., 1967. Chemistry for Sanitary Engineers. McGraw-Hill Book Co., New York, 518 pp.

Schindler, P. W., 1967. Heterogenous equilibria involving oxides, hydroxides, carbonates, and hydroxide carbonates. In: R. F. Gould (Editor), Equilibrium Concepts in Natural Water Systems. American Chemistry Society, Washington, D. C., Advances in Chemistry Series 67, pp. 196-221.

Schroeder, G. L., 1975. Nighttime material balance for oxygen in fish ponds receiving organic wastes. Bamidgeh, 27: 65-74.

Shell, E. W., 1965. Fisheries research annual report. Auburn University Agricultural Experiment Station, Auburn, Alabama, pp. 110-115.

Smith, C. E. and Piper, R. G., 1975. Lesions associated with chronic exposure to ammonia. In: W. E. Ribelin and G. Migaki (Editors), The Pathology of Fishes. University of Wisconsin Press, Madison, pp. 497-514.

Smith, L. L., Jr., Oseid, D. M., Kimball, G. L., and El-Kandelgy, S. M., 1976. Toxicity of hydrogen sulfide to various life history stages of bluegill (Lepomis macrochirus). Trans. Amer. Fish. Soc., 105: 442-449.

Snieszko, S. F., 1973. Recent advances of scientific knowledge and developments pertaining to disease of fishes. Adv. Vet. Sci. Comp. Med., 17: 291-314.

Stewart, N. E., Shumway, D. L., and Doudoroff, P., 1967. Influence of oxygen concentration on growth of juvenile largemouth bass. J. Fish. Res. Bd. Canada, 24: 475-494.

Swingle, H. S., 1945. Improvement of fishing in old ponds. Trans. North Amer. Wildl. Conf., 10: 299-308.

Swingle, H. S., 1961. Relationships of pH of pond waters to their suitability for fish culture. Proc. Pacific Sci. Congress 9 (1957), 10: 72-75.

Swingle, H. S., 1969. Methods of Analysis for Waters, Organic Matter, and Pond Bottom Soils Used in Fisheries Research. Auburn University, Auburn, Alabama, 119 pp.

Tomasso, J. R., Goudie, C. A., Simco, B. A., and Davis, K. B., 1980. Effects of environment pH and calcium on ammonia toxicity in channel catfish. Trans. Amer. Fish. Soc., 109: 229-234.

Tomasso, J. R., Simco, B. A., and Davis, K. B., 1979. Chloride inhibition of nitrite induced methemoglobinemia in channel catfish (Ictalurus punctatus). J. Fish. Res. Bd. Canada, 36: 1141-1144.

Trussell, R. P., 1971. The percent un-ionized ammonia in aqueous ammonia solutions at different pH levels and temperature. J. Fish. Res. Bd. Canada, 29: 1505-1507.

Tucker, L., Boyd, C. E., and McCoy, E. W., 1979. Effects of feeding rate on water quality, production of channel catfish, and economic returns. Trans. Amer. Fish. Soc., 108: 389-396.

Turner, W. R., 1960. Standing crops of fishes in Kentucky farm ponds. Trans. Amer. Fish. Soc., 89: 333-337.

United States Environmental Protection Agency, 1976. Methods for Chemical Analysis of Water and Wastes. Office of Technology Transfer, Cincinnati, Ohio, 298 pp.

Wallen, I. E., 1951. The direct effect of turbidity on fishes. Bull. Oklahoma A. and M. College, Vol. 48, No. 2, 27 pp.

Walters, G. R. and Plumb, J. A., 1980. Environmental stress and bacterial infection in channel catfish, Ictalurus punctatus Rafinesque. J. Fish. Biol., 17: 177-185.

Wedemeyer, G. A. and Yasutake, W. T., 1978. Prevention and treatment of nitrite toxicity in juvenile steelhead trout (Salmo gairdneri). J. Fish. Res. Bd. Canada, 35: 822-827.

Wetzel, R. G., 1975. Limnology. W. B. Saunders Co., Philadelphia, 743 pp.

Chapter 3

FERTILIZATION

3.1 INTRODUCTION

Fertilizers for fish ponds are classified as chemical fertilizers (inorganic compounds) or organic fertilizers (manures). Inorganic nutrients in chemical fertilizers stimulate phytoplankton production, thereby favoring greater abundance of fish food organisms and greater yields of fish. Phosphorus is a necessary ingredient of nearly all fish pond fertilizers because natural concentrations of phosphorus in pond waters are usually too low to foster abundant phytoplankton. Though phosphorus is normally the key nutrient to successful pond fertilization, nitrogen, potassium, and even other plant nutrients are sometimes applied to fish ponds in fertilizers.

Organic fertilizers decompose, releasing inorganic nutrients that stimulate phytoplankton growth. In this regard manures are similar to chemical fertilizers; however, organic fertilizers may also serve directly as food for invertebrate fish food organisms and fish. Organic fertilizers are usually agricultural wastes, so their use in fish culture is desirable. There is relatively little use of organic fertilizers in sportfish ponds in the United States, but they are widely used in many nations to increase yields of food fish.

3.2 PROPERTIES OF CHEMICAL FERTILIZERS
3.2.1 Primary nutrients

Fertilizers for ponds are similar or identical to those for agricultural crops. Nitrogen, phosphorus, and potassium are termed the primary nutrients in fertilizers. The fertilizer grade refers to the percentages by weight of nitrogen (as N), phosphorus (as P_2O_5), and potassium (as K_2O; called potash). Thus, a 10-10-5 fertilizer contains 10% N, 10% P_2O_5, and 5% K_2O, and a 13-38-0 fertilizer contains 13% N, 38% P_2O_5, and 0% K_2O. If the fertilizer grade is reduced by dividing by a common denominator, the fertilizer ratio is obtained. The ratio of the 10-10-5 fertilizer is 2:2:1, and the ratio of the 13-38-0 fertilizer is approximately 1:3:0. A complete fertilizer contains all three primary nutrients. The 10-10-5 fertilizer is a complete fertilizer, but the 13-38-0 fertilizer is not.

Actually, fertilizers do not contain N, P_2O_5, and K_2O. Nutrients in chemical fertilizers occur in simple inorganic compounds that ionize in water to release NO_3^-, NH_4^+, $H_2PO_4^-$, HPO_4^{2-}, or K^+, but the nutrient content of fertilizers has traditionally been expressed as percentages of equivalent N, P_2O_5, and K_2O. Recently, some workers have expressed the nutrient content of fertilizers as percentages of N, P, and K. This practice is simpler than using N, P_2O_5, and K_2O, but to prevent confusion, the traditional method of reporting fertilizer nutrients will be used here.

The nutrient content of fertilizers is usually determined by chemical analysis. Governmental regulations generally require that commercial fertilizers be analyzed by a reputable laboratory and the results of the analysis made available to the purchaser. The sale of fertilizers that do not meet the advertised grade will, in many nations, result in a stiff fine.

In some cases it may be necessary to convert percentages P and K to percentages P_2O_5 and K_2O, or vice versa. Suppose that one wants to calculate the P_2O_5 equivalence of a fertilizer that contains 10% P. Because one unit of P is equivalent to 0.5 unit of P_2O_5, a factor obtained by dividing the atomic weight of P by half the molecular weight of P_2O_5 may be used to convert P content to P_2O_5 equivalence:

$$\frac{P}{\frac{1}{2} P_2O_5} = \frac{31}{71} = 0.437$$

$$P_2O_5 = \frac{10}{0.437} = 22.9\%$$

Likewise, one can easily convert percentage P_2O_5 equivalence to percentage P as illustrated below for a fertilizer containing 46% P_2O_5:

$$\frac{\frac{1}{2} P_2O_5}{P} = \frac{71}{31} = 2.29$$

$$P = \frac{46\%}{2.29} = 20.1\%$$

The same procedures given above may be applied to potassium. Laboratory grade potassium chloride is 52.4% K; its K_2O equivalence is:

$$\frac{K}{\frac{1}{2} K_2O} = \frac{39.1}{47.1} = 0.83$$

$$K_2O = \frac{52.4\%}{0.83} = 63.1\%$$

Muriate of potash usually contains 60% K_2O; the potassium content of this substance is:

$$\frac{\frac{1}{2} K_2O}{K} = \frac{47.1}{39.1} = 1.20$$

$$K = \frac{60\%}{1.20} = 50\%.$$

3.2.2 Secondary and minor nutrients

Calcium, magnesium, and sulfur are called secondary nutrients in fertilizers. They either occur incidentally or are added. One or more of the minor nutrients (often called trace elements), copper, zinc, boron, manganese, iron, and molybdenum, may also be added in minute amounts to fertilizers. Common sources of secondary and trace elements are listed by Boyd (1979). However, aside from the application of calcium and magnesium to ponds in liming materials, there has been little use of secondary or trace elements in pond fertilization. The productivity of lakes is occasionally limited by secondary and minor elements (Goldman, 1965), hence it is conceivable that secondary or minor nutrients are also limiting in some fish ponds. The importance of secondary and minor nutrients in pond fertilization is a potentially fruitful area for research, but I will not discuss the subject further because of the paucity of information.

3.2.3 Sources of fertilizers

Jones (1979) lists an array of solid and liquid substances used as fertilizers; however, relatively few of these materials are used extensively. In the United States the most commonly employed solid fertilizers are urea, calcium nitrate, sodium nitrate, ammonium nitrate, ammonium sulfate, superphosphate, triple superphosphate, monoammonium phosphate, diammonium phosphate, and muriate of potash. Grades of the commercially available materials are given in Table 3.1. These fertilizers are usually in the form of pellets, flakes, or granules. Most particles will pass through a 4-mm screen but will be retained on a 0.86 mm screen. The commercial products are shipped in plastic or multilayer paper bags that hold 23 or 45 kg (50 or 100 pounds). Most fertilizers adsorb moisture and should be stored in a cool, dry place to prevent caking. Ammonium nitrate is extremely explosive if exposed to sparks or open flames. In fact, this material is sometimes treated with fuel oil and used as a substitute for dynamite. Sodium nitrate and urea will also support combustion; nitrogen materials and the bags in which they are shipped should be protected from flames and sparks. Solid commercial fertilizers are corrosive, and care must be taken to prevent them from corroding metals that they contact.

Liquid fertilizers are becoming increasingly important in agriculture. Liquified ammonia and urea solutions are most common, but liquid fertilizers that contain nitrogen, phosphorus, and other nutrients are available. The most common type of multinutrient liquid fertilizer is ammonium polyphosphate. Phosphoric acid, a liquid, is not applied directly to soil as a plant nutrient, but it is widely used in manufacturing other fertilizers. Phosphoric acid is suitable for

TABLE 3.1

Approximate grades of common commercial fertilizers (Jones, 1979).

Material	Percentage[a]		
	N	P_2O_5	K_2O
Urea	45	0	0
Calcium nitrate	15	0	0
Sodium nitrate	16	0	0
Ammonium nitrate	33	0	0
Ammonium sulfate	21	0	0
Superphosphate	0	20	0
Triple superphosphate	0	46	0
Monoammonium phosphate	11	48	0
Diammonium phosphate	18	48	0
Muriate of potash	0	0	60

[a]There may be some variation in grade, but the guaranteed grade is usually available from the supplier.

direct application to fish ponds. Liquid fertilizers are shipped and stored in steel tanks. Liquid ammonia is under pressure and must be handled carefully (Jones, 1979). Phosphoric acid is highly corrosive; ammonium polyphosphate is nearly neutral and does not corrode metals rapidly. Salting out of plant nutrients will occur during storage of clear, liquid ammonium polyphosphate. To prevent salting out, liquid ammonium polyphosphate is often mixed with a fine clay that does not settle rapidly. The resulting mixture is called a suspension fertilizer and is sufficiently fluid to be handled as a liquid.

Fertilizer manufacturing is discussed in detail in texts on fertilizers and soil fertility. However, a few comments on manufacturing will interest some readers. Almost all nitrogen for fertilizer manufacturing comes from compressing hydrogen and atmospheric nitrogen at high temperature to form anhydrous ammonia:

$$N_2 + 3 H_2 \rightarrow 2 NH_3$$

Anhydrous ammonia can be used in chemical processes to produce other nitrogen fertilizers. For example, ammonia may be used to produce nitric acid:

$$4 NH_3 + 5 O_2 \rightarrow 4 NO + 6 H_2O$$

$$2 \text{ NO} + O_2 \rightarrow 2NO_2$$

$$3 \text{ NO}_2 + H_2O \rightarrow 2 \text{ HNO}_3 + NO$$

Nitric acid may be reacted with ammonia to yield ammonium nitrate:

$$HNO_3 + NH_3 \rightarrow NH_4NO_3$$

Phosphorus for fertilizer manufacturing is derived from rock phosphate, which is mined from deposits in many parts of the world. Rock phosphate may be treated with sulfuric acid to produce phosphoric acid:

$$Ca_{10}F_2(PO_4)_6 + 10 \text{ H}_2SO_4 + 20 \text{ H}_2O \rightarrow 10 \text{ CaSO}_4 \cdot 2H_2O + 2 \text{ HF} + 6 \text{ H}_3PO_4$$

Likewise, treatment of rock phosphate with sulfuric acid and water in different proportions yields superphosphate:

$$Ca_{10}F_2(PO_4)_6 + 7 \text{ H}_2SO_4 + 3 \text{ H}_2O \rightarrow 3 \text{ Ca}(H_2PO_4)_2 \cdot H_2O + 7 \text{ CaSO}_4 + 2 \text{ HF}$$

Phosphoric acid may be used to produce other fertilizers; rock phosphate may be treated with phosphoric acid to obtain triple superphosphate:

$$Ca_{10}F_2(PO_4)_6 + 14 \text{ H}_3PO_4 \rightarrow 10 \text{ Ca}(H_2PO_4)_2 + 2 \text{ HF}$$

Diammonium phosphate may be produced by reacting ammonia and phosphoric acid:

$$2 \text{ NH}_3 + H_3PO_4 \rightarrow (NH_4)_2HPO_4$$

Potassium chloride (muriate of potash) is prepared through refining techniques for removing KCl from brines produced from potassium ores. Muriate of potash may be used directly as a fertilizer, or it may be used to produce other fertilizers. For example, muriate of potash reacts with nitric acid in the presence of oxygen to give potassium nitrate:

$$4 \text{ KCl} + 4 \text{ HNO}_3 + O_2 \rightarrow 4 \text{ KNO}_3 + 2 \text{ Cl}_2 + 2 \text{ H}_2O$$

3.2.4 Mixed fertilizers

Fertilizers with specific grades are made by mixing appropriate quantities of nitrogen, phosphorus, and potassium fertilizers. Ingredients needed to supply the primary nutrients for 100 kg of a particular grade seldom weigh 100 kg; a filler is added to make up the difference in weight. The filler may be an inert material, or it may be a neutralizing agent, such as limestone, to reduce acidity. Many different grades of fertilizer are commercially available. Alternatively, one may calculate the amounts of two or more fertilizers required to provide a mixed fertilizer of specific grade.

Calculations for preparation of 100 kg of 5-15-5 fertilizer from ammonium nitrate (33.5% N), triple superphosphate (46% P_2O_5), muriate of potash (60% K_2O), and limestone filler are illustrated below:

```
5 kg N/0.335          =  14.9 kg ammonium nitrate
15 kg P₂O₅/0.46       =  32.6 kg triple superphosphate
5 kg K₂O/0.60         =   8.3 kg muriate of potash
Fertilizer sources    =  55.8 kg
Limestone filler      =  44.2 kg
Total                 = 100.0 kg
```

The calculations for preparing mixed fertilizers are only slightly more difficult when one of the source materials contains two primary nutrients. The appropriate calculations for preparing 100 kg of 10-15-10 fertilizer from diammonium phosphate (18% N; 46% P_2O_5), urea (45% N), muriate of potash (60% K_2O), and limestone filler are:

```
15 kg P₂O₅/0.46 = 32.6 kg diammonium phosphate
10 kg K₂O/0.60 = 16.7 kg muriate of potash
32.6 kg diammonium phosphate X 0.19 = 5.9 kg N
10 kg N - 5.9 kg N = 4.1 kg N needed from urea
4.1 kg N/0.45 = 9.1 kg urea
32.6 kg + 16.7 kg + 9.1 kg = 58.4 kg fertilizers
100 kg - 58.4 = 41.6 kg limestone filler
```

Sometimes, it is not possible to make a particular grade of fertilizer from a given set of source materials. To illustrate, one cannot prepare 100 kg of 20-20-5 fertilizer from ammonium nitrate (33.5% N), triple superphosphate (46% P_2O_5), and muriate of potash (60% K_2O):

```
20 kg N/0.335         =  59.7 kg ammonium nitrate
20 kg P₂O₅/0.46       =  43.5 kg triple superphosphate
5 kg K₂O/0.60         =   8.3 kg muriate of potash
Fertilizer sources    = 111.5 kg
```

To prepare a 20-20-5 fertilizer, one must select fertilizer sources more concentrated in primary nutrients. For example, we could make the 20-20-5 fertilizer from
monoammonium phosphate (11% N; 55% P_2O_5), urea (45% N), and muriate of potash
(60% K_2O):

20 kg P_2O_5/0.55 = 36.4 kg monoammonium phosphate
5 kg K_2O/0.60 = 8.3 kg muriate of potash
36.4 kg monoammonium phosphate X 0.11 = 4.0 kg N
20 kg N - 4 kg N = 16 kg N needed from urea
16 kg N/0.45 = 35.6 kg urea
36.4 kg + 8.3 kg + 35.6 kg = 80.3 kg fertilizer
100 kg - 80.3 kg = 19.7 kg limestone filler

Liquid fertilizers may also be mixed to provide complete fertilizers. Liquid
fertilizer dealers store the different fertilizer sources in large tanks. Almost
any grade of mixed fertilizer may be prepared by measuring the required quantities
of two or more solutions into a large vat and blending them. Clay is often added to
the liquid mixtures to yield suspension fertilizers. Secondary elements and
micronutrients may be added to liquid or suspension fertilizers.

Unfortunately, liquid fertilizers are not yet available in many localities,
and where available, they are not packaged in small quantities for convenient use
in fish ponds.

3.2.5   Solubility of fertilizers

Fertilizers obviously must be water soluble if nutrients contained in them are to
be available to plants. Solid fertilizers are often broadcast over pond surfaces in
areas where the water is not more than 2 m deep. Boyd (1981a) determined the dissolution of primary nutrients from settling fertilizer particles by measuring the
increase in nitrogen, phosphorus, and potassium concentrations in a 2-m column of
water after known quantities of fertilizers settled through the column. The percentage dissolution of phosphorus at 29°C for selected fertilizers was: superphosphate, 4.6%; triple superphosphate, 5.1%; monoammonium phosphate, 7.1%; diammonium
phosphate, 16.8%. At the same temperature, dissolution of nitrogen from fertilizers was: monoammonium phosphate, 5.1%; diammonium phosphate, 11.7%; sodium nitrate,
61.7%; ammonium sulfate, 85.9%; ammonium nitrate, 98.8%; calcium nitrate, 98.7%.
Eighty seven percent of the potassium dissolved from muriate of potash falling
through the 2-m column. Thus, fertilizers containing phosphorus do not dissolve
appreciably while settling through 2 m of water, but nitrogen (other than compounds
containing phosphorus) and potassium sources were highly soluble. Fine granules
of diammonium phosphate (<0.42 mm in diameter) dissolved more completely while

settling through 2 m of water than did normal size (0.86-4.0 mm) particles. Unfortunately, the small granules are not commercially available.

Fertilizers that did not dissolve quickly while settling dissolved almost
completely after standing in water for 24 h. The importance of dissolution of
fertilizers before settling to the pond bottom will be discussed later. Liquid
fertilizers are almost totally water soluble if there is adequate mixing to
prevent downward density flow of the heavy fertilizer.

3.2.6 Acidity of nitrogen fertilizers

Ammonium fertilizers are sources of acidity in agricultural soils (Tisdale
and Nelson, 1956). Acidity results from nitrification, the bacterial process
whereby ammonium is oxidized to nitric acid (Alexander, 1961):

$$2 \ NH_4^+ + 3 \ O_2 \rightarrow 2 \ NO_2^- + 4 \ H^+ + 2 \ H_2O$$

$$2 \ NO_2^- + O_2 \rightarrow 2 \ NO_3^-$$

The reactions are caused by chemoautotrophic bacteria, the first reaction by
Nitrosomonas spp. and the second by Nitrobacter spp., which obtain energy from
the oxidization of reduced inorganic nitrogen. Both genera coexist in soils
and in waters, hence the two reactions proceed simultaneously, Hydrogen ion
produced in nitrification will destroy alkalinity in pond water by the following
reaction:

$$HCO_3^- + H^+ \rightarrow H_2O + CO_2$$

The maximum amounts of alkalinity theoretically destroyed by different nitrogen
fertilizers will be calculated below.

Half of the nitrogen in ammonium nitrate is fully oxidized. However, oxidation
of the ammonium in 1 mM of ammonium nitrate will release 2 meq of H^+ that will
be associated with nitrate to form nitric acid:

$$NH_4NO_3 + 2 \ O_2 \rightarrow 2 \ H^+ + 2 \ NO_3^- + H_2O$$

An amount of alkalinity (expressed as $CaCO_3$) equivalent to the H^+ released by
nitrification could potentially be destroyed. Since 1 mM of NH_4NO_3 yields 2 meq
of H^+ that react with 2 meq of alkalinity (100 mg of $CaCO_3$), 1 mg of NH_4NO_3 could
destroy 1.25 mg of alkalinity:

1 mg   x
NH_4NO_3 = 2 H^+ = $CaCO_3$
80 mg   100 mg
x = 1.25 mg alkalinity

Pure NH_4NO_3 is 35% N; each milligram of nitrogen in this substance could theoretically destroy 3.57 mg of alkalinity:

1.25 mg alkalinity per mg NH_4NO_3 ÷ 0.35 mg N per mg NH_4NO_3 = 3.57 mg alkalinity
     per mg N

Ammonium resulting from the dissociation of 1 mM of ammonium sulfate could
produce 4 meq of H^+; the H^+ would be associated with nitrate to form nitric acid
and sulfate to form sulfuric acid:

$$(NH_4)_2SO_4 + 4\ O_2 \rightarrow 4\ H^+ + 2\ NO_3^- + SO_4^{2-} + 2\ H_2O$$

Thus, each milligram of ammonium sulfate could destroy 1.52 mg of alkalinity;
1 mg of N from this compound could destroy 7.17 mg of alkalinity.

Monoammonium phosphate will, upon nitrification, result in nitric and phosphoric
acids:

$$NH_4H_2PO_4 + 2\ O_2 \rightarrow 2\ H^+ + NO_3^- + H_2PO_4^- + H_2O$$

At the pH of natural waters, phosphoric acid (H_3PO_4) is dissociated into H^+ and
$H_2PO_4^-$ ions. Thus, 2 meq of H^+ could result from the nitrification of 1 mM of
$NH_4H_2PO_4$. Each milligram of monoammonium phosphate could destroy 0.87 mg of
alkalinity, or 1 mg of N from this material could destroy 7.13 mg of alkalinity.

Nitrification of ammonium from 1 mM of diammonium phosphate could release
4 meq of H^+; 2 meq would associate with NO_3^- and 2 meq with HPO_4^{2-}. Because
only the first dissociation of H_3PO_4 is complete at the pH of most natural
waters, the acidity of diammonium phosphate may be expressed as:

$$(NH_4)_2HPO_4 + 4\ O_2 \rightarrow 3\ H^+ + 2\ NO_3^- + H_2PO_4^- + 2\ H_2O$$

Alkalinity reduction would be 1.14 mg per mg of diammonium phosphate or 5.38 mg
of alkalinity per mg of N.

Urea hydrolyzes in water to yield NH_3 and CO_2:

$$(NH_2)_2CO + H_2O \rightarrow 2\ NH_3 + CO_2$$

Ammonia is basic:

$$NH_3 + H_2O \rightarrow NH_4^+ + OH^-$$

The nitrification of ammonia from 1 mM of urea gives 4 meq of H^+; 2 meq associate with nitrate and 2 meq are neutralized by OH^-. Thus, each milligram of urea could destroy 1.67 mg of alkalinity, or 1 mg of N from urea could neutralize 3.58 mg of alkalinity.

Ammonium and polyphosphate ions are released upon dissolution of ammonium polyphosphate fertilizers, but polyphosphate gradually hydrolyzes to orthophosphate. The formula of the ammonium polyphosphate in liquid fertilizer is not available, so no attempt is made to calculate the potential loss of alkalinity resulting from the use of this fertilizer.

Hunt and Boyd (1981) measured losses of alkalinity resulting from nitrification of ammonium fertilizers in laboratory mud-water systems. Measured losses agreed well with stoichiometric calculations of potential alkalinity losses (Table 3.2), verifying that total potential acidity of ammonium fertilizers may be calculated. In ponds the actual loss of alkalinity per unit of ammonium fertilizer would be less than the potential loss. When nitrogen is added to ponds in fertilizer, it is absorbed by plants, assimilated into tissues of animals that eat plants, lost in seepage or outflow, adsorbed by muds, lost through ammonia volatilization or lost following denitrification (Boyd, 1979). Nevertheless, application of enough agricultural limestone to ponds to neutralize the total potential acidity of ammonium fertilizers (Table 3.3) would be beneficial since there are other sources of acidity.

TABLE 3.2

Losses of total alkalinity (mg/l) measured 30 days after treatment of mud-water systems with nitrogen fertilizers and stoichiometric calculations of alkalinity losses. Losses are for 4 mg/l of nitrogen (Hunt and Boyd, 1981).

Material	Measured	Calculated
Ammonium nitrate	10.9	14.3
Ammonium sulfate	26.2	28.7
Monoammonium phosphate	28.6	28.5
Diammonium phosphate	16.6	21.5
Urea	12.2	14.3
Ammonium polyphosphate	23.1	

TABLE 3.3

Amounts of agricultural limestone (neutralizing value of 100%) required to counteract the acidity of selected nitrogen fertilizers (Hunt and Boyd, 1981).

Material	Kg of agricultural limestone per 100 kg fertilizer
Ammonium nitrate (33-0-0)	118
Ammonium sulfate (21-0-0)	151
Monoammonium phosphate (11-48-0)	79
Diammonium phosphate (18-48-0)	97
Urea (45-0-0)	161
Ammonium polyphosphate (10-34-0)	72

3.3   PRIMARY NUTRIENTS IN PONDS

3.3.1   Phosphorus

The biogeochemical cycle of phosphorus in ponds is depicted in Fig. 3.1. The
dynamics of phosphorus in ponds will be described in the following paragraphs.

Filtrable orthophosphate, often termed soluble orthophosphate, is the form of
phosphorus most often measured. Concentrations of orthophosphate increase
almost immediately after ponds are fertilized, only to decline rapidly to pretreatment levels. Most pond fertilization programs require applications of
inorganic phosphorus sufficient to increase filtrable orthophosphate by 0.1-0.5
mg/l as P — provided that the fertilizer dissolves completely and mixes throughout

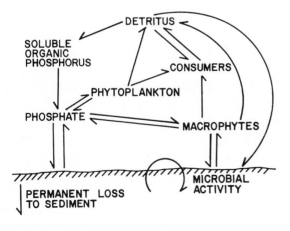

Fig. 3.1. The phosphorus cycle in a fish pond.

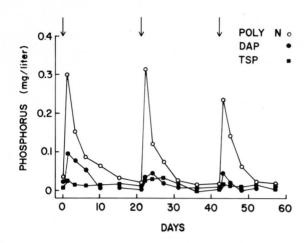

Fig. 3.2. Concentrations of filtrable orthophosphate in waters of three ponds following fertilization with three fertilizers at 9 kg/ha of P_2O_5 per application: Poly N = ammonium polyphosphate (10-34-0), DAP = diammonium phosphate (18-46-0), and TSP = triple superphosphate (0-46-0). Data are from Boyd et al. (1981).

the volume of water. If solid fertilizer is applied by broadcasting, filtrable orthophosphate concentrations will be far below potential values (Fig. 3.2). This results because the fertilizer particles quickly settle to the pond bottom without dissolving appreciably. The particles dissolve on the pond bottom where the phosphorus is adsorbed by muds. Most of the phosphorus applied in liquid fertilizer dissolves in the water, so orthophosphate concentrations approach potential values (Fig. 3.2).

The orthophosphate present in water immediately after fertilization may be absorbed by bacteria, phytoplankton, and macrophytes (Rigler, 1956, 1964; Hayes and Phillips, 1958). Studies using radioactive phosphorus demonstrated that phytoplankton can absorb orthophosphate very quickly, with a large percentage of the total uptake occurring within a few minutes (Coffin et al., 1949; Hayes and Phillips, 1958). Boyd and Musig (1981) demonstrated that phytoplankton in water samples from fish ponds absorbed an average of 41% of 0.30 mg/l additions of orthophosphate within 24 h. Phosphorus absorption by macrophytes is apparently slower than for phytoplankton (Hayes and Phillips, 1958), but macrophytes can absorb and store large amounts of phosphorus (Boyd, 1971). Gerloff and Skoog (1954) and Gerloff (1969) demonstrated that phytoplankton and macrophytes exhibit luxury consumption of phosphorus — they absorb and store more than needed for maximum growth. Phosphorus stored in aquatic plants may be used for growth at a later time (Goldberg et al., 1951; Mackereth, 1952).

Competition by different plant species for phosphorus is an important consideration in pond fertilization. If large populations of macrophytes are present, they will compete strongly with phytoplankton for applied phosphorus. Stands of macrophytes tie up comparatively large amounts of phosphorus and retain it through-out the growing season. Phytoplankton cells, on the other hand, have a short life span, and upon death, their phosphorus is released into the water for use by other cells (Fitzgerald, 1970a).

The rapid decline in filtrable orthosphate following pond fertilization is illustrated in Fig. 3.2. One would hope that most of the added phosphorus is absorbed by plants. However, phosphorus that is not absorbed by plants is rapidly adsorbed by muds (Hepher, 1958). Fitzgerald (1970b) showed that 0.4 g of dry mud could absorb 0.05 mg of orthophosphate in less than 30 min. Roughly 90% of the orthophosphate added to undisturbed mud-water systems was adsorbed by mud within 4 days (Kimmel and Lind, 1970). Boyd and Musig (1981) showed that ortho-phosphate concentrations declined logarithmetically with time in laboratory mud-water systems (Fig. 3.3). The declines in orthophosphate concentrations following fertilization of a pond and an outdoor pool were similar to those observed in laboratory mud-water systems; the loss of orthophosphate after 1 day was greater in the pond and pool than in the laboratory systems. The laboratory systems contained no plants, but the pond and the pool had moderate densities of phyto-plankton. Therefore, phosphorus uptake by phytoplankton apparently accounted for the differences in the intercepts of the phosphorus uptake graphs of the two types of systems (Fig. 3.4). Many other workers have demonstrated that muds rapidly adsorb phosphorus. In general, muds that are strongly acidic or strongly alkaline absorb phosphorus more readily than slightly acidic or neutral muds. Eren et al. (1977) presented data indicating that phosphorus concentrations in muds of fertilized ponds increased over time; they also found that these muds gradually decreased in ability to remove phosphorus from water. Further research is needed to verify this result because it suggests that phosphorus fertilization rates could be reduced in ponds with a history of fertilization.

The mechanisms of orthophosphate uptake by sediment are discussed by Boyd (1979). However, from a practical point, one only needs to know that muds rapidly adsorb orthophosphate not absorbed by plants.

In waters with high calcium concentration and elevated pH, calcium phosphate may precipitate directly from the water; phosphorus is lost without involvement of mud. Hepher (1958) assumed that $Ca_3(PO_4)_2$ (tricalcium phosphate) with a K_{sp} of 10^{-25} was the precipitating compound and calculated the concentrations of orthophosphate that could exist at different pH values and calcium concentrations. For example, at a Ca^{2+} concentration of 20 mg/l, more than 10 mg/l (as P) orthophosphate can exist in solution at pH 8, but at pH 10 the orthophosphate concentration cannot exceed 0.25 mg/l. At a Ca^{2+} concentration of 100 mg/l, the respective concentrations of orthophosphate are 2.5 and 0.01 mg/l as P at pH 8 and 10. More recent work in soil solution chemistry suggests that

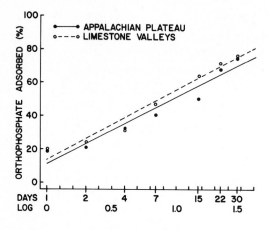

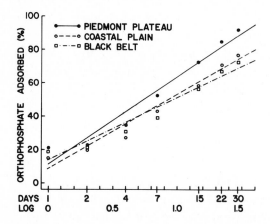

Fig. 3.3. Relationship between orthophosphate uptake by muds and time in laboratory mud-water systems. Muds were from ponds of five different soils areas of Alabama (Boyd and Musig, 1981).

$Ca_3(PO_4)_2$ does not exist in nature, and the precipitating compound is likely apatite, a more complex calcium phosphate even less soluble than tricalcium phosphate. Thus, orthophosphate concentrations will probably decline faster in ponds with hard, alkaline waters and muds than in ponds with acidic waters and muds because of the direct precipitation of phosphorus under conditions of high pH and high calcium concentration. Ammonium phosphates, rather than calcium phosphates, should obviously be used as phosphorus fertilizers in ponds with hard, alkaline waters.

In addition to orthophosphate, pond waters contain soluble organic phosphorus and particulate phosphorus. The soluble organic phosphorus and the phosphorus contained in dead particulate organic matter is mineralized by bacteria to soluble orthophosphate at an unknown rate. Phosphorus contained in living

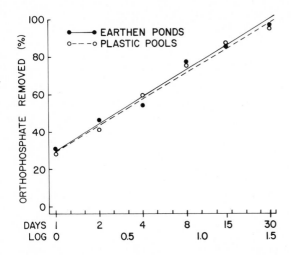

Fig. 3.4. Relationship between orthophosphate decline in ponds and in mud-water systems in outdoor, plastic pools (Boyd and Musig, 1981).

particulate matter probably has a high turnover rate because of the short life span of the planktonic organisms. The partitioning of the total phosphorus in pond waters has not been thoroughly studied, so there are no reliable data on the proportions of the total phosphorus present in soluble organic or inorganic forms, in detritus, or in living plankton. One observation is consistent: except soon after fertilizer applications, orthophosphate concentrations are only a small fraction (usually <10%) of total phosphorus concentrations. For practical purposes, the difference between total phosphorus and filtrable orthophosphate concentrations may be used as an index of the phosphorus contained in plankton and detritus. Fish and other macroscopic organisms have fairly high concentrations of phosphorus, and their combined biomass contains a rather large amount of phosphorus.

Phosphate in mud is released in large amounts to the water when iron and aluminum phosphates dissociate under reducing conditions in the hypolimnion of ponds. This phosphate is not available to plants as long as thermal stratification persists. When pond waters destratify, phosphorus from the hypolimnion is mixed throughout the water volume and is temporarily available to plants. However, the processes described above cause phosphorus concentrations to quickly return to normal.

Iron, aluminum, and calcium phosphates in aerobic sediments are slightly soluble, and a dynamic equilibrium exists between phosphate in sediments and in overlaying water. If the equilibrium state between phosphate in water and sediment is disrupted by phosphate absorption by plants, more phosphate will be released by the sediment. Many fish culturists assume that sediment is a source of phosphorus for phytoplankton growth. However, the literature on the availability of sediment phosphate is contradictory. Pomeroy et al. (1965) determined exchange rates of phosphorus between sediment and water and concluded that phosphate release was enough to maintain continued plant growth. Several workers have claimed that phosphate from sediment was responsible for phytoplankton growth during periods when dissolved orthophosphate concentrations were not adequate to support observed rates of growth (Pomeroy et al., 1956; Ragotzkie and Pomeroy, 1957; and Ryther et al., 1958). Golterman et al. (1969) obtained good growth of planktonic algae in laboratory cultures where mud was the only source of phosphate. Chiou and Boyd (1974) also found mud to be a good source of phosphate for phytoplankton in laboratory cultures, and the density of algae in the cultures increased with increasing concentrations of phosphate in the muds. Other workers have conveyed a negative opinion regarding muds as sources of phosphorus for phytoplankton. Latterell et al. (1971) found that orthophosphate concentrations in water must be extremely low before sediments will release phosphate. They concluded that sediment was a phosphate sink, and phosphate from sediment would not support abundant growth of phytoplankton. Fitzgerald (1970a, b) reported that lake muds do not provide phosphorus for growth of aquatic plants.

Hepher (1966) presented a logical assessment of the availability of phosphate from sediment. He obtained primary productivity values for fertilized and unfertilized ponds in Israel. Data on phosphorus uptake by phytoplankton were then used with the productivity data to estimate the amounts of phosphorus needed to sustain the observed primary productivity. Next, Hepher determined the rate of release of phosphate from sediments in the ponds. He concluded that the release of phosphate from sediment was an important source of this nutrient in unfertilized ponds. Calculated rates of phosphorus uptake by phytoplankton in fertilized ponds were 4.5-5.5 times greater than the amounts of phosphate released from the muds. Thus, Hepher stated that high rates of primary productivity necessary for intensive fish production depend upon frequent applications of phosphate fertilizer to keep orthophosphate concentrations above concentrations present at equilibrium.

To summarize, phosphorus from muds is important in regulating phytoplankton productivity in unfertilized ponds, and unfertilized ponds with high concentrations of phosphorus in muds will be more productive than ponds with low concentrations of phosphorus in muds. In fertilized ponds, muds act as sinks for phosphorus. Over the years, phosphorus accumulates in the muds of fertilized ponds, shifting the phosphate equilibrium in favor of the water. Nevertheless, even after many years of fertilization, phosphorus must usually be added to ponds to maintain high primary productivity (Metzger and Boyd, 1980).

Rooted macrophytes are capable of absorbing phosphorus from the sediment
(McRoy and Barsdate, 1970; Bristow and Whitcombe, 1971; Denny, 1972). Macrophytes occur above the thermocline, and the surfaces of muds beneath epilimnetic
waters are aerobic. At a depth of a few centimeters, muds are anaerobic and
concentrations of phosphate in the interstitial water increase because the low
redox potential favors the solubility of iron and aluminum phosphates. Thus,
roots of macrophytes draw upon the abundant supply of phosphorus in sediment.
Phosphorus in the anaerobic depths of sediment does not enter the overlaying
water where it could be absorbed by phytoplankton or the leaves of macrophytes.
Instead, it precipitates at the interface between anaerobic and aerobic layers
of sediment.

3.3.2 Nitrogen

The chemical equilibrium between phosphate in the mud and water dominates the
phosphorus cycle. Though the phosphorus cycle is extremely important in regulating primary productivity, most of the phosphorus in pond ecosystems exists in
inorganic combination. The nitrogen cycle (Fig. 3.5) is, by contrast, a biochemical cycle in which most transformations involve biochemical reactions, and
most of the nitrogen in a pond ecosystem is bound in living organisms and
decaying organic matter.

Forms of nitrogen in water include: nitrogen gas, nitrate, nitrite, ammonium,
ammonia, and various forms of organic nitrogen. Organic nitrogen ranges from
relatively simple dissolved compounds, such as amino acids, to complex particulate
organic matter. Nitrogen occurs in the mud in the same forms that exist in waters.

Fertilizers usually contain nitrogen in ammonium or nitrate. They dissolve
readily and the resulting ions may be absorbed by plants and assimilated into
organic nitrogen — usually in the form of protein. Plants may be consumed by
animals and the nitrogen assimilated into protein of animal tissue. Ultimately,
nitrogen incorporated into plant or animal protein will become dead organic
matter that will be decomposed by microorganisms.

Decomposition of organic matter is regulated by temperature, pH, oxygen supply,
and the nature of the organic matter. The temperature optima of microorganisms
differ among species, but decomposition is favored by warmth. Rates of decomposition generally increases over the range 5-35°C. A temperature increase of
10°C often doubles the rate of decomposition. The pH preferences of different
species of microorganisms also differ, but as a general rule, bacteria grow
best in neutral to slightly alkaline habitats while fungi flourish in more
acidic environments. Organic matter is degraded faster in neutral or alkaline
systems than in acidic systems. Aerobic decomposition requires a continuous
supply of oxygen and procedes more rapidly when dissolved oxygen concentrations
are near saturation. Decomposition also occurs under anaerobic conditions.

Some microorganisms are capable of degrading organic matter in either aerobic or anaerobic habitats (facultative anaerobic organisms), while other microorganisms grow only under anaerobic conditions (obligate anaerobic organisms). In aerobic decomposition, organic carbon is oxidized to carbon dioxide, but in anaerobic decomposition organic carbon is oxidized only to the level of simplier organic substances, such as alcohols and organic acids. The rate of degradation of organic matter is more rapid and complete in aerobic environments than in anaerobic ones. In fish ponds, organic matter concentrations in muds increase from shallow to deep water (Boyd, 1976a). This apparently results because the sediments in the deeper waters are covered during warm months by anaerobic waters of the hypolimnion.

The nature of organic matter is probably the most important factor governing decomposition at a given site. Some organic substances are more resistant to decay than others. For example, sugar is decomposed faster than cellulose and cellulose faster than lignin. Certain species of microorganisms are more effective in decomposing some compounds than others, and environmental conditions may favor decomposition of one type of organic matter over another. Nevertheless, bacteria are ubiquitous and species capable of attacking almost any kind of organic matter are present in most ecological systems. The rate of decomposition of organic matter is highest during the early stages of decomposition when the readily decomposable compounds are being utilized. Progressively slower rates of decomposition occur as microorganisms use up the easily decomposed compounds and begin to use resistant compounds.

The carbon:nitrogen ratio has a great influence on the rate of decomposition of organic matter and on the transformation of nitrogen from organic to inorganic

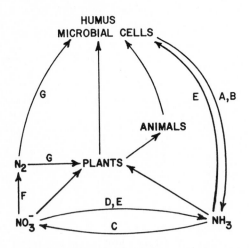

A. AMMONIFICATION
B. MINERALIZATION
C. NITRIFICATION
D. NITRATE REDUCTION
E. IMMOBILIZATION
F. DENITRIFICATION
G. N_2 FIXATION

Fig. 3.5. The nitrogen cycle.

form. Substances with a wide C:N ratio, e.g., 40% C and 0.5% N, decompose slowly; materials with a narrow C:N ratio, e.g., 40% C and 4% N, decay quickly. The C:N ratio is important because microbes are composed primarily of protein and have large percentages of carbon and nitrogen (Table 3.4). Organic matter absorbed by microbes contains more carbon than can be used for growth, and the excess is released to the environment as carbon dioxide. The percentage of the substrate carbon converted to bacterial protoplasm is called the carbon assimilation efficiency (Table 3.4). Nitrogen is also needed for growth of microbial cells. If a substrate contains a large amount of nitrogen, microbes will have plenty of nitrogen for rapid growth, and the nitrogen will be released to the environment as ammonia. This process is called mineralization of nitrogen. Microbes cannot grow rapidly on a substrate deficient in nitrogen because there is not enough nitrogen for constructing microbial cells. Inorganic nitrogen may be removed from the environment (immobilized) to offset the nitrogen deficiency of the substrate. However, unless the environment contains abundant inorganic nitrogen, decomposition of substrates with a wide C:N ratio will be slow and incomplete.

A better understanding of the role of the C:N ratio can be obtained by using the percentages of carbon and nitrogen in microbes and their substrates and carbon assimilation efficiencies of microbes (Table 3.4) to work some problems.

TABLE 3.4
Percentages of carbon and nitrogen and carbon assimilation efficiencies (percentage of substrate carbon converted to microbial carbon) for microbes.

| Microbes | % Dry Weight | | Carbon assimilation efficiency (%) |
	Carbon	Nitrogen	
Bacteria (anaerobic)	50	10	2-5
Bacteria (aerobic)	50	10	5-10
Actinomycetes	50	10	15-30
Fungi	50	5	30-40

Suppose that 100 kg of organic matter containing 40% C and 2% N are decomposed by bacteria with a carbon assimilation efficiency of 5%. Will nitrogen be mineralized or immobilized?

100 kg organic matter X 0.4 = 40 kg substrate carbon
100 kg organic matter X 0.02 = 2 kg substrate nitrogen
40 kg substrate carbon X 0.05 = 2 kg bacterial carbon
2 kg bacteria carbon ÷ 0.5 = 4 kg bacteria

4 kg bacteria X 0.1 = 0.4 kg bacterial nitrogen

2 kg substrate nitrogen - 0.4 kg bacterial nitrogen = 1.6 kg of nitrogen
    mineralized.

Assume that another substrate contains 40% C but only 0.2% N. Will nitrogen be
mineralized or immobilized if the substrate is decomposed by bacteria with a
carbon assimilation efficiency of 5%?

100 kg organic matter X 0.4 = 40 kg substrate carbon

100 kg organic matter X 0.002 = 0.2 kg substrate nitrogen

40 kg substrate carbon X 0.05 = 2 kg bacterial carbon

2 kg bacterial carbon ÷ 0.5 = 4 kg bacteria

4 kg bacteria X 0.1 = 0.4 kg bacterial nitrogen

Hence, the substrate does not contain enough nitrogen for complete decomposition,
unless nitrogen is immobilized from the environment. Of course, bacteria growing
on the substrate may die and their nitrogen be recycled.

Suppose that 100 kg of organic residue with 40% C and 2% N are decomposed by
fungi with a carbon assimilation efficiency of 35%. How does the nitrogen budget
for decomposition by fungi compare with that by bacteria?

100 kg organic matter X 0.4 = 40 kg substrate carbon

100 kg organic matter X 0.02 = 2 kg substrate nitrogen

40 kg substrate carbon X 0.35 = 14 kg fungal carbon

14 kg fungal carbon ÷ 0.5 = 28 kg fungi

28 kg fungi X 0.05 = 1.4 kg fungal nitrogen

2 kg substrate nitrogen - 1.4 kg fungal nitrogen = 0.6 kg nitrogen mineralized

See above for calculations for bacteria; the comparison follows:

	Bacteria	Fungi
Protoplasmic carbon produced (kg)	2	14
Carbon evolved as CO_2 (kg)	38	26
Protoplasmic nitrogen produced (kg)	0.4	1.4
Nitrogen mineralized (kg)	1.6	0.6

Thus, more microbial biomass is formed and less nitrogen is mineralized by fungi
than by bacteria.

The addition of organic residues to environments can have one of two consequences. Residues high in nitrogen (narrow C:N ratio) will decompose completely, and the nitrogen mineralized will aid in the decomposition of organic matter initially present. Thus, the amount of organic matter in the environment will be less after decomposition of the residue than before. This phenomenon has been aptly described by soil microbiologists as "fanning the microbial fires". Residues low in nitrogen will not decompose completely, and the amount of organic matter in the environment will increase.

The above discussion of the role of the C:N ratio is oversimplified, but the premises are valid and consistent with observations of decomposition in agricultural soils. A study by Almazan and Boyd (1978a) verified that the C:N ratio also regulates degradation of residues in aquatic habitats. Dead aquatic plants served as the sole source of nitrogen for decay in cultures enriched with all other nutrients. Rates of decomposition were estimated by the consumption of oxygen by microbes in the cultures. Oxygen consumption was greater in cultures containing aquatic plant residues with high nitrogen contents than in cultures with residues of low nitrogen contents. The addition of inorganic nitrogen to cultures containing low nitrogen content residues increased rates of oxygen consumption. Boyd (1974) also demonstrated by a bioassay technique that more nitrogen was mineralized from aquatic plant residues with high nitrogen contents than from those containing less nitrogen. Decomposing aquatic plants were the only source of nitrogen in algal cultures enriched with all other growth factors. The growth of the algae in the cultures increased as a function of the percentage of nitrogen in the residues.

The role of nitrogen in decomposition explains some commonly observed phenomena in ponds. Ponds with acidic waters tend to accumulate large amounts of organic matter because decomposition by bacteria is repressed and most decay is by fungi. When killed with herbicides, reedswamp plants decay more slowly than submersed macrophytes. Submersed macrophytes decay at a lesser rate than phytoplankton. Nitrogen content increases in the order: reedswamp plants < submersed species < phytoplankton (Boyd, 1978). Organic matter accumulates faster in muds of unfertilized ponds than in muds of fertilized ponds because nitrogen added in fertilizers favors decay of residues.

Ammonia that reaches water from fertilizers, animal excrements, or decay of organic residues exists in a pH dependent equilibrium with ammonium ion:

$$NH_3 + H_2O = NH_4^+ + OH^-$$

As pH increases, the amount of NH_3 increases and that of NH_4^+ decreases. At high pH, considerable NH_3 may be lost to the atmosphere by volatilization. Bouldin et al. (1974) found that ammonia volatilization from ponds was 2-38% per day of the total ammonia nitrogen concentrations present at the beginning of

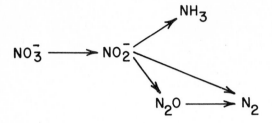

Fig. 3.6. Pathways of dentrification.

the period of measurement. The higher volatilization rates were found in ponds with the greatest total ammonia nitrogen concentrations and highest pH values.

Ammonia can be nitrified to nitrate by bacteria. Organisms that oxidize ammonia to nitrite and those that oxidize nitrite to nitrate coexist, so nitrite does not accumulate in natural environments as a result of nitrification. Data on nitrification rates in fish ponds are unavailable. In soils, nitrification is most rapid at pH 7-8 and at temperatures of 25-35°C (Alexander, 1961).

Denitrification, the bacterial process by which bacteria reduce inorganic nitrogen, occurs in anaerobic waters and sediments. Bacteria use the oxidized forms of nitrogen instead of oxygen in respiration; a process often termed nitrate respiration. In denitrification, gaseous forms of nitrogen released as metabolites are lost from the system (Fig. 3.6). Bouldin et al. (1974) found that 7-15% of the nitrate present in ponds at the beginning of the period of measurement was lost each day. The bulk of the loss was attributed to denitrification in bottom sediments.

Nitrogen fixation by bacteria associated with leguminous plants is of considerable agricultural importance. Likewise, the fixation of atmospheric nitrogen by free-living bacteria and blue-green algae is probably an important source of combined nitrogen in fish ponds. Nitrogen fixation by blue-green algae in natural aquatic ecosystems has received much study. Much of the research has focused on aerobic nitrogen fixation by heterocystous species, but other species also fix nitrogen (Fogg et al., 1973). Evidence of nitrogen fixation has been demonstrated in the non-heterocystous genera Gleocapsa, Lyngbya, Oscillatoria, and Plectonema. Fourteen genera of heterocystous blue-green algae, including the common genera Anabaena, Anabaenopsis, Calothrix, Cylindrospermum, and Nostoc, are thought to fix nitrogen. Nitrogen fixed by blue-green algae is assimilated into organic compounds and either used by the organisms or excreted into the environment. When nitrogen-fixing organisms die and decompose, nitrogen that was contained in their cells becomes available to other organisms.

Nitrogen fixation is apparently favored in waters with low concentrations of inorganic nitrogen and abundant phosphate (Fogg et al., 1973). Rates of nitrogen fixation in natural lakes range from 0 to 0.125 mg/l per day (Dugdale and Dugdale, 1962). Nitrogen fixation rates are usually higher in eutrophic waters than in oligotrophic ones (Rusness and Burris, 1970; Horne and Fogg, 1970). Nitrogen fixation rates have not been determined for fish ponds, but fish ponds are eutrophic and often contain species of blue-green algae capable of fixing nitrogen. Because of the likelihood of high rates of nitrogen fixation in ponds, it is questionable whether the input of inorganic nitrogen in fertilizer is important if phosphorus and other nutrients are in adequate supply. Differences in inorganic nitrogen concentrations and phytoplankton productivity between ponds fertilized with phosphorus and nitrogen and those fertilized with only phosphorus are often slight (Boyd and Sowles, 1978).

3.3.3 Potassium

Potassium fertilizers are highly soluble and K^+ is released upon dissolution. Potassium ions not absorbed by plants either remain in solution or participate in ion exchange reactions with sediment. The geochemical cycle for potassium in ponds is rather uneventful when compared to the phosphorus and nitrogen cycles. Potassium concentrations in natural waters usually range between 0.5 and 10 mg/l (Moyle, 1946; Arce and Boyd, 1980). Potassium is normally unimportant in pond fertilization.

3.3.4 Nutrient concentrations in ponds

Seasonal averages for nutrient concentrations in fish ponds fertilized with 10 periodic applications of 45 kg/ha of 20-20-5 fertilizer are compared with nutrient concentrations in control ponds (Table 3.5). Fertilization resulted in appreciable increases in orthophosphate and total phosphorus but smaller increases in inorganic nitrogen and potassium.

Some unfertilized ponds have higher concentrations of primary nutrients than the experiment ponds mentioned above. Unfertilized ponds in well-managed pastures in Alabama had greater concentrations of nutrients than unfertilized ponds in woods (Table 3.6). In fact, nutrient concentrations in pasture ponds were almost as high as those in fertilized ponds (monthly applications of 45 kg/ha of 20-20-5). Little of the nitrogen and phosphorus applied to pastures to increase forage production is lost in runoff (Kilmer et al., 1974). The high concentrations of these two nutrients in unfertilized pasture ponds were related to the activity of livestock on the watersheds. For example, animals grazing in pastures deposited considerable urine and manure in or near ponds. Agricultural activity also resulted in eutrophication of small natural bodies of water in Canada that were used for fish production (Barica, 1975). Surface waters in areas with fertile

TABLE 3.5

Average concentrations of primary nutrients in fertilized and unfertilized ponds. Each entry is based on the average of four replications and six periodic samples.

Variable	Unfertilized	Fertilized[a]
Filtrable orthophosphate (mg/1 as P)	0.005	0.018
Total phosphorus (mg/1)	0.026	0.175
Nitrate (mg/1 as N)	0.004	0.016
Total ammonia (mg/1 as N)	0.13	0.22
Potassium (mg/1)	1.6	1.7

[a]Ten periodic applications of 20-20-5 annually.

TABLE 3.6

Concentrations of primary nutrients for waters of unfertilized ponds on two types of watersheds (woodland and pasture) and for fertilized ponds (Boyd, 1976b).

Variable	Woods[a]	Pasture	Fertilized
Filtrable orthophosphate (mg/1 as P)	0.007	0.015	0.019
Total phosphorus (mg/1)	0.092	0.128	0.185
Nitrate (mg/1 as N)	0.075	0.099	0.073
Total ammonia (mg/1 as N)	0.05	0.10	0.12
Potassium (mg/1)	1.5	2.9	1.4

[a]Numbers of samples were: woods, 34; pasture, 53; fertilized, 26.

soils contained higher concentrations of nutrients than those in areas with infertile soils (Toth and Smith, 1960). Because of differences in natural fertility, the fertilizer requirements of ponds will obviously differ.

3.4   EFFECTS OF FERTILIZATION ON PLANTS AND INVERTEBRATES

3.4.1   Phytoplankton

Many workers have demonstrated that applications of inorganic fertilizer increase phytoplankton productivity. Data from a few of these studies will be presented to illustrate effects of fertilization on phytoplankton growth. In most of the earlier studies, samples of water were centrifuged and the weight of particulate organic matter determined. Although this was not a direct measurement of phytoplankton, the results were suggestive of phytoplankton abundance. In Alabama, Smith and Swingle (1938) reported that seasonal averages of particulate organic matter concentrations in three unfertilized ponds were 4.4, 6.0, and 8.1 mg/l. Eleven ponds fertilized with various combinations of fertilizers — all received phosphorus — had averages of 8.0-31.1 mg/l. Averages for all unfertilized and all fertilized ponds were 5.9 and 22.3 mg/l, respectively. Ball (1949) reported seasonal averages for particulate organic matter as 5.5 mg/l for two unfertilized ponds and 18.5 mg/l for two fertilized ponds at a Michigan fish hatchery. Ponds were fertilized with a complete fertilizer. Dendy et al. (1968) found that fertilization of ponds in Alabama with phosphorus alone or phosphorus plus nitrogen increased particulate organic matter concentrations two to three times above values for unfertilized ponds. Nitrogen and phosphorus fertilization was only slightly more effective than phosphorus-only fertilization in increasing concentrations of particulate organic matter. In Oregon, McIntire and Bond (1962) found that the seasonal averages for particulate organic matter concentrations were 2.7 mg/l in an unfertilized pond, 4.7 mg/l in a pond fertilized with nitrogen, and 18.6 mg/l in two ponds fertilized with nitrogen and phosphorus.

Phytoplankton abundance in fertilized and unfertilized ponds has also been measured by direct counts of organisms. The average abundance of net phytoplankton in an unfertilized lake in Ontario was 32,700 organisms per liter, while the average for three fertilized lakes was 80,400 organisms per liter (Langford, 1948). McIntire and Bond (1962) found great increases in numbers of phytoplankters following fertilization of ponds with nitrogen and phosphorus. More than 1,000,000 organisms per liter of several genera were often present. At Auburn University, unfertilized ponds usually have less than 1,000,000 phytoplankters per liter; fertilized ponds commonly have more than 10,000,000 phytoplankters per liter.

In Israel, chlorophyll a concentrations in unfertilized ponds varied from 8.8 to 115.5 µg/l; ponds fertilized with nitrogen and phosphorus had values from 103.4 to 212.3 µg/l (Hepher, 1962a). Concentrations of chlorophyll a in unfertilized experimental ponds in New York averaged 2.9 µg/l, but high rates of nitrogen and phosphorus fertilization resulted in an average of 55.5 µg/l of chlorophyll a (Hall et al., 1970). At Auburn University, chlorophyll a concentrations ranged from 5 to 30 µg/l in unfertilized ponds and from 20 to 130 µg/l in ponds fertilized with nitrogen and phosphorus (Boyd, 1973).

Gross phytoplankton productivity is also greater in fertilized ponds than in unfertilized ponds. Average gross productivity measured between 1000 and 1400 hours was 1.76 mg/l of carbon per hour in fertilized ponds and 0.18 mg/l of carbon per hour in unfertilized ponds in Alabama (Boyd, 1973). Hall et al. (1970) reported that primary productivity was 10-15 times greater in fertilized ponds than in control ponds. On an areal basis, fertilized ponds in Alabama usually

had average phytoplankton productivity values of 1-3 g/m^2 of carbon per day.
Hepher (1962a) gave average values of 3.3-6.4 g/m^2 of carbon per day for fertilize
ponds in Israel.

All of the studies mentioned above suggest that fertilization with phosphorus
or nitrogen plus phosphorus will cause great increases in phytoplankton abundance.
Because only average values were given above, data for phytoplankton abundance
on different dates in fertilized and unfertilized ponds are presented in Fig.
3.7. These data illustrate the great changes in abundance that typically occur
in fertilized ponds, but fertilized ponds are consistently more productive of
phytoplankton than unfertilized ponds.

Eutrophic bodies of water frequently develop dense blooms of blue-green algae,
so the frequent occurence of blue-green algae in fertilized fish ponds is not
surprising. However, as the following data will demonstrate, phytoplankton
communities in fertilized fish ponds are not always dominated by blue-green algae,
as often believed.

Swingle (1947) made the following statements that aptly describe phytoplankton
communities in fertilized fish ponds. "The theory that like causes produce like
effects certainly does not appear to apply in the case of the production of
plankton algae by fertilization. These differences have been especially striking
in a series of 27 adjacent, 0.25-acre ponds at Auburn. These ponds have a common
water supply and are practically identical in length, width, and depth. Yet,
when given identical fertilizer treatments, no two have the same appearance
either to the naked eye or under the microscope. On any one day these pond waters
appeared to be of various shades of green, brown, black, yellow, or red due to
the different types of plankton dominant at that particular time. When these
ponds were observed carefully, their appearance was found to change daily and
even at various times during the same day.

Water samples from 30 to 50 ponds were examined at 2- to 3-week intervals under
a microscope, and records were made over a 5-year period of the principal genera
of algae present. Where the ponds were fertilized with commercial inorganic
fertilizers, the principal algae present on any particular date in any one pond
was a mixture of 4-6 or more genera, and different genera were dominant in
different ponds receiving the same treatment. The dominant algae in practically
all ponds varied at each examination.

The algae produced by inorganic fertilization were largely genera of the
Chlorophyceae: _Scenedesmus_, _Ankistrodesmus_, _Chlorella_, _Staurastrum_, _Pandorina_,
Cosmarium, _Chlamydomonas_, _Nannochloris_, _Pediastrum_, _Coelastrum_, and others. Of
the Euglenophyceae, _Trachelomonas_, _Cryptoglena_, _Euglena_, and _Phacus_ were also
abundant and occasionally dominant. The Dinophyceae, _Glenodinium_, _Hemidinium_,
and _Peridinium_, were often present, but never in large numbers. Of the

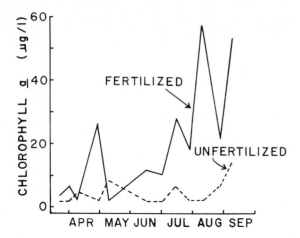

3.7. Chlorophyll <u>a</u> concentrations in fertilized and unfertilized ponds.

Chroococcaceae, or blue-greens, <u>Coelosphaerium</u> and <u>Microcystis</u> occasionally became abundant for limited periods. Diatoms, which are so abundant in the marine plankton, were relatively unimportant in these fertilized, fresh-water ponds.

Fertilization of ponds as was practiced, therefore, would appear to result in production of an unpredictable mixture of algae. It would not appear possible that all these forms of algae are equally desirable for the production of fish foods. Certainly, they are not equal from the standpoint of growth habits, appearance, and odors. The present status of pond fertilization may be likened to that of a farmer who wished to increase his production of beef cattle but ignorant of desirable pasture plants applied fertilizer to a field of grasses and weeds without previous preparation or seeding to desired species.

There is urgent need for a critical study of algal species to determine those that are most desirable for fish production, and to determine the conditions favoring production of these forms. At present it would not appear possible to raise cultures of a single species of alga in fish ponds. However, it should be possible to learn enough about the ecology of various species to seed the ponds and to maintain an abundance of the more desirable forms. It should also be possible to keep many undesirable species under control."

Since Swingle made these comments, several workers have written about phytoplankton in fertilized fish ponds, but we still have little control over the species present.

Hall et al. (1970) found the average number of species of phytoplankton to be higher in ponds in New York that received no fertilization (11.5 species) or moderate fertilization (14.5 species) than in heavily fertilized ponds (6.8 species). Diatoms were rare in all ponds. A blue-green alga, <u>Microcystis</u>

aeruginosa, was abundant in two of six ponds receiving heavy fertilization; species of green algae were the most common forms in all ponds. According to McIntire and Bond (1962), fertilized ponds in Oregon had an abundance of the following algae:

Chlorophyta: <u>Chlamydomonas</u>, <u>Cosmarium</u>, <u>Eudorina</u>, <u>Micractinum</u>, <u>Pandorina</u>, and <u>Staurastrum</u>
  Euglenophyta: <u>Euglena</u>, <u>Phacus</u>, and <u>Trachelomonas</u>
  Chrysophyta: <u>Dinobryon</u>
  Pyrrophyta: <u>Gymnodinium</u>
  Cryptophyceae: <u>Cryptomonas</u>
  Cyanophyceae: none

Diatoms were abundant in Oregon ponds not enriched with phosphorus. Boyd (1973) studied phytoplankton in three ponds fertilized with phosphorus, three fertilized with nitrogen and phosphorus, and three control ponds. Blue-green algae were never dominant in the control ponds; green algae and diatoms were most common. In ponds fertilized with phosphorus alone, blue-green were occasionally dominant, but blue-green algae were dominant on more than half of the sampling dates in ponds fertilized with nitrogen and phosphorus. The generic composition of the phytoplankton communities varied considerably among ponds and sampling dates. As few as two and as many as 24 species were recorded in individual samples. Species diversity, as calculated by the equation of MacArthur and MacArthur (1961), was 1.59 in control ponds but only 1.18 in ponds treated with nitrogen and phosphorus.

Enrichment of waters with nutrients usually does not enhance the growth of the majority of species present at the time of fertilizer application. According to Dickman and Efford (1972), a few previously rare species rapidly increase after fertilization to form an algal bloom. This striking increase in a few algal species results in a sharp reduction in community diversity. Diversity is particularly low in ponds with dense blooms of blue-green algae (Boyd, 1973).

Phytoplankton communities in six ponds in Alabama that were fertilized with nitrogen and phosphorus were examined weekly between February and October, 1973 (Boyd and Scarsbrook, 1974). Genera that comprised at least 10% of a phytoplankton community on any sampling date were:

Chlorophyta: <u>Sphaerocystis</u>, <u>Chlamydomonas</u>, <u>Dictyosphaerium</u>, <u>Coelastrum</u>, <u>Staurastrum</u>, <u>Oocystis</u>, <u>Arthrodesmus</u>, <u>Ankistrodesmus</u>, <u>Scenedesmus</u>, <u>Pectodictyon</u>, <u>Closteriopsis</u>, <u>Crucigenia</u>, <u>Tetroedron</u>, <u>Volvox</u>, and <u>Nephrocytium</u>
  Euglenophyta: <u>Euglena</u>, <u>Trachelomonas</u>, and <u>Phacus</u>
  Chrysophyta: <u>Bumilleria</u> and <u>Mallomonas</u>
  Pyrrophyta: <u>Ceratium</u> and <u>Gymnodinium</u>

Cyanophyta: <u>Anabaena</u>, <u>Oscillatoria</u>, <u>Spirulina</u>, <u>Microcystis</u>, <u>Gomphosphaeria</u>, <u>Gleocapsa</u>, <u>Rhaphidiopsis</u>, and <u>Merismopedia</u>

There was no pond in which a genus maintained an abundance of 10% of the phyto-plankton community throughout the study. Some genera were abundant for several months; others were abundant on only one or two sampling dates. The majority of abundant genera were Chlorophyta, but genera of Cyanophyta were abundant in each pond sometime during the study. One cyanophycean, <u>Rhaphidiopois</u>, was the dominant genus in one pond from early July until October. Two cyanophyceans, <u>Oscillatoria</u> and <u>Anabaena</u>, dominated the phytoplankton of another pond during May, June, and July. In a third pond, three genera of blue-green algae, <u>Anabaena</u>, <u>Microcystis</u>, and <u>Rhaphidiopsis</u>, dominated the algal community in September.

On any particular sampling date, there were large differences in the composition of the phytoplankton communities of the six ponds. For example, genera present at an abundance of 10% of the community in early July were:

Pond S-9: <u>Sphaerocystis</u>, <u>Dictyosphaerium</u>, <u>Staurastrum</u>, <u>Euglena</u>, and <u>Coelastrum</u>
Pond S-11: <u>Sphaerocystis</u>, <u>Coelastrum</u>, <u>Oocystis</u>, <u>Rhaphidiopsis</u>, and <u>Anabaena</u>
Pond S-12: <u>Sphaerocystis</u>, <u>Coelastrum</u>, <u>Scenedesmus</u>, <u>Dictyosphaerium</u>, <u>Staurastrum</u>, <u>Oscillatoria</u>, <u>Oocystis</u>, and <u>Tetraedron</u>
Pond S-13: <u>Sphaerocystis</u> and <u>Oocystis</u>
Pond S-19: <u>Closteriopsis</u>, <u>Ceratium</u>, <u>Staurastrum</u>, and <u>Chlamydomonas</u>
Pond S-22: <u>Anabaena</u>, <u>Oscillatoria</u>, and <u>Spirulina</u>

From the information presented above, it is obvious that the comments made by Swingle (1947) are still quite accurate. Fertilization results in increased phytoplankton abundance, but we have no control over the resulting generic compo-sition. Obviously, some genera are more desirable than others. For example, genera forming surface scums, those producing bad odors, and those subject to sudden die-offs are undesirable. Yet, methods for favoring one kind of alga over another have not been developed. Further, it is doubtful that such techniques will soon be developed. Nevertheless, fertilization is an effective way of increasing primary production and enhancing fish production.

3.4.2   Zooplankton

The increase in primary productivity following fertilization usually results in greater zooplankton abundance. Wiebe (1929) found 484 crustacea per liter and 1,826 rotifers per liter in a pond fertilized with phosphorus but only 263 crustacea per liter and 686 rotifers per liter in an unfertilized pond. McIntire and Bond (1962) reported that fertilization with nitrogen and phosphorus caused large increases in crustaceans and rotifers. Genera of crustaceans included

<u>Bosmina</u>, <u>Cyclops</u>, <u>Chydorus</u>, and <u>Diaphanosoma</u>, with <u>Bosmina</u> being consistently
most abundant in fertilized and unfertilized ponds. Common rotifers were
<u>Polyarthra</u>, <u>Keratella</u>, and <u>Brachionus</u>. Peak density of rotifers in a fertilized
pond was 136,000 per liter; crustacean abundance reached nearly 1,000 per liter.
In the control pond, maximum densities of rotifers and crustacea were about
10,000 per liter and 100 per liter, respectively.

Dendy et al. (1968) found the following zooplankters in Alabama ponds:

Sididae: <u>Diaphanosoma brachyurum</u>
Daphnidae: <u>Daphnia ambigua</u>, <u>Dapnia</u> spp., and <u>Ceriodaphnia</u> spp.
Bosminidae: <u>Bosmina longirostris</u>
Cyclopidae: <u>Mesocyclops edax</u>, <u>Cyclops exilis</u>, and <u>Tropocyclops prasinus</u>
Diaptomidae: <u>Diaptomus bogalusensis</u>
Rotifera: <u>Platyias quadricornis</u>, <u>P. platulus</u>, <u>Monostyla bula</u>, <u>Brachionus</u>
<u>angularis</u>, <u>B. havanaensis</u>, <u>Trichocera</u> spp., <u>Anuraeopsis fissa</u>, <u>Keratella</u> spp.,
<u>Polyarthra</u> sp., <u>Lecane</u> sp., and <u>Filina</u> sp.
Ostracoda

Ponds were fertilized with phosphorus and nitrogen, phosphorus alone, or not at
all. Total zooplankton density was similar for the two groups of fertilized
ponds and greater in fertilized than in unfertilized ponds. Estimated densities
of Cyclopidae for fertilized ponds were greater than for unfertilized ponds.
Bosminidae were more abundant in the control ponds. Other groups were present
in fertilized and unfertilized ponds in roughly equal abundance. The abundance
and composition of zooplankton were often strikingly different in samples collected on the same date from ponds treated alike or on different dates from the same
pond (Varikul, 1965).

Over a 3-year period, Hall et al. (1970) found the average biomass of zooplankton in unfertilized ponds and in ponds treated with high levels of nitrogen
and phosphorus to average 150 and 881 µg/l, respectively. There was a high turnover rate of zooplankton biomass, and the average annual production of zooplankton
was 2,767 and 7,447 µg/l for unfertilized and fertilized ponds, respectively.
Sixty-six species of zooplankton were identified in samples from the ponds, but
the cladoceran, <u>Ceriodaphnia</u>, dominated zooplankton communities in all ponds;
the most abundant rotifer was <u>Keratella</u>. The investigators made a thorough study
of the dynamics of the zooplankton communities in the ponds and concluded that
fertilization increased production of zooplankton but had little effect upon
community composition. Fish predation had profound effects on the diversity and
size distribution of the zooplankton but only affected production at lower
nutrient levels.

3.4.3   Benthos

The effects of inorganic fertilization are also reflected in benthic production.
Abundance of benthos in two unfertilized and two fertilized hatchery ponds averaged
425 and 694 organisms/m^2, respectively (Ball, 1949). At another fish hatchery,
benthic fish food organisms averaged 371 and 640 organisms/m^2 in unfertilized and
fertilized ponds, respectively (Patriarche and Ball, 1949). McIntire and Bond
(1962) found that fertilization with nitrogen and phosphorus increased the
biomass of benthic fish food organisms 7.6 times in one pond and 19.5 times in
another. Larval midges (Tendipedidae) were by far the most important group of
benthic organisms in the ponds.

Ponds in New York (Hall et al. 1970) had benthic communities composed primarily
of the following organisms:

Diptera: Chironomus tentans, Procladius sp., Ablabesmyia sp., Tanytarsini sp.,
Glypotendipes sp., Microtendipes sp., Ceratopogonidae, and Chironomus sp.

Trichoptera: Ocetis sp. and Polycentropis sp.

Ephemeroptera: Caenis simulans and Callibaetis ferrugineus

Zygoptera: Ishneura sp. and Enallagma sp.

Anisoptera: Libelludidae and Gomphidae

Amphipoda: Hyalella azteca.

Fertilization with nitrogen and phosphorus resulted in a considerable increase in
the benthic biomass. In fertilized ponds, Chironomus tentans was the most
dominant benthic species; Caenis simulans was most dominant in unfertilized ponds.
Sumawidjaja (1966) also found that fertilization increased the biomass of
benthic fish food organisms in Alabama ponds. He noted, as did Hall et al. (1970)
and McIntire and Bond (1962), that chironomid larvae were numerous in samples
from fertilized ponds.

3.4.4   Macrophytes

Aquatic macrophytes are often abundant in shallow lakes and ponds with relatively transparent waters. These plants can grow at relatively low concentrations
of dissolved nutrients, apparently because they are capable of absorbing nutrients
from muds. Therefore, bodies of water that have low levels of phytoplankton
abundance may be highly productive of macrophytes.

Macrophytes are responsible for several ecological problems in fish ponds.
They compete with phytoplankton for nutrients and light, provide cover so that
too many forage fish escape predation, interfere with fishing and seining, prevent
fish from finding feed when it is applied, increase water loss through trans-
piration, and cause dissolved oxygen deficiencies. Some common pond weeds are:

Macrophytic algae: <u>Chara</u>, <u>Nitella</u>, <u>Spirogyra</u>, <u>Rhizoclonium</u>, <u>Hydrodictyon</u>, <u>Pithophora</u>, <u>Lyngbya</u>, and <u>Cladophora</u>

Floating angiosperms: <u>Lemna</u>, <u>Spirodela</u>, <u>Wolffia</u>, and <u>Eichhornia</u>

Floating-leafed angiosperms: <u>Nymphaea</u>, <u>Nymphoides</u>, <u>Nelumbo</u>, and <u>Nuphar</u>

Submersed and emergent angiosperms: <u>Najas</u>, <u>Potamogeton</u>, <u>Ceratophyllum</u>, <u>Myriophyllum</u>, <u>Elodea</u>, <u>Heteranthera</u>, <u>Hydrilla</u>, and <u>Alternanthera</u>

Reedswamp angiosperms: <u>Typha</u>, <u>Eleocharis</u>, <u>Scirpus</u>, and <u>Juncus</u>

Macrophytic algae and submersed and emergent angiosperms often fill the water with vegetation or form dense mats at the surface. Floating and floating-leafed angiosperms cover the surface and limit light penetration into the water. Reed swamp species grow along the shallow edges and limit accessibility.

Light is especially important in regulating the distribution and growth of many aquatic macrophytes (Peltier and Welch, 1969, 1970; Martin et al., 1970). Many species disappear from aquatic ecosystems as turbidity increases. Since fertilization increases the abundance of plankton and decreases light penetration, macrophytes are often unimportant in fertilized ponds. A survey of Alabama ponds showed that ponds with troublesome infestations of aquatic macrophytes had an average Secchi disk visibility of 175 cm while Secchi disk visibility averaged 45 cm in ponds without weed problems (Boyd, 1975). The relationship to phytoplankton abundance was obvious because chlorophyll <u>a</u> concentrations averaged 13 µg/l in ponds with infestations of weeds and 86 µg/l in other ponds.

Studies of rates of photosynthesis by aquatic plants at different light intensities (Boyd, 1975) suggest that most species of submersed aquatic plants cannot grow well at depths of twice the Secchi disk visibility. Maristo (1941) presented data for Finnish lakes where maximum depths of vegetation corresponded closely to Secchi disk visibilities. These findings agree with the common experience that ponds with no water shallower than 60 cm and Secchi disk visibilities between 30 and 60 cm seldom have problems with underwater weeds. Obviously, turbidity will not control floating, floating-leafed, and emergent species.

A method for eliminating persistent infestations of submersed macrophytes was developed by Smith and Swingle (1941). They broadcast fertilizer (45 kg/ha of 20-20-5 per application) over weed beds beginning in winter and continuing at monthly intervals until weeds were covered by filamentous algae. The algae shaded the weeds, and they detached from the bottom and floated in decaying masses. Most of the weeds and macrophytic algae disappeared by late June. Nutrients from the fertilizer and the decaying weeds triggered a phytoplankton bloom that prevented regrowth of weeds. The phytoplankton bloom was maintained by periodic fertilization.

3.4.5 Water transparency as an index to fertilization

The direct influence of fertilization is to stimulate phytoplankton productivity. Few species of fish feed directly or entirely on phytoplankton, but greater abundance of phytoplankton favors higher densities of zooplankton and benthos which serve as food for fish. As a result, fish production is usually closely related to phytoplankton abundance, except in ponds to which large amounts of fish feed are applied. Further, problems with underwater weeds usually do not occur in ponds with abundant phytoplankton and associated turbidity. Thus, measurements of phytoplankton productivity or plankton abundance may be used as indices of potential fish production in ponds (Swingle and Smith, 1938; Moyle, 1946; Almazan and Boyd, 1978b).

Conventional measurements of phytoplankton productivity or biomass are too tedious and time consuming for use by practical fish culturists. In fish ponds, plankton is usually the primary source of turbidity. The Secchi disk visibility provides an estimate of water transparency (turbidity) that is generally related to plankton abundance (Barica, 1975; Almazan and Boyd, 1978b). An experienced observer can readily distinguish between plankton turbidity and other forms of turbidity. The novice must remember that plankton blooms do not always cause water to appear green; blooms may also give yellow, red, brown, or black colorations to water. Usually, plankters are large enough to be viewed against a white background and distinguished from clay particles and other forms of turbidity. It is important to always view the Secchi disk in the same manner. Different observers using the same technique may obtain different readings, but readings made by the same observer may be compared among ponds and dates of measurement. Measurements taken at different times of day by the same observer may differ appreciably because of differences in illumination and roughness of the water surface.

Fertilized ponds for culture of sportfish in the southeastern United States usually have adequate populations of fish and are free of weed problems if Secchi disk visibilities are 30-80 cm. At lower Secchi disk visibilities, plankton blooms are so dense that there is a high probability of problems with dissolved oxygen. Higher Secchi disk visibilities indicate insufficient phytoplankton productivity to support enough fish food organisms for good fish production. Water with high Secchi disk visibilities are also likely to be infested with troublesome underwater weeds. Fertilized ponds for the culture of food fish, such as Tilapia spp., require a great abundance of fish food organisms. Therefore, Secchi disk visibilities of 15-40 cm are appropriate. Most species of Tilapia are relatively tolerant to low dissolved oxygen, but oxygen depletions resulting from massive plankton blooms can result in fish kills.

Secchi disk visibilities in fertilized ponds fluctuate over time. Not infrequently, ponds must be fertilized several times in the spring before plankton

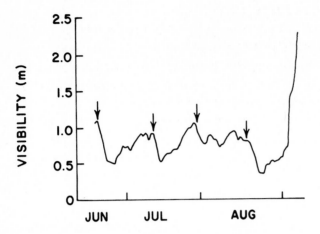

Fig. 3.8. Relationship between fertilizer applications (dates indicated by arrows) and Secchi disk visibilities (Ball and Tanner, 1951).

blooms develop. Also, plankton blooms may increase following a fertilizer appli-cation, diminish before the next application, and flourish when fertilizer is again applied. A pattern of vacillating Secchi disk visibilities reported by Ball and Tanner (1951) for a fertilized lake is given in Fig. 3.8. The fluct-uations in plankton abundance in fertilized ponds could probably be drastically reduced by applying small amounts of fertilizer at frequent intervals. Unfort-unately, it is seldom feasible to make fertilizer applications at less than 2 to 4-week intervals.

The need for fertilizer can be judged from a Secchi disk reading. For example, if an unfertilized pond in a pasture has a Secchi disk visibility of 35 cm (turbidity resulting from plankton), fertilization would not be advisable. Furthermore, if two unfertilized ponds have Secchi disk visibilities of 75 cm and 200 cm, respectively, a lower rate of fertilization might be advisable for the more turbid pond than for the other.

The Secchi disk visibility may also be used to determine if a particular fertilization program is effective in a pond. If visibility decreases after application of fertilizer and subsequent fertilization maintains Secchi disk readings in a desirable range, the program is suitable. However, if a plankton bloom fails to develop after several fertilizer applications, fertilization is ineffective. Remedial measures may be taken without having to wait until the failure of the fertilization schedule is reflected in poor fishing or low stand-ing crops of fish.

One further caution is necessary regarding Secchi disk visibility as an index of fish production. Waters in some regions are naturally less turbid than those

TABLE 3.7

Solution of Spillman's equation (Equation 3.1) for different quantities of a
growth factor (Tisdale and Nelson, 1956).

Units of growth factor X	Yield (%)	Increase in Yield (%)
0	0	0
1	50	50
2	75	25
3	87.5	12.5
4	93.75	6.25
5	96.88	3.12
6	98.44	1.56
8	99.61	0.39
10	99.90	0.10

of other areas. For example, soft waters in woodlands are often heavily stained
with humic substances, while waters with high concentrations of calcium and magnesium are often free of stains because these ions favor the precipitation of
organic colloids. At identical levels of phytoplankton abundance, the soft
water might have a Secchi disk visibility of less than 100 cm, while the value
for the hard water might exceed 200 cm. The biologist must have a basic knowledge
of the magnitude of natural turbidity in ponds, or serious error may result from
using the Secchi disk as a tool in pond fertilization.

3.5 FERTILIZER RATES AND FISH PRODUCTION

3.5.1 Growth factors and production

The use of fertilizers to increase fish yields has an agricultural analogy in
the application of fertilizers to favor greater growth of pasture grasses to
foster increased livestock production. The fish culturist should understand
some of the basic principles regulating the benefits of fertilizers in agriculture.
When a single growth factor is limiting the growth of a crop, the increase in
growth with each equal successive addition of the growth factor is progressively
smaller. This idea was developed independently by E. A. Mitscherlich and W. J.
Spillman in the early 1900's (Tisdale and Nelson, 1956). The relationship is
illustrated in Table 3.7 and defined by the equation:

$$\log(A - Y) = \log A - 0.30X \qquad (3.1)$$

where Y = yield produced by a given quantity of growth factor X and A = the maximum yield possible.

If none of the growth factor is available, X = 0 and Y = 0. But suppose 1 unit of X is present; from Equation 3.1 we see:

$$\log(100 - Y) = \log 100 - 0.301(1)$$
$$\log(100 - Y) = 2 - 0.301$$
$$\log(100 - Y) = 1.699$$
$$100 - Y = 50$$
$$Y = 50$$

The addition of 1 unit of growth factor gives 50% of maximum yield; the amount of growth factor producing 50% of maximum yield is termed 1 unit of growth factor. The calculation illustrated above may be repeated for successively greater units of growth factor. The results are tabulated in Table 3.7. Beyond 3 or 4 units of growth factor, an additional unit of growth factor causes little increase in yield.

The economic implication of the relationship between fertilizer rate and yield is clear. The fertilizer cost per unit weight of crop increases with each successive unit of fertilizer applied. Because of the diminishing returns, a point is soon reached where the cost of an additional unit of fertilizer is greater than the value of the increment of crop increase.

The concept described above can be extended to situations where more than one growth factor is involved. It has been useful in agriculture and applies equally well to fish culture. Hickling (1962) demonstrated that fish production in fertilized ponds did not increase in direct proportion to increased fertilizer additions and, above a certain level, increasing fertilizer rates did not further increase fish yields. For example, in one series of experiments, fish production averaged 97 kg/ha in unfertilized ponds, 316 kg/ha in ponds fertilized with 22.4 kg/ha of P_2O_5, and 418 kg/ha in ponds treated with 44.8 kg/ha of P_2O_5. The first 22.4 ha/ha increment of P_2O_5 resulted in an increase in fish production of 219 kg/ha, but the second 22.4 kg/ha increment of P_2O_5 yielded only an additional 102 kg/ha of fish. Hepher (1968) also stated that the concept of economic increase in production pertained to production of fish. It is difficult to assign an economic value to sport fish; nevertheless, fertilizers are a valuable resource and should be used conservatively to provide good fishing rather than wasted in trying to achieve maximum fish production. The concept of diminishing returns with increasing fertilizer rates is easily applied in commercial fish culture.

In agriculture, fertilizer rates for crops are often established for individual fields and species by soil testing (Walsh and Beaton, 1973). Soil testing procedures have been calibrated against crop response. In the simpliest terms, agronomists have determined for individual soil types, climatic regions, and crop species, the amounts of primary nutrients needed in the soil at planting to permit optimum plant growth. If the soil does not contain enough of one or more primary nutrients, techniques are available for estimating the application rate of a particular grade of fertilizer to provide the required nutrients. Many years of research are necessary to develop soil test procedures for crops in a given region (Rouse, 1968).

The nature of muds and waters in ponds no doubt varies as greatly as do the characteristics of agricultural soils, and a fertilization program that works perfectly well in ponds in Alabama may fail if applied to ponds of another region. The development of procedures for testing waters and muds from fish ponds to estimate fertilizer requirements has great appeal. Unfortunately, such methods have not been developed and are not likely to be forthcoming. No doubt, such methods could be developed in essentially the same way that soil testing methods are established. However, the requirement for experimental ponds and scientific manpower would be enormous.

Procedures are available for determining the response of bodies of water to nutrient additions (Kemmerer, 1968; United States Environmental Protection Agency, 1971). Again, these techniques work beautifully, but they are far too complicated and laborious to be of value to field biologists making fertilizer recommendations for sportfish ponds or to practical fish culturists.

For the present, results of experiments at a few research stations and the experiences of a relatively small number of workers must be used as a guide in establishing fertilizer rates for ponds.

Finally, only those nutrients that are limiting production should be added to ponds. Many commercial fertilizers contain all three primary nutrients, and these materials are often purchased and applied to fish ponds. It is foolish to add a complete fertilizer, such as 18-18-4, to a pond if only phosphorus is needed. More wisely, the desired amount of phosphorus should be added as super-phosphate or triple superphosphate.

3.5.2 Fish yields in fertilized ponds

Mortimer (1954) summarized the literature on fish pond fertilization and made the following statement: "For the fish farmer the best index of the efficacy of a manurial (fertilizer) treatment is not the effect on the plankton, bottom fauna, or on the rooted vegetation, but on the increase in fish crop over and above natural productivity." The natural productivities of waters vary greatly, and some unfertilized ponds may be just as productive as fertilized ponds. However, fertilization will generally cause large increases in fish production. For example, Mortimer (1954) reported that unfertilized carp ponds in Germany yielded 20-50 kg/ha; fertilized carp ponds yielded 200-400 kg/ha. Unfertilized ponds in

Alabama yielded 109-140 kg/ha of sunfish and fertilization increased yields to 282-484 kg/ha. Tropical lakes produced 2,240 kg/ha of fish, but fertilized ponds in tropical Africa yielded 5,135-9,000 kg/ha of Tilapia.

In the following paragraphs I will attempt to present enough data on fertilizer rates and fish yields so that the reader can make a judgement on the amount and type of fertilizer needed in a particular situation. Response to fertilization may vary considerably, so the reader must be cautious in extrapolating the findings presented here. Hasler and Einsele (1948), Neess (1946), Maciolek (1954), and Mortimer (1954) have reviewed the early research on pond fertilization. Therefore, I will confine my discussion primarily to later work. My statements will by no means constitute a review of the literature on pond fertilization and fish yields.

Hickling (1962) reported the results of extensive experimentation on pond fertilization at Malacca, Malaysia. Each treatment was replicated six times in small earthen ponds and net production over a 6-month period was measured. The primary fish in all experiments was cross-bred, hybrid, male Tilapia. In one experiment (Table 3.8) the application of superphosphate fertilizer greatly increased yields, but potassium fertilization was ineffective. In another trial (Table 3.9), phosphorus fertilization was again effective, but the inclusion of nitrogen or nitrogen plus potassium with the phosphorus did not further increase yields. Other experiments using various combinations and amounts of nitrogen, phosphorus, and potassium verified results reported in Tables 3.8 and 3.9. The optimum fertilizer application rate was 44.8 kg/ha of P_2O_5, and large increases in fish yields were obtained with only 22.4 kg/ha of P_2O_5. Hickling does not state otherwise, so it is assumed that fertilizer was applied in one dose at the beginning of experiments.

Adequate replication of treatments, as done by Hickling, is a good idea in pond fertilization research. Variation in fish production among ponds treated alike is usually great, as Hickling's work clearly demonstrates. In a treatment with average yield of 344 kg/ha, the minimum yield was 205 kg/ha and the maximum yield was 486 kg/ha. The mean for another treatment was 102 kg/ha with 50-186 kg/ha as the range. At least three replications, and preferably five, should be used in fertilization experiments.

Researchers in Israel found, by adding large doses of fertilizers to ponds, that inorganic nutrient concentrations did not exceed 0.5 mg/l for phosphorus or 2.0 mg/l for nitrogen (Hepher, 1963). They concluded that there was no reason to add more fertilizer than the amount required to give maximum nitrogen and phosphorus concentrations because any surplus would be wasted. A standard fertilizer dose of 60 kg/ha of superphosphate (11 kg/ha of P_2O_5) and 60 kg/ha of ammonium sulfate (13 kg/ha of N) was sufficient to give the maximum concentrations of nitrogen and phosphorus. The maximum concentrations only remained in waters for

TABLE 3.8

Production of fish (primarily _Tilapia_) in ponds at Malacca, Malaysia, that were fertilized with different amounts of nutrients. Each treatment was replicated 6 times; the production period was 6 months (Hickling, 1962).

Fertilizer (kg/ha)			Fish (kg/ha)
N	$P_2O_5{}^a$	K_2O	
0	22.4	0	385
0	22.4	16.8	299
0	0	16.8	114
0	0	0	104
0	44.8	0	418
0	22.4	0	287
28	22.4	0	317
0	22.4	16.8	272
0	0	0	97

^{a}Phosphorus supplied as superphosphate.

TABLE 3.9

Production of fish (primarily _Tilapia_) in ponds at Malacca, Malaysia, that were fertilized with different amounts of nutrients. Each treatment was replicated 6 times; the production period was 6 months (Hickling, 1962).

Fertilizer (kg/ha)			Fish (kg/ha)
N	$P_2O_5{}^a$	K_2O	
0	67.2	0	831
0	44.8	0	787
28	44.8	0	741
28	44.8	16.8	670
0	0	0	157

^{a}Phosphorus supplied as superphosphate.

1-2 days after fertilization, and nitrogen and phosphorus concentrations were much lower 12 days after fertilization.

From 1953 to 1958, data were collected on carp production in control ponds, ponds fertilized weekly with the standard fertilizer dose, and ponds fertilized every 2 weeks with the standard dose (Hepher, 1963). Average annual yields for controls ranged between 45 and 132 kg/ha; the average for all 6 years was 94 kg/ha. Weekly fertilization resulted in average annual yields of 643-1,305 kg/ha, with a 6-year average of 982 kg/ha. Ponds fertilized every 2 weeks had a 6-year average yield of 801 kg/ha and a range of 433-1,140 kg/ha. Fertilization increased fish production by almost an order of magnitude. The increase in yield resulting from weekly fertilization, as compared to biweekly fertilization, was not considered enough to justify weekly fertilization.

Hepher (1963) applied the standard fertilizer dose to some ponds at 2-week intervals; he added the total amount of fertilizer for the growing season to other ponds at the beginning of the growing season. Fish yields were lower in ponds where all fertilizer was applied in one initial application.

Phosphorus was the most important nutrient affecting carp yields in ponds in Israel (Hepher, 1962b). Nitrogen and phosphorus fertilization increased fish production above that obtained with phosphorus fertilization alone. For example, in 1955, carp growth in ponds fertilized with 60 kg/ha of superphosphate per application was seven times greater than in control ponds. Fish yields in ponds receiving nitrogen and phosphorus (standard fertilizer dose) were roughly nine times those of control ponds. Waters in Israel usually contain more than 5 mg/liter of potassium (Hepher, 1962b), making potassium fertilization unnecessary.

Fertilization plus feeding was employed to increase fish yields to even higher levels than achieved with fertilization alone (Hepher, 1963). This technique is used by many practical fish culturists, but it has not been studied enough to recommend as a general practice. In fact, this technique would encourage water quality problems in some fish cultures.

Ball (1949) reported fish yields at three fish hatcheries in Michigan where ponds were fertilized with a 10-6-4 fertilizer. At one hatchery, three treatment rates were established as follows: 37 kg/ha at weekly intervals, 74 kg/ha at 2-week intervals, and 112 kg/ha at 3-week intervals. At the other hatcheries, all ponds were fertilized every 3 weeks with 112 kg/ha of 10-6-4 fertilizer. Thus, all ponds received 11.2 kg/ha of N, 6.7 kg/ha of P_2O_5, and 4.5 kg/ha of K_2O. Data for plankton production showed no advantage of applying fertilizer more frequently than 3-week intervals. Combined yields of largemouth bass (_Micropterus salmoides_), creek club (_Semotilis atromaculatus_), bluegill (_Lepomis macrochirus_), and common sucker (_Catostomus commersonii_) were 167 kg/ha for unfertilized ponds and 278 kg/ha for fertilized ponds. Ball observed that the closer fish fed to the base of the food chain, the more their yield was increased by fertilization.

In New York, Hall et al. (1970) established three fertilizer treatments: eight control ponds (no fertilizer), six low nutrient ponds (0.33 kg/ha of N; 0.033 kg/ha each of P_2O_5 and K_2O), and six high nutrient ponds (3.89 kg/ha of N; 0.39 kg/ha each of P_2O_5 and K_2O). Total dry-weight standing crops of bluegill after 3 years of fertilization averaged 45 kg/ha in controls, 68 kg/ha in ponds of the low fertilizer treatment, and 114 kg/ha in ponds of the high fertilizer treatment. The yields may be multiplied by 4 to approximate live-weight standing crops.

Swingle (1947) summarized the results of pond fertilization experiments conducted at Auburn University between 1935 and 1945; some selected data from this report are summarized in Table 3.10. All three primary nutrients were applied in fertilizers, and fertilization always resulted in appreciable increases in standing crops of bluegill and largemouth bass. Applications of micronutrients with primary nutrients failed to increase fish yields. Large quantities of fertilizer were not markedly superior to modest amounts in increasing fish yields. Frequency of fertilizer application was not studied; observation on plankton response indicated that fertilizers should be applied at about monthly intervals.

Results of pond fertilization experiments (Swingle, 1947) were used by Swingle and Smith (1947) to formulate a standard fertilizer application rate for sportfish ponds in the southeastern United States. The standard fertilization program consisted of 8-14 periodic applications of 112 kg/ha of 6-8-4 fertilizer and 11.2 kg/ha of sodium nitrate. Beginning in February, applications were repeated at 3- to 4-week intervals or whenever plankton blooms diminished so that underwater objects were visible to a depth of 30 cm. This fertilization program proved effective in increasing fish production in many ponds in the southeastern United States and in many other areas. Over the years, the fertilization program suggested by Swingle and Smith has been modified slightly. Boyd and Snow (1975) gave the following modification:

1. In mid-February or early March, apply 45 kg/ha of 20-20-5 fertilizer. Follow with two additional applications at 2-week intervals.

2. Make three more applications of 45 kg/ha of 20-20-5 fertilizer at 3-week intervals.

3. Continue applications of 45 kg/ha of 20-20-5 fertilizer at monthly intervals or whenever the water clears so that a Secchi disk or a piece of white metal attached to a stick is visible to a depth of 45 cm.

4. Discontinue applications for the current year by the last week in October.

Quantities of primary nutrients per application for the fertilization program suggested by Boyd and Snow (1975) are 9 kg/ha of N, 9 kg/ha of P_2O_5, and 2.2 kg/ha of K_2O. Over a growing season 8-12 applications will be made for a total of

TABLE 3.10

Net production of fish (Lepomis macrochirus and Micropterus salmoides) in ponds treated with different amounts of fertilizer nutrients (Swingle, 1947).

Fertilizer[a] (kg/ha)			No. of ponds	Fish (kg/ha)
N	P_2O_5	K_2O		
0	0	0	3	108
486	512	256	1	392
380	461	115	1	276
148	179	45	1	341
95	115	29	3	286
68	72	36	3	252

[a]Sum of 8-12 periodic applications of fertilizer.

72-108 kg/ha of N and P_2O_5 and 18-26 kg/ha of K_2O. Although a simple, standard fertilization procedure has great appeal, it is ludicrous to assume that such a technique would be the best one to use under all circumstances. For example, the standard fertilization procedure was developed from research conducted in soft water ponds on wooded watersheds. Therefore, the use of this procedure usually results in overfertilization of pasture ponds that have more fertile waters than woodland ponds (Boyd, 1976b).

Swingle et al. (1963) determined yields of fish in control ponds, pond fertilized with 112 kg/ha per application of 0-8-2 fertilizer, and ponds fertilized with 112 kg/hectare per application of 8-8-2 fertilizer. These are the same application rates of individual nutrients called for by Boyd and Snow (1975). Fertilization resulted in large increases in fish yields over those of the controls (Table 3.11). However, nitrogen plus phosphorus fertilization was generally no more effective than phosphorus fertilization alone in increasing yields of carp; goldfish (Carassius auratus), and channel catfish (Ictalurus punctatus). Because the ponds had previously been fertilized for 15 years with a complete fertilizer, it was concluded that sufficient nitrogen for high yields of fish came from organic nitrogen and ammonium stored in muds, from nitrogen-fixing bacteria in muds and waters, from nitrogen-fixing planktonic algae, or, most probably, from a combination of all these sources. Swingle et al. (1963) also concluded that the potassium concentrations in waters of their experimental ponds were sufficiently high for high yields of fish, even without additions of potassium fertilizers. Therefore, a significant modification of the standard

TABLE 3.11

Net production (kg/ha) of three species of fish in ponds to which different fertilizers were applied. Each pond received 10 applications of 112 kg/ha of fertilizer (Swingle et al., 1963).

Species	No. of ponds	Control	0-8-2	8-8-2
Carassius auratus	2	414	615	700
Cyprinus carpio	4	125	261	296
Ictalurus punctatus	4	54	359	311

fertilization procedure is sometimes used in old ponds with a history of fertilization: make 8-12 periodic applications of 9 kg/ha of P_2O_5 (45 kg/ha of superphosphate or 20 kg/ha of triple superphosphate per application).

In another experiment conducted at Auburn University in old ponds with a history of fertilization (Swingle, 1964), an 8-8-0 treatment resulted in a 286% increase in bluegill and largemouth bass yields over controls, and a 0-8-0 treatment increased bluegill production to 213% of yields in controls. This experiment suggests some benefit of nitrogen fertilization and clearly reveals that fertilization with phosphorus alone results in large increases in fish yields.

Varikul (1965) compared the net production of Tilapia mossambica in control ponds and in ponds treated with 112 kg/ha per application of either 0-8-2 or 8-8-2 fertilizer. The ponds had been used in fertilization experiments for 22 years. Each treatment was replicated four times. Net production values were: control, 242 kg/ha; 0-8-2 fertilization, 664 kg/ha; and 8-8-2 fertilization, 653 kg/ha. Thus, phosphorus was the only nutrient required to increase fish production.

An experiment was conducted in new ponds, with low concentrations of organic matter in muds, to evaluate benefits of nitrogen plus phosphorus fertilization over phosphorus only fertilization (Boyd, 1976c). Treatments consisted of applications at 2-week intervals of 45 kg/ha of 0-20-5, 5-20-5, or 20-20-5 fertilizer. Ponds were stocked with T. aurea, and each treatment was replicated three times. Net production of T. aurea was 651 kg/ha in the 0-20-5 treatment, 947 kg/ha in the 5-20-5 treatment, and 930 kg/ha in the 20-20-5 treatment. The addition of a small amount of nitrogen (5-20-5 treatment) caused a substantial increase in net production (296 kg/ha) over that obtained with phosphorus and potassium fertilization (0-20-5 treatment). Additional nitrogen did not foster further net production. This study suggests that a small amount of nitrogen may be benefical in increasing fish production in new ponds not previously fertilized. The production of Tilapia was greater in this experiment than in the one of

Varikul (1965), apparently because twice as much fertilizer was applied to ponds —
applications twice weekly compared to monthly applications by Varikul.

Since the early 1970's, fertilizer prices have steadily escalated, primarily
because of the worldwide increases in the cost of crude oil. Therefore, a longterm
study was initiated at Auburn University to better define relationships between
fertilizer rates and fish production. Since several important findings have
resulted from this study, a general description of the experimental techniques is
provided.

Yield trials were conducted with sunfish (Lepomis spp.) in 0.04 to 0.07-ha
earthen ponds with average depths of 1 m. Ponds were filled and water levels
maintained by water from a stream that drained a wooded watershed. The stream
water contained 8-12 mg/l of total alkalinity and total hardness, about 5 μg/l
of filtrable inorganic phosphorus, and about 0.1 mg/l of inorganic nitrogen.
Ponds were limed each fall so that total alkalinity and total hardness of pond
waters were 20-40 mg/l during the growing season. Small sunfish (1-3 g live
weight) were stocked in January; treatments were replicated 3-6 times. Fertilizers
were applied 11 times each year by broadcasting solid fertilizers or by mixing
liquid fertilizer in water and splashing the solution over surfaces. Intervals
between fertilizer applications followed suggestions by Boyd and Snow (1975),
which are given above. Ponds were drained in November and fish harvested and
weighed.

In sportfish ponds in the southern United States, largemouth bass are stocked
with sunfish. This practice was not followed in experiments because of difficulties in achieving proper population balance in small ponds during one growing
season (Swingle, 1950). Because a high density of forage fish is required for
high production of largemouth bass in ponds, the amounts of sunfish growth in
experimental ponds were assumed indicative of potential production of largemouth
bass. The same assumption was made by Smith and Swingle (1938) and Swingle and
Smith (1938).

Unfertilized control ponds were not usually included in the experiments in
order to increase replication of other treatments. Because the ponds had been
used in fertilization experiments since their construction in 1971, this procedure requires justification. Previous studies indicated little residual effect
of fertilization in small ponds at Auburn University. For example, Swingle
(1964) fertilized ponds with nitrogen and phosphorus at application rates of 9
kg/ha of N and P_2O_5. These ponds had received similar N and P_2O_5 applications
for the preceding 18-22 years. Nevertheless, the 2-year production of largemouth
bass plus sunfish averaged 112 and 320 kg/ha in controls and in ponds treated
with N and P_2O_5, respectively. This finding is in agreement with those of Swingle
(1947) who found that unfertilized ponds at Auburn University typically produce
about 100 kg/ha of bass and bluegill, regardless of past fertilization.

The first experiment involved the effect of different phosphorus application rates on sunfish production (Dobbins and Boyd, 1976). The treatments consisted of 20-5-5, 20-10-5, 20-15-5, and 20-20-5 fertilization at 45 kg/ha. Results summarized in Table 3.12 show that net sunfish production increased in order of increasing phosphorus addition rates, but because of large variations in net production among ponds within a treatment, differences in net production among 20-10-5, 20-15-5, and 20-20-5 treatments were not statistically significant (P > 0.05). Ponds treated with 20-5-5 produced significantly less fish than those of the other three treatments. Phosphorus concentrations and gross phytoplankton productivity generally increased with phosphorus rates (Table 3.12). Light penetration to 1 m depth decreased with increasing phosphorus rates, but differences in percentages of pond bottoms covered by aquatic weeds did not differ greatly among treatments. Data presented in Table 3.12 suggest that high yields of fish may be obtained even in woodland ponds at a P_2O_5 application rate of 4.5 kg/ha — half of the amount recommended by Swingle and Smith (1947) and Boyd and Snow (1975).

The P_2O_5 requirements of sunfish ponds were further evaluated by Lichtkoppler and Boyd (1977) who treated six ponds with 20-10-5 and six ponds with 20-20-5 at 45 kg/ha per application. Findings of this study are summarized in Table 3.13. Phosphorus concentrations were greater in the 20-20-5 treatment than in the 20-10-5 treatment, but because of large variation, gross primary productivity did not differ significantly between the two treatments. Fish production was numerically greater in the high phosphorus treatment, but the difference was not significant (P > 0.05).

Dobbins and Boyd (1976) found that potassium concentrations were significantly greater in ponds fertilized with 20-20-5 than in ponds treated with 20-20-0 (Table 3.12). Nevertheless, differences in gross phytoplankton productivity and net sunfish production did not differ significantly between treatments (P > 0.05). Waters of the ponds treated with 20-20-0 contained an average of 1.3 mg/l of potassium; this suggests that fertilization with potassium is not necessary in waters containing 1.3 mg/l or more of this nutrient.

In another experiment, Boyd and Sowles (1978) compared sunfish production in ponds treated with 20-20-5 fertilizer to that achieved with 0-20-5 fertilization (Table 3.14). Ponds fertilized with N and P_2O_5 had significantly higher concentrations of nitrate, but not of total ammonia nitrogen, than ponds fertilized with only P_2O_5. Apparently, some of the ammonia nitrogen added in ammonium nitrate (the nitrogen fertilizer) was lost to volatilization. Nitrogen in ponds treated with only P_2O_5 apparently originated from mineralization of nitrogen in organic matter in muds and from nitrogen fixation. Blue-green algae, including genera that are capable of fixing nitrogen, were present in ponds of both treatments on all sampling dates. Aquatic macrophytes, which do not fix nitrogen, were more abundant in ponds of the nitrogen plus phosphorus treatment, apparently because of the greater concentrations of inorganic nitrogen. Phytoplankton abundance, as

TABLE 3.12

Effects of different fertilizer treatments on gross primary productivity and sunfish production in ponds. Eleven applications of 45 kg/ha of fertilizer were made between February and October (Dobbins and Boyd, 1976).

Fertilizer	Primary productivity (mg O_2/1 per 4 h)	Sunfish (kg/ha)
20-5-5	0.79	80
20-10-5	0.90	198
20-15-5	1.15	210
20-20-5	1.79	270
20-20-0	1.47	220

TABLE 3.13

Effects of two fertilizer treatments on gross phytoplankton productivity and net production of sunfish. Fertilizers were applied 11 times at 45 kg/ha, and each treatment was replicated six times (Lichtkoppler and Boyd, 1977).

Fertilizer	Primary productivity (mg O_2/1 per 4 h)	Sunfish (kg/ha)
20-10-5	1.03	322
20-20-5	1.83	360

TABLE 3.14

Effects of two fertilizer treatments on chlorophyll _a_ concentrations and net production of sunfish. Fertilizers were applied 11 times at 45 kg/ha, and each treatment was replicated four times (Boyd and Sowles, 1978).

Fertilizer	Chlorophyll _a_ (μg/1)	Sunfish (kg/ha)
0-20-5	19.3	210
20-20-5	19.2	238

measured by chlorophyll _a_ concentrations, did not differ between treatments. The slightly larger net production of sunfish in the 20-20-5 treatment was not statistically significant ($P > 0.05$).

Boyd and Sowles (1978) also compared inorganic nitrogen concentrations and phytoplankton abundance in larger ponds (0.57-10.32 ha) that were fertilized with nitrogen plus phosphorus or with phosphorus alone; application rates were 9 kg/ha for both N and P_2O_5. Nitrate concentrations, but not total ammonia nitrogen concentrations, were higher in ponds of the N plus P_2O_5 treatment. Phytoplankton abundance did not differ significantly between treatments (Table 3.15). Hence, it was assumed that nitrogen fertilization did not appreciably increase the potential for fish production in the ponds.

Liquid fertilizer was tested as a source of nitrogen and phosphorus for fish ponds (Metzger and Boyd, 1980). Liquid fertilizer (13-38-0) was applied to ponds at 5.6, 11.2, and 22.4 kg/ha per application. Inorganic phosphorus concentrations did not differ among treatments, but filtrable orthophosphate and total phosphorus concentrations increased as fertilizer application rates increased (Table 3.16). Nevertheless, chlorophyll a concentrations did not differ significantly among treatments. In earlier studies at Auburn University, average chlorophyll a concentrations ranged from 19 to 31 µg/l in ponds treated with 9 kg/ha per application of N and P_2O_5 (Boyd and Sowles, 1978; Musig and Boyd, 1980). The average chlorophyll a concentration in the low liquid fertilizer treatment (2 kg/ha per application) was 32.6 µg/l.

Net sunfish production was greater in the high treatment than in the two other treatments (Table 3.16). No solid fertilizer treatment was included in the liquid fertilizer experiment; in previous experiments in the same ponds, average net production of sunfish ranged from 238 to 397 kg/ha during different years in treatments consisting of 9 kg/ha per application of N and P_2O_5. The lowest liquid fertilizer treatment (5.6 kg/ha per application of liquid fertilizer or 2.1 kg/ha per application of P_2O_5) had a net production of 310 kg/ha of sunfish (Table 3.16). This value is within the range of values reported when four times as much P_2O_5 was applied as solid phosphate fertilizer. Only 80 kg/ha of sunfish production resulted from fertilization with 9 kg/ha per application of N and 2 kg/ha per application of P_2O_5 in solid fertilizers (Table 3.12).

The superiority of liquid fertilizer over solid fertilizer in increasing fish yields in ponds results from the greater solubility of phosphorus in liquid fertilizers. Hence, more of the phosphorus from the liquid fertilizer is available to phytoplankton. For example, 1 day after a liquid fertilizer application, filtrable orthophosphate concentrations had increased by 0.072, 0.186, and 0.348 mg/l (as P) in low, medium, and high treatments, respectively. If all of the phosphorus applied was uniformally mixed in the pond water, expected increases would be 0.10, 0.20, and 0.41 mg/l for low, medium, and high treatments. When broadcast, granules of solid phosphate fertilizers settle to the pond bottom before appreciable dissolution occurs (Boyd et al., 1981). Although the granules are water soluble, further dissolution occurs at the mud surface; this favors

TABLE 3.15

Effects of two fertilizer treatments on the plankton of large ponds. Fertilizers were applied nine times (45 kg/ha per application) to six ponds in each treatment. Plankton measurements were made at 1- to 2-week intervals (Boyd and Sowles, 1978).

Fertilizer	Chlorophyll $\underline{a}$ (μg/l)	Particulate organic matter (mg/l)
0-20-0	22.5	10.1
20-20-0	30.9	13.2

TABLE 3.16

Effects of three applications rates of liquid fertilizer (13-38-0) on water quality and net production of sunfish in ponds. Fertilizers were applied 11 times during the growing season, treatments were replicated four times. Water quality data are the averages of nine periodic measurements for each pond (Metzger and Boyd, 1980).

Variable	Fertilizer rate (kg/ha per application)		
	5.6	11.2	22.4
Chlorophyll $\underline{a}$ (μg/l)	32.6	39.5	27.2
Nitrate (mg/l as N)	0.040	0.045	0.048
Total ammonia (mg/l as N)	0.088	0.116	0.116
Filtrable orthophosphate (mg/l as P)	0.018	0.073	0.100
Total phosphorus (mg/l)	0.097	0.163	0.214
Net sunfish production (kg/ha)	310	315	418

adsorption of phosphorus by muds. Concentrations of phosphorus in pond waters following applications of liquid fertilizer, triple superphosphate, or diammonium phosphate are shown in Fig. 3.2.

Davidson and Boyd (1981) compared phytoplankton production in larger ponds (0.34-1.94 ha) treated with either 2 kg/ha per application of P_2O_5 in liquid fertilizer or 8 kg/ha per application of P_2O_5 in solid fertilizer. Results presented in Table 3.17 show that more phytoplankton was generally present in the ponds treated with solid fertilizer, but phytoplankton abundance was greater in ponds treated with liquid fertilizer than in the control ponds.

Boyd (1981b) presented data that conclusively demonstrate the value of low fertilizer application rates. Treatments and net production values for sunfish are summarized in Table 3.18. None of the values for net production differed

TABLE 3.17

Effects on chlorophyll a concentrations (μg/l) of no fertilization and fertilization with 6 kg/ha per application of liquid fertilizer (10-34-0) or with 45 kg/ha per application of granular 20-20-5. Treatments were replicated six times in ponds with areas of 0.32-1.94 ha.

Data	Fertilizer treatment		
	Solid	Liquid	None
2 Apr	15	23	
15 May	35	42	10
15 Jun	68	58	11
20 Jul	84	33	6
20 Aug	58	28	9
20 Sep	52	44	11

TABLE 3.18

Net production of sunfish in ponds that received different fertilizer treatments. Each treatment was replicated four times and fertilizers were applied 12 times during the growing season.

Fertilizer	Rate (kg/ha)	Sunfish (kg/ha)
Mixed (20-20-5)	45	228
Triple superphosphate (0-46-0)	20	298
Triple superphosphate	10	226
Diammonium phosphate (18-46-0)	10	308
Liquid fertilizer (15-25-0)	8	228

significantly (P > 0.05), even though there were considerable differences in N, P_2O_5, and K_2O application rates among treatments. Net production of sunfish in two unfertilized ponds was only 125 kg/ha — a value comparable to those reported for other unfertilized ponds in the Piedmont area of Alabama.

3.6   PRACTICAL USE OF FERTILIZERS IN PONDS

3.6.1   Selection of application rates

All researchers have found phosphorus essential and potassium non-essential in pond fertilization. Variable responses have been shown to nitrogen, but in no instance did nitrogen fertilization appear to decrease fish production.

Certainly, nitrogen is not as important as phosphorus in pond fertilization, but aside from economic considerations of low return on investment, there is no need to discourage fertilization with nitrogen unless it is known from experience that nitrogen will not stimulate fish production in a particular pond.

Fertilization rates for sportfish ponds should be established after considering the basic fertility of the pond and the fishing effort. For example, ponds on fertile watersheds, e.g., pastures, may require little or no fertilization, but ponds on less fertile watershed, e.g., woodlands, may require heavy fertilization. Likewise, ponds with heavy fishing should be fertilized at greater rates than ponds with light or moderate fishing. Results of experiments summarized above suggest that either phosphate-only fertilizers (0-1-0) or fertilizers with a nutrient ratio of about 1-3-0 are best. Of the solid fertilizers, triple super-phosphate or superphosphate may be used for phosphorus-only fertilization. Diammonium phosphate (18-48-0) has a nutrient ratio of roughly 1-3-0 and is a good source of nitrogen and phosphorus in a solid fertilizer. Alternatively, a combination of a nitrogen-only fertilizer, e.g., ammonium nitrate, and a phosphorus-only fertilizer, e.g., triple superphosphate, may be used for nitrogen and phosphorus fertilization.

Ponds often require 8-12 periodic applications of fertilizer to maintain plankton blooms. Infertile ponds with light or moderate fishing should receive 4.5 kg/ha per application of P_2O_5; 9 kg/ha of P_2O_5 per application should be applied to infertile ponds with heavy fishing. Liquid fertilizer is more effective than solid fertilizer and 2 kg/ha per application of P_2O_5 in liquid fertilizer will increase fish production appreciably. Boyd (1981c) presented several different fertilization programs for sportfish ponds and the approximate annual costs of fertilizers. Fertilizer prices vary between localities and usually increase from year to year, but these data (Table 3.19) provide an idea of the cost differentials between fertilization programs.

Ponds for production of food fish or bait minnows require heavy fertilization. Application rates even higher than 2 hg/ha per application of N and 9 kg/ha per application of P_2O_5 may be necessary in some situations.

3.6.2 Calculations of amounts of fertilizer for application

When fertilizing fish ponds, it is not necessary to purchase a mixed fertilizer or to prepare one as described earlier. To illustrate, a 1.5-ha pond could be fertilized at a rate equivalent to 50 kg/ha of 8-20-0 fertilizer using ammonium sulfate (20% N) and monoammonium phosphate (11% N and 55% P_2O_5) instead of a mixed fertilizer. Amounts of primary nutrients needed are:

N = 50 kg/ha X 0.08 X 1.5 ha = 6 kg

P_2O_5 = 50 kg/ha X 0.20 X 1.5 ha = 15 kg

The amount of monoammonium phosphate required for 15 kg of P_2O_5 is:

15 kg ÷ 0.55 = 27.3 kg

This quantity of monoammonium phosphate contains 3 kg of N, but 6 kg of N are required. The remaining 3 kg of N must be supplied in ammonium sulfate:

3 kg N ÷ 0.20 = 15 kg

Therefore, the application of 15 kg of ammonium sulfate and 27.3 kg of monoammonium phosphate to the 1.5-ha pond would be equivalent in primary nutrients to treatment with 50 kg/ha of 8-20-0 fertilizer.

Another example will be useful to some readers. An 11.2-ha pond must be fertilized with N at 4 kg/ha and P_2O_5 at 8 kg/ha using ammonium nitrate (33.5% N) and superphosphate (18% P_2O_5). The required amounts of N and P_2O_5 are:

N = 4 kg/ha X 11.2 ha = 44.8 kg
P_2O_5 = 8 kg/ha X 11.2 ha = 89.6 kg

The necessary amounts of fertilizer are:

44.8 kg ÷ 0.335 = 134 kg ammonium nitrate
89.6 kg ÷ 0.18 = 498 kg superphosphate

When applying liquid fertilizers to fish ponds, it is often simplier to measure them volumetrically. To fertilize a pond at a P_2O_5 rate of 8 kg/ha with liquid fertilizer that is 34% P_2O_5 and weighs 1.44 kg/l requires 16.3 l/ha of fertilizer. The calculations are:

8 kg/ha ÷ 0.34 = 23.5 kg liquid fertilizer
23.5 kg ÷ 1.44 kg/l = 16.3 l/ha

3.6.3 Methods of applying fertilizers

As mentioned earlier, solid fertilizers are often broadcast over pond surfaces. This practice is effective, but fertilizer should not be broadcast over deeper waters of ponds because the granules will sink into the hypolimnion. Nutrients in the hypolimnion will not become available to phytoplankton until thermal

TABLE 3.19

Annual cost of fertilizer (10 applications for fish ponds using several different fertilizers and application rates. Cost of fertilizer sources per kilogram were: liquid fertilizer, $0.272; diammonium phosphate, $0.351; triple superphosphate, $0.297; fish pond fertilizer, $0.277. Prices in United States dollars were quoted in October 1980.

Fertilization program	Rate (kg/ha per application)			Annual cost ($/ha)
	Fertilizer	N	P_2O_5	
Ponds with light or moderate fishing				
Liquid fertilizer (10-34-0)	7	0.7	2.4	19.04
Liquid fertilizer	13	1.3	4.4	35.36
Diammonium phosphate (18-46-0)	10	1.8	4.6	35.10
Triple superphosphate (0-46-0)	10	0	4.6	29.70
Ponds with heavy fishing				
Liquid fertilizer	26	2.6	8.8	70.72
Diammonium phosphate	20	3.6	9.2	70.20
Triple superphosphate	20	0	9.2	59.40
Fish pond fertilizer	45	9.0	9.0	124.65

destratification occurs.

Fertilizer platforms (Lawrence, 1954) are effective in preventing solid fertilizers from contacting bottom muds. Platforms can be easily and cheaply constructed before ponds are filled with water. Platforms should be from 30 to 40 cm underwater, and one platform with an area of about 4 m^2 is adequate for 2-4 ha of pond area. Fertilizers are poured onto the platforms and water currents distribute nutrients as they dissolve. Swingle (1965) reported that the platform method of application often reduced fertilizer requirements by 20-40%.

Boyd and Hollerman (unpublished) evaluated four methods of applying liquid fertilizers to ponds: pump, power sprayer, hand sprayer, and outboard motor. A centrifugal irrigation pump with a capacity of 400 l/min was modified to discharge liquid fertilizer. A tee was attached between the pump and suction hose on the intake side. A reducer was placed in the tee and a 1-cm inside diameter ball valve was seated in the reducer. One end of a 1.3-cm inside diameter polyvinylchloride hose was attached to the ball valve, and the other end of the hose was inserted into an open container of liquid fertilizer. The suction hose was placed in the pond, and the pump was operated to discharge water back into the pond at a site several meters from the intake. With the pump running, the ball valve was opened so that fertilizer was sucked into the incoming water, mixed, and discharged into the pond at a single site. Fertilizer flowed into the intake hose of the pump at 1.7 kg/min.

The power sprayer was operated by a 3.75-kilowatt gasoline engine. The liquid fertilizer was mixed with twice its volume of water and discharged by the sprayer at a pressure of 8.4 kg/cm^2. The mixture was sprayed over an area of about 160 m^2 in each pond.

A compression-type hand sprayer (10-liter capacity) was used to apply undiluted fertilizer. The fertilizer was applied in a band approximately 7-m wide as the operator walked around edges of ponds.

To make applications by boat, fertilizer was drained at 2 liters per minute into the propellor wake of an electric trolling motor (5 kg thrust). The boat was driven back and forth over pond surfaces as fertilizer was released.

The phosphorus fertilization rate was 9 kg/ha in all trials. Sampling grids were established in each pond, and 10 samples were taken before and 24-h after fertilization for filtrable orthophosphate analysis.

All four methods of applying liquid fertilizer were effective in appreciably increasing average filtrable orthophosphate concentrations in ponds (Table 3.20). The greatest increase in orthophosphate concentration was 0.54 mg/l in a trial using the outboard motor; the smallest increase was 0.09 mg/l in a trial with the pump. Ponds varied from 0.38 to 5.71 ha in area and from 1 to 2 m in average depth. Plankton densities at times of fertilizer applications varied among ponds; yet, averages of filtrable orthophosphate concentrations 24-h after application were remarkably similar for the different techniques of application.

The method of applying liquid fertilizer will depend upon equipment available and individual discretion, and methods different from those described above can no doubt be developed. In fact, if no equipment is on hand, liquid fertilizer may be mixed with water and splashed over pond surfaces (Metzger and Boyd, 1980). Some liquid fertilizers are neutral, but others are highly acidic. Corrosion proof pumps and sprayers must be used to apply acidic solutions. Pumps and sprayers should be flushed with plenty of water even after dispensing neutral solutions.

3.6.4 Problems encountered in fertilization

Ponds with soft acidic waters may not respond to inorganic fertilization unless they are first limed. Liming is discussed in Chapter 4.

Ponds that have waters turbid from suspended clay particles or humic substances may not respond to fertilization because light penetration is not adequate for phytoplankton growth. Methods for clearing waters of turbidity are discussed in Chapter 9. These techniques are not effective if ponds receive large amounts of

TABLE 3.20

Concentrations of filtrable orthophosphate (mg/l as P) in ponds before and 24-h after application of liquid fertilizer by four methods. Application techniques are described in the text. Fertilizers were applied at 9 kg/ha of P_2O_5.

Method	No. ponds	Area (ha)	Filtrable orthophosphate[a]	
			Before	24-h after
Pump	5	0.61-1.33	0.004-0.02	0.11-0.36
Power sprayer	5	0.76-2.02	0.002-0.02	0.11-0.67
Hand sprayer	6	0.38-1.59	0.005-0.03	0.15-0.54
Outboard motor	5	0.65-5.71	0.01 -0.04	0.18-0.55

[a]Samples were collected from 10 locations in each pond.

turbid runoff after each rain. Unless erosion of the watershed is prevented by the establishment of vegetation or the runoff diverted, fertilization is not advisable. In some ponds, problems with turbid water only occur during rainy months, so fertilizers should be applied during dry months when ponds are not turbid.

Ponds choked with aquatic macrophytes during summer should not be fertilized until weeds are brought under control. Fertilizers are usually wasted in weed-infested ponds because the nutrients are used by macrophytes rather than by phytoplankton. The technique of winter fertilization to control troublesome infestations of underwater weeds (Smith and Swingle, 1941) has already been discussed. Unfertilized ponds do not always develop macrophyte problems. Further, fertilization is not always effective in preventing the intrusion of macrophytes into ponds, especially if ponds have large expanses of shallow water. Information on chemical weed control may be found in Chapter 8.

Phytoplankton blooms may sometimes become excessive in fertilized ponds. When this occurs, one should cease fertilization until the plankton bloom diminishes. Overabundant plankton can lead to oxygen depletion and fish kills.

In cold climates, ponds freeze over for several months during the winter. As a result of decomposition of organic matter and little or no oxygen from photosynthesis beneath the ice cover, dissolved oxygen concentrations may decline to such low levels that fish kills occur. This process is frequently termed winterkill. Winterkill has been studied extensively in natural lakes (Greenbank, 1945; Barica, 1977), and methods for predicting the risk of winterkill have been advanced (Barica and Mathias, 1979). Ball (1948) and Ball and Tanner (1951) reported that winterkills in certain lakes in Michigan were the direct result of fertilization.

TABLE 3.21

Concentrations of dissolved oxygen in fertilized and unfertilized trout lakes during late winter stagnation (Ball, 1948).

Depth (m)	Dissolved oxygen (mg/l)	
	Unfertilized	Fertilized
Just beneath ice	7.8	0.8
1		0.2
3		0
5	8.2	
8	0.7	
10	0.2	

Higher levels of organic matter were present in fertilized than in unfertilized lakes. Therefore, oxygen consumption by microorganisms was greater in the lakes that had been fertilized during warm months and winterkill resulted. Concentrations of dissolved oxygen during February at different depths below the ice (Ball, 1948) are given in Table 3.21.

The turnover time of water in a pond must exceed 3-4 weeks, otherwise fertilizer nutrients will be flushed out of the pond before they produce fish food. Methods for increasing the water turnover time include diversion of excess water, enlargement of pond, or construction of another pond above the existing pond. Conventional spillways release surface water from ponds, but deep water releases (Boyd, 1979) take in water near pond bottoms and are thought by many biologists to reduce the loss of fertilizer nutrients and plankton. The value of deep water releases remains undocumented, but these releases are widely used in ponds in the southeastern United States. Some ponds have excess flow only during rainy months and may respond to fertilizers during dry weather. Finally, some ponds with short water detention times simply cannot be managed as fertilized ponds.

3.7 ORGANIC FERTILIZERS

3.7.1 Sources

A wide variety of materials are used as organic fertilizers (manures) in fish ponds. Hickling (1962) listed the following: grass, leaves and reeds; liquid manure from livestock holding facilities; sewage water; industrial wastes from distilleries, leather and milk factories, sugar refineries, and fish canning plants; livestock dung; night soil; cottonseed, groundnut, and sunflower seed cake; soybean wastes; cottonseed meal; and dry hay. Many other waste products would be equally suitable for manures.

The nature of the organic material and its prior treatment determines the moisture and primary nutrient content of manure. Concentrations of primary nutrients vary greatly among manures, but manures have much lower percentages of primary nutrients than chemical fertilizers. Concentrations of fertilizer constituents in fresh dung of farm animals are given in Table 3.22. One kilogram of diammonium phosphate (18-46-0) contains as much N as 36 kg of dairy cattle manure and as much P_2O_5 as 230 kg of this manure. Because of the diversity of manures, a listing of nutrient ratios has little value. Chemical analysis is the only sure way of ascertaining the primary nutrient content of a given organic fertilizer.

3.7.2   Influence on pond ecology

Organic fertilizers may serve as direct sources of food for invertebrate fish food organisms and fish, or they may decompose, releasing inorganic nutrients that stimulate phytoplankton growth. According to Hickling (1962), organic fertilizers are especially efficient in increasing the abundance of zooplankton and benthic organisms. Rappaport et al. (1977) compared the abundance of plankton and chironomid larvae in ponds treated with manures to the abundance of these organisms in chemically fertilized ponds and control ponds (Table 3.23). Organic fertilizer, and especially chicken droppings, was considerably more effective than chemical fertilizer in increasing the abundance of fish food organisms.

Simultaneous applications of manures and chemical fertilizers are sometimes used to increase the abundance of fish food organisms (Moav et al., 1977; Schroeder 1978). The manure itself is not a good fish food and does not produce good fish growth. Schroeder (1978) made estimates of all organisms, autotrophic and heterotrophic, pelagic and benthic, large enough to be used directly by fish in ponds treated with manure plus chemical fertilizer. He observed that the total measured production of fish food organisms did not account for even 50% of the measured fish growth. Production by the microbial community growing on the manure was sufficient to account for the rest of the measured fish growth. Therefore, he assumed that fish consumed bacteria and protozoa by ingesting small particles of manure covered by microbial growth.

Although manures usually impart color to water, waters of some ponds treated with manures were too clear for good fishing (Smith and Swingle, 1942). Manures also encouraged the growth of macrophytic algae, which are undesirable in fish ponds.

Decay of manure mineralizes nutrients, but it also requires dissolved oxygen. Collis and Smitherman (1978) found that applications of cattle manure had to be limited to 80 kg/ha per day (dry matter basis) to prevent dissolved oxygen depletion in ponds stocked with _Tilapia_. Schroeder (1974) found that the

TABLE 3.22

Fertilizer constituents in fresh manure of selected farm animals (Morrison, 1961).

Manure	Average composition (%)			
	Moisture	N	P_2O_5	K_2O
Dairy cattle	85	0.5	0.2	0.5
Beef cattle	85	0.7	0.5	0.5
Poultry	72	1.2	1.3	0.6
Swine	82	0.5	0.3	0.4
Sheep	77	1.4	0.5	1.2

TABLE 3.23

Abundance of phytoplankton in waters and chironomid larvae in muds of ponds receiving different types of manure. Results are compared with chemically fertilized and control ponds (Rappaport et al., 1977).

Treatment	Phytoplankton (No./ml)	Chironomid larvae (No./cm^2)
Chicken droppings	16,300	340
Liquid manure	5,600	82
Corral manure	3,000	38
Chemical fertilizer	4,600	43
Control	2,500	59

biochemical oxygen demand (BOD) of manure could be used to predict the decrease in dissolved oxygen following application of manure. This method is not generally useful to fish farmers because special equipment is needed to measure BOD. Experience with a particular manure usually allows fish farmers to establish application rates that will not cause dissolved oxygen depletion.

3.7.3   Fish production

Several workers have demonstrated that just as many fish can be produced with organic fertilizers as with chemical fertilizers. Hickling (1962) reported that the application of 15,000 kg/ha of cow manure resulted in an average fish yield of 300 kg/ha while the control ponds averaged 97 kg/ha of fish. In this same experiment, various treatments with chemical fertilizers resulted in average fish yields of 243-373 kg/ha. Organic fertilizers resulted in appreciable increases in bluegill production (Table 3.24) in ponds in Alabama (Smith and Swingle, 1942;

TABLE 3.24

Effects of organic fertilizers (manures) on net production of sunfish and large-mouth bass in ponds (Smith and Swingle, 1942; Swingle, 1947).

Manure	No. ponds	Manure (kg/ha)[a]	Fish (kg/ha)
None	2		111
Cottonseed meal	1	975	423
Soybean meal	1	1,500	520
Barnyard manure	1	8,000	272
Kudzu hay	1	8,000	176

[a]Sum of 4-10 applications.

Swingle, 1947). Comparison of data in Table 3.24 with those in Table 3.10 confirm that organic fertilization was comparable to chemical fertilization in increasing sunfish production. Collis and Smitherman (1978) obtained an average Tilapia yield of 1,646 kg/ha in ponds treated with cattle manure twice daily. The total input of fresh manure was 28,381 kg/ha (5,392 kg/ha dry matter). However, the application of only 3,521 kg/ha of a commercial fish feed (36% crude protein) to other ponds gave a Tilapia yield of 2,663 kg/ha. Clearly, manure is a rather low quality fish feed.

A combination of feeding with pelleted feeds and organic fertilization resulted in high yields of fish in Israel (Rappaport et al., 1977; Rappaport and Sarig, 1978). For example, the yields of carp were increased in ponds receiving pelleted feeds when chicken droppings or liquid cattle manure were applied at rates of 5 kg/ha of dry matter 5 days per week. Fresh cow dung (solid manure) had a negative effect on carp yields, and chemical fertilization was not as effective in increasing yields as chicken droppings or liquid cattle manure. Moav et al. (1977) substituted liquid cattle manure for pelleted fish feeds in polyculture systems. The average growth of fish in ponds treated exclusively with liquid cattle manure was 32 kg/ha per day as compared to 50 kg/ha per day in ponds where fish were fed a pelleted commercial feed.

In summary, results of experiments show that organic fertilizers are useful in increasing fish production. The large quantities of manure required are not always available, difficult to handle, and may cause dissolved oxygen depletion or other ecological problems. Nevertheless, in many areas chemical fertilizers are either unavailable or too expensive for use in fish ponds. In these areas, the use of manures should be encouraged because applications of organic materials may be the only available means of increasing fish production. Even in technologically advanced nations, it would be wise to use available organic wastes to increase fish production. This practice turns the waste into useful production and conserves chemical fertilizers and feeds.

Wohlfarth and Schroeder (1979) reviewed the literature on the use of manure in fish farming and concluded that maximum yields per unit are higher with high-protein feed than with manure. However, cost of high-protein feeds prohibit their use in most tropical nations.

3.7.4 Use of Wastewater for fish production

Although wastewaters such as sewage have long been used for fish production, there has recently been a revival of interest in this subject. Wastewaters provide a nutrient enriched environment for the production of fish, and the feeding of fish reduces the organic loading of the water. Thus, fish production in wastewater is viewed by some as a realistic method of water purification. This topic is beyond the scope of this discussion, but there are several excellent papers on this subject in the book "Advances in Aquaculture", which was edited by Pillay and Dill (1979).

REFERENCES

Alexander, M., 1961. Introduction to Soil Microbiology. John Wiley and Sons, New York, 472 pp.
Almazan, G. and Boyd, C. E., 1978a. Effects of nitrogen levels on rates of oxygen consumption during decay of aquatic plants. Aquat. Bot., 5: 119-126.
Almazan, G. and Boyd, C. E., 1978b. An evaluation of Secchi disk visibility for estimating plankton density in fish ponds. Hydrobiologia, 65: 601-608.
Arce, R. G. and Boyd, C. E., 1980. Water chemistry of Alabama ponds. Auburn University Agricultural Experiment Station, Auburn University, Alabama, Bulletin 522, 35 pp.
Ball, R. C., 1948. Fertilization of natural lakes in Michigan. Trans. Amer. Fish. Soc., 78: 145-155.
Ball, R. C., 1949. Experimental use of fertilizer in the production of fish-food organisms and fish. Michigan State College Agricultural Experiment Station, East Lansing, Michigan, Technical Bulletin 210, 28 pp.
Ball, R. C. and Tanner, H. A., 1951. The biological effects of fertilizer on a warm-water lake. Michigan State College Agricultural Experiment Station, East Lansing, Michigan, Technical Bulletin 223, 32 pp.
Barica, J., 1975. Summerkill risk in prairie ponds and possibilities of its prediction. J. Fish. Res. Bd. Canada, 32: 1283-1288.
Barica, J., 1977. Effects of freeze-up on major ion and nutrient content of a prairie winterkill lake. J. Fish. Res. Bd. Canada, 34: 2210-2215.
Barica, J. and Mathias, J. A., 1979. Oxygen depletion and winterkill risk in small prairie lakes under extended ice cover. J. Fish. Res. Bd. Canada, 36: 980-986.
Bouldin, D. R., Johnson, R. L., Burda, C., and Kao, C., 1974. Losses of inorganic nitrogen from aquatic systems. J. Environ. Qual., 3: 107-114.
Boyd, C. E., 1971. Phosphorus dynamics in ponds. Proc. Annual Conf. Southeast. Assoc. Game and Fish Comm., 25: 418-426.
Boyd, C. E., 1973. Summer algal communities and primary productivity in fish ponds. Hydrobiologia, 41: 357-390.
Boyd, C. E., 1974. The utilization of nitrogen from the decomposition of organic matter in cultures of Scenedesmus dimorphus. Arch. Hydrobiol., 73: 361-368.

Boyd, C. E., 1975. Competition for light by aquatic plants in fish ponds. Auburn University Agricultural Experiment Station, Auburn, Alabama, Circular 215, 19 pp.

Boyd, C. E., 1976a. Chemical and textural properties of muds from different depths in ponds. Hydrobiologia, 48: 141-144.

Boyd, C. E., 1976b. Water chemistry and plankton in unfertilized ponds in pastures and in woods. Trans. Amer. Fish. Soc., 105: 634-636.

Boyd, C. E., 1976c. Nitrogen fertilizer effects on production of Tilapia in ponds fertilized with phosphorus and potassium. Aquaculture, 7: 385-390.

Boyd, C. E., 1978. Chemical composition of wetland plants. In: R. E. Good, D. F. Whigham, and R. L. Simpson (Editors), Freshwater Wetlands, Ecological Processes and Management Potential. Academic Press, New York, pp. 155-167.

Boyd, C. E., 1979. Water Quality in Warmwater Fish Ponds. Auburn University Agricultural Experiment Station, Auburn, Alabama, 359 pp.

Boyd, C. E., 1981a. Solubility of granular inorganic fertilizers for fish ponds. Trans. Amer. Fish. Soc., 110: 451-454.

Boyd, C. E., 1981b. Comparison of five fertilization programs for fish ponds. Trans. Amer. Fish. Soc., 110: 541-545.

Boyd, C. E., 1981c. Fertilization of warmwater fish ponds. J. Soil Water Cons., 36: 142-145.

Boyd, C. E. and Musig, Y., 1981. Orthophosphate uptake by phytoplankton and sediment. Aquaculture, 22: 165-173.

Boyd, C. E. and Scarsbrook, E., 1974. Effects of agricultural limestone on phytoplankton communities of fish ponds. Arch. Hydrobiol., 74: 336-349.

Boyd, C. E. and Snow, J. R., 1975. Fertilizing farm fish ponds. Auburn University Agricultural Experiment Station, Auburn, Alabama, Leaflet 88, 8 pp.

Boyd, C. E. and Sowles, J. W., 1978. Nitrogen fertilization of ponds. Trans. Amer. Fish. Soc., 107: 737-741.

Boyd, C. E., Musig, Y., and Tucker, L., 1981. Effects of three phosphorus fertilizers on phosphorus concentrations and phytoplankton production. Aquaculture, 22: 175-180.

Bristow, J. M. and Whitcombe, M., 1971. The role of roots in the nutrition of aquatic vascular plants. Amer. J. Bot., 58: 8-13.

Chiou, C. and Boyd, C. E., 1974. The utilization of phosphorus from muds by the phytoplankter, Scenedesmus dimorphus, and the significance of these findings to the practice of pond fertilization. Hydrobiologia, 45: 345-355.

Coffin, C. C., Hayes, F. R., Godfrey, L. H., and Whiteway, S. G., 1949. Exchange of materials in a lake as studied by the addition of radioactive phosphorus. Can. J. Res., 27: 207-222.

Collis, W. J. and Smitherman, R. O., 1973. Production of Tilapia hybrids with cattle manure or a commercial diet. In: R. O. Smitherman, W. L. Shelton, and J. H. Grover (Editors), Symposium on the Culture of Exotic Fishes. Fish Culture Section, American Fisheries Section, Bethesda, Maryland, pp. 43-54.

Davidson, R. G. and C. E. Boyd, 1981. Plankton response to liquid fertilizers. Prog. Fish-Cult., 43: 126-129.

Dendy, J. S., Varikul, V., Sumawidjaja, K., and Potaros, M., 1968. Production of Tilapia mossambica Peters, plankton and benthos as parameters for evaluating nitrogen in pond fertilizers. Proc. World Symposium on Warm-Water Pond Fish Culture, FAO United Nations, Fish. Rep., 44: 226-240.

Denny, P., 1971. Sites of nutrient absorption in aquatic macrophytes. J. Ecol., 60: 819-829.

Dickman, M. and Efford, I. E., 1972. Some effects of artificial fertilization on enclosed plankton populations in Marion Lake, British Columbia. J. Fish. Res. Bd. Canada, 29: 1595-1604.

Dobbins, D. A. and Boyd, C. E., 1976. Phosphorus and potassium fertilization of sunfish ponds. Trans. Amer. Fish. Soc., 105: 536-540.

Dugdale, V. A. and Dugdale, R. C., 1962. Nitrogen metabolism on lakes: II. Role of nitrogen fixation in Sanctuary Lake, Penn. Limnol. Oceanogr., 7: 170-177.

Eren, Y., Tsur, T., and Avnimelech, Y., 1977. Phosphorus fertilization of fishponds in the Upper Galilee. Bamidgeh, 29: 87-92.

Fitzgerald, G. P., 1970a. Evaluations of the availability of sources of nitrogen and phosphorus for algae. J. Phycol., 6: 239-247.

Fitzgerald, G. P., 1970b. Aerobic lake muds for the removal of phosphorus from lake waters. Limnol. Oceanogr., 15: 550-555.

Fogg, G. E., Stewart, W. D. P., Fay, P., and Walsby, A. E., 1973. The Blue-Green Algae. Academic Press, New York, 459 pp.

Gerloff, G. C., 1969. Evaluating nutrient supplies for the growth of aquatic plants in natural waters. In: Eutrophication; Causes, Consequences, Correctives. National Academy of Science, Washington, D. C., pp. 537-555.

Gerloff, G. C. and Skoog, F., 1954. Cell contents of nitrogen and phosphorus as a measure of their availability for growth of Microcystis aeruginosa. Ecology, 35: 348-353.

Goldberg, E. G., Walker, T. J., and Whisenand, A., 1951. Phosphate utilization by diatoms. Biol. Bull. (Wood's Hole), 101: 274-284.

Goldman, C. R., 1965. Micronutrient limiting factors and their detection in natural phytoplankton populations. In: C. R. Goldman (Editor), Primary Productivity in Aquatic Environments. Mem. Ist. Ital. Idrobiol., 18 Suppl., University of California Press, Berkeley, pp. 121-136.

Golterman, H. L., Bakels, C. C., and Jakobs-Mogelin, J., 1969. Availability of mud phosphates for the growth of algae. Verh. Int. Verein. Limnol., 17: 467-479.

Greenbank, J., 1945. Limnological conditions in ice-covered lakes, especially as related to winterkill of fish. Ecol. Monogr. 15: 343-392.

Hall, D. J. Cooper, W. E., and Werner, E. C., 1970. An experimental approach to the production dynamics and structure of freshwater animal communities. Limnol. Oceanogr., 15: 839-928.

Hasler, A. D. and Einsele, W. G., 1948. Fertilization for increasing productivity of natural inland waters. Trans. N. Amer. Wildlife Conf., 13: 527-555.

Hayes, F. R. and Phillips, J. E., 1958. Lake water and sediment. IV. Radio-phosphorus equilibrium with mud, plants, and bacteria under oxidized and reduced conditions. Limnol. Oceanogr., 3: 459-475.

Hepher, B., 1958. On the dynamics of phosphorus added to fishponds in Israel. Limnol. Oceanogr., 7: 131-135.

Hepher, B., 1962a. Primary production in fishponds and its application to fertilization experiments. Limnol. Oceanogr., 7: 131-135.

Hepher, B., 1962b. Ten years of research in fish pond fertilization in Israel. I. The effect of fertilization on fish yields. Bamidgeh, 14: 29-38.

Hepher, B., 1963. Ten years of research in fishpond fertilization in Israel. II. Fertilizer dose and frequency of fertilization. Bamidgeh, 15: 78-92.

Hepher, B., 1966. Some aspects of the phosphorus cycle in fishponds. Verh. Int. Verein. Limnol., 16: 1293-1297.

Hepher, B., 1968. Some limiting factors affecting the dose of fertilizers added to fish ponds, with special reference to the Near East. In: Proc. World Symposium on Warmwater Pond Fish Culture, FAO United Nations, Fish. Rep. No. 44, 3: 1-7.

Hickling, C. F., 1962. Fish Culture. Faber and Faber, London, 295 pp.

Horne, A. J., and Fogg, G. E., 1970. Nitrogen fixation in some English lakes. Proc. Roy. Soc. Lond., B, 175: 351-366.

Hunt, D. and Boyd, C. E., 1981. Alkalinity losses from ammonium fertilizers used in fish ponds. Trans. Amer. Fish. Soc., 110: 81-85.

Jones, U. S., 1979. Fertilizers and Soil Fertility. Reston Publishing Company, Inc., Reston, Virginia, 368 pp.

Kemmerer, A. J., 1968. A method to determine fertilization requirements of a small sport fishing lake. Trans. Amer. Fish. Soc., 97: 425-428.

Kilmer, V. J., Gilliam, J. W., Lutz, J. F., Joyce, R. T., and Eklund, C. D., 1974. Nutrient losses from fertilized grassed watersheds in western North Carolina. J. Environ. Qual., 3: 214-219.

Kimmel, B. L. and Lind, O. T., 1970. Factors influencing orthophosphate concentration decline in the water of laboratory mud-water systems. Texas J.

Sci., 21: 339-445.

Langford, R. R., 1948. Fertilization of lakes in Algonquin Park, Ontario. Trans. Amer. Fish. Soc., 78: 133-144.

Latterell, J. J., Holt, R. F., and Timmons, D. R., 1971. Phosphate availability in lake sediments. J. Soil Water Cons., 26: 21-24.

Lawrence, J. M., 1954. A new method of applying inorganic fertilizer to farm fishponds. Prog. Fish-Cult., 16: 176-178.

Lichtkoppler, F. R. and Boyd, C. E., 1977. Phosphorus fertilization of sunfish ponds. Trans. Amer. Fish. Soc., 106: 634-636.

MacArthur, R. H. and MacArthur, J. W., 1961. On bird species diversity. Ecology, 42: 594-598.

Maciolek, J. A., 1954. Artificial fertilization of lakes and ponds. A Review of the Literature. U. S. Fish and Wildlife Service, Washington, D. C., Special Science Report, Fisheries No. 113, 41 pp.

Mackereth, F. J., 1952. Phosphorus utilization by _Asterionella formosa_ Hass. J. Exp. Bot., 4: 296-313.

Maristo, L., 1941. Die Seetypen Finnelands auf floristischer und vegetation-physiognomischer Grundlage. Suom. Elan-ja Kasvitiet. Seuran Vanamon Kasvitiet. Julk., 314 pp.

Martin, J. B., Bradford, B. N., and Kennedy, H. G., 1970. Relationship of nutritional and environmental factors to selected rooted aquatic macrophytes: Part I. Factors affecting growth of _Najas_ in Pickwick Reservoir. In: TVA Activities Related to Study and Control of Eutrophication in the Tennessee Valley. National Fertilizer Development Center, Tennessee Valley Authority, Muscle Shoals, Alabama pp. 7-14.

McIntire, C. D. and Bond, C. E., 1962. Effects of artificial fertilization on plankton and benthos abundance in four experimental ponds. Trans. Amer. Fish. Soc., 91: 303-312.

McRoy, C. P. and Barsdate, R. J., 1970. Phosphate absorption in eelgrass. Limnol. Oceanogr., 15: 6-13.

Metzger, R. J. and Boyd, C. E., 1980. Liquid ammonium polyphosphate as a fish pond fertilizer. Trans. Amer. Fish. Soc., 109: 563-570.

Moav, R., Wohlfarth, G., Schroeder, G. L., Hulata, G., and Barash, H., 1977. Intensive polyculture of fish in freshwater ponds. I. Substitution of expensive feeds by liquid cow manure. Aquaculture, 10: 25-43.

Morrison, F. B., 1961. Feeds and Feeding, Abridged. The Morrison Publishing Co., Clinton, Iowa, 696 pp.

Mortimer, C. H., 1954. Fertilizers in Fish Ponds. Her Majesty's Stationery Office, London, Fisheries Publication No. 5, 155 pp.

Moyle, J. B., 1946. Some indices of lake productivity. Trans. Amer. Fish. Soc., 76: 322-334.

Musig, Y. and Boyd, C. E., 1980. Comparison of polyphosphate and orthophosphate as fertilizers for fish ponds. Aquaculture, 20: 135-138.

Neess, J., 1946. Development and status of pond fertilization in central Europe. Trans. Amer. Fish. Soc., 76: 335-358.

Patriarche, M. H. and Ball, R. C., 1949. An analysis of the bottom fauna pro-duction in fertilized and unfertilized ponds and its utilization by young-of-the-year fish. Michigan State College Agricultural Experiment Station, East Lansing, Michigan, Technical Bulletin 207, 35 pp.

Peltier, W. H. and Welch, E. B., 1969. Factors affecting growth of rooted aquatics in a river. Weed Sci., 17: 412-416.

Peltier, W. H. and Welch, E. B., 1970. Factors affecting growth of rooted aquatic plants in a reservoir. Weed Sci., 18: 7-9.

Pillay, T. V. R. and Dill, W. A. (Editors), 1979. Advances in Aquaculture. Papers presented at the FAO Technical Conference on Aquaculture, Kyoto, Japan, 25 May-2 June 1976. Fishing News Books Ltd., Farnham, Surrey, England, 653 pp.

Pomeroy, L. R., Haskin, H. H., and Ragotzkie, R. A., 1956. Observations on dinoflagellate blooms. Limnol. Oceanogr., 1: 54-60.

Pomeroy, L. R., Smith, E. E., and Grant, C. M., 1965. The exchange of phosphate between estaurine water and sediments. Limnol. Oceanogr., 10: 167-172.

Ragotzkie, R. A. and Pomeroy, L. R., 1957. Life history of a dinoflagellate
bloom. Limnol. Oceanogr., 2: 62-69.
Rappaport, U. and Sarig, S., 1978. The results of manuring on intensive fish
farming at the Ginosar Station ponds in 1977. Bamidgeh, 30: 27-36.
Rappaport, U., Sarig, S., and Bejerano, Y., 1977. Observations on the use of
organic fertilizers in intensive fish farming at the Genosar Station in 1976.
Bamidgeh, 29: 57-70.
Ryther, J. H., Yentsch, C. S., Hulbart, E. M., and Vaccaro, R. F., 1958. The
dynamics of a diatom bloom. Biol. Bull. Woods Hole, 115: 257-268.
Rigler, F. H., 1956. A tracer study of the phosphorus cycle in lake water.
Ecology, 37: 550-562.
Rigler, F. H., 1964. The phosphorus fractions and the turnover time of inorganic
phosphorus in different types of lakes. Limnol. Oceanogr., 9: 511-518.
Rouse, R. D., 1968. Soil testing theory and calibration for cotton, corn, soybeans,
and coastal bermudagrass. Auburn University Agricultural Experiment Station,
Auburn, Alabama, Bulletin 375, 68 pp.
Rusness, D. and Burris, R. H., 1970. Acetylene reduction (nitrogen fixation) in
Wisconsin lakes. Limnol. Oceanogr., 15: 808-813.
Schroeder, G. L., 1974. Use of fluid cowshed manure in fish ponds. Bamidgeh,
26: 84-96.
Schroeder, G. L., 1978. Autotrophic and heterotrophic production of microorganisms
in intensely-manured fish ponds, and related fish yields. Aquaculture, 14:
303-325.
Smith, E. V. and Swingle, H. S., 1938. The relationship between plankton pro-
duction and fish production in ponds. Trans. Amer. Fish. Soc., 68: 309-315.
Smith, E. V. and Swingle, H. S., 1941. The use of fertilizer for controlling
several submerged aquatic plants in ponds. Trans. Amer. Fish. Soc., 71: 94-101.
Smith, E. V. and Swingle, H. S., 1942. Organic materials as fertilizers for fish
ponds. Trans. Amer. Fish. Soc., 72: 97-102.
Sumawidjaja, K., 1966. Influence of non-nitrogenous fertilization upon benthic
organisms in ponds stocked with different numbers of _Tilapia mossambica_ Peters.
M. S. thesis, Auburn University, Auburn, Alabama, 61 pp.
Swingle, H. S., 1947. Experiments on pond fertilization. Alabama Polytechnic
Institute Agricultural Experiment Station, Auburn, Alabama, Bulletin 264, 36 pp.
Swingle, H. S., 1950. Relationships and dynamics of balanced and unbalanced fish
populations. Alabama Polytechnic Institute Agricultural Experiment Station,
Auburn, Alabama, Bulletin 274, 74 pp.
Swingle, H. S., 1965. Fertilizing farm fish ponds. Auburn University Agricultural
Experiment Station, Auburn, Alabama, Highlights Agr. Res., 12: 1.
Swingle, H. S. and Smith, E. V., 1938. Fertilizer for increasing the natural
food for fish in ponds. Trans. Amer. Fish. Soc., 68: 126-135.
Swingle, H. S. and Smith, E. V., 1947. Management of farm fish ponds. Alabama
Polytechnic Institute Agricultural Experiment Station, Auburn, Alabama,
Bulletin 254, 32 pp.
Swingle, H. S., Gooch, B. C., and Rabanal, H. R., 1963. Phosphate fertilization
of ponds. Proc. Annual Conf. Southeast. Assoc. Game and Fish Comm., 17: 213-218.
Swingle, W. E., 1964. Pond fertilization, bluegill-bass with fertilization. In:
Fisheries Research Annual Report. Auburn University Agricultural Experiment
Station, Auburn, Alabama, pp. 62-64.
Tisdale, S. I. and Nelson, W. L., 1956. Soil Fertility and Fertilizers. The
MacMillan Co., New York, 430 pp.
Toth, S. J. and Smith, R. F., 1960. Soil over which water flows affects ability
to grow fish. New Jersey Agr., 42: 5-11.
United States Environmental Protection Agency, 1971. Algal assay procedure bottle
test. National Eutrophication Research Program, Corvallis, Oregon, 82 pp.
Varikul, V., 1965. Influence of nitrogenous fertilizer upon standing crop of
zooplankton in ponds stocked with different numbers of _Tilapia mossambica_ Peters.
M. S. thesis, Auburn University, Auburn, Alabama, 49 pp.
Walsh, L. M. and Beaton, J. D., 1973. Soil Testing and Plant Analysis. Soil
Science Society of America, Madison, Wisconsin, 491 pp.

118

Wiebe, A. H., 1929. The effects of various fertilizers on plankton production. Trans. Amer. Fish. Soc., 59: 1-8.

Wohlfarth, G. W. and Schroeder, G. L., 1979. Use of manure in fish farming — a review. Agric. Wastes, 1: 279-299.

Chapter 4

LIMING

4.1 INTRODUCTION

Pond fish will not survive in waters with pH less than 5. In waters with pH values of 5 to 6, fish will survive, but they will not grow and reproduce normally. There are many bodies of water where pH is adequate for normal growth and survival of fish, but where total alkalinity values are low and bottom muds are acidic. Here, attempts to increase fish production by inorganic fertilization often fail because there is insufficient available carbon in the alkalinity system to support high rates of phytoplankton photosynthesis, and phosphate added in fertilizer is tightly bound by muds. When phytoplankton blooms develop in waters of low alkalinity, pH may rise to undesirably high levels because of carbon dioxide removal by plants.

Problems with acid-base relationships in fish ponds can often be solved by liming. Application of liming materials is not a type of fertilization. Liming may best be viewed as a remedial procedure, necessary in some ponds, to permit normal responses of fish populations to fertilization and other management procedures.

4.2 PROPERTIES OF LIMING MATERIALS
4.2.1 Compounds

Just like fertilization, liming is an agricultural practice that has been adopted by fish culturists. Therefore, liming materials used in ponds are the same ones that are applied to agricultural soils. Compounds useful as liming materials contain either calcium or calcium and magnesium associated with an anionic radical that will neutralize acidity. The liming material most frequently used is agricultural limestone that is prepared by finely crushing either $CaCO_3$ (calcite) or $CaMg(CO_3)_2$ (dolomite). Two other common liming materials are $Ca(OH)_2$ (calcium hydroxide) and CaO (calcium oxide). Calcium hydroxide is variously referred to as hydrated lime, slaked lime, and builder's lime, while calcium oxide is often called quick lime, unslaked lime, or burnt lime. Basic slag, a by-product of steel making, contains calcium carbonate and phosphorus, so it is both a liming material and a fertilizer. Blast-furnace slag is also a by-product of steel making; it is comprised largely of calcium silicate. For reasons explained later, calcium silicate slags are not suitable for liming fish ponds. Recently there has been some use of liquid lime in agriculture. This material is an aqueous suspension of finely pulverized agricultural limestone, and it reacts very quickly to neutralize acidity. The commercial material is approximately 50% water, and application rates for liquid lime are about twice those of ordinary agricultural limestone.

Liquid lime must be transported and stored in large tanks. Agricultural limestone may be purchased in bulk form or in bags (usually 22.5 or 45 kg). Agricultural limestone in bags is usually about three times as expensive as bulk limestone
However, it is often easier to apply bags of agricultural limestone to fish ponds.
The other liming materials mentioned above are available in bags and large quantities may sometimes be purchased in bulk. Bulk liming materials occasionally
contain appreciable moisture because of outdoor storage. The moisture content
should be considered in establishing application rates of moist materials.

Reactions of liming materials with acidity are illustrated below:

$$CaCO_3 + 2 H^+ \rightarrow Ca^{2+} + H_2O + CO_2$$

$$CaMg(CO_3)_2 + 4 H^+ \rightarrow Ca^{2+} + Mg^{2+} + 2 H_2O + 2 CO_2$$

$$Ca(OH)_2 + 2 H^+ \rightarrow Ca^{2+} + 2 H_2O$$

$$CaO + 2 H^+ \rightarrow Ca^{2+} + H_2O$$

$$CaSiO_3 + 2 H^+ \rightarrow Ca^{2+} + H_2SiO_3$$

The neutralization of acidity in the first four reactions is obvious. In the fifth
reaction, silicic acid formed by the reaction of hydrogen ion and calcium silicate
is weakly dissociated, so pH rises in the medium where the reaction occurs.

Calcium containing compounds that do not neutralize acidity are not liming materials. For example, $CaSO_4 \cdot 2H_2O$ (calcium sulfate), often marketed as agricultural
gypsum, is a good source of calcium, but the sulfate radical will not neutralize
acidity.

4.2.2

The term neutralizing value refers to the relative abilities of liming materials
to neutralize acidity. Pure $CaCO_3$ is assigned a neutralizing value of 100% and is
the standard against which other materials are compared. For pure compounds, neutralizing values may be calculated. For example, the molecular weight of $CaCO_3$
is 100 and that of CaO is 56. Thus, by weight, CaO is a more effective neutralizing agent than $CaCO_3$. One unit of CaO will neutralize as much acid as 1.79 units
of $CaCO_3$ as shown by the following calculation:

$$\frac{56}{100} = \frac{1}{x}$$

x = 1.79

The neutralizing value of CaO relative to the $CaCO_3$ standard is (1.79/1) x 100= 179%. By the same reasoning, neutralizing values for other pure compounds are: $Ca(OH)_2$, 136%; $CaMg(CO_3)_2$, 109%; $CaSiO_3$, 86%.

In practice, pure compounds are not used as liming materials, and neutralizing values must be determined by chemical analysis. A 500-mg sample of finely ground liming material is placed in a 500-ml Erlenmeyer flask, and exactly 25 ml of standard 1 N HCl are added. The suspension is swirled, heated nearly to boiling, and held on a steam bath until the reaction is complete. About 100 ml of distilled water are added and the solution is boiled for 1-2 min. When cool, the solution is titrated to the phenolphthalein end point with standard 1 N NaOH. To illustrate the calculation of neutralizing value, assume the titration with standard 1 N NaOH required 16.00 ml (16 meq of NaOH). The initial amount of HCl added was 25 ml (25 meq). Hence, 9 meq of HCl were consumed by the liming material. This quantity of HCl is equivalent to 450 mg of $CaCO_3$ (9 meq X 50 mg $CaCO_3$/meq). It follows that the neutralizing value of the sample was 90% [(450/500) X 100]. A simple formula for the calculation is:

$$\% \text{ Neutralizing value} = \frac{(V - T)(N)(5,000)}{S}$$

where V = milliliters of standard acid; T = milliliters of standard base; N = normality; S = sample size in milligrams.

Liming rates are usually given in terms of $CaCO_3$ with a neutralizing value of 100%. Thus, to lime with $Ca(OH)_2$ (neutralizing value = 136%) at a rate equivalent to 2,000 kg/ha of $CaCO_3$, 2,000/1.36 = 1,470 kg/ha of $Ca(OH)_2$ are required.

4.2.3 Fineness

Calcium hydroxide and calcium oxide are, by nature of preparation, fine powders. Agricultural limestone is made up of particles of differing size, and limestone from one manufacturer may contain a greater proportion of fine particles than that from another. Smaller particles have a greater surface area relative to weight than larger particles, so small particles of agricultural limestone react faster than large particles. Particles less than 0.25 mm in size react the fastest, while particles 2.36 mm or greater in size react so slowly that they are of little value in neutralizing acidity (Tisdale and Nelson, 1956). One way of evaluating the fineness of agricultural limestone is the efficiency rating. Particle sizes are graded by sieve analysis using United States standard sieves of 8 mesh (2.36-mm openings), 20 mesh (0.855-mm openings), and 60 mesh (0.250-mm openings). Particles of limestone passing through the 60-mesh sieve are rated 100% efficient, those passing through the 20-mesh sieve and retained on the 60-mesh sieve are rated 60% efficient, those passing through the 8-mesh sieve and retained on the 20-mesh sieve are rated 20% efficient, and particles retained on the 8-mesh sieve are rated 0% efficient. The calculation of efficiency rating is illustrated below for a sample of agricultural limestone that was subjected to sieve analysis:

50% passed 60 mesh	0.50 X 100 = 50%
20% passed 20 mesh	
but not 60 mesh	0.20 X 60 = 12%
20% passed 8 mesh	
but not 20 mesh	0.20 X 20 = 4%
10% retained on 8 mesh	0.10 X 0 = 0%
	66%

Thus, the efficiency rating is 66%.

The neutralizing value and efficiency rating of agricultural limestone is used to determine how much of a particular material to apply to get the desired liming rate. For example, a batch of agricultural limestone has a neutralizing value of 92% and an efficiency rating of 85%. If the desired liming rate is 2,000 kg/ha, the amount of the particular batch of agricultural limestone required is 2,000 ÷ (0.92 X 0.85) = 2,558 kg/ha.

My experiences with liming materials applied to fish ponds indicate that the neutralizing values and efficiency ratings of these materials determine their effectiveness.

4.3 EFFECTS OF LIMING ON POND ECOSYSTEMS

4.3.1 Chemistry

There are three basic types of ponds that respond favorably to liming: (1) dystrophic ponds with waters heavily stained with humic substances and muds with large stores of slowly decaying organic matter, (2) ponds with waters of low pH and alkalinity because of moderately acidic muds and watershed soils, and (3) dystrophic ponds with waters containing mineral acidity resulting from acid-sulfate soils of watersheds. Typical pH and alkalinity values for the three types of ponds are presented in Table 4.1. Ponds with waters of low alkalinity are more common than ponds with waters having mineral acidity and no alkalinity. Because waters containing mineral acidity represent a special situation, they will be considered under a separate section.

Liming materials release ions that contribute to total alkalinity and total hardness in equivalent proportions. Therefore, liming usually results in increases in total alkalinity and total hardness as illustrated in Fig. 4.1. The increase in alkalinity and hardness following liming is obviously related to the degree

TABLE 4.1

Typical pH, total alkalinity, and mineral acidity values for three types of waters that respond to liming.

Type of water	pH	Alkalinity (mg/l CaCO$_3$)	Acidity (mg/l CaCO$_3$)
Dystrophic ponds heavily stained with humic substances	5-6	1-5	0
Ponds with moderately acidic soils on watersheds	5.5-7	3-15	0
Dystrophic ponds with acid-sulfate soils on watersheds	2-4.5	0	10-250

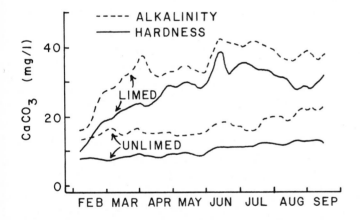

Fig. 4.1. Influence of liming on total alkalinity and total hardness concentrations in pond waters. Agricultural limestone was applied to five ponds in early February; five ponds served as unlimed controls (Arce and Boyd, 1975).

of acidity of water and mud and to the amount of liming material applied. Calcium silicate slag will increase total hardness, but because it does not contain an anion that will react with carbon dioxide, it will not increase alkalinity. Thus, silicate slags are not useful as liming materials for ponds.

Since liming neutralizes acidity, the pH of waters and muds will usually

124

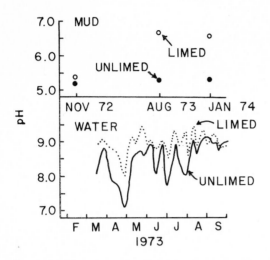

Fig. 4.2. Influence of liming on water and mud pH. Five ponds were treated with agricultural limestone in early February 1973; five ponds served as unlimed controls (Arce and Boyd, 1975).

increase after lime application (Fig. 4.2). As explained in Chapter 2, the pH of natural waters exhibits diel fluctuations because of carbon dioxide uptake or release by phytoplankton. Waters of low alkalinity are poorly buffered and daytime removal of carbon dioxide by phytoplankton may cause high pH, especially if such waters are fertilized. Liming of waters with low alkalinity will increase morning pH values, but because of the increase in alkaline reserve, waters of limed ponds are better buffered against pH change. Therefore, liming may actually result in decreased afternoon pH levels in fertilized ponds.

Because of its effect on alkalinity, liming increases the availability of carbon for photosynthesis. Data from Bachmann (1962), which are presented in Table 4.2, may be used to calculate available carbon from pH and total alkalinity. For example, if a pond has a pH of 7.0, a total alkalinity of 6 mg/l, and water temperature of 25°C, the total available carbon dioxide for photosynthesis is 6 mg/l X 0.29 (this value from Table 4.2) = 1.74 mg/l. If liming raised the pH to 8.0 and the total alkalinity to 28 mg/l, the total available carbon dioxide at 25°C would be 28 mg/l X 0.24 = 6.7 mg/l. Golterman (1975) suggested that diffusion of carbon dioxide from the atmosphere usually prevents carbon dioxide from limiting phytoplankton productivity in lakes. This is not thought to be true in fish ponds with relatively low alkalinity (Arce and Boyd, 1975).

Liming materials react with carbon dioxide when added to water, and their solubilities are to a large extent governed by carbon dioxide concentration. The reactions with carbon dioxide are:

TABLE 4.2

Factors for converting total alkalinity to milligrams of carbon per liter (Bachmann, 1962).

pH	Temperature (°C)				
	5	10	15	20	25
5.0	8.19	7.16	6.55	6.00	5.61
5.5	2.75	2.43	2.24	2.06	1.94
6.0	1.03	0.93	0.87	0.82	0.78
6.5	0.49	0.46	0.44	0.42	0.41
7.0	0.32	0.31	0.30	0.30	0.29
7.5	0.26	0.26	0.26	0.26	0.26
8.0	0.25	0.25	0.25	0.24	0.24
8.5	0.24	0.24	0.24	0.24	0.24
9.0	0.23	0.23	0.23	0.23	0.23

$$CaCO_3 + H_2O + CO_2 \rightarrow Ca^{2+} + 2HCO_3^-$$

$$Ca(OH)_2 + CO_2 \rightarrow CaCO_3 + H_2O$$

$$CaO + CO_2 \rightarrow CaCO_3$$

Obviously, $CaCO_3$ formed when $Ca(OH)_2$ or CaO react with CO_2 can react with more CO_2 to form Ca^{2+} and HCO_3^-. These reactions suggest that liming will compete with plants for CO_2 and possibly reduce photosynthetic rates. In addition to removing CO_2 from the water, excess lime that settles to the pond bottom will react with CO_2 released from the decomposition of organic matter; any CO_3^{2-} in the water will react with CO_2 that diffuses in from the atmosphere. The overall effect is higher concentrations of total available carbon dioxide within a few weeks after liming. Liming materials trap carbon dioxide that otherwise would have been lost to the atmosphere.

Concentrations of calcium and sometimes calcium and magnesium (dolomite application) increase following liming. Studies of algal cultures (Boyd and Scarsbrook, 1974) revealed that planktonic algae common in fish ponds required 5 mg/l of Ca^{2+} and 2 mg/l of Mg^{2+} for maximum growth. Assuming these proportions of Ca^{2+} and Mg^{2+} in natural water, these values correspond to a total hardness of 20.7 mg/l. Fish also require certain levels of calcium and magnesium ions in the water, or they will tend to lose these ions from their bodies. The minimum concentrations of Ca^{2+} and Mg^{2+} adequate for normal growth and survival of fish have not been established. Observations of pond fish in the southeastern United States suggest that fish do not grow normally in waters with less than 5 mg/l of total hardness.

Calcium and magnesium ions in water favor the precipitation of colloidal matter. Hasler et al. (1951) found that lime application reduced concentrations of colloidal organic matter and increased the depth of adequate light penetration for photosynthesis in bog lakes in Wisconsin. Observations of ponds in Alabama revealed that liming will reduce humic stains and lessen turbidity caused by colloidal clay particles (Boyd, 1979). Again, the degree of turbidity removal is dependent upon the lime application rate. For example, Waters (1956) observed that liming of acidic bog lakes in Michigan did not decrease color due to colloidal organic matter — apparently because lime applications were comparatively small.

Removal of turbidity increases the depth to which there is adequate dissolved oxygen for habitation by fish. Hasler et al. (1951) showed that liming a bog lake increased Secchi disk visibility from 2 m to 5 m and increased the depth at which dissolved oxygen was 4 mg/l from 2 m to 6 m. Stross and Hasler (1960) made similar observations following liming of other bog lakes.

Applications of liming materials to agricultural soils raise the pH and increase the rate of microbial activity (Alexander, 1961). A similar relationship exists in muds of fish ponds. Neess (1946) indicated that liming of European ponds stimulated bacterial decomposition of organic matter. Hansell and Boyd (1980) studied rates of carbon dioxide release from muds in laboratory mud-water systems. The lowest rates of carbon dioxide evolution were from unlimed muds with pH values of 4.7 and 5.4. The loss of carbon from these two muds over 38 days was 0.65 and 0.99%, respectively, of the carbon initially present. The greatest carbon losses were for limed muds with pH values of 6.5-7.2. One of the limed muds lost 1.37% of its initial carbon during the incubation period. Increases in bacterial decomposition favor mineralization of nitrogen and other nutrient from organic matter.

Treatment of the damp bottoms of ponds that have been drained with CaO or $Ca(OH)_2$ will destroy parasites and other undesirable organisms (Schaeperclaus, 1933; Sills, 1974). The usual treatment rate is 1,000 or 1,500 kg/ha. A period of 10-14 days should pass before ponds are refilled and stocked with fish. Fish farmers often believe that treatment with caustic lime oxidizes accumulated organic matter in damp muds. This is an erroneous belief. True, elevation of mud pH to 6.5-7 will increase microbial activity, but only a relatively small percentage of the organic matter will decay during a few days or weeks. Treatment with caustic lime usually raises pH so high that bacteria are killed, and the lime itself is not an oxidizing agent. As a result, muds are sterilized, and no decomposition results until the pH declines (Hansell and Boyd, 1980).

Increasing the pH of muds is also favorable because it increases the availability of mud phosphate. Boyd and Scarsbrook (1974) added phosphorus to limed and unlimed muds at rates of 0, 10, 50, and 100 mg/kg. After the lime and phosphorus had reacted for several weeks, small portions of the muds served as the only sources of phosphorus for growth of the alga Scenedesmus dimorphus in laboratory cultures. Additions of phosphorus to unlimed portions of muds A, D, and E resulted in little or no growth response (Table 4.3). Algal growth increased as a function of phosphorus rates for unlimed portions of mud B and C. Muds A, D, and E were more acidic, pH 5.2, 4.6, and 5.3, respectively, than muds B and C, pH 5.5 and 5.6, respectively, suggesting that increased pH favored phosphorus availability. The pH values of limed muds were between 6.3 and 6.6, and phosphorus availability increased, as evident from increased algal growth. Numbers of algal cells increased linearly with respect to phosphorus additions in limed portions of muds B, C, and D. Liming increased phosphorus availability in muds A and E, but enough phosphorus was released at low phosphorus addition rates to produce maximum algal growth.

It is difficult to extrapolate findings from laboratory studies to pond conditions, but several workers have reported that liming of ponds had favorable influences on phosphorus dynamics (Neess, 1946; Barrett, 1953; Waters, 1956). Data on filtrable orthophosphate concentrations in limed and unlimed ponds at Auburn University are presented in Table 4.4. Increases were fairly substantial even though ponds did not have extremely low alkalinity and mud pH before liming (total alkalinity, 8-14 mg/l; mud pH, 5.1-5.7). After liming, mud pH increased to 6.4-7.2 and total alkalinity rose above 20 mg/l.

4.3.2 Production of plankton and invertebrates

The initial effect of applying hydrated lime to two bog lakes was a decrease in plankton abundance (Waters, 1956). This was thought to result from loss of available carbon dioxide because of its reaction with $Ca(OH)_2$ and from high pH. After the pH declined from near 11 to about 8, plankton communities recovered. Phytoplankton and zooplankton volumes were several times greater the year after liming than before. The bog lakes were not fertilized, so the response of the plankton resulted from chemical modifications of the environment, rather than from increased supplies of nitrogen and phosphorus. Waters (1956) felt that the effects of liming on bog lakes were indirect: nutrient availability was improved due to more optimum reactions (pH) and ion concentrations, and a greater concentration of immediately available carbon dioxide resulted. The reader should recognize that bog lakes are dystrophic. Liming increases productivity by improving the chemical environment of bog lakes, and their trophic status becomes

TABLE 4.3

Growth of the alga _Scenedesmus_ _dimorphus_ in cultures where limed and unlimed muds
served as the only sources of phosphorus. Muds were treated with phosphorus at
rates of 0, 10, 50, and 100 mg/kg and allowed to react before they were placed
in algal cultures (Boyd and Scarsbrook, 1974).

Mud	pH	Algae (Thousands/ml)			
		0	10	50	100
Mud A					
Unlimed	5.2	100	120	120	120
Limed	6.3	400	480	470	600
Mud B					
Unlimed	5.5	50	100	130	200
Limed	6.4	100	200	180	450
Mud C					
Unlimed	5.6	50	100	200	550
Limed	6.3	60	150	600	850
Mud D					
Unlimed	4.6	50	75	75	150
Limed	6.6	150	300	500	700
Mud E					
Unlimed	5.3	50	150	250	185
Limed	6.5	100	1,800	1,700	1,750

TABLE 4.4

Filtrable orthophosphate concentrations (mg/l as P) in waters of limed and unlimed ponds. All ponds were treated with equivalent amounts of phosphate fertilizer (Boyd and Scarsbrook, 1974).

Date	Unlimed	Limed
1 Mar	0.005	0.006
3 Apr	0.039	0.055
10 May	0.020	0.023
7 Jun	0.003	0.010
2 Jul	0.009	0.009
4 Aug	0.006	0.011
10 Sep	0.006	0.012

oligotrophic. Inorganic fertilization would be required after liming to make bog lakes eutrophic — a condition necessary for the intensive production of warmwater fish.

Stross et al. (1961) determined the production of planktonic Crustacea in a bog lake that had been treated with $Ca(OH)_2$. Population turnover times for Daphnia measured the third summer following lime application were 2.1 weeks in the limed lake and 4.6 weeks in the unlimed lake. Slightly more biomass of Daphnia was produced in the treated lake because of the more rapid turnover; standing crops of Daphnia were actually lower in the treated lake. Failure of liming to cause a large increase in primary consumers is not surprising because fertilizers were not applied.

Zeller and Montgomery (1957) found that a number of ponds in Georgia failed to produce plankton blooms following fertilization. In most cases, waters of these ponds were slightly acidic (most pH values were 5.5-6.8) and had low total hardness (0-15 mg/1). Applications of hydrated lime or basic slag were used to increase pH and total hardness. Following liming, plankton responded favorably to fertilization. Bowling (1962) observed that liming enhanced the response of plankton to fertilization in Georgia ponds, and it increased the production of benthic fish food organisms.

Liming plus fertilization of ponds at Auburn University increased phytoplankton abundance above that obtained with fertilization alone (Boyd and Scarsbrook, 1974). Both numbers and volumes of phytoplankters were usually larger in limed ponds. Liming had no influence on the generic composition of the phytoplankton. Arce and Boyd (1975) found that treatment of fertilized ponds with agricultural limestone increased the average rate of gross primary productivity: 5.8 g carbon/m^2 per day in unlimed ponds and 6.5 g carbon/m^2 per day in limed ponds.

In summary, data on effects of liming on the production of fish food organisms are not as extensive as those for fertilization. However, liming will improve environmental conditions for plankton growth in dystrophic bog lakes and enhance the response of plankton and benthos to fertilization in soft water ponds.

4.3.3 Fish production

One of the most obvious influences of liming on fish production was obtained from unpublished records of a fish hatchery at Warm Springs, Georgia. Ponds of this hatchery were constructed on sandy, acidic soil, and the water supply had a total hardness of 3 mg/1 and a pH of 5.1. After water stood in ponds for several weeks, total hardness only increased to 5 mg/1, and the pH remained essentially unchanged. Agricultural limestone applied to ponds at 1,120 kg/ha in 1952 had little effect on hardness and pH. In 1953, ponds were treated with 11,120 kg/ha of agricultural limestone. Total hardness of pond waters increased to an average of 28 mg/l and pH rose above 7. Fish production was roughly doubled by liming even though fertilization rates remained constant (Table 4.5).

Working at the Marion Fish Hatchery, Marion, Alabama, Snow and Jones (1959) reported that the net production of bluegill was 102 kg/ha in a fertilized pond containing soft water (12 mg/l total hardness). Agricultural limestone was applied to the pond the following year at 6,700 kg/ha and bluegill production increased to 267 kg/ha.

Fish diseases had also been an important problem at the Marion Fish Hatchery. Treatment of damp muds with 1,120-2,240 kg/ha of CaO appeared to improve fish production in ponds with a history of disease problems. Snow and Jones (1959) compared affects of CaO and $Ca(OH)_2$ on pH of muds. When applied at the same rates of calcium, $Ca(OH)_2$ was just as effective as CaO in raising the pH of damp mud. Calcium percentages in CaO and $Ca(OH)_2$ are 71.4% and 54%, respectively. Thus, 1,000 kg/ha of CaO is a calcium addition rate of 714 kg/ha. An equal amount of calcium from $Ca(OH)_2$ requires 714 ÷ 0.54 = 1,322 kg/ha of $Ca(OH)_2$.

Hickling (1962) reported results of experiments in which agricultural limestone was added to unfertilized, soft water ponds at different rates (Table 4.6). Even the two highest application rates did not appreciably increase fish yields above those of unlimed ponds. In another experiment, Hickling applied agricultural limestone to 12 ponds at 2,240 kg/ha. Six of the ponds were fertilized with phosphate while the other six received no fertilization. Six more ponds were fertilized but not limed. Fish yields were: limed ponds, 104 kg/ha; fertilized ponds, 243 kg/ha; limed and fertilized ponds, 344 kg/ha. Unlimed control ponds at the Malacca Station where Hickling did his work yielded 81 kg/ha of fish (Table 4.6). Waters of unlimed ponds had alkalinity values of about 10 mg/l and pH values near 6. These results clearly show that liming is a technique for increasing the response to fertilization; it is not a substitute for fertilization.

The affect of agricultural limestone treatment (4,300-4,900 kg/ha) on production of Tilapia aurea was determined in fertilized ponds (Arce and Boyd, 1975). Alkalinities of unlimed ponds ranged from 11.6 to 18.4, but limed ponds had alkalinities of 20-40 mg/l. Net production of fish was about 25% higher in limed ponds than in unlimed ponds (Table 4.7). Liming also appeared to reduce variation in net production among ponds. The positive effect of liming was attributed to greater availability of carbon dioxide for phytoplankton growth. All ponds were heavily fertilized with phosphorus, and concentrations of total phosphorus and filtrable orthophosphate were roughly equal in limed and unlimed ponds.

All experiments have not demonstrated a positive influence of liming on fish yields. Swingle (1947) obtained slightly reduced production of fish in several ponds treated with agricultural limestone and fertilizer as compared to production in pond that were only fertilized. He concluded that calcium carbonate removed carbon dioxide and deprived plankton algae of carbon. Greene (1969) also failed

TABLE 4.5

Production of fingerling sunfish before and after applications of agricultural limestone to ponds of a fish hatchery at Warm Springs, Georgia.

Year	Limestone (kg/ha)	Sunfish	
		(No./ha)	(kg/ha)
1948	0	144,000	37
1951	0	239,000	46
1952	1,120	256,000	66
1953	11,200	314,000	136

TABLE 4.6

Yields of fish (primarily Tilapia) in unfertilized ponds treated with different amounts of agricultural limestone. Each treatment was replicated six times (Hickling, 1962).

Limestone (kg/ha)	Fish yield (kg/ha)
0	78
560	74
1,120	70
1,680	76
2,240	100
4,480	88

to show increases in production of fathead minnows (Pimephales promelas) following liming of soft waters in fertilized pools.

4.3.4   Identification of ponds needing lime

The need for liming dystropic ponds with organically stained waters is usually obvious. However, the need for liming is often not so apparent in ponds that simply have low pH and alkalinity. Many times, the response to fertilization in such ponds may diminish gradually over several years before a definite need for lime application is recognized. In other low alkalinity ponds, fertilization will increase fish production, but the pond owner may not realize that even greater production could be achieved through liming.

According to Thomaston and Zeller (1961), there was generally a positive response to lime applications by ponds with waters in the hardness range of 10-20

TABLE 4.7

Net production of _Tilapia aurea_ in limed and unlimed ponds. All ponds were fertilized twice monthly (March-September, 1973) with 45 kg/ha per application of
20-20-0 (Arce and Boyd, 1975).

Unlimed		Limed	
Pond	Fish (kg/ha)	Pond	Fish (kg/ha)
1	970	1	1,149
2	1,057	5	999
3	689	3	1,150
4	947	4	1,123
5	778	5	1,127
Average	888	Average	1,109

mg/l, but the response was not as striking as in ponds with total hardness values
below 10 mg/l. In general, the farther below 20 mg/l the total hardness, the
greater the response of ponds to liming. Observations in Alabama also indicate
that for maximum response to fertilization, ponds with less than 20 mg/l total
hardness should be limed (Boyd, 1974). However, if the total hardness is 12-15
mg/l the increase in fish production following liming may be no more than 20-25%,
and even smaller increases in fish production may result from liming ponds in the
15-20 mg/l range of total hardness. Lime application may not be worth the bother
and expense in waters with nearly 20 mg/l total hardness. Standing crops of
plankton in fertilized ponds in Alabama (Table 4.8) were related to total alkalinity.

It is unfortunate that several workers have based the need to lime ponds on
total hardness. Total alkalinity is a much better indicator of the need for
lime. In the studies mentioned above, total hardness and total alkalinity were
of almost equal magnitude, hence what has been said of hardness applies equally
well to alkalinity. There are waters where hardness may be quite high and alkalinity quite low. The reader is encouraged to measure alkalinity or both alkalinity and hardness when establishing whether or not a pond should be limed.
The wide use of total hardness apparently results from the slightly greater
difficulty of measuring total alkalinity under field conditions.

Total alkalinity or total hardness should be tested and other possible reasons
for the failure of fertilization to produce plankton blooms should be considered
before one decides to lime. The necessity for water analyses is obvious from
several studies showing that waters with alkalinities <20 mg/l and >20 mg/l may

TABLE 4.8

Relationship between total alkalinity and plankton abundance in fertilized ponds
in Alabama.

Total alkalinity (mg/l)	No. ponds	Particulate organic matter (mg/l)
<10	11	9.2
10-20	24	10.9
>20	18	15.1

be found in ponds of the same general locality (Shoup, 1944; Moyle, 1956; Mairs,
1966; Boyd and Walley, 1975). A personal experience will further emphasize the
need for water analyses before recommending liming. A fisheries biologist suggested that a pond owner apply lime to a pond near Auburn, Alabama, because fertilization did not cause a plankton bloom, and other ponds in the vicinity had
needed lime. The owner asked my opinion; an analysis of the pond water revealed
82 mg/l of total alkalinity. Further investigation revealed that the pond received the flow from a nearby limestone aquifer. Failure of fertilization to
promote a plankton bloom had resulted from excess water flowing through the pond,
not from low alkalinity and pH. Diversion of a portion of the flow of the aquifer
from the pond lengthened the retention time of fertilizer nutrients and plankton
and favored fish production.

4.3.5 Liming rates for ponds

One might conclude that the amount of liming material necessary to raise the
total hardness and total alkalinity of a pond to a specified concentration could
be directly calculated. Using such logic, the amount of $CaCO_3$ needed to increase
the alkalinity of a 1-ha pond with an average depth of 1 m from 5 to 20 mg/l would
be 15 mg for each liter of water or 15 g/m^3. Since the pond contains 10,000 m^3,
a total of 150 kg of $CaCO_3$ would be required. However, this amount of $CaCO_3$ would
hardly affect alkalinity because it would react with acidic muds and be lost
from the water.

Few fish culturists would make the above mistake because they know that much
larger amounts of liming agents must be applied to acidic agricultural soils.
In the studies summarized above, most application rates for liming materials were
1,000 kg/ha or higher. One simple technique for establishing the liming rate
for a pond is to use the same application rate employed on agricultural crops in
the vicinity or to select a rate from the literature on pond liming. If the
selected rate is adequate, total alkalinity and total hardness will be above
20 mg/l after 3 or 4 weeks. If too little liming material was applied, another

134

TABLE 4.9

Lime requirements of bottom muds based on pH and texture of muds (Schaeperclaus, 1933).

Mud pH	Lime requirement (kg/ha of CaCO$_3$)		
	Heavy loams or clays	Sandy loam	Sand
<4.0	14,320	7,160	4,475
4.0-4.5	10,740	5,370	4,475
4.6-5.0	8,950	4,475	3,580
5.1-5.5	5,370	3,580	1,790
5.6-6.0	3,580	1,790	895
6.1-6.5	1,790	1,790	0

application may be made and the alkalinity and hardness checked again in 3-4 weeks. Overliming can obviously result if the initial rate is too high.

Schaeperclaus (1933) recognized that the lime requirements of ponds differed in about the same manner as agricultural soils. Therefore, he used an agricultural procedure based on soil pH and soil texture to estimate liming rates for ponds (Table 4.9); lime requirements increased with pH and clay content of muds. Hickling (1962) reported that the method suggested by Schaeperclaus resulted in the application of more lime than needed in ponds at Malacca. Suitable liming rates for ponds there were estimated from the effects of different application rates on water chemistry (Hickling, 1962). This procedure was time consuming and costly, and results were directly applicable only to ponds in the experiment.

Recently, a lime requirement procedure used by soil testing laboratories was modified for fish ponds (Boyd, 1974). This technique permits highly reliable liming rates for individual ponds. The soil chemistry background and the essential features of the lime requirement test will be discussed below.

4.4   EXCHANGE ACIDITY AND LIME REQUIREMENT

4.4.1   Cation exchange

Colloidal particles of organic matter and clay minerals in muds and soils have negative charges and attract swarms of cations. An equilibrium exists between concentrations of cations in interstitial water and concentrations of these cations adsorbed onto colloidal particles (Fig. 4.3). If a large amount of some cation, say K^+, is added to the interstitial water of the system

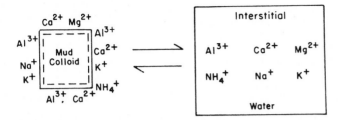

Fig. 4.3. Equilibrium for cations adsorbed on mud colloids and cations dissolved in interstitial water (Boyd, 1979).

illustrated in Fig. 4.3, it will disrupt the equilibrium and concentrations of adsorbed cations and cations in interstitial water will change to establish a new equilibrium between adsorbed ions and ions in the interstitial water. At the new equilibrium, there will be greater concentrations of all cations in solution and a smaller concentration of all cations, except K^+, adsorbed on mud colloids. Increased concentrations of ions other than K^+ in solution results from their displacement from colloids by K^+.

Cations on mud colloids and in interstitial water are termed exchangeable cations, and the sites of adsorption on colloids are referred to as exchange sites. Some cations are held more tightly on exchange sites than others. In general, the order of attraction is: trivalent cations > divalent cations > monovalent cations. Thus, Al^{3+} in interstitial water would be more effective in replacing ions on exchange sites than Ca^{2+}, and Ca^{2+} in interstitial water would be a stronger competitor for exchange sites than K^+. The quantity of cations that is adsorbed on exchange sites of soil or mud is expressed as milliequivalents of cations per 100 g of dry soil or mud and is referred to as the cation exchange capacity (CEC). The CEC of agricultural soils varies from 1 to 100 meq/100 g or more. The magnitude of CEC in soils is related to the type of clay mineral, clay content, and organic matter content. Boyd (1970) found that muds from Alabama ponds had CEC values of 0.5-26 meq/100 g. Muds with high proportions of sand had low CEC values, while those with high proportions of organic matter, clay, or both had higher values for CEC. Muds in Alabama ponds usually had higher CEC values than soils of surrounding watersheds.

4.4.2 The nature of exchange acidity

The acidity of mud may be visualized in two ways. The acidity of mud as measured with a pH electrode reflects the hydrogen ion activity in water surrounding mud particles. The pH is an intensity factor, but it provides no information on the capacity of the mud to yield acidity (hydrogen ions). A mud has potential or exchange acidity resulting from acidic cations on exchange sites. Exchange acidity is a capacity factor that indicates how much H^+ a mud can yield. Exchange acidity and pH may be likened to heat content and temperature. Temperature is an intensity factor, and heat content is a capacity factor. A beaker of water may be at 80°C and a lake at 25°C. Though the intensity of heat is greater in the beaker, the lake contains more heat.

Acidic cations include Al^{3+}, Fe^{3+}, and H^+, but little Fe^{3+} and H^+ occur on exchange sites. Basic cations are Ca^{2+}, Mg^{2+}, K^+, Na^+, and NH_4^+. The fraction of the total cation exchange capacity filled by acidic cations is termed base unsaturation. For example, an analysis of a mud gives: Ca^{2+}, 5 meq/100 g; Mg^{2+}, 2 meq/100 g; K^+, 1 meq/100 g; Na^+, 0.25 meq/100 g; NH_4^+, 0.1 meq/100 g; Al^{3+}, 4 meq/100 g. Summation of the concentrations of ions gives 12.35 meq/100 g, the CEC. Basic ions amount to 8.35 meq/100 g and acidic ions account for 4 meq/100 g; base unsaturation is 4 ÷ 12.35 = 0.320. Some authors prefer to divide the concentration of basic ions by the CEC to obtain the base saturation. However, I will use base unsaturation in the following discussion.

The acidic reaction of Al^{3+} may be visualized as follows:

$$Al\text{-mud} \;=\; Al^{3+} + 3\;H_2O \;=\; Al(OH)_3 \downarrow + 3\;H^+$$

The aluminum compound that precipitates could be several related aluminum hydroxides, but I will use $Al(OH)_3$ (gibbsite) as a representative compound. Because aluminum hydroxides are naturally abundant in muds and soils, hydrogen ion introduced into the interstitial water will dissolve aluminum hydroxide and increase the concentration of Al^{3+} in the interstitial water. Aluminum ions in interstitial water are in equilibrium with exchangeable aluminum on cation exchange sites in mud. Obviously, little H^+ can exist as an exchangeable cation because H^+ in solution reacts with aluminum hydroxide. Furthermore, at equilibrium, the concentration of H^+ in interstitial water is a function of the Al^{3+} concentration; the concentration of Al^{3+} is determined by the amount of Al^{3+} held on exchange sites in the mud. The reactions mentioned above hold for both inorganic and organic muds. High concentrations of organic acids in organic muds react with aluminum as follows:

$$RCOOAl \;=\; Al^{3+} + 3H_2O \;=\; Al(OH)_3 \downarrow + 3H^+$$

Thus, the statement that acidic muds are aluminum muds and aluminum muds are acidic muds aptly describes exchange acidity of muds.

From the preceding discussion, it is obvious that the pH of the water surrounding mud particles is closely related to the degree of base unsaturation of the mud particles (Fig. 4.4). This pH measurement is called the mud pH, even though a pH meter will only sense hydrogen ions in solution. The magnitude of the potential acidity (exchange acidity) of a mud depends more on the size of

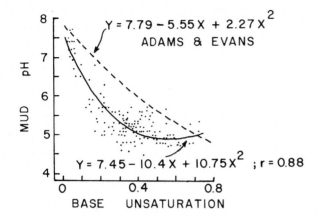

Fig. 4.4. Relationship between base unsaturation and pH of muds in Alabama ponds, and the relationship between base unsaturation and pH of agricultural soils used by Adams and Evans (1962) in calculating liming rates. Data are from Boyd (1974).

the CEC than on the degree of base unsaturation of the mud. Two muds with different CEC values may have the same pH and the same degree of base unsaturation, but the mud with the greatest CEC will have the largest exchange acidity. This results because the mud with the greatest CEC will have the largest quantity of acidic cations. To illustrate this point, consider that two muds each have a base unsaturation of 0.6 and a corresponding pH of 5.3 (Fig. 4.4). One mud has a CEC of 5 and the other has a CEC of 20. The exchange acidity of the first mud is 5 meq/100 g X 0.6 = 3 meq/100 g; the exchange acidity of the second mud is four times larger — 20 meq/100 g X 0.6 = 12 meq/100 g. Remember, base unsaturation is simply the proportion of acidic cations to total cations on exchange sites.

4.4.3 Neutralization of exchange acidity

If the pH of a mixture of 1 part water and 1 part acidic mud is measured and enough base added to neutralize the acidity of the water in the mixture, the pH may briefly rise to neutrality, but it will soon return nearly to the initial value. To affect a permanent change in pH, enough base must be added to neutralize the exchange acidity, or in the case of acid-sulfate muds and soils, the acidity resulting from further oxidation of pyrite.

The neutralization by calcium carbonate of the exchange acidity in a mud is illustrated in Fig. 4.5. Neutralization of H^+ by $CaCO_3$ causes the reaction involving Al^{3+} and $Al(OH)_3$ to proceed to the right with the release of Al^{3+} from exchange sites in the mud and the precipitation of $Al(OH)_3$. Calcium ions released by the action of H^+ on $CaCO_3$ replace Al^{3+} on exchange sites. The net effect is that H^+ in interstitial water is neutralized, causing a rise in pH,

138

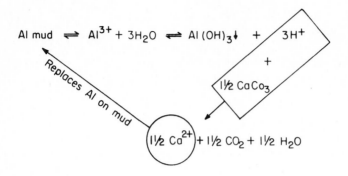

Fig. 4.5. A qualitative model of the neutralization of acidic mud by calcium carbonate (Boyd, 1979).

and the exchange acidity of the mud decreases because replacement of Al^{3+} on exchange sites by Ca^{2+} lowers base unsaturation.

4.4.4 Direct calculation of lime requirement

If data on pH, CEC, and the relationship between pH and base unsaturation (Fig. 4.4) are available, the lime requirement may be calculated. To illustrate, a sample of soil has a pH of 5.0 and a CEC of 10 meq/100 g. It is desired to lime the field represented by the sample to raise the soil pH to 6.5. Reference to Fig. 4.4 indicates that the soil has an initial base unsaturation of 0.75; a base unsaturation of 0.25 corresponds to pH 6.5. Therefore, the base unsaturation should be decreased from 0.75 to 0.25. Because complete base unsaturation corresponds to 1.0, it follows that enough calcium carbonate must be added to neutralize an amount of acidity equal to half the CEC. This quantity may be calculated as follows:

$$\text{Acidity to neutralize} = \frac{0.75 - 0.25}{1.0} \times 10 \text{ meq/100 g} = 5 \text{ meq/100 g.}$$

One milliequivalent of $CaCO_3$ is 50 mg, so 5 meq/100 g X 50 mg/meq = 250 mg/100 g of $CaCO_3$ must be applied to raise the pH to 6.5. Liming materials are usually thought to react in the upper 15-cm layer of agricultural soils, and according to Jackson (1958), 1 ha of soil 15 cm deep weighs about 2.2 X 10^6 kg. For the example above, 250 mg/100 g of $CaCO_3$ is the same as 2.5 g/1,000 g of $CaCO_3$ or 0.0025 kg/kg of $CaCO_3$. Therefore, 0.0025 kg/kg of $CaCO_3$ X 2.2 X 10^6 kg/ha of soil = 5,500 kg/ha of $CaCO_3$. However, the reaction of liming materials in soils is slow and incomplete, so a liming factor of 1.5 is often used (Adams and Evans, 1962). The adjusted liming rate is 5,500 kg/ha of $CaCO_3$ X 1.5 = 8,250 kg/ha of

$CaCO_3$.

4.4.5 Buffer methods for lime requirements of soils

The direct calculation of lime requirement serves well for illustration, but it is seldom used because the analysis of CEC is time consuming. A number of buffer methods for calculating lime requirements of soils with exchange acidity are available (Peech and Bradfield, 1948; Shoemaker et al., 1961; Adams and Evans, 1962; Yuan, 1974) for rapid determination of lime requirement. The procedure developed by Adams and Evans (1962) will be described below. The pH change caused by the addition of a known quantity of soil to a buffered solution is used to estimate the exchange acidity. Each pH change of 0.1 unit in 20 ml of the buffered solution corresponds to 0.08 meq of exchange acidity. For example, if 10 g of soil causes 20 ml of buffered solution to decrease in pH from 8.0 to 7.5, the exchange acidity is 0.08 meq X 5 = 0.4 meq/10 g or 4 meq/100 g. The initial base unsaturation for the sample is estimated from the initial soil pH (Fig. 4.4), as is the base unsaturation value for the desired pH. Hence, the amount of acidity to neutralize to give the desired pH is found by:

$$\text{Acidity to neutralize} = \text{Exchange acidity} \times \frac{\text{Initial base unsaturation} - \text{Desired base unsaturation}}{\text{Initial base unsaturation}} \quad (4.1)$$

The factor multiplied by the exchange acidity represents the proportion of the exchange acidity that must be neutralized to produce the desired pH.

To further illustrate the procedure, suppose that one desires to lime a soil to pH 6.5 from an initial pH of 5.2. The initial pH indicates a base unsaturation of 0.65, and a pH of 6.5 corresponds to a base unsaturation of 0.25 (Fig. 4.4). A 10-g sample of soil changes the pH of 20 ml of buffer by 0.7 pH units. The acidity to neutralize is calculated by Equation 4.1.

$$\text{Acidity to neutralize} = 0.08 \times 7 \times \frac{0.65 - 0.25}{0.65} = 0.34 \text{ meq/10 g}$$

The above computation is for 10 g of soil and must be converted to kilograms per hectare of $CaCO_3$ as follows:

$$0.34 \text{ meq} \times 50 \text{ mg/meq} \times \frac{1,000 \text{ g/kg}}{10 \text{ g}} = 1,700 \text{ mg/kg of } CaCO_3$$

0.0017 kg of $CaCO_3$/kg of soil X 2.2 X 10^6 kg/ha = 3,740 kg/ha of $CaCO_3$.

Finally, multiplication by a liming factor of 1.5 gives 5,610 kg/ha of $CaCO_3$.

In practice, a table of lime requirement values is calculated for all combinations of soil-water pH (initial soil pH) and soil-buffered solution pH. The soil-buffered solution pH may be used instead of the pH change of the buffered solution because the buffered solution is prepared with an initial pH of 8.0. This permits direct interpolation of lime requirement from two pH readings. Tables of lime requirement values may be prepared for any desired pH. Furthermore, the same soil sample may be used to measure the soil-water pH and the soil-buffered solution pH.

4.4.6 Buffer lime requirement for ponds

The Adams-Evans lime requirement technique for agricultural soils has often been used to determine the lime requirements of muds from fish ponds (Swingle, 1969). However, liming materials are applied to raise the total hardness and total alkalinity of pond water above 20 mg/l — not to raise the mud pH to a specified level. Boyd (1974) made an extensive study of mud and water chemistry of ponds in the major physiographic regions of Alabama and used the findings to modify the Adams-Evans lime requirement procedure for use in ponds. It was found that the total hardness of pond waters was correlated with mud pH (as measured in a 1:1 mixture of dry, pulverized pond mud and distilled water) as illustrated in Fig. 4.6. When the mud pH exceeded 5.9, almost all total hardness values for the corresponding pond waters exceeded 20 mg/l. Therefore, if a dried mud sample from a pond had a mud pH above 5.9, the pond needed no lime because 20 mg/l total hardness is considered suitable for good fish production. Incidentally, total alkalinity values for pond waters were slightly greater than total hardness. Next, it was found that the total hardness of pond waters was closely correlated with the base unsaturation of pond muds (Fig. 4.7). This indicated that lowering the base unsaturation of muds by liming could be expected to increase the total hardness of pond waters. When ponds had muds with base unsaturation values of 0.2 or less, waters had total hardness values above 20 mg/l (Fig. 4.7). Finally, the relationship between mud pH and the base unsaturation of pond muds was highly significant, but the equation for this relationship was quite different from the one relating pH and base unsaturation of agricultural soils (Fig. 4.4). This resulted because pond muds contained more organic matter and had higher CEC values than the agricultural soils used by Adams and Evans (1962).

The lime requirement for a fish pond should represent the amount of calcium carbonate required to raise the pH of the mud to 5.9 so that base unsaturation will be 0.2 or less and the total hardness (and alkalinity) will be above 20 mg/l. The equation for mud pH versus base unsaturation of mud (Fig. 4.4) was used to construct a table of lime requirement values for fish ponds (Table 4.10). No changes in the laboratory aspects of the Adams-Evans procedure were necessary;

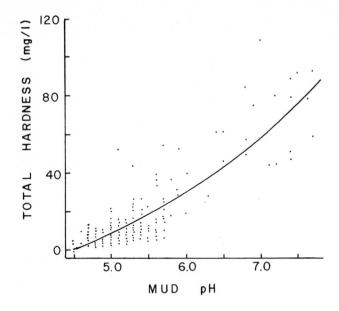

Fig. 4.6. Influence of mud pH on total hardness of waters in Alabama ponds (Boyd, 1974).

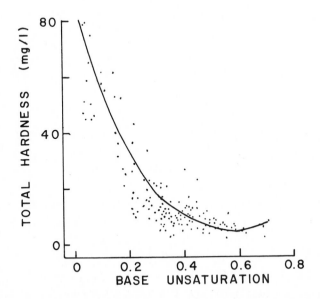

Fig. 4.7. Influence of base unsaturation of muds on total hardness of waters in Alabama ponds (Boyd, 1974).

the procedure is given later.

Originally, lime was assumed to react to a depth of 15 cm in muds, and the weight of the upper 15-cm layer of mud in ponds was taken as 2.2 X 10^6 kg/ha (Boyd, 1974). Later, Boyd and Cuenco (1980) showed that liming materials did, in fact, react to depths of at least 15 cm. Mud cores were collected from 16 ponds, and the air dry weights of the upper 15-cm layers were determined. There was considerable variation among ponds in the weights of the upper 15-cm layers of mud (650,000-2,009,000 kg/ha; mean = 1,407,000 kg/ha). The lightest muds contained a large proportion of organic matter, and the heaviest muds were comprised almost entirely of inorganic substances. For preparation of Table 4.10, I used a weight of 1.5 X 10^6 kg/ha for the weight of a 15-cm layer of pond mud. Thus, lime requirement values in Table 4.10 are about a third less than those given originally (Boyd, 1974).

The lime requirement of soils and muds is associated with colloidal-sized particles of clay and organic matter, rather than with the larger particles of gravel, sand, and silt. This results because only the colloidal particles possess negative charges necessary for the adsorption of cations. In fish ponds, there is a gradient in particle size distribution with water depth. Smallest proportions of sand and gravel and largest proportions of silt and clay are in muds from deeper water (Table 4.11). Sand and gravel in runoff entering ponds settle quickly near shallow water edges, but smaller silt and clay particles remain in suspension longer, resulting in their deposition being more uniform. Organic matter accumulation is also greater in deep water than in shallow water (Table 4.11). Decomposition of organic matter is much slower under anaerobic than under aerobic conditions, and muds beneath the thermocline are usually anaerobic during warm months. The net result of differences in particle size distribution and organic matter concentration is that samples of mud from shallow water have lower CEC values than samples from deeper water. Hence, lime requirements are greater for mud samples from deeper areas of ponds (Table 4.11).

Variation in lime requirement values also occurs among samples taken from the same depth but from different horizontal positions in the same pond. Therefore, samples should be taken at random from a number of areas and equal volumes of each composited to give one sample upon which to make the lime requirement determination (Boyd and Cuenco, 1980).

The sample for lime requirement determination should be spread in a thin layer on a plastic sheet and dried at room temperature. The dry mud should then be gently pulverized with a mortar and pestle and the material that passes a 20-mesh screen (0.85-mm openings) saved for analysis. For most accurate results, the proportion of the entire sample that passes the 20-mesh screen should be estimated and the liming rate based only on the estimated weight of mud represented by this fraction. For example, if 75% of the sample passes a 20-mesh screen, the lime

TABLE 4.10

Lime requirement in kilograms per hectare of $CaCO_3$ (neutralizing value = 100%) to increase total hardness and total alkalinity of pond water to 20 mg/l or more (Boyd, 1974).

Mud pH in water	$CaCO_3$ (kg/ha) according to mud pH in buffered solution									
	7.9	7.8	7.7	7.6	7.5	7.4	7.3	7.2	7.1	7.0
5.7	91	182	272	363	454	544	635	726	817	908
5.6	126	252	378	504	630	756	882	1,008	1,134	1,260
5.5	202	404	604	806	1,008	1,210	1,411	1,612	1,814	2,016
5.4	290	580	869	1,160	1,449	1,738	2,029	2,318	2,608	2,898
5.3	340	680	1,021	1,360	1,701	2,042	2,381	2,722	3,062	3,402
5.2	391	782	1,172	1,562	1,948	2,344	2,734	3,124	3,515	3,906
5.1	441	882	1,323	1,765	2,205	2,646	3,087	3,528	3,969	4,410
5.0	504	1,008	1,512	2,016	2,520	3,024	3,528	4,032	4,536	5,040
4.9	656	1,310	1,966	2,620	3,276	3,932	4,586	5,242	5,980	6,552
4.8	672	1,344	2,016	2,688	3,360	4,032	4,704	5,390	6,048	6,720
4.7	706	1,412	2,116	2,822	3,528	4,234	4,940	5,644	6,350	7,056

TABLE 4.11

Texture, organic matter concentration, and lime requirement of muds from different depths in a pond (Boyd, 1977).

Depth (m)	Mineral fraction (%)				Organic matter (%)	Lime requirement (kg/ha of $CaCO_3$)
	Gravel	Sand	Silt	Clay		
0.1	12	53	17	18	0.8	600
0.33	10	68	14	8	0.7	700
0.67	4	40	38	18	1.5	1,200
1.0	2	20	52	26	2.8	2,000
1.33	0	12	60	28	3.5	2,400
1.67	0	10	60	30	4.0	3,000
2.0	0	8	57	35	4.5	3,200
2.33	0	4	59	37	5.5	2,800

requirement based on the 20-mesh sample may be reduced by 25%. Correction of data for particle size is generally not necessary unless gravel is abundant.

The buffered solution for the lime requirement procedure is prepared as follows: dissolve 20 g of p-nitrophenol, 15 g of boric acid, 74 g of potassium chloride, and 10.5 g of potassium hydroxide in distilled water and dilute to 1,000 ml in a volumetric flask. Weigh 20.0 g of dry mud that passed the 20-mesh screen into a 100-ml beaker, add 20 ml of distilled water, and stir intermittently for 1 h. Measure the pH of the mud-water mixture with a glass electrode while stirring. This value is the mud pH. Next, add 20.0 ml of the buffered solution to the mud-distilled water mixture and stir intermittently for 20 min. Set the pH meter at pH 8.0 with a 1:1 mixture of buffered solution and distilled water. Determine the pH of the mud-distilled water-buffered solution mixture while stirring vigorously. Select the appropriate liming rate from Table 4.10. If the pH of the mud-distilled water-buffered solution mixture is below 7.0, repeat the analysis with 10.0 g dry mud and double the liming rate from Table 4.10. Lime requirements from Table 4.10 are for $CaCO_3$ with 100% neutralizing value and efficiency rating.

4.4.7 Effectiveness of the lime requirement for ponds

A total of 52 ponds at Auburn University were treated with agricultural limestone at rates established by the modified Adams-Evans lime requirement technique. Initial total alkalinities ranged from 5-12 mg/l and lime requirements were between 1,000 and 5,000 kg/ha. Total alkalinity and total hardness values 6 months after liming were 17.5-48 mg/l. Values were above 20 mg/l in all but five ponds. These five ponds seeped excessively, and the ions from liming were apparently lost in seepage. The pH of mud in limed ponds ranged from 6-7. The lime requirement procedure has also been used with almost complete success for many privately-owned ponds in the southeastern United States. Liming rates were usually 2,000-6,000 kg/ha, but rates of 8,000-14,000 kg/ha were obtained for ponds with high concentrations of organic matter in mud. Failure of the procedure to estimate adequate liming material only occurred when mud samples were not representative of pond bottoms and when ponds had excessive water loss to seepage or spillway discharge.

The lime requirement procedure was developed for use in the southeastern United States, but it should be applicable to ponds in most warm climates. For best results, workers in other regions should determine the relationship between base unsaturation and mud pH for a representative series of ponds, ascertain the base unsaturation and mud pH corresponding to a total hardness of 20 mg/l, and use these findings to prepare a table of lime requirement values. Alternatively, workers in other areas can use the double buffer method of Yuan (1974) for determining lime requirement. The Yuan method does not require data on the relationship between base unsaturation and mud pH.

4.5   APPLICATION OF LIMING MATERIALS TO PONDS

4.5.1 Selection of liming materials and time of application

Any of the common liming materials, other than silicate slags, mentioned earlier may be used in fish ponds. When applied in equivalent amounts, all liming materials produced similar increases in total alkalinity (Table 4.12). The reaction with acidity is faster with calcium oxide and calcium hydroxide than with basic slag and agricultural limestone. However, calcium hydroxide and calcium oxide are unpleasant to handle because they are highly caustic, and they may cause the water pH to rise to levels toxic to fish. Of course, the water pH will decrease to acceptable levels within a few weeks, and fish may be stocked. Therefore, basic slag or agricultural limestone are generally safer to use than calcium oxide and hydroxide. Based on early experiences, basic slag is usually considered to contain about 10% P_2O_5 and a neutralizing value of about 80%. Wolt and Adams (1978) found that recent changes in the steel-making process have altered the composition of basic slag. The new basic slag contains less phosphorus and has a lower neutralizing value than the old basic slag (Table 4.13). Thus, it requires 3,600 kg/ha of the new basic slag to be equivalent to 2,000 kg/ha of calcium carbonate (neutralizing value = 100%). Agricultural limestone is generally the safest, cheapest, and most effective liming material for ponds.

Treatment with liming materials has several immediate undesirable effects on water quality. Most of the liming material does not dissolve at once and as it settles through the water, phosphorus reacts with it and is lost from solution. The pH rises and appreciable free carbon dioxide cannot exist in the water. Nevertheless, within a few weeks, the liming material reacts with mud to increase the mud pH and enhance the availability of phosphate fertilizer and with carbon dioxide to increase the alkalinity and the carbon dioxide reserve. In temperate climates, liming materials should be applied after fertilization has been discontinued in late fall or winter. In the tropics and subtropics, liming materials should be added a few weeks before fertilizer applications are initiated. In ponds with low concentrations of organic matter, the addition of readily decomposable organic matter at the time of liming will hasten the dissolution of liming materials and the stabilization of water quality. This results because carbon dioxide released by decay of organic matter will react with calcium carbonate, calcium oxide, or calcium hydroxide. Hence, abundant carbon dioxide prevents hydroxide or carbonate ions from occurring in the water in appreciable concentration, thereby lowering the pH. In some ponds, precipitation of colloidal materials from water following liming may reduce turbidity and encourage the growth of underwater weeds (Boyd and Scarsbrook, 1974). Clear water is normally a temporary problem that is corrected by turbidity resulting from plankton after a few applications of inorganic fertilizer.

TABLE 4.12

Effects of equivalent application rates of four liming materials on total alkalinity (Boyd, 1974).

Liming material	Total alkalinity (mg/l)	
	Before liming	After liming
None	11	13
Hydrated lime	9	55
Basic slag	13	54
Dolomitic limestone	11	42
Calcitic limestone	12	35

TABLE 4.13

Comparison of old and new forms of basic slag (Wolt and Adams, 1978).

Property	1957 slag (%)	1975 slag (%)
Available phosphorus (P_2O_5)	10.1	1.3
Total phosphorus (P_2O_5)	10.9	2.1
Limestone equivalent ($CaCO_3$)	78.0	55.0
Passing 100-mesh screen	80.0	80.0

4.5.2 Methods of application

New ponds can best be limed before they are initially filled with water. The lime requirement of soil from the bottoms of new ponds should be determined on representative samples. The required amount of liming material should be spread evenly over the pond bottom; a disc harrow may be used to incorporate the liming material into the pond bottom. Discing is not mandatory, but it will hasten the neutralization of acidity in pond bottoms.

The bottoms of older ponds that are drained for fish harvest or renovation may be allowed to dry and limed in the same manner as new ponds. Liming is obviously more difficult when ponds are full because the liming material must be spread over the entire surface.

For small ponds, a relatively small amount of liming material is required, and bagged liming material may be spread from a boat as it moves over the pond surface. In fact, ponds at some research facilities are small enough that their entire surfaces may be covered by broadcasting liming materials from the water's edge. Bulk liming materials are less expensive than bagged materials and should be used when large amounts are necessary.

Waters (1956) used a raft and pump system for applying hydrated lime. The apparatus consisted of a raft 3 m long by 1.8 m wide, supported in back by the shore and in front by two floating steel drums. A plywood mixing tank was lowered through a rectangular hole in the raft. A hopper was constructed at the top of the mixing tank for introduction of lime. The intake hose of the pump was placed in the mixing tank and the lime and water were pumped up and discharged into the lake.

Stross and Hasler (1960) modified the method used by Waters (1956) so that hydrated lime could be applied over the surface rather than at one point. They attached the mixing tank to the side of a boat and used a pump attached to the boat to discharge the slurried lime as the boat moved about the surface.

The simplist method for spreading bulk agricultural limestone is to construct a platform on the end of a large boat or between two smaller boats — a single sheet of plywood will usually suffice as a platform. Limestone may be spread with a shovel as the boat moves about the surface. A tractor with a front-end loader may be used to speed the loading of limestone. A 5.5 m long boat with a maximum width of 1.2-1.5 m will safely carry 500 kg of agricultural limestone. Four workers (one boat operator, one front-end loader operator, and two shovelers) can apply 30-40 tons of limestone per day.

Workers of the Fisheries Section of the Alabama Department of Conservation limed several large lakes (>20 ha). They used a raft that would carry 1 ton of limestone. The raft was powered by an outboard motor; a pump and spray nozzle provided a stream of pond water to wash limestone from the raft.

If means for distributing liming materials over pond surfaces are not available, some benefit may be obtained by dumping piles of liming materials along the shallow water edges of ponds. Waves must break over the piles of limestone to make this application technique effective.

Calcium oxide or hydroxide may be applied to the water supplies of ponds. Liming mills that monitor lime into water at specified rates are commonly used in treating potable water before distribution in pipe lines. Such devices have been used to lime the water supplies of ponds.

4.5.3 Residual effects of liming

Hickling (1962) stated that an application of liming material would last indefinitely in a pond with no outflow. Most ponds lose water to overflow, and all earthen ponds lose water through seepage. Thomaston and Zeller (1961) found that treatment of ponds in Georgia with 2,000 kg/ha of agricultural limestone had beneficial effects on productivity for 2-4 years. In an experiment conducted in ponds with different rates of outflow, liming at a rate established by the lime

requirement test was ineffective in Grier's pond, a small pond with a water exchange time of 3 weeks (Fig. 4.8). In four other ponds (S-11, S-12, S-13, and
S-19), total hardness declined considerably within 1 year after liming but was
still about 20 mg/l nearly 3 years after liming. These four ponds lost water to
overflow only during periods of heavy rainfall, and they did not seep excessively.
The decline in total hardness of the water in the spring of 1974 and 1975 occurred
during periods of heavy rainfall. The other pond (S-6) had some overflow throughout the year; the increase in total hardness following liming and the residual
effect of liming in S-6 were intermediate between Grier's pond and S-11, S-12,
S-13, and S-19.

Five ponds that originally had waters with less than 12 mg/l total hardness
were limed in the winter of 1973. The following autumn these ponds were drained
and refilled with runoff. Three months after refilling the total hardness of
water in the ponds varied from 19.2-38.4 mg/l. Therefore, the beneficial effect
of liming is not destroyed by a single draining. Results of an experiment conducted with laboratory mud-water systems (Fig. 4.9) indicated that 10 water re-
placements might be tolerated before liming is again needed (Boyd and Cuenco, 1980)
This does not suggest that a pond may be drained 10 times before liming is again
in order. Considerable water is usually lost to overflow or seepage between
drainings.

A procedure for liming small experimental ponds that are drained annually was
developed at Auburn University. Enough agricultural limestone was initially
applied to ponds to satisfy the lime requirements of muds (about 4,400 kg/ha).
Since then, I have applied agricultural limestone at 1,100 kg/ha each year following
refilling. This procedure has been in use for 8 years and has maintained satisfactory total hardness, total alkalinity, and mud pH.

Hansell and Boyd (1980) found that alkalinity and hardness could be increased
by small additions of hydrated lime during dry summer months to ponds that had
such great overflow during wetter months that conventional applications of agricultural limestone were ineffective. Ponds were treated with an amount of hydrated
lime calculated to raise the total alkalinity to 25 mg/l:

Hydrated lime in mg/l = (25 mg/l - Initial alkalinity) (0.74)

where 0.74 is a factor relating hydrated lime concentration to total alkalinity.
The hydrated lime was broadcast over pond surfaces. The treatment was effective
in maintaining total alkalinity above 20 mg/l for 8 weeks.

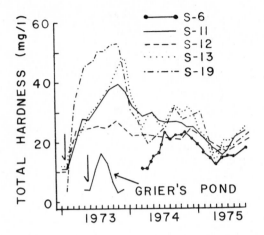

Fig. 4.8. Residual effect of liming on water hardness in six ponds. Grier's pond has a water retention time of 3 weeks, pond S-6 has year-around outflow, and the other ponds have outflow only during rainy weather. Arrows indicate dates of agricultural limestone application (Boyd, 1976).

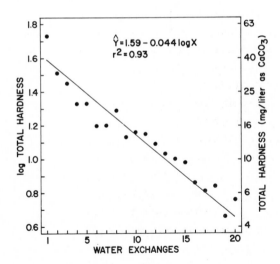

Fig. 4.9. Relationship between water exchange and total hardness in laboratory mud-water systems treated with enough agricultural limestone to satisfy the lime requirement of the muds (Boyd and Cuenco, 1980).

4.6 ACID-SULFATE SOILS

4.6.1 Chemistry

Exchange acidity will not account for pH values less than 4-4.5. Lower pH values usually indicate that sulfuric acid is present in soils. In mining areas sulfide containing minerals, i. e., pyrite (FeS_2), pyrrhotite ($Fe_{0.858}S$), and chalcopyrite ($CuFeS_2$) are exposed on the surface (Sorensen et al., 1980). Upon exposure to air and water, these minerals oxidize to form sulfuric acid. The oxidation of pyrite is as follows:

$$FeS_2 + H_2O + 3\tfrac{1}{2} O_2 \rightarrow FeSO_4 + H_2SO_4 \tag{4.2}$$

$$2 FeSO_4 + \tfrac{1}{2} O_2 + H_2SO_4 \rightarrow Fe_2(SO_4)_3 + H_2O \tag{4.3}$$

$$FeS_2 + 7 Fe_2(SO_4)_3 + 8 H_2O \rightarrow 15 FeSO_4 + 8 H_2SO_4 \tag{4.4}$$

According to Sorensen et al. (1980), the production of ferric sulfate from ferrous sulfate is greatly accelerated by the activity of bacteria of the genus Thio-bacillus, and under acidic conditions, the oxidation of pyrite by ferric sulfate is very rapid. In addition, ferric sulfate may also hydrolyze as shown:

$$Fe_2(SO_4)_3 + 6 H_2O = 2 Fe(OH)_3 + 3 H_2SO_4 \tag{4.5}$$

Sulfuric acid dissolves large amounts of heavy metals (aluminum, manganese, zinc, copper, etc.), so runoff or seepage from mine spoils is highly acidic and contains potentially toxic ions. The potential for acid production in mine spoils depends largely on the amount and particle size of the pyritic material, the availability of exchangeable bases and neutralizing minerals (primarily carbonates), the exchange of oxygen and solutes with the sulfide minerals, and the abundance of Thiobacillus. Because the exchange of oxygen and solutes and the abundance of Thiobacillus are restricted with depth, the control of mine spoil acidity is essentially a surface problem.

Waterlogging of mine spoils restricts the availability of oxygen, and sulfuric acid production does not occur in anaerobic muds. In fact, sulfate is reduced to sulfide under anaerobic conditions by bacteria of the genus Desulfovibrio (Connell and Patrick, 1968, 1969). However, ponds formed by flooding mine spoils may have problems with sulfuric acid formation in bottom muds exposed to oxygenated water.

Soil developed from marine sediments containing sulfide minerals is often called "cat's clay". Rickard (1973) described the process of cat's clay formation. When rivers and runoff carrying a heavy load of sediment emptied into the sea, sediment was deposited near shore. After the deposits rose above mean low water level, vegetation became established. As deposition continued, the coast slowly accreated, and a swamp forest developed. In the swamp forest, tree roots trapped organic and inorganic debris; decomposition in dense masses of organic debris resulted in anaerobic conditions; sulfur reducing bacteria became abundant. Sulfides produced by bacteria accumulated in pore spaces as hydrogen sulfide or combined with iron to form precipitates of iron sulfides. The iron sulfides underwent further chemical reaction to form iron disulfides that crystallized to form iron pyrite. The reactions may be summarized as:

$$2\ CH_2O\ (organic\ matter) + SO_4^{2-} \rightarrow H_2S + 2\ HCO_3^-$$

$$Fe(OH)_2 + H_2S \rightarrow FeS + 2\ H_2O$$

$$FeS + S \rightarrow FeS_2\ (pyrite)$$

As long as sediments containing pyrites are submerged and anaerobic, they remain reduced and change little. However, if they are drained and exposed to the air, oxidation results, and sulfuric acid is formed (see Equations 4.2-4.5). After drainage and ensuing acidification, the sediment is called an acid-sulfate soil. For example, Fleming and Alexander (1961) reported that some soils of the South Carolina tidal marsh area developed high acidity when drained. The pH of soil samples from these areas decreased as much as 3 units on drying. The pH values for dry samples ranged from 2.0 to 3.0, with an occasional value below 2.0. The soils contained up to 5.5% total sulfur. Field identification of cat's clays in South Carolina could sometimes be made by the smell of hydrogen sulfide from disturbed soil, but often it was necessary to determine pH before and after drying. Soils that will become acid-sulfate soils if drained and aerated are called potential acid-sulfate soils.

4.6.2 Lime requirement of acid-sulfate soils

Several procedures are also available for determining the lime requirement of acid-sulfate soils (Sorensen et al., 1980). The procedures all involve a method of determining the buffer lime requirement, and a technique for estimating the amount of calcium carbonate required to neutralize all of the acid that could result from the oxidation of pyrite. The unmodified buffer lime requirement procedure of Adams and Evans (1962) is recommended for determining the exchange acidity lime requirement. A suitable procedure for the potential acidity of pyrite was developed by G. W. Akin and R. I. Barnhisel of the University of Kentucky. In this procedure, sulfide is oxidized to sulfuric acid by hydrogen peroxide treatment, and the amount of sulfuric acid formed is determined by titration with a standard base.

The Akin-Barnhisel procedure requires the following reagents: 30% reagent grade hydrogen peroxide, phenolphthalein indicator solution, and standard sodium hydroxide (known normality between 0.01 and 0.05 N). The sample should be passed through a 20-mesh sieve (0.85-mm openings). The proportion of the material passing the 20-mesh sieve is the reactive fraction. Grind the reactive fraction further so that it passes a 60-mesh sieve (0.250-mm openings). Place 5.00 g of the 60-mesh material in a 500-ml tall form beaker. Add 20 ml of 30% hydrogen peroxide, and heat the mixture to about 40°C or until a noticeable reaction similar to boiling occurs. Once the reaction starts, remove the beaker from the heat, and let the reaction continue. Once the reaction stops, add 10 ml of 30% hydrogen peroxide and again heat to 40°C. Continue adding hydrogen peroxide and heating until no reaction occurs at 40°C. Add distilled water to a volume of about 100 ml and heat the solution for 30 min on a water bath to remove any excess hydrogen peroxide. After the beaker and contents have cooled, add 5 drops of phenolphthalein solution and titrate with standard sodium hydroxide. At the endpoint, a faint pink color will persist for at least 30 sec. The following equation is used:

$$\text{Potential acidity in meq/100 g} = \frac{\text{(ml of NaOH) (N) (100 g)}}{\text{Weight sample in grams}}$$

The liming rate is calculated from potential acidity: 1 meq/100 g of acidity requires 1 meq/100 g X 50 mg/meq of $CaCO_3$ X 10 = 500 mg/kg of $CaCO_3$. The liming factor of 1.5 and the reactive fraction (proportion of sample passing a 20-mesh sieve) must be included in the computation:

$CaCO_3$ in mg/kg = Potential acidity in meq/100 g X 750 X Reactive fraction

The reactive fraction must be used as a decimal fraction.

To determine the liming rate, the buffer lime requirement and the lime requirement due to sulfide are summed. The procedure outlined above is intended for use on materials of watersheds that oxidize and acidify runoff. When liming materials are applied to such soils they react with acid according to well known stoichiometry illustrated below for calcium carbonate:

$$CaCO_3 + H_2SO_4 \rightarrow CaSO_4 + H_2O + CO_2$$

The pyrite in soil is not destroyed by liming; the liming material destroys any sulfuric acid present at the time of application, and the residual liming material continues to react with sulfuric acid produced by subsequent oxidation of pyrite.

Lime requirements of pond muds containing sulfides are not meaningful. As long as muds are flooded, little sulfuric will be produced by oxidation because the redox potential of muds is low. The buffer lime requirement may be used to

establish rates for such muds, but the potential acidity of pyrite should not be
included because overliming would result.

4.6.3 Acid-sulfate soils and fish production

Seepage from mine spoils frequently reaches natural waters. Acidic mine drainage may result in low productivity of natural waters or even cause complete destruction of fish populations. In some instances, mine spoil may be covered with
soil that does not contain pyrite and vegetation established, thereby preventing
acidic drainage from the spoil. In other situations, it is necessary to treat
mine spoils with agricultural limestone to neutralize sulfuric acid resulting
from the oxidation of pyrite. It is possible, at a reasonable cost, to greatly
reduce or even prevent problems of acidic mine drainage.

Old coal strip-mines may even be converted to lakes that will support fish
populations. Waller and Bass (1967) found that conversion of strip-mines to
productive lakes required that all of acid-sulfate spoils on the watershed, including lake banks, be treated to prevent acidic seepage. Next, agricultural
limestone was applied to lakes at the rate of 25 mg/l of $CaCO_3$ for each milligram
per liter of boiling point acidity. Several strip-mine lakes treated as above
maintained pH values near 7, measureable alkalinity, and had satisfactory fish
production (Scheve, 1971).

In Malaysia, a drought caused mangrove swamps to dry out and acid-sulfate soil
conditions resulted. When rains came, drainage from the acid-sulfate soils reached
a river and caused a fish kill (Dunn, 1965). Thus, drainage from areas of cat's
clay is potentially harmful to fish populations.

Problems with acid-sulfate soils may also occur in ponds constructed in cat's
clay formations. For example, at the Brackishwater Aquaculture Center, Leganes,
Iloilo, The Phillippines, surface soils where ponds were constructed were not
highly acidic, but unfortunately, subsurface soils were potential acid-sulfate
soils (unpublished memo). In the years since drainage, pyrites in the surface
soils had oxidized and the resulting sulfuric acid had leached out. Ponds were
excavated with their bottoms constructed of acid-sulfate soil, and much of the
soil of the surrounding dikes was acid-sulfate. Upon initial filling, the water
in the ponds was not acidic. However, pyrite in the dikes was exposed to the air
and oxidized, forming sulfuric acid. Rains washed the sulfuric acid from the
dikes into ponds and caused fish kills. Furthermore, acidity prevented vegetation
from growing on the dikes and erosion ensued.

The lime requirement of some dikes was as high as 116 tons/ha. A program for
liming and sodding dikes was initiated so that fish could be reared in the ponds.

154

REFERENCES

Adams, F. and Evans, C. E., 1962. A rapid method for measuring lime requirement of red-yellow podzolic soils. Soil. Sci. Soc. Amer. Proc., 26: 355-357.

Alexander, M., 1961. Introduction to Soil Microbiology. John Wiley and Sons, New York, 472 pp.

Arce, R. G. and Boyd, C. E., 1975. Effects of agricultural limestone on water chemistry, phytoplankton productivity, and fish production in soft water ponds. Trans. Amer. Fish. Soc., 104: 308-312.

Bachmann, R. W., 1962. Evaluation of a modified C-14 technique for shipboard estimation of photosynthesis in large lakes. Great Lakes Research Publication No. 8, 61 pp.

Barrett, P. H., 1952. Relationships between alkalinity and adsorption and regeneration of added phosphorus in fertilized trout lakes. Trans. Amer. Fish. Soc., 82: 78-90.

Bowling, M. L., 1962. The effects of lime treatment on benthos production in Georgia farm ponds. Proc. Annual Conf. Southeast. Assoc. Game and Fish Comm., 16: 418-424.

Boyd, C. E., 1970. Influence of organic matter on some characteristics of aquatic soil. Hydrobiologia, 36: 17-21.

Boyd, C. E., 1974. Lime requirements of Alabama fish ponds. Auburn University Agricultural Experiment Station, Auburn, Alabama, Bulletin 459, 20 pp.

Boyd, C. E., 1977. Organic matter concentrations and textural properties of muds from different depths in four fish ponds. Hydrobiologia, 53: 277-279.

Boyd, C. E., 1979a. Water Quality in Warmwater Fish Ponds. Auburn University Agricultural Experiment Station, Auburn, Alabama, 359 pp.

Boyd, C. E., 1979b. Lime requirement and application in fish ponds. In: T. V. R. Pillay and W. A. Dill (Editors), Advances in Aquaculture. Papers presented at the FAO Technical Conference on Aquaculture, Kyoto, Japan, 26 May-2 June 1976. Fishing News Books Ltd., Farnham, Surry, England, pp. 120-122.

Boyd, C. E. and Cuenco, M. L., 1980. Refinements of the lime requirement procedure for fish ponds. Aquaculture, 21: 293-299.

Boyd, C. E. and Scarsbrook, E., 1974. Effects of agricultural limestone on phytoplankton communities of fish ponds. Arch. Hydrobiol., 74: 336-349.

Boyd, C. E. and Walley, W. W., 1975. Total alkalinity and hardness of surface waters in Alabama and Mississippi. Auburn University Agricultural Experiment Station, Auburn, Alabama, Bulletin 465, 16 pp.

Connell, W. E. and Patrick, W. H., Jr., 1968. Sulfate reduction in soil: effects of redox potential and pH. Science, 159: 86-87.

Connell, W. E. and Patrick, W. H., Jr., 1969. Reduction of sulfate to sulfide in waterlogged soil. Soil Sci. Soc. Amer. Proc., 33: 711-714.

Dunn, I. C., 1965. Notes on mass fish death following drought in Malaya. Malaysian Agric. J., 45: 204-211.

Fleming, J. F. and Alexander, L. T., 1961. Sulfur acidity in South Carolina tidal marsh soils. Soil Sci. Soc. Amer. Proc., 25: 94-95.

Golterman, H. L., 1975. Physiological Limnology. Elsevier Scientific Publishing Company, Amsterdam, 489 pp.

Greene, G. N., 1969. Effects of water hardness on fish production in plastic pools. Proc. Annual Conf. Southeast. Association Game and Fish Comm., 23: 455-461.

Hansell, D. A. and Boyd, C. E., 1980. Uses of hydrated lime in fish ponds. Proc. Annual Conf. Southeast. Assoc. Fish and Wildl. Agencies, 34: in press.

Hasler, A. D., Brynildson, O. M., and Helm, W. T., 1951. Improving conditions for fish in brown-water bog lakes by alkalization. J. Wildl. Manag., 15: 347-352.

Hickling, C. F., 1962. Fish Culture. Faber and Faber, London, 295 pp.

Jackson, M. L., 1958. Soil Chemical Analysis. Prentice-Hall, Englewood Cliffs, New Jersey, 498 pp.

Mairs, D. F., 1966. A total alkalinity atlas for Maine lake waters. Limnol. Oceanogr., 11: 68-72.

Moyle, J. B., 1956. Relationships between the chemistry of Minnesota surface waters and wildlife management. J. Wildl. Manag., 20: 303-320.

Neess, J. C., 1946. Development and status of pond fertilization in Central Europe. Trans. Amer. Fish. Soc., 76: 335-358.

Peech, M. and Bradfield, R., 1948. Chemical methods for estimating lime needs of soils. Soil Sci., 65: 35-55.

Rickard, D. T., 1973. Sedimentary iron formation. In: H. Dost (Editor), Proceedings of the International Symposium on Acid Sulfate Soils, Volume I. Institute for Land Reclamation and Improvement, Wageningen, The Netherlands, pp. 28-65.

Schaeperclaus, W., 1933. Textbook of Pond Culture. U. S. Fish and Wildlife Service, Washington, D. C., Leaflet 311, 206 pp.

Scheve, J. W., 1971. Limnological and fisheries investigations of strip-mine lakes in southeast Kansas. M. S. thesis, Kansas State College of Pittsburg, Pittsburg, Kansas, 171 pp.

Shoemaker, H. E., McLean, E. O., and Pratt, P. F., 1961. Buffer methods for determining lime requirement of soils with appreciable amounts of extractable aluminum. Soil. Sci. Soc. Amer. Proc., 25: 274-277.

Shoup, C. S., 1944. Geochemical interpretation of water analyses from Tennessee streams. Trans. Amer. Fish. Soc., 74: 223-229.

Sills, J. B., 1974. A review of the literature on the use of lime ($Ca(OH)_2$, CaO, $CaCO_3$) in fisheries. U. S. Fish and Wildlife Service, Washington, D. C., 30 pp.

Snow, J. R. and Jones, R. O., 1959. Some effects of lime applications to warmwater hatchery ponds. Proc. Annual Conf. Southeast. Assoc. Game and Fish Comm., 13: 95-101.

Sorensen, D. L., Knieb, W. A., Porcella, D. B., and Richardson, B. Z., 1980. Determining the lime requirement for the Blackbird Mine spoil. J. Environ. Qual., 9: 162-166.

Stross, R. G. and Hasler, A. D., 1960. Some lime-induced changes in lake metabolism. Limnol. Oceanogr., 5: 265-272.

Stross, R. G., Neess, J. C., and Hasler, A. D., 1961. Turnover time and production of the planktonic crustacea in limed and reference portions of a bog lake. Ecology, 42: 237-245.

Swingle, H. S., 1947. Experiments on pond fertilization. Alabama Polytechnic Institute Agricultural Experiment Station, Auburn, Alabama, Bulletin 264, 30 pp.

Swingle, H. S., 1969. Methods of Analysis for Waters, Organic Matter, and Pond Bottom Soils Used in Fisheries Research. Auburn University, Auburn, Alabama, 119 pp.

Thomaston, W. W. and Zeller, H. D., 1961. Results of a six-year investigation of chemical soil and water analysis and lime treatment in Georgia fish ponds. Proc. Annual Conf. Southeast. Assoc. Game and Fish Comm., 15: 236-245.

Tisdale, S. I. and Nelson, W. L., 1956. Soil Fertility and Fertilizers. The MacMillan Co., New York, 430 pp.

Waller, W. T. and Bass, J. C., 1967. Pre- and post-improvement limnological analyses of certain strip-mine lakes in southeast Kansas. Kansas Forestry, Fish and Game Commission, Topeka, Kansas, 94 pp.

Waters, T. F., 1956. The effects of lime application to acid bog lakes in Northern Michigan. Trans. Amer. Fish. Soc., 86: 329-344.

Wolt, J. D. and Adams, F., 1978. Whatever happened to basic slag? Auburn University Agricultural Experiment Station, Auburn, Alabama, Highlights of Agricultural Research, 25, No. 1: 15.

Yuan, T. L., 1974. A double buffer method for the determination of lime requirement of acid soils. Soil Sci. Soc. Amer. Proc., 38: 437-440.

Zeller, H. D. and Montgomery, A. B., 1957. Preliminary investigations of chemical soil and water relationships and lime treatment of soft water in Georgia farm ponds. Proc. Annual Conf. Southeast. Assoc. Game and Fish Comm., 11: 71-76.

Chapter 5

DYNAMICS OF DISSOLVED OXYGEN

5.1   INTRODUCTION

   Problems with low concentrations of dissolved oxygen are infrequent in fertilized ponds, even though these ponds are eutrophic. However, when fish culture is
intensified through feeding, problems with dissolved oxygen increase in frequency
and severity. In ponds receiving feed, standing crops of fish are quite high and
metabolic wastes provide nutrients to encourage heavy plankton blooms. Thus, photosynthesis and respiration proceed at rapid rates, and factors favoring respiration
over photosynthesis for brief periods may cause dissolved oxygen deficiencies that
stress or kill fish. Phytoplankton plays a dominant role in the dissolved oxygen
dynamics of fish ponds, so some knowledge of phytoplankton ecology is essential
for those involved in intensive fish culture.

5.2   DIFFUSION

   The atmosphere contains a vast amount of oxygen, some of which will diffuse
into pond waters when they are undersaturated with oxygen. Likewise, oxygen
will be lost to the atmosphere when pond waters are supersaturated with oxygen.
The driving force causing net transfer of oxygen between air and water is the
difference in the tension between oxygen in the atmosphere and oxygen in the
water. Once equilibrium is reached, oxygen tensions in air and water are the
same, and net transfer of oxygen ceases. The oxygen deficit (D) or the oxygen
surplus (S) may be expressed as:

$$D = DO_e - DO_m$$

$$S = DO_m - DO_e$$

where DO_e = the equilibrium concentration (saturation) of oxygen in water and DO_m
= the measured concentration of oxygen in water.
   Oxygen must enter or leave a body of water at the air-water interface, and for
the very thin film of water in contact with air, the greater D or S, the faster
oxygen will enter or leave the film. For undisturbed water the net transfer of oxygen will depend upon D or S, the area of the air-water interface, the temperature,
and the time of contact (Haney, 1954; Knight, 1965). Even when D or S is great,
the rate of net transfer is slow. Water of the surface film quickly reaches equilibrium with oxygen, and further net transfer requires that oxygen diffuse from the
film to the greater body of water or from the greater body of water to the film.

Natural bodies of water are never completely quiescent, and oxygen transfer is regulated by the amount of turbulence (Welch, 1968).

For simplicity, S can be considered as a negative D and the rate of change in D with respect to time (t) may be expressed for a completely mixed system as:

$$\frac{dD}{dt} = -K_d D$$

where K_d = the overall transfer coefficient. The overall transfer coefficient is a constant only for specific conditions, and according to Knight (1965), K_d can best be expressed as:

$$K_d = K \times \frac{A}{V} \times t$$

where K = a constant for a particular amount of turbulence; A = area of the air-water interface; V = the volume of water; t= time of contact between air and water. The air-water interface varies with turbulence, and neither variable can be estimated accurately. Nevertheless, it is possible to calculate K_d empirically between t_1 and t_2 because integration of Equation 5.1 gives:

$$K_d = \frac{\ln D_1 - \ln D_2}{t_1 - t_2} \qquad (5.2)$$

Various units may be used in Equation 5.2, but for convenience, K_d is often expressed as grams of oxygen transferred per square meter of pond surface per hour. A plot of the natural logarithms of D against time for a throughly mixed body of water or the natural logarithms of D, as calculated from dissolved oxygen profiles, for a less than thoroughly mixed body of water gives a straight line, for which K_d is the slope (Fig. 5.1).

Measurements of K_d in laboratory tanks range from 0.03 to 0.08 g/m^2 of O_2 per h in still water to as high as 0.74 g/m^2 of O_2 per h in turbulent water. An accurate measurement of K_d is virtually impossible in natural waters because biological processes are continually adding or removing oxygen during the period of measurement, and complex circulation patterns in natural water are difficult to assess. Schroeder (1975) reported K_d values of 0.01-0.05 g/m^2 of O_2 per h for each 30 mm of Hg (0.2 atmosphere) oxygen saturation deficit for fish ponds in Israel. In other words, if the dissolved oxygen tension of the water is 99.2 mm of Hg, the deficit in saturation is 159.2 - 99.2 = 60 mm of Hg. Thus, oxygen will enter the water at 0.02-0.1 g/m^2 per h. If the pond is 1 m in average depth, these K_d values will correspond to 0.02-0.1 g/m^3 of O_2 per h or 0.02-0.1 mg/l of oxygen. Wind is the primary source of turbulence in waters of fish ponds, hence

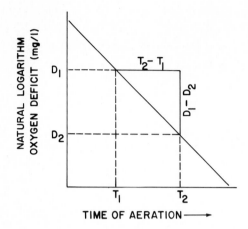

Fig. 5.1. Change in oxygen deficit with time during aeration.

the minimum and maximum K_d values reported by Schroeder (1975) apparently represent low turbulence (little wind) and high turbulence (strong wind), respectively. Results reported by Welch (1968) for a fish pond in Georgia were similar to those of Schroeder. During calm weather, K_d values were about 0.1 g/m^2 of O_2 per h at 100% departure from saturation. The K_d values increased to around 0.5 g/m^2 of O_2 per h during windy weather.

It is difficult to predict rates of oxygen transfer in ponds because dissolved oxygen concentrations are constantly changing. Early in the morning, dissolved oxygen concentrations may be below saturation, but later in the day supersaturation may result from photosynthesis. Thus, oxygen diffuses into the water early in the morning and out of the water later in the day. Likewise, early in the night waters may be supersaturated with oxygen, but after a few hours, respiration by the pond biota results in undersaturation and a change in the direction of net transfer of oxygen. Data presented by Schroeder (1975) were transformed to show transfers of dissolved oxygen during 12 h of darkness under average wind conditions for ponds of 1 m average depth with different initial oxygen saturation (Table 5.1). If pond water is at 50% saturation at dusk, diffusion will add 1.69 mg/l of oxygen during the night. The oxygen concentration in the water will probably not increase by this amount because some of the incoming oxygen will be used in respiration. In a pond initially at saturation at dusk, there will be a gain of 0.44 mg/l during the night. This gain results because respiratory processes will cause an oxygen deficit during the night even though the water was initially at saturation. The losses of oxygen from waters initially supersaturated with oxygen increase with increasing initial saturation. Values in Table 5.1 are for ponds

TABLE 5.1

Approximate rates of oxygen transfer between pond surfaces and atmosphere during 12 h of darkness. Ponds were assumed to be 1 m deep. Data were modified from oxygen transfer data presented by Schroeder (1975).

Dissolved oxygen at dusk (% Saturation)	Oxygen transfer (mg/1)	Dissolved oxygen at dusk (% Saturation)	Oxygen transfer (mg/1)
50	+ 1.69	160	- 1.64
60	+ 1.49	170	- 1.82
70	+ 1.18	180	- 1.98
80	+ 1.00	190	- 2.11
90	+ 0.77	200	- 2.37
100	+ 0.44	210	- 2.42
110	+ 0.16	220	- 2.54
120	- 0.18	230	- 2.67
130	- 0.55	240	- 2.76
140	- 0.94	250	- 2.91
150	- 1.48		

1 m deep, but they may be adjusted for other depths.

Halverson et al. (1980) reported nightly diffusion losses of oxygen up to 3.19 mg/1 in ponds at Auburn University. The magnitude of values increased with initial percentage saturation and wind velocity.

5.3 PHOTOSYNTHESIS

Rates of photosynthesis in fish ponds are related to phytoplankton abundance and light intensity. Assuming equal light intensities, the photosynthetic production of dissolved oxygen will increase as a function of phytoplankton abundance. In fish ponds, phytoplankton is the major source of turbidity so light penetration is generally related to phytoplankton abundance (Table 5.2). Hence, phytoplankters are limited to shallower depths as their abundance increases, and there is a strong vertical stratification of photosynthetic rates and dissolved oxygen concentrations.

Gross primary productivity rates of 1-4 mg/1 of O_2 per hour were observed in the upper strata of fish ponds at Auburn University (Boyd, 1973). Nevertheless, because of abundant plankton, light penetration was greatly restricted and rates of primary productivity declined rapidly with depth (Fig. 5.2). The compensation points, the depths at which the amount of oxygen produced in photosynthesis just

TABLE 5.2

Light penetration in ponds with different densities of the alga <u>Microcystis</u> sp. (Beasley, 1963).

Pond	<u>Microcystis</u> (colonies/ml)	Light (% of incident)		
		15 cm	75 cm	150 cm
S-1	28,900	31.6	0.4	0
S-3	7,000	79.6	28.0	4.4
S-8	3,700	68.5	9.5	1.2
S-6	700	75.5	35.1	12.1
S-14	400	80.9	29.8	9.4

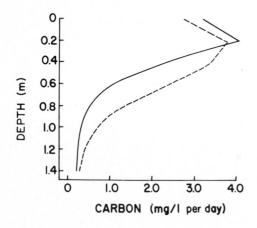

Fig. 5.2. Rates of gross primary productivity at different depths in two fish ponds (solid and broken lines) with relatively dense phytoplankton blooms.

equals the amount of oxygen used in respiration, ranged from 40 to 75 cm. When data were intergrated with depth, oxygen production in fish ponds ranged from 4 to 12 g/m^2 of O_2 per day. For a pond of 1 m average depth, these values correspond to 4-12 mg/l of O_2 per day.

Hepher (1962) also noted a marked vertical stratification of photosynthesis in fish ponds in Israel. Maximum rates of photosynthesis occurred at light intensities of 1,500-8,000 foot candles (16,140-86,080 lux). Photosynthesis decreased rapidly at lower light intensities because of inadequate light; photosynthesis was 80% of maximum at 1,000 foot candles (10,760 lux) and 50% of maximum at 500

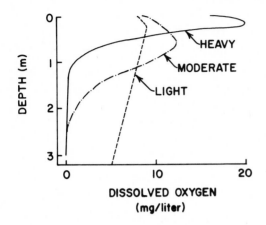

Fig. 5.3. Concentrations of dissolved oxygen at different depths in ponds with light, moderate, and heavy phytoplankton blooms.

foot candles (5,380 lux). Light intensities above 8,000 foot candles (86,080 lux) retarded photosynthesis; rates were 50% of maximum at 15,000 foot candles (161,400 lux). Photosynthesis was usually about 80-90% of maximum near the surface, maximum at 10-12 cm, and around 50% of maximum at 30 cm. These observations led Hepher to conclude that as fish ponds become more enriched with nutrients, primary productivity increases in upper layers of water, where favorable light conditions exist, but decreases in lower layers, where overshading by the plankton reduces light penetration.

Abundant plankton in surface waters and resulting attenuation of light causes shallow thermal stratification of fish ponds (Beasley, 1963). Therefore, even though large quantities of oxygen are produced in surface waters, the oxygen is not mixed with deeper waters. High oxygen concentrations in surface waters favor diffusion of oxygen to the air, but photosynthetic rates usually exceed diffusion rates and surface waters are strongly supersaturated with dissolved oxygen. The net effect of the interaction between light and phytoplankton abundance is a rapid decline in dissolved oxygen concentration with depth (Fig. 5.3). The depth of 0 mg/l dissolved oxygen will vary with plankton abundance, wind mixing, and pond size, but it usually between 0.5 and 2 m.

On clear days, photosynthesis rates increase rapidly after sunrise and remain high until almost sundown, although afternoon rates may be somewhat less than morning rates (Verduin, 1957; Harris, 1973). Cloudy skies cause a decrease in photosynthetic rates (Romaire and Boyd, 1979).

The pattern of dissolved oxygen stratification with depth may be opposite of that described above in ponds with macrophytes growing in deep water. These

ponds contain little phytoplankton, so greater photosynthetic rates and oxygen
concentrations often occur in the weed beds in deep water.

5.4 RESPIRATION

Although oxygen is only evolved by macrophytes or phytoplankton, all aerobic
organisms use oxygen in respiration. Furthermore, respiration goes on continuously, while photosynthesis occurs only during daylight. Rates of respiration
increase with plankton density and warmth, and values as high as 0.5 mg/l of O_2
per h have been reported for plankton communities in pond waters of 30°C (Boyd
et al., 1978a). Over 24 h, this rate amounts to 12 mg/l. Either Equation 2.11
or Equation 2.12 may be used to calculate respiration rates of plankton.

Oxygen consumption by fish was discussed in Chapter 2; Equations 2.9 and 2.10
may be used to estimate how much oxygen will be consumed by fish.

Mezainis (1977) reported that oxygen uptake by muds in two channel catfish
ponds in Alabama ranged from 8 to 70 mg/m^2 of O_2 per h and from 20 to 114 mg/m^2
of O_2 per h, respectively, during a growing season. Fish ponds in Israel had
benthic respiration values of 42-125 mg/m^2 of O_2 per h (Schroeder, 1975). In
simpler terms, if mud in a 1-m deep pond uses oxygen at the rate of 30 mg/m^2
per h for 12 h, a total of 360 mg of oxygen is used by each square meter of mud
surface. Since 1 m^3 of water lays above 1 m^2 of mud, this represents a reduction
in dissolved oxygen of 0.36 mg/l in 12 h. Ponds studied by both Mezainis and
Schroeder received large applications of nutrients and no doubt had high rates
of benthic respiration. The median value for the two studies was 61 mg/m^2 of
O_2 per h. Since little is known about factors affecting rates of benthic respiration, and it is difficult to obtain reliable measurements of the process, the
median value will be taken as an approximation of benthic respiration in ponds.
Of course, the rate of benthic respiration is dependent upon the oxygen supply,
and aerobic respiration cannot continue in anaerobic muds. Thus, muds of the
hypolimnion will not normally affect oxygen dynamics.

5.5 DIEL CHANGES IN DISSOLVED OXYGEN CONCENTRATIONS

Because of the effects of respiration and photosynthesis and of the slow rates
of diffusion, dissolved oxygen concentrations continually change over a 24-h
period. Dissolved oxygen concentrations are usually lowest near dawn, increase
during daylight hours to a peak during the afternoon, and decline again during
nighttime (Fig. 5.4). The highest concentrations of dissolved oxygen in the
afternoon are usually found in ponds with the greatest abundance of plankton.
However, waters of these ponds also have high rates of respiration, hence they
also have the lowest concentrations of dissolved oxygen in the early morning.
Ponds used for the commercial culture of channel catfish typically have dissolved

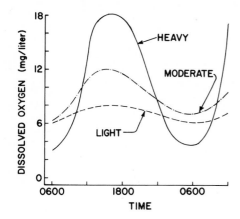

Fig. 5.4. Diel changes in dissolved oxygen concentrations in surface waters (0-0.5 m) of ponds with light, moderate, and heavy plankton blooms.

oxygen concentrations above 15 mg/l in the afternoon and below 3 mg/l at dawn (Boyd et al., 1979a).

Cloudy weather has an unfavorable influence on the diel patterns of dissolved oxygen concentrations. On cloudy days, photosynthesis does not proceed as rapidly as on clear or partly cloudy days. Therefore, concentrations of dissolved oxygen are not as high at dusk following a cloudy day as a clear day. This means that dissolved oxygen concentrations will decline more during nights following cloudy days than clear days. A few consecutive cloudy days may cause depletion of dissolved oxygen in ponds with abundant plankton (Fig. 5.5).

5.6   PREDICTING DECLINE IN OXYGEN CONCENTRATIONS
5.6.1 Channel catfish ponds

From a management standpoint, it is often desirable to predict how low dissolved oxygen will fall during a given night. Boyd et al. (1978a) used the following equation to predict the decline in dissolved oxygen in channel catfish ponds:

$$DO_t = DO_{dusk} \pm DO_{df} - DO_f - DO_m - DO_p \qquad (5.3)$$

where DO_t = dissolved oxygen concentration after t hours of darkness; DO_{dusk} = dissolved oxygen concentration at dusk; DO_{df} = gain or loss of oxygen to diffusion; DO_f = oxygen used by fish; DO_m = loss of oxygen to respiration of organisms in mud; DO_p = oxygen consumed by the planktonic community. The DO_{dusk} term was measured, DO_{df} was taken from Table 5.1, DO_f was calculated from Equation 2.9

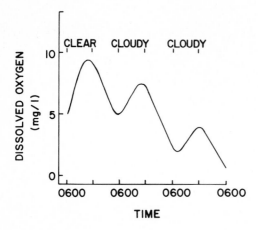

Fig. 5.5. Effects of cloudy weather on dissolved oxygen concentrations in a pond.

(required estimates of the number and average weight of fish), DO_m was assumed to be 61 mg/m^2 per hour, and DO_p was estimated by either Equation 2.11 or Equation 2.12. To simplify computations, regression equations and associated terms necessary to solve Equation 5.3 were programmed into a computer. Equation 5.3 was successful in predicting the nighttime decline in dissolved oxygen on five dates in two channel catfish ponds (Boyd et al., 1978a). In comparisons of measured and calculated values where plankton respiration was estimated from COD data, the smallest differences between measured and calculated dissolved oxygen concentrations were 0.01 mg/l in Pond A and 0.13 mg/l in Pond B. The greatest differences were 0.49 mg/l in Pond A and 0.98 mg/l in Pond B. Percentage differences (disregarding sign) in calculated and measured dissolved oxygen concentrations ranged from 0.24 to 11.25% with and average of 6.31%. Equation 5.3 underestimated measured dissolved oxygen six times and overestimated it four times. When Secchi disk visibility was used to estimate plankton respiration, the smallest discrepancies in measured and calculated dissolved oxygen concentrations were 0.22 mg/l in Pond A and 0.15 mg/l in Pond B. The greatest differences were 0.97 and 0.94 mg/l for Pond A and B, respectively. The difference in measured and calculated values averaged 10.40%. Equation 5.3 underestimated measured dissolved oxygen nine of ten times. Obviously, from a management standpoint, underestimations are more desirable than overestimations.

The accuracy of Equation 5.3 in predicting the nighttime decline in dissolved oxygen was further evaluated in five channel catfish ponds during summer, 1978 (Boyd et al., 1979b). A total of 30 comparisons between predicted and measured concentrations of dissolved oxygen were made, and the correlation coefficient

TABLE 5.3

Critical Secchi disk values (cm) for 1-m deep ponds containing 3,400 kg/ha of channel catfish. A smaller Secchi disk value for any combination of temperature and dissolved oxygen concentration at dusk will cause dissolved oxygen to fall below 2.0 mg/l by dawn. Dissolved oxygen concentration will not fall below 2.0 mg/l for entries designated S.

°C	Dissolved oxygen concentration at dusk (mg/l)					
	2	4	6	8	10	12
20	79	S	S	S	S	S
22	100	42	S	S	S	S
24	100	69	26	S	S	S
26	100	90	48	21	S	S
28	100	100	66	37	16	S
30	100	100	79	53	32	S
32	100	100	90	66	48	26

(r) between predicted and measured values was 0.95 (P<0.01). The average difference between measured and predicted dissolved oxygen concentrations, disregarding sign, was 0.47 mg/l.

In channel catfish ponds, emergency aeration is often used if dissolved oxygen falls below 2 mg/l. Equation 5.3 was used to determine, for different standing crops of channel catfish, dissolved oxygen concentrations at dusk, and water temperatures, the Secchi disk visibilities corresponding to 2 mg/l of dissolved oxygen at dawn. Results of the calculations were used to prepare tables that may be used by fish farmers to predict if dissolved oxygen depletion will occur during a given night. A sample table is presented (Table 5.3), and tables for other standing crops of fish are available (Romaire and Boyd, 1978). To illustrate the use of the table, suppose that the temperature is 24°C and the dissolved oxygen concentration at dusk is 6 mg/l. Reference to Table 5.3 gives a Secchi disk value of 26 cm. Thus, if the Secchi disk visibility in the pond is greater than 26 cm, dissolved oxygen will not drop below 2 mg/l. The dissolved oxygen may be expected to fall below 2 mg/l if the Secchi disk visibility is 26 cm or less.

Boyd et al. (1978a) observed that the decline in dissolved oxygen concentration during the night was essentially linear with respect to time. If dissolved oxygen is measured at dusk and again after 2-3 h, the two dissolved oxygen concentrations can be plotted versus time and a straight line through the two points projected to estimate dissolved oxygen at other times during the night or at dawn (Fig. 5.6).

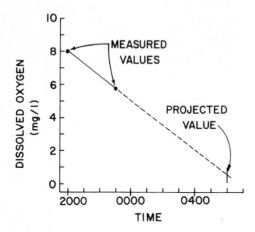

Fig. 5.6. The projection method for estimating nighttime decline in dissolved oxygen concentrations in fish ponds (Boyd et al., 1978a).

This procedure was almost as reliable as Equation 5.3 in predicting dissolved oxygen concentrations in the two ponds mentioned above. The smallest difference between measured and predicted values was 0.13% and the greatest difference was 20.83%. The average difference was 10.01%, and the projection method overestimated dissolved oxygen nine of ten times.

Channel catfish farmers usually find it necessary to monitor dissolved oxygen concentrations on a daily basis during much of the growing season and especially during months when water temperatures are above 26°C (Boyd et al., 1979a). The procedures outlined above have been used successfully by some farmers, but many have, through experience, developed their own ways of predicting the likelihood of oxygen depletion. Most of the methods used by fish farmers are similar to the one described by Boyd et al. (1979a). Dissolved oxygen concentrations were measured at a depth of approximately 15 cm with a polarographic oxygen meter at one or two locations in each pond. Measurements were made at dawn and mid-afternoon each day between May and October. The dissolved oxygen probe was attached to a fiber glass rod to allow readings to be taken from pond banks. A graph of dawn and afternoon dissolved oxygen concentrations was prepared for each pond. If the dissolved oxygen concentration at dawn was above 5 mg/1 and the afternoon value was as high or higher than the previous day, dissolved oxygen was not measured during the night. If the dissolved oxygen concentration at dawn dropped below 5 mg/1 or the afternoon value was markedly lower than for the previous day, dissolved oxygen was measured a 2- to 3-h intervals during the night. The slope of the oxygen curve was used to predict if concentrations would fall below 2 mg/1 before

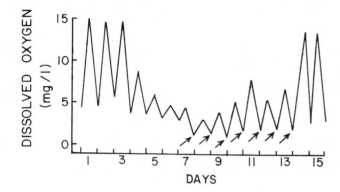

Fig. 5.7. Afternoon and early morning concentrations of dissolved oxygen in a pond with a chronic dissolved oxygen problem. Arrows indicate dates when emergency aeration was used (Boyd, et al., 1979a).

dawn. An example of one of the oxygen graphs is given in Fig. 5.7. This procedure was used on a fish farm with 36 ponds totaling 220 ha; considerable labor was obviously required.

5.6.2 Tilapia ponds

The decline in dissolved oxygen concentration during darkness was also predicted in <u>Tilapia</u> ponds with Equation 5.3 (Romaire et al., 1978). The fish respiration term (DO_f) for Equation 5.3 was obtained from Equation 2.10. Estimates of plankton respiration were obtained from Equation 2.12. Some of the ponds were treated with cow manure. For these ponds, the oxygen consumption of manure was taken from data in Table 5.4. Again, Equation 5.3 successfully predicted the decline in oxygen concentrations. The average absolute deviations between calculated and measured dissolved oxygen concentrations were 0.49 mg/l for unmanured ponds and 0.38 mg/l for manured ponds.

5.6.3 Trout ponds

Rainbow trout (<u>Salmo</u> <u>gairdneri</u>) have been successfully cultured during winter in raceways and ponds that were used in the summer for channel catfish production (Hill et al., 1972; Halverson et al., 1980). This double-cropping system permits year-around use of warmwater facilities. The nighttime dissolved oxygen equation (Equation 5.3) was also successful in predicting the nighttime decline in dissolved oxygen. The DO_f term in Equation 5.3 was obtained by use of an equation for trout respiration presented by Muller-Feuga et al. (1978):

Oxygen consumption (mg O_2/kg per h) = A X W^b X 10^{ct}

where W = weigh of fish in grams; t = temperature in °C; A = 75 (4 to 10°C) or A = 249 (12 to 22°C); b = -0.196 (4 to 10°C) or b = -0.142 (12 to 22°C); C = 0.055 (4 to 10°C) or C = 0.024 (12 to 22°C). Plankton respiration (DO_p) was calculated from an equation relating COD and oxygen consumption by plankton at 20°C and assuming a Q_{10} = 2. The equation was:

DO_p in mg/l per h = 0.00848 + 0.00264C

where C = COD. This approach to predicting overnight decline in oxygen would be useful in summer in coldwater ponds.

5.7   OXYGEN BUDGETS OF FISH PONDS

The important variables contributing to the nighttime oxygen budgets of fish ponds are apparent from the nighttime oxygen prediction equation (Equation 5.3). However, it is beneficial to know something of the magnitudes of the different terms. Therefore, I will prepare an oxygen budget for a channel catfish pond: 400 g fish, 8,000 fish/ha, water temperature of 28°C, COD of 75 mg/l, and a dissolved oxygen concentration at dusk of 15 mg/l. The pond has an area of 1 ha

TABLE 5.4
Oxygen demand of fresh cow manure in grams oxygen per kilogram of manure per hour as related to percentage dry matter in the manure and the temperature. Modified from data presented by Schroeder (1974).

°C	Dry matter (%)				
	11	13	15	17	19
15	0.050	0.133	0.200	0.288	0.371
20	0.067	0.175	0.267	0.383	0.492
25	0.100	0.263	0.400	0.575	0.738
30	0.133	0.350	0.533	0.767	0.983

and an average depth of 1 m. The calculations are given below.

Diffusion:
At a temperature of 28°C, the solubility of oxygen in water is 7.75 mg/l. Thus, the percentage saturation is (15 ÷ 7.75) X 100 = 194%. From Table 5.1, oxygen

loss to diffusion will be 2.11 mg/l.

Fish Respiration:
   The amount of oxygen used by fish will be computed with Equation 2.9:

$\log$ mg O_2/g per h $= - 0.999 - 0.000957(400) - 0.0000006(400)^2 + 0.0327(28) +$
   $0.0000087(28)^2 + 0.0000003(400)(28)$
$\log$ mg O_2/g per h $= - 0.552$
mg O_2/g per h $= 0.280$

The pond contains 8,000 fish X 0.4 kg = 3,200 kg of fish. Assuming a 12-h night, this quantity of fish would consume 0.000280 kg O_2/kg per h X 12 h X 3,200 kg = 10.75 kg of oxygen. The pond contains 10,000 m^3 of water, and 1 g/m^3 = 1 mg/l. Hence, 10,750 g of O_2 ÷ 10,000 m^3 = 1.08 g/m^3 or 1.08 mg/l. Therefore, the fish would remove 1.08 mg/l of dissolved oxygen during the night.

Benthic Respiration:
   For lack of a better estimate, a value of 61 mg/m^2 of O_2 per h will be accepted. Thus, each square meter of mud will remove 61 mg/m^2 of O_2 per h X 12 h = 732 mg/m^2 of oxygen. Because the pond is 1 m average depth, this corresponds to 732 mg/m^3, or 0.73 mg/l. Benthic respiration would require 0.73 mg/l of dissolved oxygen.

Plankton Respiration
   The amount of oxygen used by plankton will be computed with Equation 2.11:

Plankton respiration in mg/l per h $= - 1.006 - 0.00148(75) - 0.0000125(75)^2 +$
   $0.0766(28) - 0.00144(28)^2 + 0.000253(75)(28)$
Plankton respiration $= 0.36$ mg/l per h

During the night, plankton will remove 0.36 mg/l per h X 12 h = 4.32 mg/l of dissolved oxygen.

Total:

Source	mg/l	% of total
Diffusion	2.11	25.6
Fish	1.08	13.1
Benthos	0.73	8.9
Plankton	4.32	52.4
Total	8.24	100.0

TABLE 5.5

Nighttime dissolved oxygen for rainbow trout ponds at Auburn, Alabama (Halverson et al., 1980).

Pond	Water temperature (°C)	Respiration (mg/l)			Diffusion (mg/l)
		Fish	Plankton	Benthos	
E-39	10	0.07	0.28	0.42	-1.13
E-55	8	0.20	0.32	0.39	-3.19
E-51	10	0.22	0.51	0.46	1.09

Schroeder (1975) evaluated the nighttime balance for oxygen in manured fish ponds in Israel. He stated that the primary sinks for oxygen varied from test to test among three factors: BOD of water (plankton respiration), fish respiration, and diffusion of oxygen to the atmosphere. Benthic respiration, including the decay of manure, was only a minor factor in overnight oxygen consumption. The studies by Boyd et al. (1978a) and Romaire et al. (1978) corroborate Schroeder's findings.

The oxygen budgets for trout ponds during winter (Halverson et al., 1980) differ from the budget discussed above. Because of low water temperatures, respiration by fish and plankton was comparatively low and diffusion was the dominant variable (Table 5.5).

Daytime budgets for oxygen in ponds contain the same variables as nighttime budgets but with the addition of oxygen production in photosynthesis. As pointed out earlier, the amount of oxygen produced in photosynthesis is a function of both phytoplankton abundance and light intensity. Hepher (1962) reported that fertilize ponds in Israel had hourly primary productivity rates of 4.1 to 11.5 mg C/mg chlorophyll $\underline{a}$, with an average of 7.6. Assuming that 1 mole of oxygen is released in photosynthesis for every gram atomic weight of carbon fixed, the values may be converted to O_2 by multiplying them by 32/12. Thus, an average of 20.3 mg O_2 was produced each hour by each mg of chlorophyll $\underline{a}$. If the chlorophyll $\underline{a}$ concentration was 100 µg/l, each liter contained 0.1 mg of chlorophyll $\underline{a}$, and 2.03 mg of oxygen were produced. Over a 12-h period, 24.4 mg/l of dissolved oxygen were produced.

An equation for predicting the change in dissolved oxygen during a daily photoperiod was developed by Romaire and Boyd (1979). We measured dissolved oxygen concentrations at dawn and dusk and then added the estimated fish respiration to the change in dissolved oxygen concentration. Data on dissolved oxygen concentration at dawn, solar radiation, and either chlorophyll $\underline{a}$ concentration or Secchi disk visibility were used as independent variables in multiple regression equations for predicting the daytime dissolved oxygen change. Fish respiration may be subtracted from the predicted daytime change in dissolved oxygen to make the equation applicable to any fish culture system. This approach is general provided one accepts the premises that diffusion and benthic respiration are constants. The statistical models were as follows:

$$DO_{change} = b_0 + (b_1)(Rad) + (b_2)(Rad)^2 + (b_3)(Ch_a) + (b_4)(Ch_a)^2 + (b_5)(Sat) +$$
$$(b_6)(Sat)^2 + (b_{13})(Rad)(Ch_a) + (b_{35})(Ch_a)(Sat) \qquad (5.4)$$

$$DO_{change} = b_0 + (b_1)(Rad) + (b_2)(Rad)^2 + (b_3)(Sd) + (b_4)(Sd)^2 + (b_5)(Sat) +$$
$$(b_6)(Sat)^2 + (b_{13})(Rad)(Sd) + (b_{35})(Sd)(Sat) \qquad (5.5)$$

where DO_{change} = dissolved oxygen change (mg/1 per day) adjusted for fish respiration; b_0 = intercept; b_1, ..., b_{35} = partial regression coefficients; Rad = solar radiation in langleys/day (range: 60-600 langleys/day); Ch_a = chlorophyll a in μg/1 (range: 8-280 μg/1); Sat = percentage dissolved oxygen saturation at dawn (range: 10-115%); Sd = Secchi disk visibility in cm (range: 14-180 cm). The coefficients of multiple determination (R) were 0.91 for Equation 5.4 and 0.89 for Equation 5.5. The partial regression coefficients (b_i) for both equations are given in Table 5.6. In view of the complexity of pond ecosystems and the difficulty in obtaining highly precise estimates for the variables of interest, these equations are considered acceptable for predictive purposes.

Data in Table 5.7 are estimates of daily dissolved oxygen changes in ponds with different concentrations of chlorophyll a and different light regimes.

In order to simulate dissolved oxygen concentrations at dawn and dusk, Equation 5.5 was coupled with the nighttime dissolved oxygen equation (Equation 5.3). Results of simulations were used to determine the number of consecutive days necessary for dissolved oxygen concentrations to decline to 2 mg/1 in ponds for various solar radiation values and Secchi disk visibilities (Table 5.8). Results clearly show that the combination of abundant plankton (as estimated by Secchi disk visibility) and low solar radiation has adverse effects on oxygen regimes in fish ponds.

5.8   ALGAL DIE-OFFS

Die-offs of phytoplankton and related fish kills are common in fish ponds (Swingle, 1968; Abeliovich, 1969; Boyd et al., 1975) and other small, eutrophic bodies of water (Barica, 1975a). Die-offs are characterized by sudden death of all or a great portion of the phytoplankton followed by rapid decomposition of

TABLE 5.6
Partial regression coefficients for Equations 5.4 and 5.5 (see text).

Coefficient	Equation 5.4	Equation 5.5
b_0	- 3.240	4.780
b_1	0.0124	0.0211
b_2	- 0.0000120	- 0.0000160
b_3	0.0582	- 0.0853
b_4	- 0.000144	0.000192
b_5	0.0858	- 0.0084
b_6	- 0.000651	- 0.000325
b_{13}	0.0000520	- 0.0000520
b_{35}	- 0.000355	0.000462

TABLE 5.7
Daily changes in dissolved oxygen concentrations (mg/1) in ponds with different chlorophyll a concentrations and solar radiation. Values are approximate because they were estimated from Fig. 1 of Romaire and Boyd (1979).

Chlorophyll a (µg/1)	Solar radiation (langleys/day)				
	100	200	300	400	500
20	0.8	1.4	2.3	2.7	2.9
60	2.1	3.4	4.3	5.1	5.5
100	3.3	4.8	5.9	6.9	7.5
140	4.2	6.0	7.3	8.5	9.3

the dead algae. Dissolved oxygen concentrations will decline drastically because of low rates of photosynthesis and high rates of decay, and oxygen depletion may result.

Abeliovich and Shilo (1972) reported that photooxidative death in laboratory cultures of Anacystis nidulans was induced at both high (35°C) and low temperatures (4-15°C) under conditions of high pH, high oxygen concentration, carbon dioxide depletion, and high light intensity. When carbon dioxide was added to the medium, photooxidative death was prevented at high temperature, indicating the action of enzymes in the process. The enzyme superoxide dismutase protects aerobic organsims against toxic effects of oxygen. Abeliovich et al. (1974) found that photo-

TABLE 5.8

Number of consecutive days (simulated) necessary for dissolved oxygen concentrations to decline to 2.0 mg/l in ponds with varying amounts of solar radiation and Secchi disk visibilities[a] (Romaire and Boyd, 1979).

Secchi disk visibility (cm)	Solar radiation (langleys/day)					
	50	100	150	200	300	400
30	0	0	0	0	0	0
40	1	1	1	1	1	1
50	1	1	1	1	1	3
60	1	1	1	1	2	4
70	1	1	1	1	2	5
80	1	1	1	2	3	6

[a]Assumptions: initial dissolved oxygen at dusk was 10.0 mg/l, pond was 1 m deep, 2,240 kg/ha of channel catfish, and water temperature of 30°C at dusk and 28°C at dawn.

oxidative death in cultures of A. nidulans corresponded to a decline in superoxide dismutase activity. These findings suggest that die-offs of natural algal blooms are related to photooxidation. Boyd et al. (1978b) reported that die-offs of blue-green algae can be expected when buoyant blue-green algae form surface scums during calm, clear, warm weather. Conditions in surface scums are similar to those occurring in cultures where photooxidative death was observed.

There has been considerable interest in die-offs of phytoplankton in prairie pothole lakes in Canada and the effects of these die-offs on fish farming. Barica (1975b) noted that mid summer collapses of Aphanizomenon flos-aquae take place more or less regularly each year. Following a mild winter, he also noted collapses of blooms of diatoms (Cyclotella, Nitzschia, and Synedra), green algae (Coccomyxa, Chlamydomonas, and Lauterborniella) and of blooms of other blue-green algae (Microcystis, Anabaena, and Merismopedia). According to Barica, the algae quickly reached their exponential phase of growth with chlorophyll a values of 100-200 µg/l, dissolved oxygen concentrations above 15 mg/l, and Secchi disk visibilities of 20-40 cm. At this time, inorganic phosphorus and ammonia concentrations were very low. Within a few days, the whole mass of algae started sinking, resulting in clearing of surface waters. The algal mass began to decay resulting in a decrease in oxygen concentration and an increase in ammonia and inorganic phosphorus levels. Periods of oxygen depletion lasted for 1-2 weeks. Barica (1975b) also noted a great increase in ammonia and inorganic phosphorus in anaerobic bottom waters before the bloom collapsed. No cause of the die-offs was identified, but possible causes were listed as: cyanophage attack, autodestruction by toxins (alleopathy), damage to gas vacuoles, upwelling of reductive lake sediments by wind action, inadequate light, nutrient deficiency, or a combination of two or more of these factors.

Barica (1975a) reported that fish kills only occurred in prairie pothole lakes with specific conductances of 800-2,000 μmho/cm, where chlorophyll a concentrations exceeded 100 μg/l. He observed: when summer chlorophyll a concentrations were below 100 μg/l, Secchi disk visibilities were 40 cm or greater, and dissolved oxygen ranged from 6-15 mg/l, lakes could be safely used for fish culture. Further, lakes having NH_3-N concentrations above 1 mg/l and minimum dissolved oxygen concentrations below 1 mg/l in winter should not be used for fish farming.

Events surrounding an almost complete die-off of Anabaena variabilis in a catfish pond at Auburn, Alabama, were documented by Boyd et al. (1975). The pond contained a bloom of A. variabilis that had been uniformly dense throughout the water column during windy days in March and April, 1974. In late April, a succession of clear, calm days resulted in a surface scum on 29 April. On the afternoon of 29 April, algae in the scum began to deteriorate and blotches of blue-green substances were seen in a few places on the pond surface. Algae had a bleached appearance and in some areas, the water was brown with dead algae. The entire pond surface appeared brown on 30 April, and microscopic examination revealed that filaments of Anabaena were breaking up and turning yellow-green or brown. Live phytoplankters were scarce in water samples taken between 30 April and 5 May (Fig. 5.8). During this period, the water was turbid with decaying algae and photosynthesis was essentially nil. A rapid increase in phytoplankton abundance occurred between 5 May and 8 May, but the new phytoplankton community consisted of green algae rather than blue-green algae.

Dissolved oxygen concentrations quickly dropped to 0 mg/l following the die-off of the Anabaena bloom (Fig. 5.9). While dissolved oxygen values were low, total ammonia nitrogen and carbon dioxide concentrations increased to peak levels of 2 and 20 mg/l, respectively. The pH of surface waters had been above 9 during daytime before the die-off, but daytime pH values were between 6 and 7 while carbon dioxide was abundant. Once algal density began to increase, dissolved oxygen concentrations and pH increased and carbon dioxide and ammonia levels declined. The similarity between the shapes of the phytoplankton abundance and dissolved oxygen concentration curves (Figs. 5.8 and 5.9) is particularly impressive. Emergency measures, aeration and release of oxygenated water into the pond, prevented massive mortality of fish.

All phytoplankton die-offs are not as dramatic as the one described by Boyd

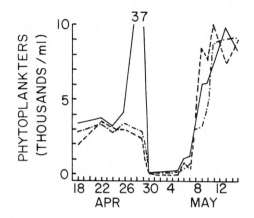

Fig. 5.8. Abundance of phytoplankton in a fish pond before and after a phytoplankton die-off (Boyd et al., 1975). Solid line = surface; dashes = 1 m depth; dots and dashes = 2 m depth.

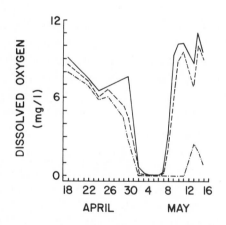

Fig. 5.9. Dissolved oxygen concentrations in a fish pond before and after a phytoplankton die-off (Boyd et al., 1975). Solid line = surface; dashes = 1 m depth; dots and dashes = 2 m depth.

et al. (1975). For example, die-offs of A. variabilis which occurred on 2 May 1975, in two other ponds at Auburn, Alabama, were described by Boyd et al. (1978b). The two die-offs occurred after surface scums of Anabaena formed during calm, clear, warm weather — as in the earlier case study. However, the two die-offs in 1975 did not result in complete mortality of the phytoplankton bloom and

dissolved oxygen depletion was not as severe as in the earlier study; minimum
concentrations at the surface were 3.5 and 5 mg/l.

Phytoplankton blooms were examined frequently during the springs of 1974, 1975,
and 1976 in ponds at Auburn University (Boyd et al. 1978b). Heavy blooms (1,000
individuals/ml or more) of blue-green algae were present in 34.8% of ponds examined in 1974, 31.2% in 1975, and 25.0% in 1976. Die-offs were observed in most
ponds with heavy blooms of blue-green algae. However, only in five instances,
two in 1974, two in 1975, and one in 1976, did dissolved oxygen concentrations
drop below 1 mg/l following die-offs. All die-offs occurred on warm, clear,
calm days when heavy scums of blue-green algae formed on the surface. Fortunately
depressions of dissolved oxygen concentrations after die-offs were seldom great
enough to kill fish.

Dobbins and Boyd (1976) also noted that die-offs of macrophytic algae may
occur in fish ponds. Die-offs of dense mats of _Spirogyra_ occurred in four of 20
ponds in a fertilization experiment. All die-offs followed a similar pattern.
Mats of _Spirogyra_ growing on pond bottoms formed gas bubbles and floated to the
surface. Filaments of _Spirogyra_ were initially bright green and appeared healthy.
After 2 or 3 days at the surface, filaments yellowed, died, and began to decay.
Dissolved oxygen concentrations reached minimum values of 1 to 3 mg/l in ponds
1 to 3 days after die-offs.

Sudden increases in turbidity may also result in mortality of underwater weeds
and oxygen depletion. I have seen dissolved oxygen depletion occur in ponds after
silt-laden runoff made waters turbid and killed underwater weed communities.
Similar oxygen depletions may result from herbicide treatment of ponds.

5.9 OVERTURNS

I have already mentioned that abundant plankton in fish ponds results in shallow
thermal stratification. Plankters have a short life span, hence there is a steady
rain of dead plankton into the hypolimnion. Oxygen is soon depleted and waters
of the hypolimnion contain high concentrations of reduced substances, e. g.,
ferrous iron and organic matter, that have a high oxygen demand. The condition
described above is not usually detrimental to fish populations. However, if
thermal stratification is disrupted, dilution of oxygenated water with anaerobic
water from the hypolimnion and high rates of oxygen removal by reduced substances
can lead to oxygen depletion. Fish kills following overturns (thermal destratification) are commonly encountered, but this problem has apparently received
little study.

According to Swingle (1968), there are several causes of overturns. A sharp
drop in air temperature may chill surface water, causing it to sink and force
hypolimnetic water to the surface. This phenomenon is most likely to occur in
late summer or early fall when the first cold air masses move southward. Upwelling

may also result from heavy winds that blow the surface water towards the opposite bank, pulling hypolimnetic waters to the surface on the windward side. Overturns may follow cold rains that cool surface waters, causing them to sink and displace hypolimnetic water. Heavy, cold rains on watersheds may chill stream water entering ponds; density currents of cold water flow along pond bottoms, causing upwelling of hypolimnetic waters.

5.10   IDENTIFICATION OF OXYGEN PROBLEMS

Much has already been said about the necessity of monitoring oxygen concentrations in ponds for intensive fish culture. Observations of the appearance of water and the behavior of fish may alert fish farmers to oxygen problems when equipment for measuring oxygen is not available. When algal scums suddenly change from a green to a brown or gray color, phytoplankton die-offs should be suspected. Decaying algal scums are usually apparent on pond surfaces after die-offs. Large numbers of fish at the surface, often gasping for air, suggest oxygen depletion.

Dendy (1965) noted that recently cut surfaces of certain light-colored woods were noticeably stained upon exposure for 30-45 minutes or less to water containing about 0.1-0.2 mg/l of dissolved oxygen. This resulted from the reaction of tannin in the wood with ferrous iron in anaerobic water. The best woods for detecting oxygen depletion were American chestnut, Chinese chestnut, red oak, and white oak. Dendy also found black locust, black walnut, cherry, dogwood, larch, mahogany, redwood, and sycamore to be suitable for detecting dissolved oxygen depletion.

REFERENCES

Abeliovich, A., 1969. Water blooms of blue-green algae and oxygen regime in fish ponds. Verh. Int. Verein. Limnol, 17: 594-601.
Aveliovich, A. and Shilo, M., 1972. Photo-oxidative death in blue-green algae. J. Bacteriol., 111: 682-689.
Abeliovich, A., Kellenberg, D., and Shilo, M., 1974. Effect of photooxidative conditions on levels of superoxide dimutase in Anacystis nidulans. Photoochem. Photobiol., 19: 379-382.
Barica, J., 1975a. Collapse of algal blooms in prairie pothole lakes: their mechanism and ecological impact. Verh. Internat. Verein. Limnol., 19: 606-615.
Barica, J., 1975b. Summerkill risk in prairie ponds and possibilities of its prediction. J. Fish. Res. Bd. Canada, 32: 1283-1288.
Beasley, P. G., 1963. The penetration of light and the concentration of dissolved oxygen in fertilized pond waters infested with Microcystis. Proc. Annual Conf. Southeast. Assoc. Game and Fish Comm., 17: 222-226.
Boyd, C. E., 1973. Summer algal communities and primary productivity in fish ponds. Hydrobiologia, 41: 357-390.
Boyd, C. E., Prather, E. E., and Parks, R. W., 1975. Sudden mortality of a massive phytoplankton bloom. Weed Sci., 23: 61-67.
Boyd, C. E., Romaire, R. P., and Johnston, E., 1978a. Predicting early morning dissolved oxygen concentrations in channel catfish ponds. Trans. Amer. Fish. Soc., 107: 484-492.

Boyd, C. E., Davis, J. A., and Johnston, E., 1978b. Die-offs of the blue-green alga, Anabaena variabilis, in fish ponds. Hydrobiologia, 61: 129-133.

Boyd, C. E., Steeby, J. A., and McCoy, E. W., 1979a. Frequency of low dissolved oxygen concentrations in ponds for commercial culture of channel catfish. Proc. Annual Conf. Southeast. Assoc. Fish and Wildl. Agencies, 33: 591-599.

Boyd, C. E., Romaire, R. P., and Johnston, E., 1979b. Water quality in channel catfish production ponds. J. Environ. Qual., 8: 423-429.

Dendy, J. S., 1965. Use of woods to determine the depths of oxygen distribution in ponds. Prog. Fish-Cult., 27: 75-78.

Dobbins, D. A. and Boyd, C. E., 1976. Phosphorus and potassium fertilization of sunfish ponds. Trans. Amer. Fish. Soc., 105: 536-540.

Halverson, C. J., Jensen, J. W., and Boyd, C. E., 1980. Water quality in standing-water ponds for winter production of rainbow trout in Alabama. Trans. Amer. Fish. Soc., 109: 310-313.

Haney, P. D., 1954. Theoretical principles of aeration. J. Amer. Water Works Assoc., 46: 353-376.

Harris, G. P., 1973. Diel and annual cycles of net plankton photosynthesis in Lake Ontario. J. Fish. Res. Bd. Canada, 30: 1779-1787.

Hepher, B., 1962. Primary production in fish ponds and its application to fertilization experiments. Limnol. Oceanogr., 7: 131-135.

Hill, T. K., Chesness, J. L., and Brown, E. E., 1972. Utilization of rainbow trout, Salmo gairdneri Richardson, in a double-crop fish culture system in south Georgia. Proc. Annual Conf. Southeast. Assoc. Game and Fish Comm., 26: 368-376.

Knight, R. S., 1965. Performance of a Cage Rotor in an Oxidation Ditch. M. S. thesis, Iowa State University, Ames, Iowa, 83 pp.

Mezainis, V. E., 1977. Metabolic Rates of Pond Ecosystems under Intensive Catfish Cultivation. M. S. thesis, Auburn University, Auburn, Alabama, 107 pp.

Muller-Feuga, A., Petit, A., and Sabbaut, J. J., 1978. The influence of temperature and wet weight on the oxygen demand of rainbow trout (Salmo gairdneri R.) in fresh water. Aquaculture, 14: 355-363.

Romaire, R. P. and Boyd, C. E., 1978. Predicting nighttime oxygen depletion in catfish ponds. Auburn University Agricultural Experiment Station, Auburn, Alabama, Bulletin 505, 32 pp.

Romaire, R. P. and Boyd, C. E., 1979. Effects of solar radiation on the dynamics of dissolved oxygen in channel catfish ponds. Trans. Amer. Fish. Soc., 108: 473-478.

Romaire, R. P., Boyd, C. E., and Collis, W. J., 1978. Predicting nighttime dissolved oxygen decline in ponds used for tilapia culture. Trans. Amer. Fish. Soc., 107: 804-808.

Schroeder, G. L., 1974. Use of fluid cowshed manure in fish ponds. Bamidgeh, 26: 84-96.

Schroeder, G. L., 1975. Nighttime material balance for oxygen in fish ponds receiving organic wastes. Bamidgeh, 27: 65-74.

Swingle, H. S., 1968. Fish kills caused by phytoplankton blooms and their prevention. Proc. World Symposium on Warm-Water Pond Fish Culture, FAO United Nations, Fish. Rep. No. 44, 5: 407-411.

Verduin, J., 1957. Daytime variations in phytoplankton photosynthesis. Limnol. Oceanogr., 2: 333-336.

Welch, H. E., 1968. Use of modified diurnal curves for the measurement of metabolism in standing water. Limnol. Oceanogr., 13: 679-687.

Chapter 6

FEEDING

6.1 INTRODUCTION

A wide variety of feedstuffs are employed in fish culture. These feeds range
in quality from rations that supply all of the nutrient requirements of fish to
materials such as agricultural waste, industrial by-products, leaves, and grasses
that merely supplement natural food supplies. The conversion of feed to fish,
termed the pond conversion value or S-value by Swingle (1968), is calculated as
follows:

$$S = \text{Feed applied} \div \text{Net production} \tag{6.1}$$

Pond conversion values of 2.0 or less are commonly achieved with high quality
feeds, but S-values become higher as food quality decreases. In ponds where
feeding is practiced, uneaten feed and metabolic waste represent nutrient enrichment, so feeding leads to increased plankton production. Wastes from feeding
and plankton exert an oxygen demand, and nitrogenous materials resulting from
feeding accumulate in pond waters. Therefore, as feeding rates increase in ponds,
water quality becomes poorer and finally limits the production of fish.

6.2 FEEDING AND FISH PRODUCTION

Swingle (1968) pointed out that the greatest production of fish in fertilized
ponds was obtained for those species with the shortest food chains. Maximum
annual production obtained in fertilized ponds at Auburn University for species
with different feeding habits were as follows:

Species	Feeding habit	Production (kg/ha)
Micropterus salmoides	picivorous	196
Ictalurus punctatus	insectivorous	370
Lepomis macrochirus	insectivorous	560
Tilapia mossambica	plankton-feeder	1,612

Feeding may be used to increase production above that possible in fertilized
ponds. Prather (1956) reported that the production of golden shiners (Notemigonus
chrysoleucas) in seven fertilized ponds ranged from 428 to 644 kg/ha with an
average of 453 kg/ha. The combination of fertilization plus feeding at 22.4 kg/ha
per day increased the average production in three ponds to 791 kg/ha. The production of fathead minnows (Pimephales promelas) was raised from 166 to 1,330

kg/ha through the use of fertilizer and feed instead of fertilizer alone (Prather et al., 1953). Pond conversion values for fathead minnows were 2.3.-3.8.

Maximum annual production of Java tilapia (Tilapia mossambica) in ponds receiving applications of feeds and fertilizer was given as 13,340-17,920 kg/ha in Thailand, 1,190-2,800 kg/ha in Malaysia, and 3,289 kg/ha in Taiwan (Swingle, 1960). In ponds at Auburn University, the Java tilapia produced 1,660 kg/ha in fertilized ponds and 2,010-4,920 kg/ha with fertilization and feeding (Swingle, 1960). Pond conversion values for Java tilapia ranged from 0.4 to 1.1. The low S-values resulted because much of the measured fish production resulted from natural fish food organisms, which were abundant in ponds receiving feeds and fertilizers. The Nile tilapia (T. nilotica) produced 2,670-4,483 kg/ha with the combination of fertilization and feeding. Pond conversion values ranged from 0.7 to 1.4. All tilapia growth trials conducted by Swingle (1960) were for 191 days or less, so greater annual production could be achieved in tropical climates.

Production of channel catfish (Ictalurus punctatus) in fertilized ponds is normally less than 400 kg/ha (Swingle, 1968). By using high protein, pelleted feeds, channel catfish production may be easily increased to 3,000-4,000 kg/ha (Prather and Lovell, 1971, 1973). The S-values in feeding experiments with channel catfish usually ranged from 1.2 to 2.0 (Prather and Lovell, 1971; Lovell et al., 1974). The S-values for channel catfish are much higher than those for tilapia because channel catfish utilize relatively little of the natural food in ponds. Chuapoehuk (1977) applied pelleted feed for channel catfish in three ponds, and in three other ponds he applied the same amount of feed in finely pulverized form so that the catfish could not eat it. Fish production in ponds receiving the pulverized feed was only 8.3% of that obtained where pelleted feed was used.

Swingle (1960) reported that common carp (Cyprinus carpio) production ranged from 302 to 504 kg/ha in fertilized ponds. The combination of feeding plus fertilization increased carp production to 1,120-1,460 kg/ha. The S-values for carp ranged from 2.2 to 2.6.

The combination of several species (polyculture) results in higher yields of fish than possible with one species (monoculture) because food organisms not consumed by one species may be used by another species. If the proper species combinations are selected, there will be little competition between the polyculture species. For example, in channel catfish ponds where feeds are applied, species that utilize natural food organisms but not pelleted feed will increase total fish production. Data presented by Dunseth and Smitherman (1977) clearly demonstrate that polycultures of channel catfish, tilapia (Tilapia aurea), grass carp (Ctenopharyngodon idellus), and silver carp (Hypophthalmichthys molitrix) will increase fish production above that achieved with channel catfish alone. Further, none of the combinations of species greatly affected production of channel catfish, the primary culture species. Moav et al. (1977) reported a total yield of 6,282 kg/ha of common carp, silver carp, grass carp, and tilapia in 126 days in ponds receiving pelleted, high protein feed. The pond conversion value was 2.46.

The data presented above represent only a minute sample of the literature on fish production in ponds receiving feeds. However, the material presented clearly demonstrates that feeding or feeding plus fertilization can increase fish production over that possible with fertilization alone. The data presented above were for stagnant-water ponds without continuous aeration. The combination of feeding plus aeration (see Chapter 7) may be used to further increase fish production.

There is a large body of information on the nutritional requirements of fish and on the preparation and composition of fish feeds. Practical papers on feeding practices abound. The purpose here is to discuss the relationships between fish feeding and water quality, so I will not stray into other areas.

6.3   FATE OF NUTRIENTS IN FEEDS

Although S-values (Equation 6.1) are suitable for economic purposes, they are misleading in considerations of water quality. A pond stocked with channel catfish might have a net production of 4,000 kg/ha resulting from 6,000 kg/ha of total feed applied; S = 6,000 ÷ 4,000 = 1.5. Feeds are usually dry (90-95% dry matter) while fish contain only 20 to 25% dry matter (Boyd, 1974). Assuming 95% and 25% dry matter for feed and fish in the preceding example, 5,700 kg/ha of dry feed resulted in 1,000 kg/ha of dry fish; S = 5,700 ÷ 1,000 = 5.7. But everyone knows that you buy dry feed and sell wet fish, and the S-value for dry weight may appear silly. However, consider that 5,700 kg/ha of substance was applied to the pond in feed and only 1,000 kg/ha of substance was removed from the pond in fish. Thus, 4,700 kg/ha of substance (dry weight) reached the water in metabolic and digestive waste from fish — assuming all of the feed was consumed. In our example 4.7 kg of wastes capable of enriching the pond resulted from each kilogram of fish produced. This waste included organic compounds that contributed directly to oxygen demand and mineral nutrients that indirectly contributed to oxygen demand by increasing phytoplankton growth.

To further illustrate why fish feeding pollutes pond waters, I will prepare a materials budget with fish production data from Lovell et al. (1974). The average net production of channel catfish was 3,370 kg/ha in ponds receiving 4,450 kg/ha of feed (S = 1.32). The feed was approximately 95% dry matter, and fish were about 25% dry matter. Hence, 4,228 kg/ha of dry matter in feed produced 842 kg/ha of dry matter in fish. Therefore, 3,386 kg/ha of dry matter reached the ponds as metabolic waste or uneaten feed. Much of the waste was in the form of carbon dioxide, but considerable nitrogen and phosphorus were included. The feed contained 5.76% nitrogen and 1.26% phosphorus on a dry weight basis and channel catfish had average nitrogen and phosphorus contents of 11.17% and 4.11%,

respectively. Therefore, 244 kg/ha of nitrogen and 53 kg/ha of phosphorus were
applied to ponds in feed, but only 94 kg/ha of nitrogen and 35 kg/ha of phosphorus
were contained in the net production at fish harvest. The nitrogen and phosphorus
contributions to ponds in wastes were 150 and 18 kg/ha, respectively. This amount
of phosphorus is equivalent to 41.2 kg/ha of P_2O_5 and is roughly equal to half of
the amount of phosphorus fertilizer added to sunfish-bass ponds for maximum fish
production (Boyd and Snow, 1975). Nitrogen added in wastes is nearly twice that
added in fertilizers for maximum production of sunfish and bass. Nutrients reach
the waters of ponds that receive feed on a continuous basis and are no doubt more
effective in promoting plankton growth than nutrients from fertilizers applied at
2- to 4-week intervals.

Boyd (1973) reported a mean rate of carbon fixation by photosynthesis of 2.55
g/m^2 of carbon per day during the growing season in four channel catfish ponds
that received an average of 2,800 kg/ha of feed. Assuming that dry phytoplankton
is 48% carbon (Boyd and Lawrence, 1966), 5.32 g/m^2 of dry matter were produced
daily by photosynthesis. This is 53 kg/ha per day or 9,540 kg/ha in a 180-day
growing season. The COD of phytoplankton averaged 1.29 kg of oxygen/kg dry weight,
so the COD production by phytoplankton in the four ponds averaged 12,300 kg/ha.
Thus, 1 kg of feed resulted in an average of 4.4 kg of COD in phytoplankton. The
feed had a COD of 1.14 kg of oxygen/kg, so the COD input in feed was 3,192 kg/ha.
Channel catfish had a COD of 1.4 kg of oxygen/kg dry weight. The average net
production of fish was 2,100 kg/ha (2,100 X 0.25 = 525 kg/ha dry weight). Thus,
the COD of the net fish production was 735 kg/ha. The difference in COD of feed
and fish, 3,192 kg/ha - 735 kg/ha = 2,457 kg/ha, was the approximate COD of
wastes — including oxygen used in oxidation of feed by fish for energy. The
total COD resulting from feeding may be roughly estimated as the sum of the COD
of phytoplankton and waste: 12,300 kg/ha + 2,457 kg/ha = 14,757 kg/ha. This
comes to 5.3 kg of COD for each kilogram of live fish. Notice that the COD of
phytoplankton was roughly 5 times greater than the COD of waste. The waste is,
nevertheless, responsible for the large production of COD in channel catfish ponds
because the inorganic nutrients from the waste stimulate photosynthesis. More
thorough COD budgets for fish culture systems are badly needed.

6.4   WATER QUALITY AND FEEDING RATES

6.4.1 Temporal changes

The following comments on feeding rates and water quality are based on studies
of channel catfish. The principles advanced are general and will hold for other
culture systems.

Ponds are normally stocked with small fish and feeds are applied daily at a
certain percentage of the weight of fish in ponds. Feeding rates are adjusted

periodically for weight gains by fish. For example, channel catfish are usually fed at 3-4% of body weight per day during the first few weeks. Later in the growing season feeding rates are often lowered to 2% of body weight. The feeding rates are usually adjusted at 2-week intervals for weight gain as illustrated in Table 6.1 with data from Prather and Lovell (1971). Some fish culturists sample fish by seining to estimate weight gain, but the usual procedure in fish farming is to assume a pond conversion value (based on past experience) and estimate fish standing crops from the amount of feed that has been applied. This procedure is usually just as reliable but less laborious than sampling. Obviously, feeding rates increase with time because standing crops of fish increase.

Boyd (1974) monitored changes in water quality in nine ponds stocked with channel catfish where feeding rates were gradually increased to a maximum of 45 kg/ha per day. A total of 4,480 kg/ha of feed was applied to each pond. Concentrations of nitrate, total ammonia nitrogen, organic nitrogen, filtrable ortho-phosphate, total phosphorus, COD, standard BOD, and chlorophyll $\underline{a}$ gradually increased as feeding rates increased. Maximum concentrations of these variables occurred in late August when both water temperature and feeding rates were high. Concentrations of most of the variables declined slightly in September, when waters began to cool. Average concentrations of water quality variables for an early June and a mid-August sampling date are presented in Table 6.2. Dissolved oxygen concentrations were not routinely measured in the ponds, but no oxygen depletions occurred.

A more thorough examination of water quality in channel catfish ponds was conducted by Boyd et al. (1979a). Five ponds with surface areas of 0.89-8.9 ha and average depths of 1.5-2 m were stocked with 7,400 fingerling channel catfish per hectare in March 1978. Fish were fed a commercial, floating-pellet feed (35% crude protein), usually at 3% of body weight per day, 6 days per week. Average daily feeding rates for different time intervals are presented in Table 6.3. Feeding rates were reduced in September to prevent fish from exceeding ideal marketable size.

Water temperatures gradually increased until late May and then remained relatively constant until late September, after which they gradually decreased (Fig. 6.1). Secchi disk visibility, chlorophyll $\underline{a}$ concentration, and numbers of phytoplankton generally increased as the growing season progressed. Data for mid-May and mid-September are presented in Table 6.4. Genera of phytoplankton comprising >10% of the phytoplankton community on a particular date in a given pond included: Anabaena, Ankistrodesmus, Closterium, Coelastrum, Cosmarium, Euastrum, Microcystis, Oocystis, Oscillatoria, Peridinium, Rhaphidiopsis, Scenedesmus, Schroederia, Selenastrum, Sphaerocystis, and Staurastrum. This list is similar to the list of algal genera observed in fertilized ponds (see Chapter 3). The

TABLE 6.1

Data of growth of channel catfish and feeding rates during a single growing season.

Period	Weight of fish at beginning of period (kg/ha)	Feed applied per day during period (kg/ha)
11 Mar-12 Apr	45	1.1
13 Apr-30 Apr	72	2.8
1 May-20 May	111	5.6
21 May-10 Jun	197	8.4
11 Jun- 2 Jul	333	17.9
3 Jul- 5 Aug	636	28.0
6 Aug-30 Sep	1,368	33.6
1 Oct- 4 Nov	2,816	44.8

TABLE 6.2

Average concentrations of selected water quality variables in nine channel catfish ponds in June when the feeding rate was 8.4 kg/ha per day and in August when the feeding rate was 33.6 kg/ha per day.

Variable	Concentration (mg/1)	
	June	August
Nitrate-nitrogen	0.035	0.060
Total ammonia nitrogen	0.12	0.22
Organic nitrogen	1.60	1.21
Filtrable orthophosphate (as P)	0.005	0.008
Total phosphorus	0.040	0.075
Chemical oxygen demand	15.1	36.5
Biological oxygen demand	2.2	6.2
Chlorophyll a	0.012[a]	0.050[a]

[a] 12 and 50 µg/1.

percentage of the phytoplankton communities comprised of blue-green algae increased from spring to fall; compare May and September (Table 6.4).

Total ammonia nitrogen increased to concentrations in excess of 1 mg/1 by late

TABLE 6.3

Average daily feeding rates for five channel catfish ponds at Auburn, Alabama. Feed was applied six days per week.

Period	Feed applied (kg/ha per day)	Period	Feed applied (kg/ha per day)
6 Mar-18 Apr	3.7	11 Jul-24 Jul	41.3
9 Apr- 2 May	8.8	25 Jul- 7 Aug	41.6
3 May-15 May	5.4	8 Aug-21 Aug	61.1
16 May-28 May	13.1	22 Aug- 5 Sep	70.9
29 May-11 Jun	20.2	6 Sep-18 Sep	47.5
12 Jun-26 Jun	28.2	19 Sep- 2 Oct	30.0
27 Jun-10 Jul	40.5	3 Oct-31 Oct	20.1

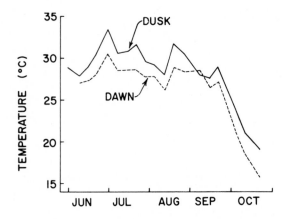

Fig. 6.1. Water temperatures at dawn and dusk in fish ponds at Auburn, Alabama (Boyd et al., 1979a).

summer (Table 6.4). Afternoon pH values were usually between 8.5 and 9.5 and early morning pH values were between 6.5 and 7.5. Assuming 30°C, 1 mg/l of total ammonia nitrogen, pH 7 in the morning, and pH 9 in the afternoon, un-ionized ammonia concentrations ranged between 0.01 and 0.45 mg/l (as N) during a 24-h period in late summer and early fall. The afternoon concentrations were not high enough to be lethal, but they were higher than concentrations that have been reported to cause reduction in growth (see Chapter 2). Filtrable orthophosphate

TABLE 6.4

Average concentrations of water quality variables on mid-May and mid-September sampling dates in five channel catfish ponds. See text for stocking and feeding rates.

Variable	May	September
Chlorophyll a (μg/l)	10	170
Secchi disk visibility (cm)	160	25
Blue-green algae (% of total)	18	95
Total phytoplankton (log No./ml)	3.2	5.0
Total ammonia nitrogen (mg/l)	0.12	0.51
Nitrate (mg/l as N)	0.03	0.09
Nitrite (μg/l as N)	10	4.0
Carbon dioxide (mg/l)	1.0	7.7
Chemical oxygen demand (mg/l)	16	77
Filtrable orthophosphate (μg/l as P)	3.0	2.5
Total phosphorus (mg/l)	0.05	0.18

concentrations were always quite low; average values never exceeded 0.01 mg/l as P on a given date. Total phosphorus concentrations increased as the season progressed, but averages never exceeded 0.2 mg/l.

Concentrations of carbon dioxide increased with time (Table 6.4). During the summer carbon dioxide averaged >4 mg/l in the early morning, and values for individual ponds were >10 mg/l. Later in the day, carbon dioxide usually declined below a measurable concentration because of its removal by plants. Carbon dioxide was not directly toxic to fish, but high concentrations were undesirable when dissolved oxygen levels were low.

The COD of pond waters increased during the growing season (Table 6.4). Average values in late summer were above 50 mg/l, and individual ponds had COD values as high as 100 mg/l.

Dissolved oxygen concentrations exhibited strong vertical stratification during summer in all ponds. The depths of 0 mg/l dissolved oxygen ranged from 1.0 to 2.0 m in all ponds.

Dissolved oxygen concentrations in the surface waters (upper 50 cm) were generally above saturation at dusk. Concentrations of oxygen at dawn were much lower than concentrations at dusk (Fig. 6.2). During August and much of September, average dissolved oxygen concentrations at dawn were around 2 mg/l, and individual ponds had even lower concentrations on some dates. Problems with low dissolved oxygen occurred when water temperatures were above 26°C and feeding rates were

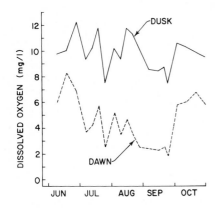

Fig. 6.2. Average dissolved oxygen concentrations at dawn and dusk in five channel catfish ponds at Auburn, Alabama (Boyd et al., 1979a).

high (Tables 6.3 and 6.4; Fig. 6.2). Emergency aeration was occasionally necessary to prevent fish mortality in oxygen-depleted ponds.

Examination of data presented above reveals that water quality gradually de-
teriorated as the season progressed. Simple linear correlations were determined
between daily feeding rates on each sampling date (X) and measured variables (Y)
on those dates. Linear correlations were also obtained for total feed applied
before a particular sampling date (X) and measured variables (Y). The highest
correlation coefficients (r) were always realized using the total feed applied
before a given date as the X-variable. This was expected because substances
originating from metabolic and digestive wastes are related to both the feed
applied on a particular day and the accumulation of wastes from previous days.
Highly significant correlations (P < 0.01) were for regressions between feeding
rates and COD, total phosphorus, Secchi disk visibility (negative r), percentage
blue-green algae, dissolved oxygen at dawn (negative r), phytoplankton abundance,
and chlorophyll a.

The five ponds were stocked and managed in almost identical manner, but there
were large differences in the highest and lowest concentrations of each variable
on the different sampling dates. This variation is illustrated by presenting the
minimum and maximum coefficients of variation (CV) for individual sampling dates:

Variable	CV (%)
Blue-green algae (%)	1.2-111.0
$\log_{10}$ phytoplankton numbers	1.5- 12.8
Dissolved oxygen at dusk	3.1- 33.3

Variable	CV (%)
COD	8.1- 36.5
Nitrate	15.7- 68.6
Dissolved oxygen at dawn	16.7- 53.5
Carbon dioxide	20.7-115.2
Secchi disk visibility	21.8- 56.1
Total phosphorus	28.9- 43.6
Chlorophyll a	29.2- 71.3
Filtrable orthophosphate	30.5- 96.5
Total ammonia nitrogen	59.7-121.6

6.4.2. Relationship to maximum feeding rate

Tucker et al. (1979) conducted an experiment in 0.04-ha earthen ponds stocked with channel catfish fingerlings at 5,000, 10,000, and 20,000 fish per hectare. Daily feeding rates were gradually increased to maximum values of 34, 56, and 78 kg/ha per day in ponds of the low, medium, and high stocking rates, respectively, on 2 August and continued at these rates until fish harvest on 24 October.

Temperature data for ponds were as follows:

Date	°C at dawn	Date	°C at dawn
1 Jun	25.7	21 Aug	29.7
13 Jun	27.3	6 Sep	26.4
26 Jun	28.9	18 Sep	27.0
10 Jul	29.2	2 Oct	19.7
24 Jul	29.3	16 Oct	15.1
7 Aug	27.3		

Concentrations of chlorophyll a, COD, total ammonia nitrogen, and nitrate increased and dissolved oxygen concentrations at dawn and Secchi disk visibilities decreased as daily feeding rates increased in ponds of all three treatments. These observations are in agreement with findings of two other studies (Boyd, 1974; Boyd et al., 1978).

Ponds with the lowest maximum daily feeding rate usually had the best water quality, and ponds with the highest maximum daily feeding rate normally had the poorest water quality. This fact is illustrated with water quality data from a mid-September sampling date (Table 6.5).

Plankton abundance and COD were substantially greater in ponds with the highest feed application rate than in other ponds because more nutrients were available from metabolic and digestive wastes.

Nitrite concentrations were a function of feeding rate, but the toxic threshold

TABLE 6.5

Average concentrations of water quality variables in mid-September for channel
catfish ponds receiving one of three maximum daily feed application rates: low,
34 kg/ha per day; medium, 56 kg/ha per day; high, 78 kg/ha per day. Each feeding
rate treatment was replicated six times.

Variable	Feeding rate		
	Low	Medium	High
Secchi disk visibility (cm)	31	35	22
Chlorophyll a (µg/l)	62	74	155
Chemical oxygen demand (mg/l)	42	50	75
Total ammonia nitrogen (mg/l)	0.25	1.1	1.5
Nitrite (µg/l or N)	3	13	15
Afternoon pH	8.2	7.8	7.6
Dissolved oxygen at dawn (mg/l)	4.5	1.9	1.1

for nitrite was not reached in any of the ponds. Average total ammonia nitrogen
concentrations were always below 0.5 mg/l in the low treatment. However, concentrations of total ammonia nitrogen often exceeded 1 mg/l in ponds of the other
two treatments. Un-ionized ammonia concentrations fluctuated daily because pH
was normally about 7 in the early morning and about 9 in the afternoon. The
greatest measured un-ionized ammonia concentration was 0.94 mg/l in a pond of the
high treatment. Fish in this pond were observed in distress at the surface even
though dissolved oxygen concentrations were high. Examination of some of the fish
failed to reveal parasite or disease organisms to cause the condition, but thick-
ening of gill epithelia, such as observed as a clinical sign of exposure to high
un-ionized ammonia levels, was noted.

Minimum concentrations of dissolved oxygen occurred in all treatments between
1 July and 18 September when water temperatures ranged between 25 and 30°C at
dawn. Dissolved oxygen seldom fell below 4.0 mg/l in the low treatment or below
2.0 mg/l in the medium treatment. However, they were usually less than 2.0 mg/l
at dawn in the high treatment and sometimes as low as 0-0.5 mg/l. Of 270 determinations per treatment, dissolved oxygen was <2.0 mg/l at dawn 49%, 29%, and
2% of the time in ponds of the high, medium, and low treatments, respectively.
Emergency aeration was not used to prevent fish mortality when oxygen depletion
occurred. Dead fish were removed, counted, and weighed.

Fish did not normally come to the surface and exhibit signs of oxygen stress
unless dissolved oxygen concentrations were below 1 mg/l. Fish were fed in the

TABLE 6.6

Summary of channel catfish production data from ponds that received different maximum daily feeding rates: low, 34 kg/ha per day; medium, 56 kg/ha per day; high, 78 kg/ha per day. Each treatment was replicated six times.

Variable	Treatment		
	Low	Medium	High
Harvest weight (kg/ha)	2,990	4,100	4,860
Survival (%)	99	93	83
Mean weight of individual fish (g)	601	443	284
S-value[a]	1.3	1.7	2.5

[a]Total feed applied ÷ net production.

afternoon, and they did not eat well in ponds where the oxygen concentration had been below 1.0 mg/l during the morning of the same day. No fish mortality resulted from oxygen depletion in ponds of the low treatment. In one pond of the medium treatment, 11% of the fish succumbed to oxygen depletion. Oxygen depletions resulted in 7-32% mortality of fish in three ponds of the high treatment.

Fish production data are summarized in Table 6.6. The medium treatment was clearly superior to the low treatment. Although average yield was greater in the high treatment, the increased cost of production and the smaller size of fish at harvest made this treatment less attractive economically than the medium treatment. Data for the medium and high treatments (Fig. 6.3) showed that harvest weights were usually less in ponds with low concentrations of dissolved oxygen at dawn than in ponds with higher oxygen levels at dawn.

Findings of this study reveal that oxygen depletion and other water quality problems are not likely if maximum daily feeding rates do not exceed about 35-40 kg/ha. At maximum daily feeding rates of about 60 kg/ha, some water quality problems may occur. However, emergency aeration can be used to prevent fish mortality (see Chapter 7). At feeding rates of 80 kg/ha per day or above, problems with dissolved oxygen and un-ionized ammonia will be severe. Without continuous nightly aeration (see Chapter 7) or high water flushing rates, it is doubtful that such high feeding rates would be as economical as moderate feeding rates.

6.4.3. Effects of weather on maximum feeding rate

Hollerman and Boyd (1980) repeated the high stocking and feeding rate treatment

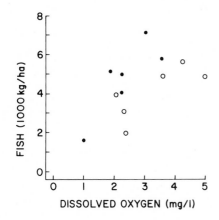

Fig. 6.3. Average dissolved oxygen concentrations at dawn and net production of channel catfish. Solid dots and open circles indicate stocking rates of 20,000 and 10,000 fish per hectare, respectively (Tucker et al., 1979).

TABLE 6.7
Comparison of fish production data for 2 years in ponds stocked at 20,000 channel catfish per hectare. Data are the average of six replications (Tucker et al., 1979; Hollerman and Boyd, 1980).

Variable	1978	1979
Harvest weight (kg/ha)	4,860	1,400
Survival (%)	83	40
Mean weight of individual fish (g)	284	112
S-value[a]	2.5	6.3

[a]Total feed applied ÷ net fish production.

of Tucker et al. (1979). The harvest weights of fish were strikingly different for the two years (1978 and 1979) as shown in Table 6.7. Differences in harvest weights resulted primarily from more problems with oxygen depletion and associated fish kills in 1979 than in 1978. For example, Tucker et al. (1979) reported that 49% of their dissolved oxygen measurements at dawn were <2 mg/l in 1978. In 1978, 66% of the dissolved oxygen concentrations measured at dawn were <2 mg/l. Differences in oxygen concentrations at dawn for the two years were apparently related to solar radiation differences. Solar radiation values for 15 June to 15 October revealed that the majority of days (82 of 122) in 1978 received >400 langleys

TABLE 6.8

Average daily solar radiation, as measured with a solarimeter, during August and September at Auburn, Alabama.

Year	Langleys/day		Year	Langleys/day	
	August	September		August	September
1970	391	401	1976	511	410
1971	436	397	1977	482	364
1972	463	383	1978	425	348
1973	412	445	1979	394	255
1974	335	243	1980	486	389
1975	419	313			

while most days in 1979 received <400 langleys. The average solar radiation for the time interval was 414 langleys/day in 1978 and 344 langleys/day in 1979. Romaire and Boyd (1979) showed a high positive correlation between the concentration of dissolved oxygen at dawn and the amount of solar radiation per day.

The amount of solar radiation at a given location will usually vary considerably for measurements taken during the same time period for different years. This is illustrated in Table 6.8 with solar radiation data collected during August and September at Auburn, Alabama. The influence of solar radiation on fish farming has not been seriously considered. Examination of this phenomenon might explain variation in yields among years. Furthermore, year to year variation in solar radiation could result in problems in extrapolating research findings to other years. For example, the relative freedom from dissolved oxygen problems in ponds of the medium treatment (maximum daily feeding rate of 56 kg/ha) of Tucker et al. (1979) might not have occurred if the experiment had been conducted in 1979 instead of 1978.

6.5 Commercial channel catfish ponds

In experiments, it is relatively easy to develop clear-cut relationships between feeding rates and water quality and to estimate feeding rates that are safe for research ponds. However, for a number of reasons, it is difficult to extrapolate findings directly to commercial fish farms. In research, ponds are normally drained each year for fish harvest. Thus, the nutrient and organic matter-laden water is discharged and replaced with better quality water before the next crop of fish is stocked. During draining, much of the loose, nutrient-enriched sediment is brought into suspension and also discharged. Many commercial catfish farmers do not drain their ponds each year. Instead, they harvest fish with large seines or trap them and replace the harvested fish with small fish. This procedure undoubtedly leads to greater nutrient enrichment over time than the practice of draining ponds each year, but no research has been conducted to establish the rate of nutrient enrichment. When ponds are not drained and restocked each year, it is virtually impossible to accurately estimate standing crops of fish. Fish farmers usually judge the feeding rate from consumption of feed by fish, and accurate data on feed inputs are seldom available for a given pond.

Experiments on water quality in channel catfish ponds have usually been conducted in ponds where water levels were maintained without overflow at the tops of standing drain pipes. In other words, just enough water was added to replace evaporation and seepage. Many fish farmers have large wells as water supplies for ponds. When water quality begins to deteriorate, they will drain water from the bottoms of ponds and replace the outflow with well water. Thus, considerable amounts of accumulated nutrients and organic matter are released. Higher feeding rates would be required to cause the same degree of water quality deterioration in ponds with appreciable water exchange than in ponds without water exchange. A thorough examination of the practice of water exchange is badly needed in order to develop quantitative relationships among water exchange rates, water quality, and feeding rates.

Pamatmat and Mezainis (1977) observed that deep, sheltered ponds were more susceptible to dissolved oxygen depletion than shallow, exposed ponds. In shallow, exposed ponds, wind forces are adequate to prevent appreciable thermal stratification. At night, oxygen, which can be absorbed only at the surface, is mixed throughout the volume of water. Not only does diffusion result in higher oxygen concentrations in a shallow, exposed pond, but a hypolimnion with associated oxygen deficit does not develop. Large volumes of oxygen deficient waters may cause dissolved oxygen depletion if sudden overturns occur during summer. The ideal depth for fish ponds is not known, but Pamatmat and Mezainis estimated that the maximum depth of a sheltered pond should not exceed 1.2 m.

The water supply for ponds is also important in establishing maximum feeding rates. For example, a pond filled by runoff from pastures may have highly fertile water capable of producing dense algal blooms irrespective of nutrients resulting from feed applications (see Chapter 2). Research on feeding rates and water quality has been conducted in ponds filled with nutrient impoverished runoff from woodland. Well waters occassionally have high concentrations of phosphorus that favor plankton production.

In some instances, it is possible for researchers to study water quality in commercial fish ponds. Boyd et al. (1979b) were able to obtain data on dissolved oxygen problems in 36 ponds used for the commercial production of channel catfish

TABLE 6.9

Average concentrations of dissolved oxygen on selected dates in 36 channel catfish production ponds in Tallahatchie County, Mississippi. Numbers of ponds with con- cencentrations <2.0 mg/l at dawn are also provided.

Date	Dissolved oxygen (mg/l)		<2.0 mg/l at dawn (No. of ponds)
	Dawn	Mid-afternoon	
17 Apr	5.6	10.2	0
23 May	4.4	11.4	0
24 Jun	3.7	14.3	1
25 Jul	4.5	12.8	4
10 Aug	3.8	11.3	7
10 Sep	2.7	12.9	13
1 Oct	5.7	10.9	0

in Mississippi. The ponds contained fish of two sizes: marketable size and small fish that were being reared to marketable size. Marketable fish were periodically removed by seining. Estimated average standing crops of fish ranged from a low of 2,350 kg/ha in June to a high of 3,950 kg/ha in September. Individual ponds contained up to 6,170 kg/ha of fish. Fish were fed a daily ration of high protein- content pellets at approximately 2% of estimated standing crops. Feeding rates for individual ponds were sometimes >100 kg/ha per day.

Average concentrations of dissolved oxygen at dawn and in mid-afternoon on selected dates are presented in Table 6.9. The number of ponds with dissolved oxygen concentration <2.0 mg/l at dawn on selected dates is also given in Table 6.9. Dissolved oxygen concentrations below 2.0 mg/l were first observed on 21 May, and the frequency of values below 2.0 mg/l was usually quite high (10-40%) between 20 June and 12 September. A frequency of 80% was recorded on 9 September, following a spell of cloudy weather. Problems with low dissolved oxygen were slight after 15 September. Water temperatures were above 26°C at dawn during the period when dissolved oxygen concentrations below 2.0 mg/l were recorded. Boyd et al. (1978) and Tucker et al. (1979) also found that most oxygen depletion problems occurred when water temperatures were above 26°C. Nevertheless, phyto- plankton die-offs and associated oxygen depletions have been observed at temper- atures below 26°C.

Brown and Boyd (unpublished) monitored water quality in 24 ponds for commercial production of channel catfish. Ponds, located in western Alabama, were 1-10 ha in area and 1-1.5 m average depth. Maximum daily feeding rates ranged from 34

TABLE 6.10

Summary of water quality data on an August sampling date for 28 ponds in western Alabama for commercial production of channel catfish.

Variable	Minimum	Average	Maximum
Chemical oxygen demand (mg/l)	25	51	180
Chlorophyll a (μg/l)	18	135	375
Total ammonia nitrogen (mg/l)	0.10	0.99	5.98
Nitrite (mg/l as N)	0	0.019	0.11

to 112 kg/ha. A summary of water quality data for one August sampling date is presented in Table 6.10. In general, the higher the feeding rate, the greater the concentrations of COD, total ammonia nitrogen, nitrite-nitrogen, and chlorophyll a.

6.6 EFFLUENTS FROM FISH PONDS

In the United States, effluents from fish ponds are considered potential sources of pollution (United States Environmental Protection Agency, 1974). This agency developed tentative effluent limitation values for native pond fish culture systems. The primary restriction was that maximum instantaneous concentrations of settleable solids in effluents could not exceed 3.3 ml/l. The settleable solids represent the volume of material that settles from water during 1 h while the water is held in an Imhoff cone (American Public Health Association et al., 1975). Little is known about the quality of effluents from catfish ponds or about ways of treating effluents to improve their quality, so fish farmers in the United States have been justifiably concerned over effluent limitations.

Boyd (1978) gathered data on the quality of effluents during harvest of channel catfish from eight ponds at Auburn University. Pond waters were discharged through drain pipes extending through bases of dams from the deepest points in ponds. Fish harvest involved two phases. In the draining phase, about 95% of the water was discharged and the drain was closed. During the seining phase, fish were harvested with a large seine. Drains were reopened one to three times during the seining phase to further lower the water level to facilitate the capture of fish.

Concentrations of all potential pollutants were comparatively low during the draining phase, and most importantly, settleable matter values were always below 3.3 ml/l in all eight ponds. However, during the seining phase, activity of wading workers and frightened fish stirred fine particles of sediment into the small volume of water (Fig. 6.4). The result was a marked increase in concentrations of all measured variables except nitrate. Nearly all settleable matter

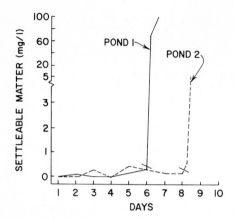

Fig. 6.4. Settleable matter concentrations in two channel catfish ponds during fish harvest. The oblique dashes indicate the beginning of seining to remove fish (Boyd, 1978).

TABLE 6.11

Quality of effluents from channel catfish ponds during the two phases of fish harvest.

Variable	Harvest phase	
	Draining	Seining
Settleable matter (ml/l)	0.08	28.5
Biochemical oxygen demand (mg/l)	4.3	28.9
Chemical oxygen demand (mg/l)	30	342
Filtrable orthophosphate (μg/l as P)	16	59
Total phosphorus (mg/l)	0.11	0.49
Total ammonia nitrogen (mg/l)	0.98	2.34
Nitrate (mg/l as N)	0.16	0.14

values exceeded 3.3 ml/l during the seining phase. Average concentrations of water quality variables during the two phases of fish harvest are summarized in Table 6.11. Obviously, considerable reduction in the release of pollutants could be affected by not releasing water after seining is initiated.

The importance of fish ponds as point sources of pollution is not known. Even waters discharged during the draining phase of fish harvest had higher levels of settleable matter, BOD, COD, total phosphorus, and total ammonia nitrogen than

small streams in the vicinity of Auburn, Alabama (Boyd, 1978). However, the po-
llutional effects of effluents will differ with volumes discharged from ponds and
with flow rates and water quality characteristics of receiving streams.

6.7   OFF-FLAVOR

Odors and flavors described as "earthy-musty" are often detected in potable
waters taken from lakes, streams, or reservoirs. Most workers indicate that
species of actinomycetes and blue-green algae are responsible for these undesirable
sensory characteristics of certain waters (Silvey, 1966; Maloney, 1966; Rosen et
al., 1970; Weete et al., 1977).

Thayson (1936) first described the earthy-musty flavor in fish from rivers in
Scotland. He concluded that actinomycetes that grew in muds synthesized the
earthy-musty compounds, and trout absorbed the compounds from the water. In
Israel, off-flavor in the flesh of carp has been attributed to the blue-green alga
Oscillatoria tenuis (Aschner et al., 1969). Lovell (1971) found that channel
catfish raised on fish farms in the United States frequently had such intensive
off-flavor that they were unsuitable for marketing. A survey of the catfish processing industry in 1971 (Lovell, 1973) revealed that over 50% of ponds tested
before draining by several processing firms contained fish with such intense off-
flavor that draining and harvesting were postponed until flavor improved.

Several compounds with earthy-musty odors have been isolated from cultures of
organisms and from natural waters. The compound geosmin ($C_{12}H_{22}O$) has a strong
earthy-musty odor and is synthesized and excreted into the water by actinomycetes
and blue-green algae (Gerber and Lechevalier, 1965; Medsker et al., 1968;
Safferman et al., 1967). Other compounds with earthy-musty odors that have been
isolated from cultures of actinomycetes and from natural waters are mucidone
(Dougherty et al., 1966) and 2-methylisoborneol (Rosen et al., 1970). These
compounds are similar to geosmin in structure.

Lovell and Sackey (1973) cultured samples of the geosmin-producing blue-green
algae Symploca muscorum and Oscillatoria tenuis in the laboratory. When channel
catfish were placed directly in algal culture tanks, they acquired a distinct
earthy-musty flavor similar to the odor of the algae within 2 days, and the intensity of the flavor reached a maximum after 10 days of exposure. When fish
that had been in the algal culture tanks for 14 days were transferred to flowing
water that did not contain earthy-musty odors, the off-flavor in their flesh disappeared after 10 days. Fish held in tanks containing algae-free filtrate from
the algae culture tanks acquired off-flavor at a slower rate than fish held
directly in the algal culture tanks. This indicated that the fish could absorb
the off-flavor compounds without ingesting the algae — possibly by absorption
across gill membranes.

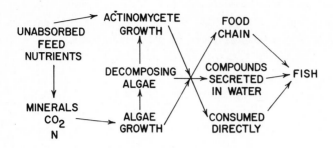

Fig. 6.5. Pathways through which geosmin and other compounds responsible for off-flavor reach fish (Lovell, 1979).

Blue-green algae are autotrophic and do not require organic matter for growth. Therefore, fish feeding does not contribute directly to their growth. However, as pointed out earlier, inorganic nutrients derived indirectly from feeds favor the growth of algae, and blue-green algae are often abundant in ponds. Actinomycetes are heterotrophic and must have a supply of organic matter, so unconsumed feed, fecal material, and dead algae serve as substrate for growth of these organisms. Nutrient enrichment from either fertilization or feeding favors proliferation of organisms responsible for off-flavor, but off-flavor in fish is not restricted to nutrient-enriched waters (Lovell, 1979). The mechanisms by which off-flavor compounds may reach fish tissues are given in Fig. 6.5.

Lovell (1979) reported results of a survey made to identify environmental conditions and organisms associated with off-flavor in pond-reared channel catfish. Fish were collected from commercial ponds where off-flavor fish had been reported. The fish were dressed, wrapped in aluminum foil, and cooked without seasoning for 15 min at 250°C. A panel of sensory evaluators tested the fish and assigned each sample a score of 1 to 10 according to the following scoring system: 10 = no off-flavor, 8 = slight, 6 = distinct, 4 = intense, and 2 = extreme. Environmental data collected from ponds included: date, location, water temperature, total hardness, condition of plankton bloom, predominant algae, and presence of odorous actinomycetes.

Of the 42 ponds, most contained fish with slight to extreme off-flavor of the geosmin-type. Lovell found little conclusive information, but he was able to make several useful generalizations. Off-flavor was found throughout the growing season. Ponds on sandy soils with low total hardness and productivity, and ponds on fertile loam and clay soils with high total hardness and productivity contained off-flavor fish. The occurrence of off-flavor was not related to plankton abundance or to plankton die-offs. Furthermore, off-flavor was not consistently related to a specific alga or actinomycete. The phytoplankton communities of ponds

TABLE 6.12

Average sensory panel scores for channel catfish, initially with intense off-flavor, held in clear, flowing water at 25°C for various lengths of time.

Holding time (days)	Sensory score[a]
0	3.2
3	5.7
6	6.7
10	8.7
15	9.0

[a]10 = no off-flavor; 2 = extreme off-flavor.

with off-flavor fish were similar in generic composition to those of ponds where off-flavor did not occur. Odor-producing actinomycetes were found with equal frequency in ponds with off-flavor fish and in ponds where fish were not off-flavor. Ponds on sandy soils with soft water usually had off-flavor fish in the spring or fall when water temperature was about 20°C. Ponds on more fertile soil with hard water had off-flavor during all months of the growing season.

Channel catfish from 40 ponds at Auburn University were removed at various times during the year and tested by the sensory panel. Fish from three ponds had distinct off-flavor in the spring. All three ponds had heavy blooms of the blue-green alga Anabaena circinalis. Lovell held fish initially without off-flavor in cages in one of the ponds with an A. circinalis bloom. After 7 days, fish in the cages had developed off-flavor. In the late autumn off-flavor fish were found in one pond with a heavy bloom of A. circinalis and in two ponds with intense growth of the green alga Volvox aureus. No other cases of off-flavor were observed in the 40 ponds.

Off-flavor may be removed from fish by holding them in flowing water free of off-flavor compounds (Lovell, 1979). Results of one test of off-flavor removal are summarized in Table 6.12. Thus, depending upon water temperature and degree of off-flavor, compounds causing off-flavor in channel catfish can be removed in 5-15 days. Lovell reported weight losses of 9-17% while purging fish of off-flavor. The weight losses resulted because fish could not be fed during the purging procedure.

Lovell (1979) also recommended practices to reduce problems with off-flavor in pond fish culture. Feed wastes should be minimized by using good feeds without overfeeding. When possible, water in the culture system should be exchanged to lessen the potential for growth of off-flavor causing organisms. Chemical control of phytoplankton was suggested. However, this practice is questionable because it can result in oxygen depletion (see Chapter 8). Lovell also reported that increasing turbidity of water through mechanical agitation or with bottom-feeding fish will suppress phytoplankton growth. This is also a questionable practice.

REFERENCES

American Public Health Association, American Water Works Association, and Water Pollution Control Federation, 1975. Standard Methods for the Examination of Water and Wastewater, 14th edition. American Public Health Association, Washington, D. C., 1193 pp.

Aschner, M., Laventer, C., and Chorin-Kirsch, I., 1969. Off-flavor in carp from fish ponds in the coastal plain and the Gelid. Bamidgeh, 19: 23-25.

Boyd, C. E., 1973. Summer algal communities and primary productivity in fish ponds. Hydrobiologia, 41: 357-390.

Boyd, C. E., 1974. Water quality in catfish ponds. J. Mar. Sci. Ala., 2: 19-30.

Boyd, C. E., 1978. Effluents from catfish ponds during fish harvest. J. Environ. Qual., 7: 59-62.

Boyd, C. E. and Lawrence, J. M., 1966. The mineral composition of several fresh-water algae. Proc. Annual. Conf. Southeast. Assoc. Game and Fish Comm., 20: 413-424.

Boyd, C. E. and Snow, J. R., 1975. Fertilizing farm fish ponds. Auburn University Agricultural Experiment Station, Auburn, Alabama, Leaflet 88, 8 pp.

Boyd, C. E., Romaire, R. P., and Johnston, E., 1978. Predicting early morning dissolved oxygen concentrations in channel catfish ponds. Trans. Amer. Fish. Soc., 107: 484-492.

Boyd, C. E., Romaire, R. P., and Johnston, E., 1979a. Water quality in channel catfish production ponds. J. Environ. Qual., 8: 423-429.

Boyd, C. E., Steeby, J. A., and McCoy, E. W., 1979b. Frequency of low dissolved oxygen concentrations in ponds used for commercial culture of channel catfish. Proc. Annual Conf. Southeast. Assoc. Fish and Wildl. Agencies, 33: 591-599.

Chuapoehuk, W., 1977. Nutritional contribution of natural pond organisms to channel catfish growth in intensively-fed ponds. M. S. thesis, Auburn University, Auburn, Alabama, 56 pp.

Dougherty, J. D., Campbell, R. D., and Morris, R. L., 1966. Actinomycetes: isolation and identification of agent responsible for musty odors. Science, 152: 1372.

Dunseth, D. and Smitherman, R. O., 1977. Pond culture of catfish, tilapia, and silver carp. Auburn University Agricultural Experiment Station, Auburn, Alabama, Highlights of Agricultural Research, 24, No. 3: 4.

Gerber, N. N. and Lechevalier, H. A., 1965. Geosmin, an earthy-smelling substance isolated from actinomycetes. App. Microbiol., 13: 935.

Hollerman, W. D. and Boyd, C. E., 1980. Nightly aeration to increase production of channel catfish. Trans. Amer. Fish. Soc., 109: 446-452.

Lovell, R. T., 1971. The earthy-musty flavor in intensively-cultured catfish. Proc. Assoc. South. Agric. Workers, 67: 102.

Lovell, R. T., 1973. Environment-related off-flavours in intensively cultured fish. Paper presented at FAO United Nations Technical Conference on Fishery Products, Tokyo, Japan, 4-11 December 1973, 7 pp.

Lovell, R. T., 1979. Flavour problems in fish culture. In: T. V. R. Pillay and W. A. Dill (Editors), Advances in Aquaculture. Papers presented at the FAO Technical Conference on Aquaculture, Kyoto, Japan, 26 May-2 June 1976. Fishing News Books Ltd., Farnharm, Surry, England, pp. 186-190.

Lovell, R. T. and Sackey, L. A., 1973. Absorption by channel catfish of earthy-musty flavor compounds synthesized by cultures of blue-green algae. Trans. Amer. Fish. Soc., 102: 774-777.

Lovell, R. T., Prather, E. E., Tres-Dick, J., and Chhorn, L., 1974. Effects of addition of fish meal to all-plant feeds on the dietary protein needs of channel catfish in ponds. Proc. Annual Conf. Southeast. Assoc. Game and Fish Comm., 28: 222-228.

Maloney, T. E., 1966. Research on algal odor. J. Amer. Water Works Assoc., 55: 481-486.

Medsker, L. L., Jenkins, D., and Thomas, J. F., 1968. Odorous compounds in natural waters: An earthy-smelling compound associated with blue-green algae and actinomycetes. Environ. Sci. Tech., 2: 461-464.

Moav, R., Wohlfarth, G., Schroeder, G. L., Hulata, G., and Barish, H., 1977. Intensive polyculture of fish in freshwater ponds. I. Substitution of expensive feeds by liquid cow manure. Aquaculture, 10: 25-43.

Pamatmat, M. M. and Mezainis, V., 1977. Disadvantages of deep and sheltered ponds for intensive catfish culture. Auburn University Agricultural Experiment Station, Auburn, Alabama, Highlights of Agricultural Research, 24, No. 4: 3.

Prather, E. E., 1956. Experiments on the commercial production of golden shiners. Proc. Annual Conf. Southeast. Assoc. Game and Fish Comm., 10: 150-155.

Prather, E. E. and Lovell, R. T., 1971. Effect of vitamin fortification in Auburn No. 2 fish feed. Proc. Annual Conf. Southeast. Assoc. Game and Fish Comm., 25: 479-483.

Prather, E. E. and Lovell, R. T., 1973. Response of intensively fed channel catfish to diets containing various protein-energy ratios. Proc. Annual Conf. Southeast. Assoc. Game and Fish Comm., 27: 455-459.

Prather, E. E., Fielding, J. R., Johnson, M. C., and Swingle, H. S., 1953. Production of bait minnows in the Southeast. Alabama Polytechnic Institute Agricultural Experiment Station, Auburn, Alabama, Circular 112, 72 pp.

Romaire, R. P. and Boyd, C. E., 1979. Effects of solar radiation on the dynamics of dissolved oxygen in channel catfish ponds. Trans. Amer. Fish. Soc., 108: 473-478.

Rosen, A. A., Mashni, C. I. and Safferman, R. S., 1970. Recent developments in the chemistry of odor in water: the cause of earthy-musty odor. Water Treatment and Examination, 19: 106-119.

Safferman, R. S., Rosen, A. A., Mashni, C. I. and Morris, M. E., 1967. Earthy-smelling substance from a blue-green alga. Environ. Sci. Tech., 1: 429-430.

Silvey, J. K. G., 1966. Tastes and odors-effects of organisms. J. Amer. Water Works Assoc., 58: 706-715.

Swingle, H. S., 1960. Comparative evaluation of two tilapias as pondfishes in Alabama. Trans. Amer. Fish. Soc., 89: 142-148.

Swingle, H. S., 1968. Estimation of standing crops and rates of feeding fish in ponds. Proc. World Symposium on Warm-Water Pond Fish Culture, FAO United Nations, Fish. Rep. No. 44, 3: 416-423.

Thaysen, A. C., 1936. The origin of an earthy or muddy taint in fish. Ann. Appl. Biol., 23: 99-109.

Tucker, L., Boyd, C. E., and McCoy, E. W., 1979. Effects of feeding rates on water quality, production of channel catfish, and economic returns. Trans. Amer. Fish. Soc., 108: 389-396.

United States Environmental Protection Agency, 1974. Development document for proposed effluent limitations guidelines and new source performance standards for the fish hatcheries and farms. National Field Investigations Center, Denver, Colorado, 237 pp.

Weete, J. D., Blevins, W. T., Wilt, G. R., and Durham, D., 1977. Chemical, biological, and environmental factors responsible for the earthy odor in the Auburn city water supply. Auburn University Agricultural Experiment Station, Auburn, Alabama, Bulletin 490, 48 pp.

Chapter 7

AERATION

7.1 INTRODUCTION

Dissolved oxygen is probably the most important single variable regulating production of fish in intensive culture. The dynamics of dissolved oxygen are strongly influenced by phytoplankton density, which in turn, is regulated primarily by the rate fish are fed. Thus, the density of phytoplankton and the frequency and severity of problems with low dissolved oxygen increase with feeding rate, and the intensification of fish culture is ultimately limited by the amount of feed that can be applied to ponds without causing oxygen depletion.

Aeration may be used to mechanically increase concentrations of dissolved oxygen in ponds. There are several types of aeration. Emergency aeration is employed to prevent fish from dying during periods of oxygen depletion. For example, fish farmers are careful to maintain feeding rates at levels that will not cause oxygen depletion under normal conditions. However, in spite of conservative feeding practices, oxygen depletion may occur during prolonged periods of cloudy weather or following phytoplankton die-offs. Emergency aeration is then used to prevent fish from dying until conditions improve for natural aeration by phytoplankton. Aeration is sometimes applied to prevent thermal and oxygen stratification in ponds in an effort to reduce the risk of oxygen depletion. Wells are occasionally the primary water supplies for ponds. Because well water is normally devoid of oxygen, it should be aerated before it flows into ponds. Stocking and feeding rates may be increased in ponds if natural oxygen supplies are supplemented by aeration. Thus, aeration on a nightly basis — sometimes even on a continuous basis — has been a means of intensifying fish culture.

In this chapter, I will discuss the principles of aeration, types of aerators, and the benefits of aeration. The treatment is based on a few selected studies and my experiences, and it is not to be taken as a literature review.

7.2 PRINCIPLES OF AERATION

The only way that dissolved oxygen can be transferred from air to water is by diffusion. The process of diffusion was discussed in Chapter 5. In general, the rate of diffusion depends primarily on three factors: the oxygen deficit in the water, the amount of water surface exposed to the air, and the degree of turbulence. Aeration devices function to increase the amount of air-water interface so that more oxygen can enter the water. Most aerators also increase turbulence so that oxygen entering at the air-water interface is mixed throughout the volume of water. One method of increasing the air-water interface is to mechanically agitate surface water. This creates a greater surface area and also causes mixing

of the water. There are many ways of agitating surface water. The water may be
splashed into the air with paddle wheels, sprayed into the air with pumps, or
stirred by various other devices. A second method for increasing the air-water
interface is to release bubbles of air beneath the water, and as the bubbles rise
to the surface, oxygen will diffuse across the air bubble-water interface.

According to Wheaton (1977) there are four basic types of aerators: gravity,
surface, diffuser, and turbine. Gravity aerators work on the principle that the
air-water interface may be increased as water falls to lower elevation. For example, waterfalls are natural aerators because the water breaks up into droplets
and spray as it falls. Water flowing down an inclined plane that has a corrugated
surface is agitated enough to increase the air-water interface and effect aeration.
Surface aerators break up or agitate the water surface to increase the air-water
interface; a paddle wheel aerator splashes water into the air and causes turbulence at the surface. Diffuser aerators inject bubbles of air or oxygen into the
water. The common pump and air stone diffuser used in aquaria is an example.
Turbine aerators employ a propeller to circulate water and effect aeration at the
surface.

Aerators are normally tested in tap water of 20°C and initially with 0 mg/l
dissolved oxygen. Stukenberg et al. (1977) describe standard procedures for
evaluating aeration equipment. A tank of water — tank sizes vary to accomodate
aerators under consideration — is deoxygenated by the addition of sodium sulfite:

$$Na_2SO_3 + \tfrac{1}{2} O_2 \rightarrow Na_2SO_4$$

Theoretically, 7.9 mg/l of sodium sulfite are needed to remove 1 mg/l of dissolved
oxygen. However, because the aeration device is used to mix the sodium sulfite,
some oxidation of sulfite occurs during the mixing period. Approximately 1.5-2
times the theoretical quantity of sodium sulfite is normally added to assure complete deoxygenation. Cobalt chloride at 0.05-0.2 mg/l as Co is used to catalyze
the oxidation of sodium sulfite. Once the water is deoxygenated, the aerator is
operated to raise the oxygen concentration in the aeration basin. Dissolved
oxygen concentrations are measured at different locations in the test basin while
the aerator is running. At least six sets of measurements should be made while
the dissolved oxygen concentration increases from 10 to 70% of saturation. The
plot of the natural logarithm of the saturation deficit versus time should give a
straight line (Fig. 7.1); the slope is the transfer coefficient (see Chapter 2).
Unless the graphs of data taken at the different sampling sites are similar,
mixing in the tank was incomplete and results questionable. The following equation
is used to calculate the transfer coefficient:

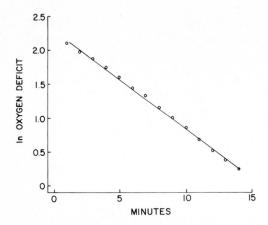

Fig. 7.1. Graph of the natural logarithm of the oxygen deficit versus time of aeration during an aerator test.

$$(K_La)20 = \frac{\ln(C_s - C_1) - \ln(C_s - C_2)}{t_2 - t_1}$$ (7.1)

where $(K_La)20$ = transfer coefficient (h^{-1}); C_s = saturation with oxygen (mg/l); C_1 = initial oxygen concentration (mg/l); C_2 = final oxygen concentration (mg/l); t_1 = time at beginning of aeration (h); t_2 = time at end of aeration (h). The K_La value for 20°C $[(K_La)20]$ may be used to calculate K_La values for other temperatures $[(K_La)]$:

$$(K_La)T = (K_La)20 \times 1.024^{t-20}$$

where t = the temperature of interest.

The amount of oxygen transferred per unit time at standard conditions (tap water at 20°C; 0 mg/l dissolved oxygen) may be obtained by the following equation:

$$(OT)20 = [(K_La)20 \times C_s \times \text{tank volume in liters}) \div 10^6$$ (7.2)

where (OT)20 = oxygen transfer (kg/h) at 20°C.

The efficiency of an aerator in terms of oxygen transferred per unit of power is:

$$[OT]20 = (OT)20 \div kw$$ (7.3)

where kw = kilowatts of power used in 1 h.

To illustrate the evaluation of aeration equipment, suppose that an aerator was tested under standard conditions in a tank containing 20 m^3 of water. The following data were obtained: C_1 = 0.0 mg/l, C_s = 8.84 mg/l, C_2 = 7.20 mg/l, t_1 = 0900 h, t_2 = 0930 h, and power requirement = 0.25 kw. The transfer coefficient is calculated with Equation 7.1:

$$(K_La)20 = \frac{\ln(8.84 - 0) - \ln(8.84 - 7.20)}{0.5 \text{ h}}$$

$$(K_La)20 = \frac{2.18 - 0.49}{0.5}$$

$$(K_La)20 = 3.38 \text{ h}^{-1}$$

The $(K_La)20$ value is used in Equation 7.2 to give the oxygen transfer:

$$(OT)20 = 3.38 \text{ h}^{-1} \text{ X } 8.84 \text{ mg/l X } 20,000 \text{ l} \div 10^6 \text{ mg/kg}$$

$$(OT)20 = 0.60 \text{ kg/h}$$

The transfer rate may be based on energy expenditure with Equation 7.3:

$$[OT]20 = 0.60 \text{ kg/h} \div 0.5 \text{ kw} = 1.2 \text{ kg/kw·h}$$

In practice, the transfer rate is lower than the one obtained under standard conditions. This results because temperatures may not be 20°C, concentration of dissolved oxygen may be greater than 0 mg/l, and the water under aeration may not absorb oxygen at the same rate as tap water. Substances contained in water lower the rate of oxygen absorption and the oxygen saturation concentration slightly. The oxygen transfer correction (α) is calculated as:

$$\alpha = \frac{(K_L'a)20}{(K_La)20}$$

where $(K_L'a)20$ = value for water being aerated and $(K_La)20$ = value for standard conditions. The oxygen saturation correction (β) is:

$$\beta = \frac{(C_s')20}{(C_s)20}$$

where $(C_s')20$ = oxygen saturation at 20°C for water being aerated and $(C_s)20$ = value for tap water. Wheaton (1977) reported that for domestic sewage, α values were between 0.80 and 0.95 and β values were between 0.95 and 1.00.

Eckenfelder and Ford (1968) presented the following equation for prediction of transfer of oxygen under pond conditions:

$$OT' = [OT]20\left[\frac{\beta C_s - C_d}{8.84} (1.024)^{T-20}\alpha \right] \tag{7.4}$$

where OT' = kg O_2/kw·h transferred under pond conditions; $[OT]20$ = kg O_2/kw·h transferred under standard conditions; β = oxygen transfer correction; α = oxygen saturation correction; C_s = oxygen saturation for existing temperature and pressure; C_d = design dissolved oxygen concentration; T = temperature in °C. Alpha and beta values have not been determined for pond waters, but one would expect the values to be similar in magnitude to those of domestic sewage.

To illustrate the utility of Equation 7.4, suppose that an aerator is rated under standard conditions to transfer 2 kg O_2/kw·h (such data are generally supplied by manufacturers). The aerator is to be used in a fish pond where dissolved oxygen concentrations must be maintained above 4 mg/l and the temperature is 28°C. Assuming that α = 0.90 and β = 0.98, Equation 7.4 may be used to obtain the amount of oxygen transferred under pond conditions:

$$OT' = 2 \times \left[\frac{(0.98)(7.75) - 4}{8.84} (1.024)^{28-20}(0.90) \right]$$

$$OT' = (2)(0.407)(1.209)(.90)$$

$$OT' = 0.886 \text{ kg/kw·h}$$

The design dissolved oxygen concentration — the concentration of oxygen under operating conditions — usually causes the greatest difference between oxygen transfer under standard conditions and oxygen transfer under pond conditions. The reduction in oxygen transfer with increasing concentrations of dissolved oxygen in ponds is illustrated in Fig. 7.2. Colt and Tchobanoglous (1979) presented standard oxygen transfer rates for various types of aeration techniques for fish culture systems (Table 7.1).

Pure oxygen systems are also used in fish culture. When using pure oxygen, the C_s term in the transfer equations is simply increased to account for the new partial pressure of oxygen:

TABLE 7.1

Typical rates of oxygen transfer under standard conditions[a] for aeration systems used in fish culture (Colt and Tchobanoglous, 1979).

Aeration system	Transfer rate (kg O_2/kw·h)
Diffused-air systems	
Fine bubble	1.2- 2.0
Medium bubble	1.0- 1.6
Coarse bubble	0.6- 1.2
Low-speed surface aerator (with or	
without draft tube)	1.2- 2.4
High-speed floating aerator	1.2- 2.4
U-tube aerator	4.5-45.6
Gravity aerator	1.2- 1.8
Venturi aerator	1.2- 2.4
Static tube systems	1.2- 1.6

[a]20°C; 0 mg/l dissolved oxygen; $\alpha = 1.0$; $\beta = 1.0$.

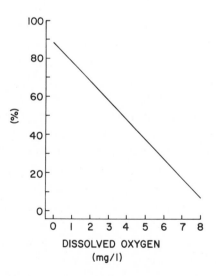

Fig. 7.2. Percentage reduction in oxygen transfer rates of aerators in waters of 28°C with different dissolved oxygen concentrations.

$$C_s' = C_s \ X \ \frac{760 \text{ mm Hg}}{159.2 \text{ mm Hg}}$$

where C_s' = the solubility of oxygen from a pure oxygen atmosphere; 760 mm Hg = the partial pressure of oxygen in the pure gas at standard conditions; 159.2 mm Hg = the partial pressure of oxygen in the atmosphere at standard conditons (see Chapter 2). The transfer of oxygen in diffused-air systems may also be enhanced by introducing compressed air. The C_s' term may be calculated for compressed air by multiplying C_s for standard conditions by a factor obtained by dividing the pressure of compressed air by atmospheric pressure.

A diffused-air system is illustrated in Fig. 7.3. The efficiency of oxygen transfer is related to bubble size; small bubbles offer a greater air-water inter-face than large bubbles. Furthermore, a greater concentration gradient between oxygen in the bubble and oxygen in the water may be achieved using pure oxygen or greater compression of air. In addition to releasing air or pure oxygen at the pond bottom and allowing it to rise as in Fig. 7.3, the diffuser may be placed beneath a downflow aerator so that bubbles are forced downward and then permitted to rise to the surface. Venturi aerators suck air into water so that bubbles are formed (Fig. 7.4). Speece (1969) described a U-tube aerator like the one illustrated in Fig. 7.5. The U-tube is usually 15-20 m deep, hence bubbles have a long contact period with water. Unless adequate head is available, water must be pumped through the U-tube. Diffused-air systems are particularly useful when oxygen concentrations in the water are relatively high, because pure oxygen or compressed air increase the oxygen saturation value (C_s).

Spray-type aerators (Fig. 7.6) and paddle wheels are typical surface aerators. Another type of surface aeration is a nozzle for spraying water into the air. These aerators break water into turbulent, thin layers and drops that have high transfer coefficients and large surface to volume ratios. The principle theo-retical disadvantage is the relatively short exposure time of water to air in the falling water. According to Haney (1954), water in a jet rising 3 m and then falling has only a 2-sec exposure to the air. On the other hand, a bubble of air the size often employed in injection aerators has very little acceleration, and a bubble rising 3 m has a contact time of 10 sec. Nevertheless, there are many practical disadvantages to diffused-air systems in ponds: cost of installing the diffuser system over the pond bottom, obstruction to fish harvest by the diffusers, and clogging of pores in diffusers when not in operation. Therefore, surface-type aerators are more widely used in fish culture than diffused air systems.

Gravity aerators were studied by Chesness and Stephens (1971). Water was aerated by allowing it to fall over a weir onto a splash board (Fig. 7.7), paddle wheel, or brush and by allowing it to flow down various types of inclined planes

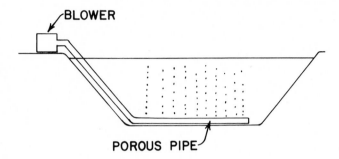

Fig. 7.3. Diffused-air system for pond aeration.

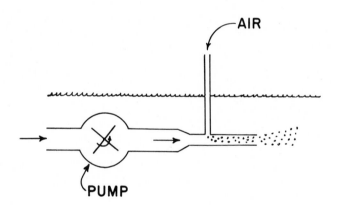

Fig. 7.4. Venturi for oxygenating water.

(Fig. 7.8). In another kind of gravity aeration system, water was pumped to the top of a vertical pipe (riser) and allowed to fall through perforated aprons. The effectiveness of gravity aerators was determined from the equation:

$$E = 100 \times \frac{C_b - C_a}{C_s - C_a} \qquad (7.5)$$

where E = aeration effectiveness (%); C_a = oxygen concentration in water above aerator, C_b = oxygen concentration in water below aerator; C_s = oxygen concentration at saturation. The effectiveness of seven gravity flow aerators studied

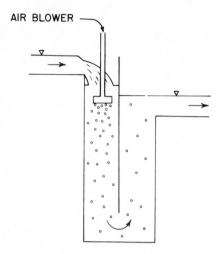

Fig. 7.5. A U-tube aerator (Speece, 1969).

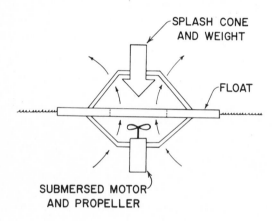

Fig. 7.6. Spray-type surface aerator.

by Chesness and Stephens are given in Table 7.2.

Gravity flow aerators are inexpensive to operate when natural head is available. For example, if water from an artesian well is available above the pond surface, well water may be passed over a gravity aerator before it flows into the pond. Obviously, it will cost more for gravity aeration if the water must be pumped from lower elevation to the top of the gravity aerator.

TABLE 7.2

Aeration effectiveness of seven gravity aerator designs (Chesness and Stephens, 1971).

Aerator design	Aeration effectiveness[a] (%)
Weir with splash board	24.1
Weir with paddle wheel	24.2
Weir with rotating brush	23.9
Corrugated inclined plane — no holes	25.3
Corrugated inclined plane — with holes	30.1
Lattice	34.0
Riser with perforated aprons	31.7

[a]Head loss = 0.3 m. Equation 7.5 was used to calculate aeration effectiveness.

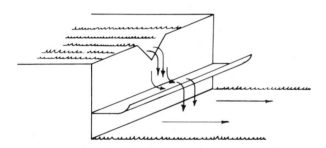

Fig. 7.7. Weir and splash board for aeration by gravity flow.

7.3 EMERGENCY AERATION

Emergency aeration is frequently employed to prevent fish kills during periods of dissolved oxygen depletion. Many biologists and fish farmers feel that emergency aeration is necessary when dissolved oxygen concentrations in warmwater fish ponds fall below 2 mg/l. In emergency aeration, it is necessary to quickly raise dissolved oxygen concentrations, so rather powerful aerators are required if ponds are large. In large ponds it is often not possible to raise oxygen concentrations throughout the pond volume. However, if one or more areas of oxygenated water are provided, fish will usually locate these havens and avoid suffocation.

A multitude of different devices are used to effect emergency aeration. Pumps may be used by placing intakes 25–50 cm below the surface and releasing the water

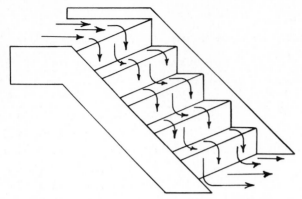

Fig. 7.8. Inclined plane for aeration by gravity flow.

onto the pond surface. Some oxygenation occurs when the water splashes against the surface, and additional oxygenation results from currents set in motion at the pond surface. Even greater aeration will result if the pump is used to discharge water at the top of an inclined plane aerator. Obviously, the effectiveness of this technique will depend upon pump capacity. Most fish farmers employ 10 to 30-cm diameter pumps with discharge capacities of 4-20 m^3/min. A 20 m^3/min pump would discharge the entire volume of a 1-ha pond of 1 m depth in 8.3 h.

Another technique utilizing pumps is that of pumping oxygenated water from an adjacent pond into the pond with oxygen-depleted water. The effectiveness of this procedure also varies with pump capacity. Furthermore, water must be available to replace the water transferred from the adjacent pond, or back-pumping must be employed to refill the adjacent pond.

When plenty of well water is available, water may be released from the bottom of ponds with dissolved oxygen problems and replaced with well water. Because well water is normally devoid of oxygen, it should be passed over a gravity-flow aerator as it flows to a pond.

High discharge, low head pumps such as the Crisafulli pump (Crisafulli Pump Company, Glendale, Montana) may be fitted on the intake side with a vertical pipe capped with a perforated cone. The pump is mounted on a trailer and may be backed into a pond and powered by the power-take-off of a farm tractor. The discharge of the pump must pass through the perforated cone so that it is sprayed into the air before falling onto the pond surface.

Paddle wheel aerators are also popular emergency aeration devices. One such aerator is manufactured by the Clark Livingston Machine Shop, Greensboro, Alabama. The paddle wheels are mounted on the axle of a truck differential which, in turn, is mounted at the end of a trailer. The trailer may be backed into a pond and the paddle wheels rotated by a drive shaft connected to the power-take-off of a tractor. Twelve paddles, each 35 cm long by 15 cm wide, are attached to each wheel. The paddle wheel aerator is usually positioned so that paddles on the undersides of wheels extend 25-30 cm into the water. Paddle wheels are usually rotated at about 120 rpm. The paddle wheels splash water into the air and effect strong currents in surface water.

There are two basic disadvantages of tractor-powered aerators: a tractor is required for each aerator, and most farm tractors have more power than needed to rotate the paddle wheels. Therefore, one recent trend is to mount the axle and paddle wheels on a float and power them with an electric motor. Large paddle wheels are usually rotated by 3.7-7.5-kw electric motors. Although the electrically -powered aerators represent a savings in operational cost, they have to be positioned at one location. This is a great disadvantage because fish will be located in the area of the pond where oxygen concentrations are highest, and the electrically -powered aerators cannot be moved to the most advantageous location. Paddle wheel aerators may also be propelled by a hydraulic pump. A centrally-located hydraulic pump can power several aerators, but mobility of aerators is decreased. There are many different ways of mounting paddles of various sizes and shapes on wheels and shafts. Most paddle wheel aerators have been constructed by ingenious fish farmers, and few have been tested for aeration effectiveness.

Spray-type surface aerators are usually rated at 0.75 to 3.75 kw. These aerators may be used to provide emergency aeration in small ponds. However, in larger ponds, spray-type aeration is not a feasible means of emergency aeration.

In the event that emergency aeration equipment such as that described above is unavailable, agitation by an outboard motor may improve dissolved oxygen concentrations. A boat equipped with a 7.5-kw motor, twisting and turning at high speed for 4 h effected enough agitation in a 0.4-ha pond to raise dissolved oxygen concentrations from 0.3 to 2 mg/l and prevent suffocation of fish (Swingle, 1968).

Treatments of ponds with up to 6 mg/l of potassium permanganate is frequently recommended to alleviate oxygen depletion (Lay, 1971). However, recent studies by Tucker and Boyd (1977), which are discussed in Chapter 9, showed that potassium permangante treatment was ineffective in treating dissolved oxygen depletions. In fact, potassium permanganate treatment retards oxygen production by phytoplankton, thus prolonging oxygen depletion. Carbon dioxide concentrations, which may be excessive during oxygen depletion, may be reduced by treatment with calcium hydroxide, as is also explained in Chapter 9. Calcium hydroxide has no other benefical effect on water quality in oxygen-depleted ponds. The effectiveness of phosphate fertilization to increase photosynthesis during times of low oxygen concentration, as suggested by Swingle (1968), has never been evaluated.

Techniques of emergency aeration have been developed through practical experience rather than research. Therefore, Boyd and Tucker (1979) compared the effectiveness of several techniques of emrgency aeration. The tests were conducted in 0.57-ha ponds where phytoplankton blooms were killed with algicides to effect low concentrations of dissolved oxygen (0.70-2.92 mg/l at 0.5 m depth just before testing). Slight changes in concentrations of dissolved oxygen were measured in samples of water incubated in BOD bottles suspended in ponds during tests of aeration equipment. However, these changes did not exceed ± 0.1 mg/l during 4 h, and oxygen changes in pond waters reflected the effect of aeration devices.

Three sizes (0.25, 2.2, and 3.7 kw) of electrical, spray-type surface aerators each failed to appreciably increase dissolved oxygen concentrations in ponds within 4 h. Obviously, several 3.7-kw aerators would be required to quickly raise dissolved oxygen concentrations in a 0.57-ha pond. Spray-type surface aerators are best suited for small ponds. For example, a 0.25-kw spray-type surface aerator quickly raised dissolved oxygen concentrations and prevented fish kills in 0.04-ha ponds stocked with channel catfish (Dunseth, 1977).

A 30.5-cm Crisafulli pump and a 15.2-cm Rainmaster pump (Construction Machinery Company, Waterloo, Iowa) with discharges of 18.9 and 3.8 m^3/min, respectively, were used to circulate oxygen-deficient pond waters. Intakes were placed just below pond surfaces, and the water was discharged back onto the surfaces, thereby inducing water circulation. The small pump (3.8 m^3/min) only raised oxygen concentrations in the upper 1-m of water by 0.46 mg/l during 4 h, but the larger pump (18.9 m^3/min) raised oxygen concentrations in the upper 1-m by 1.46 mg/l during the same period. Average dissolved oxygen concentrations in the discharges of the two pumps (points where water splashed onto pond surfaces) were 2.5 mg/l for the small pump and 3.5 mg/l for the large pump. The large pump created an oxygen-enriched zone of 1,000 m^2, and the small pump created an oxygen-enriched zone of 300 m^2. The oxygen-enriched zones had oxygen concentrations that were appreciably higher than those in other areas of the ponds.

Both pumps were also used to transfer oxygen-enriched water from an adjacent pond into a pond with oxygen-depleted waters. The large pump discharged water averaging 7.8 mg/l of dissolved oxygen. After 4 h of operation, the average dissolved oxygen concentration in the pond with oxygen-depleted waters had increased by 2 mg/l. The oxygen-enriched zone had an area of 1,600 m^2. Success would have been even greater if water could have been drained from the bottom of the oxygen-depleted pond while the oxygenated water was released at its surface. The small pump discharged water averaging 8.5 mg/l of dissolved oxygen into an oxygen depleted pond. Average dissolved oxygen concentrations increased by less than 1 mg/l during 4 h. However, an oxygen enriched zone of 1,000 m^2 was formed by the discharge.

The hose was removed from the outlet of the Crisafulli pump and replaced with a sprayer. The sprayer was a 30.5-cm pipe that extended above the pump. The end of the pipe was closed by a cone into which was cut 127 holes of 1.2 cm diameter, six large slots (7 cm X 1 cm), and six small slots (4 cm X 1 cm) on the side

TABLE 7.3

Amounts of oxygen added to 0.57-ha ponds during a 4-h period by different techniques of emergency aeration (Boyd and Tucker, 1979).

Type of emergency aeration	Oxygen added (kg)	Relative efficiency (%)
Paddle wheel aerator	31.9	100
Crisafulli pump with sprayer	19.9	64
Crisafulli pump discharging water from adjacent pond	12.1	39
Spray-type surface aerator (3.75 kw)	9.7	31
Crisafulli pump circulating pond water	7.5	24
Spray-type surface aerator (2.25 kw)	7.2	23
Rainmaster pump circulating pond water	6.8	22
Rainmaster pump discharging water from adjacent pond	3.8	12
Spray-type surface aerator (0.25 kw)	2.5	8

facing the pond. The pump was then used to spray oxygen-deficient water into the air to affect its aeration. The force of the spray striking the surface and the intake of water by the pump induced strong currents that favored absorption of oxygen by the surface water. Average dissolved oxygen concentrations in the pond increased by about 3 mg/l following 4 h of aeration with the Crisafulli pump and sprayer. Water caught just before it struck the pond surface had an average oxygen concentration of 5.02 mg/l. The oxygen-enriched zone was 500 m^2 in area.

A tractor-powered paddle wheel aerator of the type described above was also tested. The paddle wheel aerator raised dissolved oxygen concentrations in the pond by 4 mg/l during the 4-h test period. Water from in the spray of the aerator contained 6.2 mg/l of dissolved oxygen. The oxygen-enriched zone was 900 m^2 in area. However, the aerator provides strong mixing and oxygen concentrations were much higher at all areas in the pond than when other aerators were tested. Additional data on the effectiveness of the paddle wheel aerator were obtained in two channel catfish production ponds. It raised the average dissolved oxygen concentration in the surface 1-m stratum from 1.2 to 3.5 mg/l in a 0.89-ha pond in 3 h and from 1.0 to 3.5 mg/l in a 1.12-ha pond in 5 h. Both tests were conducted at night, so dissolved oxygen increases were not influenced by photosynthesis.

The summary of the emergency aeration tests (Table 7.3) gives the amounts of oxygen added by each device and the relative effectiveness of each. These values are corrected for increases or decreases in dissolved oxygen resulting from photosynthesis and respiration. The paddle wheel aerator was considerably more effective than the other techniques for adding dissolved oxygen to pond water. The Crisafulli pump with sprayer was the next most effective technique. The other procedures were considerably less effective. If the amount of dissolved oxygen added to ponds was evaluated in terms of oxygen per kilowatt, the spray-type surface aerators would be much more efficient than the tractor-powered equipment. However, for emergency aeration the amount of dissolved oxygen added per unit of power is relatively unimportant because it is imperative to increase dissolved oxygen concentrations quickly to prevent fish mortality. The new electrically-powered paddle wheel aerators that have essentially the same aeration capacity as the tractor-powered paddle wheel aerators are obviously more energy efficient.

Tests conducted by Boyd and Tucker were for 0.57-ha ponds (except for two tests of the paddle wheel aerator), and dissolved oxygen concentrations would have increased less in larger ponds and more in smaller ponds. Even when emergency aeration is not effective in increasing dissolved oxygen concentrations throughout a pond, zones of oxygen-enriched water are produced. Fish quickly find these areas and avoid suffocation. In large ponds (5-10 ha) emergency aeration devices should be operated at two or more locations to help fish locate aerated zones.

Emergency aeration is a vital management tool in the commercial production of channel catfish — and other species. Fish farmers monitor dissolved oxygen concentrations, and when they suspect that concentrations will fall below 2 mg/l, emergency aeration is usually initiated. Boyd et al. (1979) conducted a study during the 1978 growing season to determine the frequency of oxygen depletion and emergency aeration practices on a channel catfish farm in Tallahatchee County, Mississippi. Thirty-two ponds had areas of 6.1 ha; the other four ponds had areas of 2.8, 4.9, 8.1, and 8.9 ha. Standing stocks of fish and feeding rates varied among ponds and over time, but some ponds had standing stocks over 5,000 kg/ha and feeding rates above 100 kg/ha per day. Emergency aeration was initiated in a pond when the graph of the nighttime dissolved oxygen concentrations suggested that values would fall below 2 mg/l before dawn. Aeration was applied in one of three manners: paddle wheel aerators operated from the power-take-offs of farm tractors, lift pumps that pumped oxygenated water from an adjacent pond into the pond with the dissolved oxygen problem, and Crisafulli pumps that sprayed oxygen-deficient water into the air so that it fell onto the pond surface. When oxygenated water from an adjacent pond was pumped into a pond with oxygen-deficient water, an equal volume of water was returned to the adjacent pond after the oxygen crisis. Four paddle wheel aerators, three Crisafulli pumps with sprayers, and two lift pumps were available for use in the 36 ponds.

Emergency aeration was not required until 15 May and comparatively few ponds had to be aerated until 15 June. Between 16 June and 15 September, there were only four nights during which no ponds were aerated. A maximum of nine ponds was aerated on a single night. However, on a few dates, more than nine ponds had dissolved oxygen concentrations below 2 mg/l. On these dates, only the ponds with the most rapidly declining dissolved oxygen concentrations were aerated. Emergency aeration was generally initiated between midnight and dawn and continued during daylight until phytoplankton photosynthesis had produced adequate dissolved oxygen to prevent stress of fish. The duration of emergency aeration was usually 3-4 h (range = 1-10 h). Emergency aeration was generally effective, and oxygen-related fish kills occurred in only three ponds. Fish mortality was estimated at 4,000 kg in one pond and 2,000 kg in the other two ponds. This was a comparatively small loss of fish, for the 220 ha of ponds had a maximum standing stock of about 1,000,000 kg.

During the 154-day period 1 May through 1 October emergency aeration was used 410 times out of a possible 5,544 times (7.4% of possible times). All ponds required emergency aeration on at least three nights, but none were aerated more than 27 nights. The number of consecutive nights of aeration seldom exceeded three, but one pond was aerated on nine consecutive nights. In summary, most ponds required aeration less than 20 nights and aeration was seldom continued for more than three consecutive nights.

In the study described above, a maximum of 75% of the ponds had dissolved oxygen levels below 2 mg/l on a single date. Nevertheless, no fish kills resulted on that date even though emergency aeration was employed in only a portion of the ponds with dissolved oxygen concentrations below 2 mg/l. These were the ponds with the most rapidly declining dissolved oxygen concentrations. This finding suggests that enough emergency aeration equipment to aerate 25% of the ponds on a fish farm is adequate to prevent most oxygen-related fish kills provided the aerators are used judiciously. Emergency aeration units of the type used on the Mississippi fish farm are mobile and one unit could be used in more than one pond on the same night, thereby providing a margin of safety.

Tractor-powered emergency aeration units are quite expensive because a tractor is needed for each unit. The development of self-powered aerators, several of which could be moved among ponds by a single tractor, would be of great benefit to commercial fish farmers.

7.4 SUPPLEMENTAL OR CONTINUOUS AERATION

7.4.1. Evaluation of pond aeration techniques

Fish farmers have been ingenious in devising methods for aerating pond waters. Unfortunately, they are generally unable to determine the effectiveness of their aeration systems and to define their operating characteristics. Since most pond aeration systems have been designed through practical experience rather than

research, this area deserves more attention by researchers. It would be helpful
to clearly define relationships among aeration, stocking and feeding rates, fish
production, and economic returns. Presently, many fish farmers simply adopt some
aeration system and assume that it will provide benefits. Many times, the system
may not be the best for the particular operation, and the assumed benefits may
be minimal.

In the two studies discussed below, aeration systems for commercial aquaculture
enterprises were tested to determine which were best for existing circumstances
Later, I will give some guidelines for calculating aeration needs, but pilot
studies of the type described below provide valuable information for those select-
ing aeration systems.

In Israel, Marek and Sarig (1971) and Rappaport and Sarig (1975) showed that
yields of carp and tilapia could be increased 5-6 fold over those possible with
conventional culture methods by applying aeration. Therefore, Rappaport et al.
(1976) evaluated five methods of aeration to determine which were potentially useful on fish farms. Test ponds had volumes of 200 m^3, and the volume of water was
exchanged with fresh water every 10 days. The aeration systems are described
below:

An air blower (5.8 kw) with a 7.6-cm diameter outlet pipe was connected in
test ponds to permeable plastic pipes. The porous pipe released small air bubbles
at low pressure to enable efficient oxygen absorption by the water. Air was
supplied through these pipes at 0.08-0.25 m^3/min and 460-600 mm Hg.

An injector (venturi) method was tested in which water passed through a jet
that drew air through a pipe whose outlet was above the water surface. Pressure
was 1,526-1,900 mm Hg, and the 4-mm jet was rated at 1 m^3/h.

Paddle wheel aerators consisted of two water wheels turned by an electric motor.
Two sizes (0.19 kw and 0.38 kw) of paddle wheels were tested.

A spray-type surface aerator (0.25 kw) that drew water from the lower layer of
oxygen-deficient water and jetted it into the air for oxygen enrichment was
evaluated.

An air blower was used to introduce air from a 20-mm diameter pipe at one point
in a pond. The air flow rate was 0.17-0.20 m^3/min.

Three crops of fish were produced annually in ponds. The effectiveness of
aerators was rated by average percentage saturation just before sunrise (Table
7.4). Best results were for paddle wheels and the spray-type surface aerator.
These aerators effected aeration by splashing water into the air; the less effective aerators released air bubbles near pond bottoms. According to Rappaport
and coworkers, a 20% oxygen saturation level is the threshold below which fish

TABLE 7.4

Average percentages of oxygen saturation just before sunrise in experimental ponds (Rappaport et al., 1976).

Aeration device	Season		
	1	2	3
Japanese water mill (0.38 kw)	97	82	99
Japanese water mill (0.19 kw)	84	68	60
Floating aerator (0.25 kw)		67	63
Blower and plastic pipe	50	34	27
Standard blower	39	17	19
Injector venturi	27	12	11

mortality may occur within 2-3 h. Oxygen concentration in all ponds dropped below threshold levels occasionally but not long enough to cause fish mortality.

The greatest fish yields were obtained with the spray-type surface aerator. This was surprising because the paddle wheel aerators were more effective in increasing oxygen concentrations. However, all methods of aeration gave much higher levels of fish production than could be achieved without aeration. Of course, water exchange used in these tests permitted greater fish production than could have been realized in static ponds.

Mitchell and Kirby (1976) also evaluated pond aeration systems. They tested the aeration systems described below in ponds of 0.033-0.17 ha:

An air blower was used to force air through 12 lengths of DuPont Viaflo porous tubing fixed horizontally about 10 cm from the pond bottom. Each piece of tubing was 1.2 m long and received air at 1.7 m^3/h.

Water jet exhausters (Schutte-Koerting Type 484; 3.8 cm) were located near the pond bottom in a horizontal position. A pump drawing suction from near the pond center supplied water to the exhausters.

Two types of spray-type surface aerators were tested. The Fresh-Flo unit was a float-mounted device that pumped water through a vertical cylinder using a propeller-type impeller. Water was discharged through a series of slots in the vertical cylinder above the water line. The unit was rated at 0.38 kw and pumped 1.14 m^3/min of water. The Air-O-Lator unit was a propeller type that picked up water near the surface and discharged it against a cone to create a circular spray pattern and considerable surface turbulence. Two sizes of Air-O-Lator, 0.25 kw and 0.75 kw, were tested.

TABLE 7.5

Performance characteristics of pond aeration devices in a 0.06-ha pond with a volume of 590 m^3 (Mitchell and Kirby, 1976).

Device	Oxygen transfer	
	(kg/hr)	(kg/kw·h)
Mechanical entrainment		
Air-O-Lator		
0.75 kw	1.15	0.48
0.25 kw	0.50	0.50
Fresh-Flo (0.37 kw)	0.24	0.24
Porous diffusion (Viaflo)	0.29	0.96
Jet exhausters and eductors		
Type 484 water jet exhausters		
Four units per pond	0.64	0.16
Two units per pond	0.45	0.22
Type 264 water jet eductors		
Two 3.8-cm units per pond	0.67	0.32
One 7.6-cm unit per pond	0.79	0.35
Two 3.8-cm units plus one		
7.6-cm unit per pond	1.48	0.34

Water jet eductors (Schutte-Koerting Type 264; 3.8 cm and 7.6 cm sizes) that aspirated air and pumped water were situated in ponds like the exhausters.

Performance characteristics of the pond aeration devices in a 0.06-ha pond. with a volume of 590 m^3 are summarized in Table 7.5. Mitchell and Kirby concluded that the Air-O-Lator unit was an effective and economical aeration device. It required no unusual supporting system and was easily mobile. Mobility is important in multiple pond operations because all ponds do not need aeration simultaneously. In ponds where the water depths were less than 0.7 m, the Air-O-Lator disturbed the bottoms and caused turbidity. The Viaflo tubing was the most energy efficient system, but it required a complex and expensive piping and compressor system that appeared to have significant maintenance problems. For example, during periods of inactivity, algae grew on the surface of the tubing and had to be removed by hand. The water jet exhauster and eductor units transferred considerable oxygen to the water, but their energy consumption was high. They were also susceptible to plugging by foreign material. Mitchell and Kirby suggested that the Air-O-Lator

TABLE 7.6

Summary of data collected during an experiment on aeration of white catfish ponds. Treatments were replicated four times; water quality variables were measured monthly during the 236-day experiment (Loyacano, 1974).

Variable	Air volume (m^3/min per ha)		
	0	6.9	10.4
Dissolved oxygen[a] (mg/l)	3.1	3.9	4.5
Chemical oxygen demand (mg/l)	59	62	51
Total ammonia nitrogen (mg/l)	0.6	2.2	1.0
Turbidity (Jackson turbidimeter units)	92	158	170
Net fish production (kg/ha)	2,740	4,560	5,510

[a]Measured near dawn.

would probably be the best choice of aerator for small ponds, provided these devices do not disturb bottoms and create excessive turbidity.

7.4.2 Aeration of channel catfish ponds

Loyacano (1974) studied the effect of aeration on the production of white catfish (Ictalurus catus) in 0.04-ha ponds. Aeration was effected by rotary positive blowers that forced air through 2.54-cm diameter polyvinylchloride (PVC) pipes. A 2.54-cm air line was directed horizontally down the middle of each pond approximately 15 cm from the pond bottom. Two 2.54-cm openings (7 m apart, equidistant from pond edges, and directed upward) permitted release of air from each air line. Three aeration treatments, 0, 6.9, and 10.4 m^3/min per ha were each replicated four times. Aeration was continuous for 143 days. Ponds were stocked with 20,000 fish/ha and feed was applied 6 days weekly. Maximum daily rations were 145 kg/ha in unaerated ponds and 196 kg/ha in aerated ponds. There were no appreciable differences in pH, carbon dioxide, or temperature in the ponds, but dissolved oxygen concentrations and turbidity increased with the degree of aeration (Table 7.6). Increased turbidity apparently resulted from disturbance of bottom muds by aeration. Total ammonia nitrogen was highest in the intermediate aeration treatment and lowest in the unaerated treatment. Chemical oxygen demand was lowest in the high aeration treatment. Average survival rates were 88, 93, and 99% in ponds receiving air volumes of 0, 6.9, and 10.4 m^3/min per ha. Average net production of fish increased with rate of aeration (Table 7.6).

TABLE 7.7

Harvest weight of channel catfish, S-values, and net economic returns for aerated and unaerated ponds. Each treatment was replicated twice (Parker, 1979).

Fish stocked (No./ha)	Harvest weight (kg/ha)	S-value	Net returns (U.S.$/ha)
Unaerated			
5,000	3,214	2.0	531
Aerated			
5,000	4,278	1.75	42
10,000	2,863	3.25	- 1,885
20,000	10,416	2.0	154
40,000	15,837	1.7	2,478

Aeration permitted the introduction of quantities of feed in excess of those possible in unaerated ponds. Loyacano concluded that volumes of air greater than those used in his study might produce larger improvements in water quality and further increases in fish yields. Unfortunately, data were not subjected to economic analysis.

Parker (1979) stocked duplicate 0.02-ha ponds with channel catfish at 5,000, 10,000, 20,000, and 40,000 fish/ha in April. Ponds were aerated continously with air-lift pumps (5-cm diameter; 3.3-m vertical entrainment) that moved 0.11 m^3/min of water with 0.06 m^3/min of air. The pumps added about 1 mg/l of oxygen when water contained 3-4 mg/l of oxygen and 0.3 mg/l of oxygen when the dissolved oxygen concentration in the water was 5-6 mg/l. When additional aeration was required, it was supplied with 0.25-kw spray-type surface aerators. Each pond received 16.3 m^3/day of fresh water inflow. Fish were fed daily at a rate of 3% of body weight per day for 204 days. Fish production data and net returns for each treatment are summarized in Table 7.7. The unaerated treatment was more profitable than all aerated treatments except the aerated treatment with the highest stocking rate (40,000 fish/ha). Half of the fish had to be harvested from the ponds of the higest stocking rate after 142 days because of difficulties in maintaining water quality. The remaining fish were harvested after 204 days. Production and economic data were based on the total harvest. Ponds had volumes of 200 m^3 and water exchange rates of 16 m^3/day, thus the water in the ponds was exchanged about every 2 weeks — a rate which is seldom possible in commercial fish ponds.

Plemmons (1980) stocked channel catfish at rates of 18,500, 25,000, and 31,000 fish/ha in ponds that were continuously aerated with spray-type surface aerators

TABLE 7.8

Average dissolved oxygen concentrations at dawn in aerated and unaerated ponds stocked with different densities of catfish. Each treatment was replicated three times (Plemmons, 1980).

Treatment	Dissolved oxygen (mg/l)					
	Apr	Jun	Jul	Aug	Sep	Nov
Unaerated						
5,000 fish/ha	3.7	4.8	4.2	3.3	4.7	6.4
Aerated						
18,500 fish/ha	6.9	4.6	3.8	2.5	4.8	6.6
25,000 fish/ha	6.6	4.4	3.8	1.8	3.1	6.5
31,000 fish/ha	6.5	4.4	3.7	1.9	3.7	5.5

rated at 5.5 kw/ha; unaerated control ponds were stocked at 5,000 fish/ha. Fish were stocked in March and harvested in November. Treatments were replicated three times. Feed was applied daily; the maximum feeding rates of 28 kg/ha per day in unaerated ponds and 206 kg/ha per day in the aerated treatment with the greatest stocking density were attained in October.

Average concentrations of dissolved oxygen at dawn for selected months are presented in Table 7.8. In spite of aeration, dissolved oxygen concentrations often dropped below 2 mg/l in ponds of all treatments, and especially in ponds with the highest stocking rates. For example, dissolved oxygen concentrations averaged below 2 mg/l on 13 mornings in unaerated ponds and on 11, 28, and 26 mornings, respectively, in aerated ponds with low, medium, and high stocking rates. Thus, emergency aeration with a Crisafulli pump was employed to prevent fish mortality during periods of critically low dissolved oxygen. In addition, water was occasionally flushed through all ponds to improve water quality. The ponds had volumes of 1,560 m^3 and the maximum volume of water added was 7,100 m^3 — more than four times the pond volume. Unfortunately, Plemmons did not provide complete data on emergency aeration and water exchange.

Total ammonia nitrogen concentrations usually averaged at least 1 mg/l in all ponds, and in September average values were above 2 mg/l in ponds of aerated treatments. The highest total ammonia nitrogen concentration for an individual pond was 4.75 mg/l. Even greater total ammonia nitrogen concentrations would have resulted had water not been flushed through ponds when un-ionized ammonia levels at dawn reached 0.3 mg/l. Afternoon pH values were often above 8.5, so un-ionized ammonia concentrations were frequently above 1 mg/l during afternoons.

TABLE 7.9

Channel catfish production data for unaerated and aerated ponds. Each treatment was replicated twice (Plemmons, 1980).

Variable	Treatment and stocking densities (fish/ha)			
	Unaerated	Aerated		
	5,000	18,500	25,000	30,100
Survival (%)	90	80	79	77
Harvest weight (kg/ha)	2,518	8,544	11,108	12,846
Average weight of individual fish (kg)	0.57	0.58	0.57	0.55
S-value	1.27	1.59	1.59	1.68

Although no fish mortality was attributed to ammonia toxicity, high levels of un-ionized ammonia probably had adverse effects on growth.

Disease caused by the bacterium Flexobacter columnaris was noted on two separate occasions within a 6-day period following dissolved oxygen concentrations less than 2 mg/l. Two other disease outbreaks were related to low oxygen levels. However, Plemmons felt that most problems with disease were triggered by rapid water temperature fluctuations caused by cold fronts and associated cold rain.

Data on survival, harvest weight of fish, average size of fish at harvest, and feed conversion are summarized in Table 7.9. More than four times as much net fish production was obtained in the aerated treatment with the high stocking rate than in the unaerated treatment. However, the increased production in aerated ponds cannot be attributed solely to the surface aerators, for emergency aeration and water exchange were also employed.

Plemmons made an economic analysis of the production systems. Gross returns were calculated as the value of the harvested fish minus costs of fingerlings, feed, electricity, aerators (initial cost depreciated over 10 years), chemicals for disease treatment, and pumping. Gross returns were:

Treatment	(U.S.$/ha)
Unaerated, 5,000 fish/ha	1,737
Aerated, 18,500 fish/ha	4,121
Aerated, 25,000 fish/ha	5,956
Aerated, 31,000 fish/ha	6,558

The cost of aeration was estimated to range from $0.13 to $0.19 per kilogram of fish. Of course, profit (net return) would be much less because labor, equipment, and fixed costs would have to be subtracted from gross returns.

A study was conducted at Auburn University to determine if nightly aeration of ponds with high feeding rates would reduce the risk of dissolved oxygen depletion and allow greater production of channel catfish than possible in unaerated ponds (Hollerman and Boyd, 1980). Twelve earthen ponds (0.02-0.04 ha) were stocked in February with 20,000 channel catfish fingerlings per hectare. Fish were fed a commercial ration (35% crude protein; floating pellet) 6 days per week at 3% of body weight adjusted periodically for weight gain and observed mortality. Maximum daily feeding rates reached 71 kg/ha per day in unaerated ponds and 90 kg/ha per day in aerated ponds. A 0.25-kw spray-type surface aerator (Air-O-Lator Corp., Kansas City, Missouri) was placed in each of six ponds, and the other six ponds were unaerated controls. Beginning on 1 July, aeration was applied from 0400 to 0600 h. From 1 August until 7 August, aerators were operated from 0200 to 0600 h. Aeration was applied from 0000 to 0600 h from 8 August until the fish were harvested on 16 October. Water was only added to ponds to replace evaporation.

The average of all dissolved oxygen measurements between 3 July and 10 October was 1.52 and 7.29 mg/l at dawn and dusk, respectively, for unaerated ponds and 4.64 and 8.25 mg/l at dawn and dusk for aerated ponds. For individual dates, average dissolved oxygen concentrations at dawn were always above 3.5 mg/l in the aerated ponds and often below 2 mg/l in the unaerated ponds (Fig. 7.9). Fish were generally observed in distress when dissolved oxygen concentrations were below 1.0 mg/l, and mortalities usually occurred when dissolved oxygen at dawn was below this level for two or more consecutive days. All unaerated ponds had fish kills attributed to low dissolved oxygen concentrations, but no oxygen-related fish kills occurred in aerated ponds.

A comparison of the diel pattern of dissolved oxygen concentrations for the aerated and unaerated ponds indicated an abrupt leveling of the nighttime dissolved oxygen decline when aeration began (Fig. 7.10). Afterwards, dissolved oxygen concentrations remained stable during the period of aeration.

Average total ammonia nitrogen concentrations were usually between 0.5 and 1.0 mg/l after mid-July. After aeration was initiated, total ammonia nitrogen values were higher in aerated ponds than in unaerated ponds. This probably resulted from disturbance of sediments by mixing, and from greater feeding rates in aerated ponds near the end of the experiment. Concentrations of total ammonia nitrogen never exceeded 1.29 mg/l in individual ponds. Although un-ionized ammonia concentrations were never lethal to fish, afternoon concentrations were frequently above 0.2 mg/l and probably had adverse effects on growth.

226

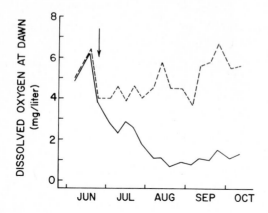

Fig. 7.9. Average oxygen concentrations at dawn on different dates in aerated (dashed line) and unaerated (solid line) ponds. Each treatment was replicated six times. The arrow indicates start of aeration (Hollerman and Boyd, 1980).

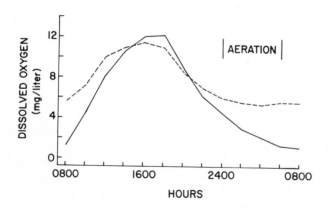

Fig. 7.10. Average dissolved oxygen concentrations for a 24-h period in unaerated (solid line) and aerated (dashed line) ponds. Each treatment was replicated six times. Aeration was applied between 0000 and 0600 h (Hollerman and Boyd, 1980).

Nitrite-nitrogen concentrations averaged below 0.06 mg/l in both aerated and unaerated ponds until 1 August. Afterwards, nitrite values increased rapidly in aerated ponds; concentrations averaged 0.02 and 0.20 mg/l as N in unaerated and aerated ponds, respectively, in mid-September. The greater accumulation of nitrite in aerated ponds apparently resulted from nitrite produced by denitrification in the bottom muds being mixed throughout the pond waters by the action of the aerators. Nitrite was oxidized in the water as obvious from the observation on

TABLE 7.10

Summary of fish production in aerated and unaerated ponds that were stocked with 20,000 channel catfish per hectare. Treatments were replicated six times (Hollerman and Boyd, 1980).

Variable	Treatment	
	Unaerated	Aerated
Survival (%)	40	92
Average weight of individual fish (kg)	0.11	0.28
S-value[a]	6.3	1.7
Harvest weight (kg/ha)	1,400	5,307

[a]Total feed applied ÷ net fish production.

3 October that aerated ponds had an average of 0.33 mg/l nitrate-nitrogen as compared to 0.03 mg/l in unaerated ponds. However, nitrite-nitrogen remained at high concentration in aerated ponds because of nightly mixing by aeration. Methemoglobinemia resulting from elevated nitrite concentration was not observed in fish of either treatment.

Carbon dioxide concentrations were regularly higher in unaerated ponds. In the early morning when carbon dioxide concentrations were above air saturation, aeration favored diffusion of carbon dioxide into the air.

Parasites including Scyphidia sp., Cryptobia branchialis, Costia sp., and Trichophyra sp. were found on fish from aerated and unaerated ponds. An infection of Aeromonas hydrophila occurred on fish in one aerated pond. Because no dissolved oxygen depletions occurred in aerated ponds, the average mortality of 8% was attributed to parasites and disease. Fish mortality in unaerated ponds could not be attributed solely to dissolved oxygen depletion since disease and parasite problems were plentiful.

Data on fish production are summarized in Table 7.10. Harvest weight, survival, and average weight of individual fish were all significantly greater in the aerated ponds. In three unaerated ponds, fish mortality ranged from 85 to 100% and there was no net production.

A basic budget analysis was performed by procedures developed by Crawford and McCoy (1977) to estimate profits for the aerated ponds. Net return was estimated at $1,500 per hectare. Because concentrations of dissolved oxygen never fell below the minimum acceptable value of 2 mg/l (Meyer et al., 1973), a higher stocking and feeding rate would likely have resulted in greater production and net returns. Tucker et al. (1979) reported that a stocking rate of 10,000 channel catfish per hectare and a maximum daily feeding rate of 56 kg/ha in unaerated ponds returned a profit of $1,303 per hectare. Thus, nightly aeration with aerators rated at 2.5 kw/ha only increased profits by $193 per hectare over that reported in unaerated ponds.

The economic analysis by Hollerman and Boyd suggests that nightly aeration might be a useful management tool. However, direct extrapolation of the economic data to larger ponds, as done in the budget analysis, is not valid for commercial fish ponds. The number and sizes of aerators for optimum aeration in larger ponds is not known and placing one large aerator in a pond, as assumed in the budget, is questionable at best. Depending on the size, configuration, and location of ponds, wiring costs for aerators would be highly variable. Even costs for disease and parasite control, maintenance, and harvest are not known to increase in direct proportion to pond size. Studies of the economics of aeration in commercial ponds will ultimately be required.

7.5 DESTRATIFICATION

Photosynthetic production of oxygen is great in surface waters of ponds used for intensive fish culture. However, as pointed out in Chapter 5, considerable amounts of oxygen are lost by diffusion from supersaturated surface waters. Further, the high densities of plankton restrict light penetration and increase temperature of surface layers, resulting in shallow thermal and oxygen stratification. Large volumes of oxygen-depleted hypolimnetic waters in fish ponds are undesirable because sudden thermal destratification (overturns) of such fish ponds can cause low oxygen concentration and fish kills.

Circulation of surface waters with paddle wheel aerators will mix oxygen-enriched surface waters with deeper waters of lower oxygen concentration (Busch et al., 1978). Busch and Flood (1979) used six paddle wheel aerators, powered by 0.19-kw electric motors, to provide circular water movement in a 0.53-ha pond stocked with channel catfish. Aerators were operated 5 h each day (0100-0600 h). The influence of the aerators was to increase oxygen concentrations in deep waters and reduce slightly oxygen levels in surface water. The energy consumption for the aerators was only 0.26 kw·h/day of fish produced. However, net fish production was only 2,610 kg/ha; a level of fish production not uncommon in ponds that are not aerated.

Busch (1980) constructed 0.065-kw paddle wheel aerators that provided a slow horizontal water current with a minimum of surface spraying and splashing. The inlet to the wheel's channel restricted all surface flow, bringing in water from about 50-cm depth. Most of the discharge was in the surface 20 cm. Two such paddle wheel aerators were installed in a 0.73-ha pond. Based on velocity and discharge data, the two paddle wheels pumped a volume equal to the pond volume every 20 h. More importantly, they provided a change of surface water every 2.4 h. Surface circulation was 5 m/min on the paddle wheel side of the pond and 2 m/min for the returning flow on the opposite side. Four paddle wheel operation schedules were tested: nighttime circulation, daytime circulation, day and night circulation, and no circulation. Busch concluded from oxygen measurements that paddle wheel aerators may serve to increase or decrease dissolved oxygen levels depending upon dissolved oxygen concentrations at the time of operation. Daytime stirring, through the reduction of the thermal gradient, can be effective in increasing overnight dissolved oxygen concentrations near the pond bottom. Day and night circulation and nighttime circulation can decrease the dissolved oxygen gradient that will form when aerators are not operated. Energy consumption by the two aerators for daytime operation was 1.95 kw·h/day.

Another method for affecting aeration of deep water is by down-flow aeration. Quintero and Garton (1973) built an axial flow (a pump in which most of the head produced by the propeller is from the pushing of the vanes), low head pump for lake destratification that created a down flow of well-oxygenated surface water. The Quintero-Garton pump had a capacity of 0.67 m^3/sec and was driven by a 0.37-kw electric motor. The apparatus consisted of an electric motor, a belt-drive reduction gear, a propeller, and an orifice shroud. It operated like a vent fan, except it moved water rather than air. The pump had a rounded subsurface entrance section made of sheet metal, a short sheet metal throat, a 1.07-m diameter propeller (seven-bladed aluminum crop drying fan), and a non-rigid diffuser of nylon-reinforced neoprene to recover the velocity head (Fig. 7.11). Various modifications of the Quintero-Garton pump are possible. The non-rigid diffuser was a mechanical means to recover exit velocity head, one of the major components of head loss. However, the massive diffuser increases construction cost and causes difficulties in installation. Therefore, Garton et al. (1977) recommended that the diffuser be omitted, and the loss in flow compensenated for by increasing propeller speed.

A modified Quintero-Garton pump was operated for 120 days on a 40-ha lake in Oklahoma (Garton et al., 1977). The pump had a 1.82-m diameter propeller located 1.8 m below the water line. The pump produced a flow of 1.72 m^3/sec (12.9% of the total lake volume per day) at 17 rpm with a 0.75-kw electric motor. Four days of operation eliminated thermal stratification and maintained isothermal conditions throughout the summer. Dissolved oxygen at 5 m increased from 0.2 to 4.3 mg/l after the first day of pumping. Afterwards, dissolved oxygen concentrations at 5 and 9 m were above levels observed during previous years when aeration had not been employed. Pumping also reduced the BOD of lake waters.

Modified Quintero-Garton pumps, similar to the one used by Garton et al. (1977), have been tested in channel catfish production ponds in Alabama by H. D. Kelly

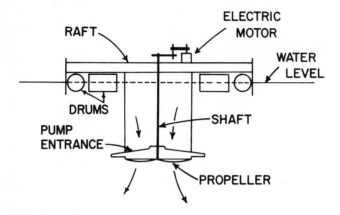

Fig. 7.11. A Quintero-Garton pump for destratifying lakes and ponds (Garton et al., 1977).

of the Soil Conservation Service of the United States Department of Agriculture. He found that the pumps eliminated thermal and oxygen stratification in ponds. Concentrations of oxygen in surface waters were lower in ponds containing pumps than in unaerated control ponds because the oxygen-enriched surface waters were mixed with deeper waters. However, the total oxygen supply in ponds was increased by pumping because continual down flow of surface waters reduced oxygen loss through diffusion.

Mixing of oxygen-enriched surface waters with deeper waters appears beneficial in ponds used for intensive fish culture. Pumps of the Quintero-Garton type appear to be a more suitable means of destratification in large ponds than the small paddle wheel aerators described by Busch (1980). However, the Quintero-Garton pump must be operated in water that is 3-4 m deep or disturbance of the bottom will create turbidity. Therefore, the small paddle wheel aerators would likely be effective in small, shallow ponds. Of course, if ponds are large, shallow, and not protected from the wind, natural wind mixing will often reduce problems of thermal and oxygen stratification. Further research is needed to ascertain if mixing of oxygen-enriched surface water with deeper water will reduce the risk of oxygen depletion.

7.6 PRACTICAL CONSIDERATIONS

The studies discussed above clearly demonstrate that emergency aeration is a sound management tool. Many types of emergency aeration have been used to successfully abort oxygen-related fish kills, but paddle wheel aerators, either tractor-powered or electrically driven, appear to be the best devices for emergency aeration. When compared to other emergency aerators, paddle wheels have superior oxygen transfer characteristics and are less expensive, more reliable, and easier to operate. Emergency aeration permits stocking and feeding rates to be raised to the maximum possible under normal conditions, for emergency aeration will prevent fish mortality when abnormal conditions (thermal destratification, phytoplankton die-offs, and prolonged cloudy weather) arise. Without emergency aeration, stocking and feeding rates must be considerably less because conditions conducive to oxygen depletion occur fairly frequently.

Aeration may be used on a more or less continual basis to increase fish production in ponds. However, the economics of continuous aeration are not clearly established. In arid regions where water is scarce or in densely populated regions where space for pond construction is scarce, continuous aeration is thought to be an effective management tool in small ponds. For example, fish farmers in Israel (arid climate) and Japan (high population density) use continuous aeration to intensify fish production. Research to document the benefits of aeration is often conducted in ponds where water exchange is employed to further improve water quality. For example, studies of aeration by Israeli workers (Rappaport et al., 1976) were made in ponds where water was exchanged every 10 days. Disposal of nutrients and organic matter in outflowing water undoubtedly permitted greater intensification of fish culture than would have been possible through the aeration of stagnant water ponds. Likewise, Plemmons (1980) and Parker (1979) flushed relatively large volumes of water through small ponds where the effects of aeration on channel catfish production were evaluated. They obtained much greater production of channel catfish than was reported in studies of aeration in stagnant water ponds by Hollerman and Boyd (1980).

Although aeration is widely practiced, research is needed to quantitatively define relationships among aeration rates, water quality, fish production, and economic returns. Such data would allow fish farmers to make more intelligent decisions about aeration. Furthermore, research needs to be conducted in such a manner that the benefits of other measures of improving water quality (water exchange, emergency aeration, etc.) can be separated from the benefits accrued from continuous aeration. For practical reasons, research on aeration is normally conducted in small ponds and there is no certainty that results so obtained may be extrapolated directly to larger ponds. Thus, many of the benefits of aeration expounded by researchers may not be realized in practical application.

In the southern United States there has been a continuing interest in aeration of commercial channel catfish ponds in spite of the fact that there is no conclusive proof that any type of aeration other than emergency aeration is profitable. One common practice is to locate one or two 3.73-kw spray-type surface aerators in large production ponds (5-10 ha). The aerators are often operated continuously. During daylight hours, pond waters are supersaturated with oxygen, and aeration only serves to increase the rate of diffusion of oxygen to the atmosphere. During the night, or at other times when the water is below saturation with oxygen, the aerators transfer oxygen to the water. However, most fish farmers and many individuals with training in fish culture have no idea how much oxygen is being transferred by the aerators. Usually, it is simply assumed that the aerators are transferring enough oxygen to benefit the fish.

The oxygen transfer rates of the aerators may be calculated. For illustration, suppose that a 10-ha pond with an average depth of 1.5 m is being continuously aerated by two 3.73-kw surface aerators that are rated at 2 kg O_2/kw·h under standard conditions. Assuming that the water temperature is 28°C and that the average dissolved oxygen concentration during the night is 4 mg/l, we can determine the oxygen transfer rate for the aerators under pond conditions with Equation 7.4. In the following computation, β and α values will be taken as 0.97 and 0.90, respectively:

$$OT' = 2 \left[\frac{0.97(7.75 - 4)}{8.84} (1.024)^8 (0.90) \right]$$

$$OT' = 0.866 \text{ kg } O_2/\text{kw·h}$$

Therefore, the two 3.73-kw aerators will transfer 0.866 kg O_2/kw·h X 3.73 kw X 2 = 6.46 kg O_2/h. In 12 h, the aerators will transfer 77.52 kg of oxygen. The pond contains 150,000 m^3 of water, so the quantity of oxygen transferred by the aerators will be equivalent to 77,520 g ÷ 150,000 m^3 = 0.52 g/m^3 or 0.52 mg/l. This amount of oxygen would obviously have little effect on fish production. Furthermore, during the day, the aerators probably cause an oxygen loss equivalent to the nighttime gain.

Although aeration of the type described above has little influence on dissolved oxygen concentrations, the practice has resulted in the intensification of channel catfish culture. Fish farmers had confidence to increase stocking and feeding rates because they assumed a large influence of the aerators. Dissolved oxygen problems still occurred after installation of the surface aerators, but emergency aeration was employed to prevent fish kills. In reality, the surface aerators had no real effect, but their use resulted in greater profits because income from higher stocking and feeding rates more than compensated for the cost of aeration. Over the years, many fish farmers have discovered that the aerators were not actually beneficial. They have discontinued the use of the aerators, but have not reduced feeding and stocking rates to previous levels.

The aeration requirements to maintain oxygen concentrations above a specified level will be calculated to demonstrate that the aeration of large ponds requires considerable energy. Let us assume that a 10-ha pond of 1.5 m average depth ($150,000$ m^3) will be stocked with 10,000 channel catfish per hectare. We will further assume that the fish will reach 400 g each by late summer when water temperature will be 28°C and when COD may be as high as 150 mg/l. Benthic respiration will be assigned a value of 61 mg O_2/m^2 per h. It is desired to locate enough spray-type surface aerators in the pond to prevent dissolved oxygen concentrations from falling below 4 mg/l (51.7% of air saturation at 28°C). The 3.73-kw aerators are rated at 1.8 kg $O_2/kw\cdot h$ under standard conditions.

In order to solve this problem, we will calculate the rate of oxygen loss from the pond water, calculate the oxygen transfer rate of aerators, and determine the number of aerators needed. The calculations follow:

<u>Plankton respiration</u> (Equation 2.11; C = COD; T = °C)

O_2 in mg/l per h = $- 1.006 - 0.00148$ C $- 0.0000125$ $c^2 + 0.0766$ T $- 0.00144$ $T^2 +$ 0.000253 CT

$$= - 1.006 - 0.222 - 0.281 + 2.145 - 1.129 + 1.063$$

O_2 consumption = 0.57 mg/l per h

<u>Fish respiration</u> (Equation 2.9; W = fish weigh in grams; T = °C)

log O_2/g of fish per h = $- 0.999 - 0.000957$ W $+ 0.0000006$ $W^2 + 0.0327$ T $-$ 0.0000087 $T^2 + 0.0000003$ WT

$$= - 0.999 - 0.383 + 0.096 + 0.916 - 0.007 + 0.003$$
$$= - 0.374$$

O_2 consumption = 0.423 mg/g per h

This is equivalent to 0.423 mg O_2/g of fish per h X 400 g/fish X 100,000 fish = 16,920 g O_2/h, and 16,920 g O_2/h $\div$ 150,000 m^3 = 0.113 g O_2/m^3 per h or 0.113 mg/l per h.

<u>Benthic respiration</u>

61 mg O_2/m^2 per h $\div$ 1.5 m = 40.7 mg O_2/m^3 per h
This quantity is equal to 0.041 mg/l per h.

<u>Diffusion</u>

Aerators are tested in tanks open to the atmosphere and natural diffusion of oxygen is included in the oxygen transfer rating of the aerator. Of course, ponds receive more wind mixing than aeration tanks, but we will not attempt to calculate natural diffusion. Any natural aeration will serve as a safety factor.

<u>Oxygen loss</u>

The total oxygen loss from the pond water is 0.57 + 0.113 + 0.041 mg O_2/l per h = 0.724 mg O_2/l per h. If aerators are turned on when the dissolved oxygen concentration is at 4 mg/l, they must transfer 0.724 mg/l per h to prevent further decline in oxygen levels. This rate of oxygen transfer is equivalent to 0.724 g O_2/m^3 per h X 150,000 m^3 = 108,600 g O_2/h or 108.6 kg O_2/h.

Aerator requirements

Aeration requirements may now be estimated by Equation 7.4, assuming α = 0.90 and β = 0.98:

$$OT' = 1.8 \left[\frac{(0.98)(7.75 - 4)}{8.84} \quad (1.024)^8 (0.90) \right]$$

OT' = 0.797 kg O_2/kw·h

Thus, the aeration requirement is 108.6 kg O_2/h ÷ 0.797 kg O_2/kw·h = 136 kw·h. The aerators are rated at 3.73 kw each, so 37 aerators will be required.

Obviously, it would be very expensive to aerate a large pond at a rate suffi-cient to maintain oxygen concentrations above 4 mg/l at night when fish and plankton density are high and water is warm. A more reasonable approach is to use supplemental aeration at night to increase the carrying capacity for fish under normal conditions and rely on emergency aeration to prevent fish kills when oxygen-depletion results. Based on earlier calculations, two 3.73-kw spray-type surface aerators would, under average conditions (28°C; 4 mg/l dissolved oxygen), transfer about 6.59 kg O_2/h to a 10-ha pond of 1.5 m depth. If channel catfish in the pond weigh 400 g each, their rate of oxygen consumption would be 0.423 mg O_2/g of fish per h or 0.423 g O_2/kg of fish per h (see example above). Hence, the aerators supply enough to meet the respiratory requirements of 6,590 g O_2/h ÷ 0.423 g O_2/kg of fish per h = 15,579 kg of fish or about 1,500 kg/ha of fish. Unfortunately, this method of expressing the benefits of aeration is misleading because each kilogram of fish produced results in about 5.3 kg of COD (see Chapter 6). Therefore, the COD of ponds would be higher at greater fish density and oxygen concentrations would be lower at night as a result of increased stocking and feeding rates, even though enough aeration was applied to theoretically fulfill the respiratory needs of the additional fish. More research will be required before we can estimate the relationship between the amount of aeration applied and the degree of intensification of fish culture permissible under normal conditions. Of course, emergency aeration equipment must be available or fish kills may result following phytoplankton die-offs, overturns, or cloudy weather.

Steeby (1976) aerated a 1.4-ha channel catfish pond with a total of 0.96 m^3/min of compressed air released through 25 diffusers located over the pond bottom. The pond was heavily stocked with fish and fed at a high rate. Fish survival and growth was excellent under normal weather conditions. However, plankton density was high in response to feeding, and a massive fish kill occurred during a prolonged period of cloudy weather in September — only a few weeks before fish were to have been harvested. Incidentally, the aeration system was operating at full capacity when the fish kill occurred. It simply could not supply enough oxygen to meet the requirements of the pond biota when photosynthetic rates were low.

When high quality surface or ground water is available, it may be added to ponds with low dissolved oxygen to increase the oxygen supply and to flush out accumulated organic matter. Ground water that is aerated by gravity aeration is most commonly employed. This practice is highly successful in small ponds, but usually decreases in effectiveness as pond size increases. For example, suppose that a well with a discharge of 4 m^3/min is available to supply gravity aerated water at 7.5 mg/l of dissolved oxygen. The discharge will contain 7.5 g/m^3 of dissolved oxygen or 7.5 g/m^3 X 4 m^3/min X 60 min/h X 12 h = 21,600 g or 21.6 kg of oxygen in 12 h. If the receiving pond has an area of 0.5 ha and a depth of 1 m (5,000 m^3 volume), the added oxygen will be equivalent to 21,600 g ÷ 5,000 m^3 = 4.32 g/m^3 or 4.32 mg/l. Further, the total discharge will be 4 m^3/min X 60 min/h X 12 h = 2,880 m^3 or (2,880 m^3 ÷ 5,000 m^3) X 100 = 57.6% of the pond volume. The discharge would obviously have a tremendous influence on water quality. On the other hand, if the pond has an area of 10 ha and an average depth of 1.5 m (150,000 m^3 volume), the oxygen equivalent of the inflowing water will be only 21,600 g ÷ 150,000 m^3 = 0.14 g/m^3 or 0.14 mg/l. The total discharge would be (2,880 m^3 ÷ 150,000 m^3) X 100 = 1.92% of the pond volume. Thus, the discharge would not appreciably improve water quality during a 12-h period.

REFERENCES

Boyd, C. E. and Tucker, C. S., 1979. Emergency aeration of fish ponds. Trans. Amer. Fish. Soc., 108: 299-306.
Boyd, C. E., Steeby, J. A., and McCoy, E. W., 1979. Frequency of low dissolved oxygen concentrations in ponds for commercial culture of channel catfish. Proc. Annual Conf. Southeast. Assoc. Fish and Wildl. Agencies, 33: 591-599.
Busch, C. D., 1980. Circulation for pond aeration and energy conservation. In: J. W. Avault (Editor), Proc. World Mariculture Soc., 11: in press.
Busch, C. D. and Flood, C. A., Jr., 1979. Pond water movement can improve natural aeration. Auburn University Agricultural Experiment Station, Auburn, Alabama, Highlights of Agricultural Research, 26, No. 1: 8.
Busch, C. D., Flood, C. A., Jr., and Allison, R., 1978. Multiple paddlewheels' influence on fish pond temperature and aeration. Trans. Amer. Soc. Agric. Eng., 21: 1222-1224.
Chesness, J. L. and Stephens, J. L., 1971. A model study of gravity flow aerators for catfish raceway systems. Trans. Amer. Soc. Agric. Eng., 14: 1167-1169.
Colt, J. and Tchobanoglous, G., 1979. Design of aeration systems for aquaculture. Department of Civil Engineering, University of California, Davis, California, 25 pp.
Crawford, K. W. and McCoy, E. W., 1977. Budgeting for selected aquacultural

236

enterprises. Auburn University Agricultural Experiment Station, Auburn, Alabama, Bulletin 495, 51 pp.

Dunseth, D. R., 1977. Polyculture of channel catfish, Ictalurus punctatus, silver carp, Hypothalmichthys molitrix, and three all-male tilapias, Sarotherodon spp. Ph.D. dissertation, Auburn University, Auburn, Alabama, 72 pp.

Eckenfelder, W. W., Jr. and Ford, D. L., 1968. New concepts in oxygen transfer and aeration. In: E. F. Gloyna and W. W. Eckenfelder, Jr. (Editors), Advances in Water Quality Improvement. University of Texas Press, Austin, pp. 215-236.

Garton, J. E., Strecker, R. G., and Summerfelt, R. C., 1977. Performance of an axial flow pump for lake destratification. Proc. Annual Conf. Southeast. Assoc. Game and Fish Comm., 31: 336-347.

Haney, P. D., 1954. Theoretical principles of aeration. J. Amer. Water Works Assoc., 46: 353-376.

Hollerman, W. D. and Boyd, C. E., 1980. Nightly aeration to increase production of channel catfish. Trans. Amer. Fish. Soc., 109: 446-452.

Lay, B. A., 1971. Applications for potassium permanganate in fish culture. Trans. Amer. Fish. Soc., 100: 813-815.

Loyacano, H. A., 1974. Effects of aeration in earthen ponds on water quality and production of white catfish. Aquaculture, 3: 261-271.

Marek, M. and Sarig, S., 1971. Preliminary observations of super-intensive fish culture in the Berth-Shean Valley in 1969-1970. Bamidgeh, 23: 93-99.

Meyer, F. B., Sneed, K. E., and Eschmeyer, P. G., 1973. Second report to the fish farmers. U. S. Bureau of Sport Fisheries and Wildlife, Washington, D. C., Resource Publication 113, 123 pp.

Mitchell, R. E. and Kirby, A. M., Jr., 1976. Performance characteristics of pond aeration devices. In: J. W. Avault (Editor), Proc. World Mariculture Soc., 7: 561-581.

Parker, N. C., 1979. Channel catfish production in continuously aerated ponds. Research Workshop Summary of Papers, Catfish Farmers of America Annual Meeting, 31 January-3 February, 1979, Jackson, Mississippi, 44 pp.

Plemmons, B. P., 1980. Effects of aeration and high stocking density on channel catfish production. M. S. thesis, Louisiana State University, Baton Rouge, Louisiana, 35 pp.

Quintero, J. E. and Garton, J. E., 1973. A low energy lake destratifier. Trans. Amer. Soc. Agric. Eng., 16: 973-978.

Rappaport, A. and Sarig, S., 1975. Results of tests in intensive growth of fish at the Genosar station ponds in 1974. Bamidgeh, 27: 75-82.

Rappaport, U., Sarig, S., and Marek, M., 1976. Results of tests of various aeration systems on the oxygen regime in the Genosar experimental ponds and growth of fish there in 1975. Bamidgeh, 28: 35-49.

Speece, R. E., 1969. U-tube oxygenation for economical saturation of fish hatchery water. Trans. Amer. Fish. Soc., 89: 789-795.

Steeby, J. A., 1976. Effects of compressed air aeration in a heavily-fed farm pond stocked with channel catfish. M. S. thesis, Auburn University, Auburn, Alabama, 49 pp.

Stuckenburg, J. R., Wahbeh, V. N., and McKinney, R. E., 1977. Experiences in evaluating and specifying aeration equipment. J. Water Poll. Cont. Fed., 49: 66-82.

Swingle, H. S., 1968. Fish kills caused by phytoplankton blooms and their prevention. Proc. World Symposium on Warm-Water Pond Fish Culture, FAO United Nations, Fish. Rep. No. 44, 5: 407-411.

Tucker, C. S. and Boyd, C. E., 1977. Relationships between potassium permanganate treatment and water quality. Trans. Amer. Fish. Soc., 106: 481-488.

Tucker, L., Boyd, C. E., and McCoy, E. W., 1979. Effects of feeding rate on water quality, production of channel catfish, and economic returns. Trans. Amer. Fish. Soc., 108: 389-396.

Wheaton, F. W., 1977. Aquacultural Engineering. Wiley-Interscience, New York, 708 pp.

Chapter 8

AQUATIC PLANT CONTROL

8.1   INTRODUCTION
   The importance of aquatic plants in fish ponds has been continually emphasized
in the preceding chapters. Aquatic plants are the base of the food chain in ponds
where fish derive their nutriment from aquatic organisms. Dissolved oxygen in
most ponds results from photosynthesis by aquatic plants, and imbalances in photosynthesis and respiration lead to oxygen depletion and fish kills. Overabundance
of phytoplankton, sometimes a cause of oxygen depletion in fertilized ponds,
suggests that too much fertilizer is being applied. In ponds where fish are fed,
excessive phytoplankton abundance is the natural consequence of high feeding
rates necessary for large yields of fish. Normally, fish production in intensive
culture is limited by the amount of feed that can be applied without phytoplankton
blooms becoming so dense that dissolved oxygen problems cannot be managed.
   Macrophytes are also common inhabitants of fish ponds. In fertilized ponds,
and even in some ponds where feeding is practiced, low or moderate abundance of
macrophytes can be tolerated. However, if macrophyte communities become extensive
they may cause serious ecological problems. They compete with phytoplankton for
nutrients, provide cover so that forage fish escape predation, interfere with
fishing and fish harvest, increase water loss through evapotranspiration, prevent
fish from finding feed which is applied, and cause problems with dissolved oxygen.
   Because of the problems caused by phytoplankton and macrophytes, there is
considerable interest in their control. Various chemical, mechanical, and biological techniques have proven effective in controlling aquatic vegetation. However, none of the control methods are effective under all conditions and the control
of aquatic plants in ponds is often a difficult task.

8.2   CHEMICAL CONTROL
8.2.1 Restrictions on chemicals
   In the United States, the Federal Environmental Pesticide Act of 1972 requires
that all chemical uses in fish culture be covered by registration granted by the
United States Environmental Protection Agency or by the United States Food and
Drug Administration (Cumming, 1975). This legislation extends to all chemicals
applied to ponds, but it has particularly affected chemical control of aquatic
plants. Because a large body of information is required to prove that a particular chemical is safe, both to the environment and to humans consuming fish from
waters treated with the chemical, and the market for chemicals in fish culture is
small, there is little incentive for the manufacturer of a chemical to seek its

clearance for use in fish ponds. Therefore, the United States Fish and Wildlife Service has devoted considerable effort towards securing clearance for use of chemicals in fisheries (Meyer et al., 1976).

Chemicals used in fisheries fall into several possible categories of registration (Meyer et al., 1976) as follows:

Petition for Exemption from Registration: Fishery use does not constitute use of the compound as a pesticide and is therefore exempt from registration requirements.

Generally Regarded as Safe: Fishery use is generally regarded as safe because of a long history of demonstrated safety in a related, nonfishery field.

Not New Drug Monograph: Compound is not a new drug and has been used for desired purpose for many years.

Petition for Exemption from Tolerance: Registration is required, with possible exemption from tolerance because of the low levels used or because the residual levels present after use are low.

New Animal Drug Application: Any drug or anesthetic used in the production of animals for human food must be registered.

Food Use Registration: Registration is required and a maximum residue tolerance must be established that cannot be exceeded; withdrawal times after treatment are often specified.

Nonfood Use Registration: Registration is required but use is limited to nonfood fishes.

Experiment Use Permits: Permits are required for field studies in which a pesticide or other experimental compound is used in an area larger than 0.40 ha.

Meyers et al. (1976) indicated that the following chemicals had been registered: antimycin*, rotenone (Noxfish®, Pronoxfish®, and Chem-Fish Regulator®)*, Bayluscide®*, 3-trifluoro-methyl-4-nitrophenol (TFM)*, TFM-Bayluscide mixture*, Finquel® (MS-222)*, trichlorfon (Masoten®)*, sodium chloride, nitrofurpirinol (Furanace®)*, Terramycin , sulfamerazine, copper sulfate, dichlobenil (Casoron®)*, dimethylamine salt of 2, 4-dichlorophenoxy acetic acid (DMA-2, 4-D), diquat bromide (Diquat®), endothall (Aquathol®, Hydrothol®, Hydout®, and Q-Dril®), simazine (Aquazine®), and calcium hydroxide and oxide (lime). Fertilizers, liming materials, gypsum, and alum are apparently exempt from registration because fishery use is generally regarded as safe because of a long history of demonstrated safety in a related nonfishery field. Private pond owners may, at their own risk, apply unregistered chemicals to sportfish ponds, but employees of governmental agencies

---

*Nonfood fish only.

in the United States cannot legally recommend the use of chemicals that are not registered. Lack of registration does not imply that a particular chemical is unsafe for use in fisheries. Rather, lack of registration indicates that documentation is lacking to prove that the chemical is safe. Furthermore, registration does not imply that a chemical is effective for the intended uses.

All of the discussion applies to fish culture in the United States. I am not familar with restrictions on chemicals used in fish culture in other nations.

8.2.2 Phytoplankton control with copper sulfate

Copper sulfate has a long history of use as an algicide. Many workers have determined the toxicity of copper sulfate to algae. For example, Maloney and Palmer (1956) evaluated the toxicity of copper sulfate to 30 species of algae. The concentration required to control a particular species was defined as the concentration that killed all treated individuals. Copper sulfate concentrations of 0.25, 0.5, 1.0, and 2.0 mg/l controlled 0, 13, 37, and 53%, respectively, of all species tested. Appreciable mortality of algae will result at concentrations lower than those required for complete kill (Bartlett et. al., 1974). Palmer (1962) reviewed data on the toxicity of copper sulfate to algae and ranked genera as being susceptible or resistant to this chemical. Fitzgerald and Faust (1963) demonstrated that the toxicity of copper sulfate to algae was greater in some culture media than in others. Bartsch (1954) found that the toxicity of copper sulfate to algae decreased with increasing pH and total alkalinity. Algae also develop a resistance to copper sulfate upon repeated application (Fitzgerald, 1959). Therefore, the toxicity of copper sulfate to algae will vary depending upon water quality, species, and previous exposure of algae to copper sulfate.

Copper sulfate is also highly toxic to fish, so concentrations that are required to control algae must be below the threshold toxicity for fish. The effect of copper sulfate on fish has been widely investigated, and the results of these studies were reviewed by McKee and Wolf (1963) and Jackson (1974). Discrepancies exist in the literature regarding the toxicity of this chemical. Concentrations from 0.002 to 200 mg/l have been reported lethal to various species of fish in different waters. As expected, some species are more susceptible to copper sulfate than others. For example, McKee and Wolf (1963) reported the highest concentrations of copper sulfate tolerated by different species as follows: trout, 0.14 mg/l; carp, 0.33 mg/l; suckers, 0.33 mg/l; catfish, 0.40 mg/l; pickerel, 0.40 mg/l; goldfish, 0.50 mg/l; perch, 0.67 mg/l; sunfish, 1.35 mg/l; and black bass, 2.0 mg/l. McKee and Wolf did not give corresponding data on water temperature, water quality, exposure time, or scientific names of fish. Wide differences also exist between toxicity data for a single species as reported by different authors (Jackson, 1974). Many of these discrepancies no doubt resulted from differences in experimental conditions. Lloyd (1965) found that temperature, the concentrations of calcium and dissolved oxygen in the water, and the activity of fish affected the toxicity of copper sulfate. Copper sulfate is more toxic in water of low alkalinity than in water of high alkalinity. Because magnitudes of hardness and alkalinity are often similar, many workers have erroneously attributed the degree of toxicity to water hardness rather than to alkalinity. Inglis and Davis (1972) found the 96-h LC50 for copper sulfate to bluegill (Lepomis macrochirus) to be 1.0 mg/l at a total hardness of 5.2 mg/l, 1.72 mg/l at 209 mg/l total hardness, and 2.55 mg/l at 365 mg/l total hardness. In these experiments, total alkalinity increased with increasing total hardness, and the reduction in toxicity was related to alkalinity instead of hardness. The toxicity of copper to fish also decreases with increasing pH (Pagenkopf et al., 1974).

In natural waters, there is little Cu^{2+} ion present at equilibrium, for most copper is associated with inorganic ions (ion-pairs) or organic substances (complexes). For example, at the pH and alkalinities of natural waters, there will be 2-200 times as much of the copper carbonate ion-pair as Cu^{2+} (Boyd, 1979). Add to copper in inorganic ion-pairs the copper complexed with organic substances, and only a minute fraction of the total copper will be Cu^{2+} (Stiff, 1971a, b). Pagenkopf et al. (1974) suggested that Cu^{2+} was the toxic form of copper to fish. However, Shaw and Brown (1974) claimed that both copper ion and the copper carbonate ion-pair are toxic to fish, and the toxicity of copper is related to its total concentration. Further evidence that Cu^{2+} is the toxic form of copper is afforded by the fact that complex formation with glycine and humic substances reduced the toxicity of copper to fish (Stiff, 1971b). Sprague (1968) suggested that the chelating agent NTA (nitrilotriacetic acid) could be used as an antipollutant to protect fish from copper poisoning. Chelated copper herbicides are often recommended for application to soft water ponds to prevent copper poisoning in fish.

Care must obviously be used when copper sulfate is applied as an algicide, for fish mortality can result from direct toxicity of copper. However, copper applied to ponds in algicides quickly disappears from the water. Some of the copper is absorbed by plants, but most is precipitated as insoluble tenorite (CuO) or malachite $[Cu_2(OH)_2CO_3]$ (Stumm and Morgan, 1970) or adsorbed by bottom muds (Riemer and Toth, 1970). The influence of copper sulfate treatment on copper concentrations in pond water is shown in Fig. 8.1.

Applications of copper sulfate may be quite effective in reducing phytoplankton abundance in lakes and ponds. For example, Sohacki et al. (1969) applied 2 mg/l of copper sulfate to a pond in Michigan with a total alkalinity of 80 mg/l and phytoplankton photosynthesis declined markedly. However, the treatment did not have appreciable residual effect and phytoplankton photosynthesis quickly returned to pretreatment levels. Similar observations have been reported by many workers and there is no doubt that copper sulfate is an excellent algicide, but it is

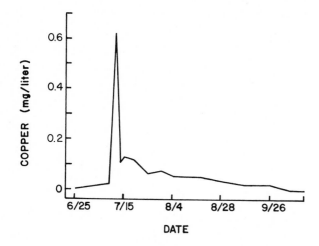

Fig. 8.1. Effect of copper sulfate treatment of a pond on copper concentrations in water.

without appreciable residual toxicity. Application rates vary from 0.025 mg/l to more than 1 mg/l (Jackson, 1974). Montgomery (1961) used 0.5-1.0 mg/l copper sulfate in farm ponds in Georgia. Bartsch (1954) found that 0.33 mg/l of copper sulfate was effective in controlling phytoplankton in lakes in the midwestern United States where total alkalinity values were below 50 mg/l. However, 2 mg/l of copper sulfate were needed in waters where total alkalinity exceeded 50 mg/l. Toth and Riemer (1968) also found that the same dosage rate for copper sulfate was not suitable for all ponds; however, methods for determining the best dosage rate are not available.

Crance (1963) used copper sulfate at the rate of 0.84 kg/ha to "thin" Microcystis blooms in fish ponds. This low concentration of copper sulfate greatly reduced the abundance of Microcystis, but Microcystis soon increased in abundance and retreatment was necessary. Because of the successful use of copper sulfate at low concentrations to reduce Microcystis blooms, many biologists in the southern United States recommend the application of 0.84 kg/ha of copper sulfate for "thinning" phytoplankton blooms of all types. However, Tucker and Boyd (1978) found that application of 0.84 kg/ha of copper sulfate to channel catfish ponds at 2-week intervals was not effective in reducing total phytoplankton abundance. No Microcystis or other species of scum-forming algae occurred in the ponds treated with copper sulfate; this observation is not conclusive because no algal scums formed in untreated ponds. Kessler (1969) found that localized applications of copper sulfate were effective in killing phytoplankton in surface scums, but his treatment rates were considerably greater than 0.84 kg/ha.

Several techniques have been used to apply copper sulfate to ponds. Some workers have put copper sulfate crystals in burlap bags and towed the bags behind a
boat while the chemical dissolved. Others have placed the copper sulfate in cloth
bags and suspended the bags in ponds for the copper sulfate to gradually dissolve.
Copper sulfate may be broadcast over pond surfaces, or it may be dissolved in
water and sprayed over surfaces. Button et al. (1977) distributed copper sulfate
into a water supply reservoir at the rate of 4 kg/ha from a hopper mounted on a
boat.

The decomposition of algae killed following copper sulfate application may
result in depletion of dissolved oxygen. Sohacki et al. (1969) reported a marked
decline in dissolved oxygen following treatment of a pond with 2 mg/l of copper
sulfate, and McIntosh and Kevern (1974) reported that treatment of a pond with 3
mg/l copper sulfate caused oxygen depletion. Copper sulfate applications kill
large numbers of invertebrate fish food organisms (Crance, 1963; McIntosh and
Kevern, 1974), but the populations of these organisms increase again soon after
treatment.

Chelation of copper is thought to protect it for a time from precipitation.
The chelate dissociates to release more copper as plants absorb copper from the
water. Furthermore, the toxicity of the copper in a chelated compound to fish is
less than that of an equal concentration of copper applied as copper sulfate.
Hence, species of fish with a high susceptibility to copper are less apt to be
harmed by treatment with chelated copper; this is especially true for treatment
of acidic waters. Nevertheless, manufacturers of chelated copper algicides
caution that use of high concentrations of these algicides may cause fish mortality
in waters of low alkalinity.

An example of a chelated copper algicide is Cutrine® (Applied Biochemists,
Inc., Mequon, Wisconsin). Cutrine is a copper triethanolamine complex in water;
it contains the equivalent of 7.1% elemental copper. The manufacturer recommends
for phytoplankton control the use of enough Cutrine to provide a copper concentration of 0.2 mg/l. A suitable chelated copper algicide can be made by mixing
1 part by weight of copper sulfate and 2 parts by weight of citric acid in water.
Chelated copper algicides are considerably more expensive than copper sulfate per
unit of copper, and it remains to be seen if they are appreciably more effective
over a wide range of conditions.

8.2.3 Phytoplankton control with simazine

Simazine [2-chloro-4, 6-bis (ethylamino)-s-triazine] is a powerful inhibitor
of photosynthesis and is extremely toxic to phytoplankton. Simazine is not toxic
to fish at concentrations normally used for phytoplankton control (Mauck, 1974).

In the United States, a commercial formulation of simazine called Aquazine® (Ciba-Geigy Corporation, Greensboro, North Carolina) is marketed for phytoplankton control. The manufacturer recommends the use of Aquazine at 0.60 mg/liter for light infestations of phytoplankton and up to 1.25 mg/l for heavy infestations. The Aquazine treatments should be made in the spring before water temperature reaches 24°C and before algal blooms become extremely dense. Retreatment with Aquazine is recommended if blooms develop during summer. An alternative to periodic applications of Aquazine is to treat pond bottoms with 10-18 kg/ha of Aquazine before filling the ponds in the spring.

The manufacturer claims that Aquazine provides effective and selective control of blue-green algae. They also noted that dissolved oxygen concentrations usually begin to decline about 3 days after treatment with Aquazine and reached minimum levels about 2 weeks after treatment. Sutton et al. (1965) also observed that simazine was toxic to algae and caused oxygen concentrations to decline.

Although simazine is recommended by many biologists for phytoplankton control in fish ponds, there is little information to justify this recommendation. The most thorough evaluation of simazine application to ponds is that of Tucker and Boyd (1978, 1979). In one experiment (Tucker and Boyd, 1978), channel catfish fingerlings were stocked in eight ponds at the rate of 10,000 per hectare and fed 7 days per week at 3% of body weight adjusted periodically for weight gain. Four of the ponds were treated with 0.80 mg/l of simazine on 26 April 1976, and subsequent applications of 0.25 mg/l were made on 20 July and 26 August. The other four ponds served as untreated controls. Simazine treatment caused a drastic reduction in phytoplankton (Fig. 8.2). Chlorophyll a concentrations were 3-10 times lower in treated ponds than in control ponds. Simazine disappeared from the water rapidly; less than 50% of that applied remained after 16 days. Regrowth of phytoplankton following initial treatment was not obvious until early June when simazine concentrations in pond water were about 0.25 mg/l. During August and September, some regrowth of phytoplankton occurred even though simazine concentrations in the water were between 0.3 and 0.4 mg/l. Nevertheless, these findings verify that simazine is an extremely powerful algicide.

Unfortunately, dissolved oxygen concentrations were adversely affected by simazine treatment (Fig. 8.3). Average concentrations of dissolved oxygen measured between 0800 and 0900 h were never above 80% of air saturation in simazine-treated ponds, and concentrations were below 50% of saturation during most of the growing season. Concentrations of dissolved oxygen were usually near air saturation in control ponds. In spite of high feeding rates, early morning dissolved oxygen levels were never dangerously low in the control ponds. As a result of low dissolved oxygen levels, fish fed poorly in treated ponds for up to 2 weeks following each application of simazine. Furthermore, on the morning following the simazine

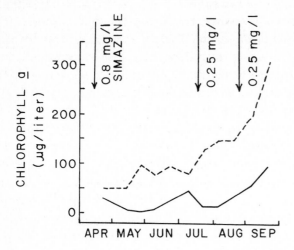

Fig. 8.2. Chlorophyll a concentrations in channel catfish ponds following treatment with simazine; arrows indicate simazine treatments. After Tucker and Boyd (1978).

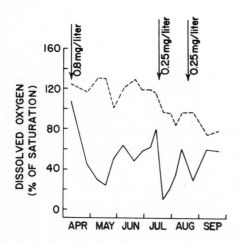

Fig. 8.3. Dissolved oxygen concentrations measured between 0800 and 0900 h in channel catfish ponds following treatment with simazine; arrows indicate simazine treatments. After Tucker and Boyd (1978).

treatment on 20 July, oxygen depletion in one treated pond killed about a third the fish. Emergency aeration prevented further mortality. At harvest, control ponds yielded an average of 2,643 kg/ha of channel catfish; the yield for the simazine-treated ponds averaged only 2,107 kg/ha. The difference was statistically significant (P<0.05). Results of this study suggest that simazine should not be applied to catfish ponds for "thinning" phytoplankton blooms.

In the other study (Tucker and Boyd, 1979), simazine was applied to the bottoms of three ponds at the rate of 13.4 kg/ha on the day before filling the pond with water. The treated ponds and three untreated ponds were stocked with 7,400 fingerling channel catfish per hectare, and fish were fed at 3% of body weight adjusted periodically for weight gain. Simazine concentrations in the treated ponds remained above 0.2 mg/l for 4 months. This prolonged persistence of simazine resulted in lower levels of phytoplankton abundance and lower concentrations of dissolved oxygen as compared to untreated control ponds. Catfish yields averaged 3,495 and 2,832 kg/ha in control and treated ponds, respectively. The reduction in fish yield in the simazine-treated ponds was statistically significant (P<0.01).

8.2.4 Generalizations about algicides

Both copper sulfate and simazine are very effective algicides. However, problems with low dissolved oxygen concentrations following treatment with these algicides limit their usefulness in fish culture. Although "spot applications" of copper sulfate to scums of phytoplankton are effective, it is doubtful that small, periodic applications of copper sulfate or simazine — or for that matter, any algicide — can be employed effectively to limit phytoplankton abundance in nutrient-enriched fish ponds. The use of algicides to limit phytoplankton growth in ponds used for intensive fish culture is analogous to a human losing weight by taking periodic, sublethal doses of a toxin instead of reducing his food intake. Although he may lose weight, he will not be very healthy after losing the weight, for he continues to overeat and must continue to ingest the toxin to keep from gaining back weight. In the fish ponds, nutrients that stimulate phytoplankton continually reach the water because feeds are applied for the fish. An algicide treatment may reduce phytoplankton. However, as soon as the algicide concentration diminishes to a non-toxic level, phytoplankton abundance will increase.

Further investigations of chemical methods for preventing overabundant phytoplankton growth in eutrophic ponds should not be initiated in haste. Results from studies of copper sulfate and simazine cast serious doubts on the use of algicides as chemostats on phytoplankton growth in ponds used for intensive fish culture. Algicides are useful in reducing the abundance of phytoplankton in bodies of water where dense phytoplankton blooms are intolerable and low dissolved oxygen concentrations are not of primary concern: swimming pools, ponds and lakes used for water sports, and water supply reservoirs.

8.2.5 Macrophytes

Chemical methods of weed control are widely practiced, and there is a voluminous literature on the subject. Excellent reviews of chemical control of macrophytes are available (Davison et al., 1962; Little, 1968; Lawrence, 1968; Blackburn, 1974), so I will only make some comments on the practical use of herbicides.

Whitwell and Bayne (undated) gave an excellent summary of herbicides and treatment rates to control weeds in lakes and ponds:

Weed	Herbicide	Active ingredient
Macrophytic algae	Copper sulfate	0.5-3.0 mg/l
	Simazine	1.25 mg/l
Potamogeton and Najas	Diquat	0.25-2.0 mg/l
	Endothal	2.0 -5.0 mg/l
	Simazine	1.0 -3.0 mg/l
Ceratophyllum	Diquat	0.25-2.0 mg/l
	Endothal	2.0 -5.0 mg/l
Utricularia and Elodea	Diquat	0.25-2.0 mg/l
Myriophyllum	2, 4-D granules	22 kg/ha
Azolla, Lemna, and Wolffia	Diquat	0.25-1.0 mg/l
	2, 4-D amine	5 kg/ha
Eichhornia	2, 4-D amine	5 kg/ha
Nymphaea, Nuphar, and Nelumbo	Dichlobenil	7.0 -9.0 kg/ha
Brasenia	2, 4-D granules	40 kg/ha
Polygonum and Sagittaria	2, 4-D amine	9 kg/ha
Eleocharis and Hydrocotyle	Diquat	0.5 kg/ha
Typha, reedswamp plants, and grasses	Dalapon	6.0 -22.0 kg/ha

Johnson (1965) made an extensive study of chemical weed control in farm ponds in Ontario. He found that two or three applications of 1 mg/l of copper sulfate, spaced 2 or 3 days apart, was effective in controlling Cladophora and Spirogyra. Applications of 3 mg/l of copper sulfate were required to kill Chara. Endothal at 1-3 mg/l was effective against filamentous algae and submerged aquatics but not against floating-leafed aquatics or Chara. Silvex at 2-3 mg/l killed submerged aquatic plants and some floating-leafed plants but not Chara. The combination of equal amounts of Endothal and Silvex at 1-3 mg/l was no more effective on submerged plants than either herbicide used alone, but the mixture had a greater effect on mixed populations of submergent and floating-leafed plants. Paraquat and Diquat at 3 mg/l were effective against submerged plants but not Chara. Fenac (17 kg/ha), 2, 4-D (34-45 kg/ha), and simazine (22 kg/ha) were effective against underwater weeds. Herbicide application did not directly harm fish and had no major effects on populations of fish food organisms. However, some fish were killed because of oxygen depletion when heavy growths of Chara and other algae were killed.

Proper application of herbicides is essential. Liquid herbicide can be applied to submerged weeds by injecting the liquid into the water behind a boat. Granules can be broadcast by hand or with a hand-cranked spreader. Crystals may be put in burlap bags and towed through the water to effect dissolution. Herbicides should generally be applied to the foliage of plants with leaves above the water. Liquid herbicide may be applied to foliage with a back-pack sprayer as one walks along the water's edge. Motorized sprayers may be operated from boats.

The leaves of many floating and emergent aquatic plants have thick, waxy coatings that cause herbicide-water mixtures or solutions to bead and run off; this reduces penetration of the leaf surface by the active ingredient. Surfactants may be added to herbicide-water solutions to favor spreading of the solutions on plant surfaces. Household detergent is a suitable surfactant. When oil soluble herbicides are mixed with water, an emulsifying agent should be added and the mixture constantly agitated to prevent separation of the oil and water. Oil soluble herbicides can also be dissolved in fuel oil, kerosene, or diesel fuel. Such solutions frequently exhibit improved herbicidal action because the oil aids in penetration of the waxy coating and because the oils themselves are phytotoxic.

When used according to recommendations provided by the manufacturer, herbicides are seldom directly toxic to fish. However, decay of plants killed by herbicides may lead to oxygen depletion. If a pond contains extensive areas of weeds, the pond should be divided into two or more segments and the vegetation in different segments killed at different times. With this method, there is usually not enough vegetation decaying at one time to cause dissolved oxygen depletion. Obviously, the risk of oxygen depletion following herbicide treatment is greatest during hot weather when decomposition rates are highest and the solubility of oxygen in water is lowest. Herbicides applied to kill macrophytes may also kill phytoplankton; this further contributes to oxygen problems. Simazine and Karmex, which are sometimes applied to kill macrophytes, are especially toxic to phytoplankton.

Herbicides are quite effective in killing aquatic weeds. However, once the concentration of herbicide has declined to a non-toxic level, plants will begin to grow once more. For example, suppose a pond is infested with Potamogeton. Treatment of the pond with Diquat would eliminate the Potamogeton, but once the Diquat concentration declines, Potamogeton or some other submerged weed will re-infest the pond. In other words, a given habitat is suitable for growth of particular types of plants and nothing short of changing the environment will alter the dominant type of vegetation. It is true that herbicide treatment will keep clear ponds free of underwater weeds, but repeated applications will be necessary. However, if fertilizer is applied to the pond in which Potamogeton was killed with a herbicide, a phytoplankton bloom will develop. Turbidity from the phytoplankton will prevent regrowth of submerged plants without additional herbicide applications. Hence, the environment has been changed to favor another type of vegetation.

8.3 BIOLOGICAL CONTROL

Plankton-feeding fish are considered by many as potential phytoplankton control agents. There has not been enough research in this area to make clear cut statements about phytoplankton control by fish. Experiments on the influence of tilapia (Tilapia aurea), silver carp (Hypophthalmichthys molitrix), and big head carp (Aristichthys nobilis) on phytoplankton populations in ponds used for intensive culture of channel catfish were inconclusive (Malca, 1976; Dunseth, 1977). However, these experiments showed that total fish production was much greater in the polyculture systems (channel catfish and plankton-feeding fish) than in ponds stocked only with channel catfish. There was no apparent competition of the plankton-feeding fish with the channel catfish. Further research in this area has considerable promise. Even if fish species capable of preventing excessive phytoplankton abundance in channel catfish are not found, the technique provides a potential means of converting at least a portion of the unwanted phytoplankton production into edible fish flesh.

There has been some interest in the possibility of cultivating certain species of aquatic plants in eutrophic aquatic systems to remove inorganic nutrients and limit phytoplankton growth (Boyd, 1976; Rogers and Davis, 1972; Steward, 1970). Boyd (1976) demonstrated that water hyacinth (Eichhornia crassipes) stands absorbed an average of 3.4 kg/ha of nitrogen and 0.34 kg/ha of phosphorus per day during rapid growth. McVea and Boyd (1975) established levels of water hyacinth cover of 0, 5, 10, and 25% of pond surfaces in nutrient-enriched ponds at Auburn, Alabama. Phytoplankton abundance was less in ponds with 10 and 25% cover than in ponds with 0 and 5% cover. Competition of water hyacinth with phytoplankton involved shading and the removal of nutrients. Further research on using water hyacinths and other aquatic macrophytes to reduce the potential for phytoplankton in ponds for intensive fish culture might have practical application.

Grass carp (Ctenopharyngodon idella) has received much publicity for its ability to eat large quantities of aquatic macrophytes and thereby control weeds in ponds. The grass carp, or white amur, is a native of those rivers of Siberia, Manchuria, and China which ran into the Pacific Ocean from latitudes 50°N to 23°N (Cross, 1969). It has been successfully introduced into a number of countries in Southeast Asia, Africa, Europe, and North America.

Cross (1969) gave the following list, in approximate order of preference, of plants eaten by grass carp: Elodea canadensis, Ceratophyllum demersum, Chara sp., Lemna minor, Potamogeton natans, Lemna trisulea, Myriophyllum sp., Potamogeton pectinatus, Typha latifolia, Phragmites communis, Juncus effusus, Carex nigra,

TABLE 8.1

Quantities of aquatic weeds consumed by grass carp and growth of carp (Singh et al., 1969).

Weed	Consumption by fish[a] (g/day)	Weight gain per fish (g/day)
Hydrilla verticillata	903	9.6
Najas indica	813	4.5
Ceratophyllum demersum	757	8.9
Spirodella polyrhiza	260	6.8
Lemna trisulca	200	7.7
Utricularia stellaris	479	3.4
Salvinia cucullata	155	2.5

[a]Initial weights of fish ranged from 124 to 958 g.

TABLE 8.2

Effect of grass carp on weed infestations in ponds (Singh et al., 1969).

Weed infestation	Weed standing crop (tons/ha)	Grass carp (No./ha)	(g/fish)	Days to eliminate weeds
Hydrilla verticillata and Najas indica	68	654	113	42
Ceratophyllum demersum	6	400	2,640	5
Ceratophyllum demersum	37	250	974	49
Nechamandra alternifolia	7	250	1,830	43
Spirodela polyrhiza	6	1,250	474	20
Lemna trisulca	2	1,000	1,124	11

Hydrocharis morsus-ranae, Nasturtium officinale, Potamogeton lucens, and Carex pseudocyperus. Singh et al. (1969) found that grass carp could successfully eliminate most aquatic weeds from ponds; the only plants not actively eaten were Eichhornia, Pistia, Nymphoides, and Nymphaea. Data on daily consumption of weeds and growth of grass carp are presented in Table 8.1. Selected data on the control of weeds in ponds are given in Table 8.2. Kilgen and Smitherman (1971) reported that grass carp stocked alone at rates of 45 per hectare effectively eliminated

Chara spp., Potamogeton diversifolius, and Myriophyllum spicatum from 0.04-ha
ponds in less than 99 days. Grass carp reduced the amounts of water hyacinths in
ponds. The diet of grass carp consisted primarily of macrophytes (75-95%), but
mature insects were found in the guts of some fish. Similar results were obtained
when the grass carp were stocked with other species of fish. Kilgen and Smitherman
concluded: grass carp do not pose a threat as a competitor for food organisms
later by other species; grass carp are excellent game and food fish; grass carp
are a biological means of controlling weeds in ponds.

Because the studies mentioned above and others indicate that grass carp are
effective in eliminating aquatic vegetation, there has been considerable use of
grass carp as biological weed control agents. Past experience has indicated that
introductions of exotic animals often result in ecological disasters. Therefore,
there has been much concern, especially in the United States, over the introduction
of grass carp. Many scientists fear that grass carp may have undesirable effects
on native fish and wildlife populations. The American Fisheries Society recently
published a group of papers on grass carp in the United States in the "Transactions
of the American Fisheries Society." Guillory and Gasaway (1978) revealed that grass
carp were in 35 states and in a number of river systems, but no natural reproduction
had been documented. However, since that symposium evidence is mounting that grass
carp have successfully reproduced in the Mississippi River. Some workers indicated
that grass carp reduced the production of primary culture species (Forester and
Avault, 1978; Forester and Lawrence, 1978), while other researchers reported no
such reduction (Kilgen, 1978; Bailey, 1978). Mitzner (1978) showed that grass
carp reduced the shore line vegetation, and the hours of shore fishing more than
doubled. Unfortunately, there are still not enough data for evaluation of the
potential influence of grass carp on native habitats where aquatic macrophytes are
often a desirable component of the ecosystem. Many states in the United States
forbid by law the introduction of grass carp, and it will be many years before the
grass carp controversy is resolved.

Fish farmers and sportfish pond owners continue to use grass carp for weed
control. Every effort should be made to prevent the fish from escaping into
natural waters. Ponds that flood should not be stocked. Ponds that have spillway
discharge should have effective screens or barriers to prevent escape of grass
carp. Whitwell and Bayne (undated) recommend the use of grass carp in sportfish
ponds and channel catfish production ponds in the southeastern United States.
Their recommendations are summarized in Table 8.3. These stocking rates are
probably applicable to other types of pond fish culture.

Lawrence (1968) reported that common carp (Cyprinus carpio) in sufficient
numbers (400 per hectare or more) stirred bottom sediments and caused enough turbidity to prevent submerged weed growth. He also stated that the Israeli strain
of the common carp in limited numbers (55 per hectare) could control Pithophora

TABLE 8.3

Stocking rates for grass carp to control aquatic weeds in fish ponds. After Whitwell and Bayne (undated).

Fish in pond	Degree of infestation		
	Slight	Moderate	Heavy
Predaceous fish[a]	6	10-18	18-22
Non-predaceous fish[b]	7-10	12-20	20-25

[a]Stock 20-30 cm grass carp.
[b]Stock 5-15 cm grass carp.

and other macrophytic algae. Shell (1962) reported that tilapia (Tilapia nilotica, T. mossambica, and T. melanopleura) were of some value in controlling aquatic weeds in ponds.

A number of species of aquatic insects attack aquatic plants. Hence, there has been a continuing interest in the possibility of controlling aquatic weeds with these insects (Center, 1975). The value of insects in controlling weeds in ponds has not been established.

The use of inorganic fertilizers to promote phytoplankton blooms and eliminate underwater weed by shading is an effective biological method. This practice is discussed thoroughly in Chapter 3.

8.4 MECHANICAL CONTROL

Emergent weeds and some submerged species may be controlled by periodic cutting. Normally, if fertilization is practiced, 2 years of cutting will completely elim-inate submerged weeds. Emergent weeds must be removed on a routine basis. A deepened pond edge (no water less than 0.5 m in depth) is recommended as a con-struction feature for ponds (Lawrence, 1968). In old fertilized ponds, repeated removal of marginal weeds and soil will gradually deepen the edges and prevent weed infestation. Several species of macrophytic algae have been successfully eliminated from fertilized ponds by beating the surface masses with a cane pole or other suitable rod. Macrophytic algae may also be removed from ponds with seines or rakes.

Eicher (1946) reported that aniline (nigrosine) dye could be used to limit light penetration into natural waters and thereby reduce the growth of underwater weeds. Dye was applied to lakes at 1.2 mg/l, and Secchi disk visibilities were reduced from more than 4 m before treatment to 2.4 m or less soon after treatment. The dye was stable in water; concentrations declined by only 50% during 1 year.

252

Underwater weeds did not grow to lake surfaces of dye-treated lakes as they had in previous years. Surber and Everhart (1950) used 305.4 mg/l of nigrosine dye to control underwater weeds in hatchery ponds. They noted no harmful influence of dye on fish. In contrast to the favorable results mentioned above, Levardsen (1953) reported that nigrosine dye was ineffective in controlling underwater weeds. The dye caused low dissolved oxygen and high carbon dioxide concentrations. Dye disappeared from the water too rapidly to effect weed control. A dye mixture with the trade name Aquashade® (Aquashade Inc., Eldred, New York) has been used to control aquatic weeds in swimming ponds, golf course ponds, industrial ponds, cooling towers, and fountains.

REFERENCES

Bailey, W. M., 1978. A comparison of fish populations before and after extensive grass carp stocking. Trans. Amer. Fish. Soc., 107: 207-212.
Bartlett, L. F., Rabe, F. W., and Funk, W. H., 1974. Effects of copper, zinc and cadmium on Selenastrum capricornutum. Water Res., 8: 179-185.
Bartsch, A. F., 1954. Practical methods for control of algae and water weeds. U. S. Public Health Rep., 69: 749-757.
Blackburn, R. D., 1974. Chemical control. In: D. S. Mitchell (Editor), Aquatic Vegetation and Its Use and Control. UNESCO, Paris, pp. 85-98.
Boyd, C. E., 1976. Accumulation of dry matter, nitrogen and phosphorus by cultivated water hyacinths. Econ. Bot., 30: 51-56.
Boyd, C. E., 1979. Water Quality in Warmwater Fish Ponds. Auburn University Agricultural Experiment Station, Auburn, Alabama, 359 pp.
Button, K. S., Hostetter, H. P., and Mair, D. M., 1977. Copper dispersal in a water supply reservoir. Water Res., 11: 539-544.
Center, T. C., 1975. The use of insects for the biological control of water-hyacinth in the United States. In: P. L. Brezonik and J. L. Fox (Editors), Water Quality Management through Biological Control. Department of Environ. Engineering Sci., University of Florida, Gainesville, Florida, pp. 57-59.
Crance, J. H., 1963. The effects of copper sulfate on Microcystis and zooplanton in ponds. Prog. Fish-Cult., 25: 198-202.
Cross, D. G., 1969. Aquatic weed control using grass carp. J. Fish. Biol., 1: 27-30.
Cumming, K. B., 1975. History of fish toxicants in the United States. In: P. H. Eschmeyer (Editor), Rehabilitation of Fish Populations with Toxicants: a Symposium. North Central Division, American Fisheries Society, Spec. Publ. No. 4, pp. 5-21.
Davison, V. E., Lawrence, J. M., and Compton, L. V., 1962. Waterweed control on farms and ranches. U. S. Department of Agriculture, Farmer's Bull. 2181, U. S. Government Printing Office, Washington, D. C., 22 pp.
Dunseth, D. R., 1977. Polyculture of channel catfish, Ictalurus punctatus, silver carp, Hypophthalmichthys molitrix, and three all-male tilapias, Sarotherodon spp. Ph. D. dissertation, Auburn University, Auburn, Alabama, 62 pp.
Eicher, G., 1947. Analine dye in aquatic weed control. J. Wildl. Manag., 11: 193-197.
Fitzgerald, G. P., 1959. Bactericidal and algicidal properties of some algicides for swimming pools. Appl. Microbiol., 7: 205-211.
Fitzgerald, G. P. and Faust, S. L., 1963. Factors affecting the algicidal and algistatic properties of copper. Appl. Microbiol., 11: 345-351.
Forester, J. S. and Avault, J. W., Jr., 1978. Effects of grass carp on freshwater red swamp crawfish in ponds. Trans. Amer. Fish. Soc., 107: 156-160.
Forester, T. S. and Lawrence, J. M., 1978. Effects of grass carp and carp on populations of bluegill and largemouth bass in ponds. Trans. Amer. Fish. Soc.,

107: 172-175.

Guillory, V. and Gasaway, R. D., 1978. Zoogeography of the grass carp in the United States. Trans. Amer. Fish. Soc., 107: 105-112.

Inglis, A. and Davis, E. L., 1972. Effects of water hardness on the toxicity of several organic and inorganic herbicides to fish. U. S. Fish and Wildlife Service, Washington, D. C., Technical Paper 67, 22 pp.

Jackson, G. A., 1974. A Review of the Literature on the Use of Copper Sulfate in Fisheries. U. S. Fish and Wildlife Service, Washington, D. C., Report No. FWS-LR-74-06, 88 pp.

Johnson, M. G., 1965. Control of aquatic plants in farm ponds in Ontario. Prog. Fish-Cult., 27: 23-30.

Kessler, S., 1960. Eradication of blue-green algae with copper sulfate. Bamidgeh. 12: 17-19.

Kilgen, R. H., 1978. Growth of channel catfish and striped bass in small ponds stocked with grass carp and water hyacinths. Trans. Amer. Fish. Soc., 107: 176-180.

Kilgen, R. H. and Smitherman, R. O., 1971. Food habits of the white amur stocked in ponds alone and in combination with other species. Prog. Fish-Cult., 33: 123-127.

Lawrence, J. M., 1968. Aquatic weed control in fish ponds. Proc. World Symposium on Warm-Water Pond Fish Culture, FAO United Nations, Fish. Rep. No. 44, 5: 76-91.

Levardsen, N. O., 1953. Experiments with nigrosine dye in aquatic plant control. Prog. Fish-Cult., 15: 109-113.

Little, E. C. S., 1968. The control of water weeds. Weed Res., 8: 79-105.

Lloyd, R., 1965. Factors that affect the tolerance of fish to heavy metal poisoning. In: C. D. Tarzwell (Editor), Biological Problems in Water Pollution. U. S. Department of Health, Education, and Welfare, Washington, D. C., p. 181.

Malca, R. P., 1976. Polyculture systems with channel catfish as the principal species. Ph. D. dissertation, Auburn University, Auburn, Alabama, 202 pp.

Maloney, T. E. and Palmer, C. M., 1956. Toxicity of six chemical compounds to thirty cultures of algae. Water and Sewage Works, 103: 509-513.

Mauck, W. L., 1974. A Review of the Literature on the Use of Simazine in Fisheries. U. S. Fish and Wildlife Service, Washington, D. C., Report No. FWS-LR-74-16, 46 pp.

McIntosh, A. W. and Kevern, N. R., 1974. Toxicity of copper to zooplankton. J. Environ. Qual., 3: 166-170.

McKee, J. E. and Wolf, H. W. (Editors), 1963. Water Quality Criteria, 2nd edition. State of California, State Water Quality Control Board, Sacramento, Publication 3-A, 548 pp.

McVea, C. and Boyd, C. E., 1975. Effects of waterhyacinth cover on water chemistry, phytoplankton and fish in ponds. J. Environ. Qual., 4: 375-378.

Meyer, F. B., Schnick, R. A., and Cumming, K. B., 1976. Registration status of fishery chemicals, February, 1976. Prog. Fish-Cult., 38: 3-7.

Mitzner, L., 1978. Evaluation of biological control of nuisance aquatic vegetation by grass carp. Trans. Amer. Fish. Soc., 107: 135-145.

Montgomery, A., 1961. Control of aquatic weeds in farm ponds. J. Soil and Water Conserv., 16: 69-70.

Pagenkopf, G. K., Russo, R. C., and Thurston, R. V., 1974. Effect of complexation on toxicity of copper to fishes. J. Fish. Res. Bd. Canada, 31: 462-465.

Palmer, C. M., 1962. Algae in Water Supplies. U. S. Public Health Service, Publ. No. 657, 88 pp.

Riemer, D. N. and Toth, S. J., 1970. Adsorption of copper by clay minerals, humic acid and bottom muds. J. Amer. Water Works Assoc., 62: 195-197.

Rogers, H. H. and Davis, D. E., 1971. Nutrient removal by water-hyacinth. Weed Sci., 20: 423-428.

Shaw, T. L. and Brown, V. M., 1974. The toxicity of some forms of copper to rainbow trout. Water Res., 8: 377-382.

Shell, E. W., 1962. Herbivorous fish to control _Pithophora_ sp. and other aquatic weeds in ponds. Weeds, 10: 326-327.

Singh, S. B., Sukumaran, K. K., Pillai, K. K., and Chakrabarti, P. C., 1969. Observations on efficacy of grass carp, *Ctenopharyngodon idella* (Val.) in controlling and utilizing aquatic weeds in ponds in India. Proc. Indo-Pacific Fish. Coun., 12: 220-235.

Sohacki, L. P., Ball, R. C., and Hooper, F. F., 1969. Some ecological changes in ponds from sodium arsenate and copper sulfate. Mich. Acad. Sci., 1: 149-162.

Sprague, J. B., 1968. Promising anti-pollutant: chelating agent NTA protects fish from copper and zinc. Nature, 220: 1345-1346.

Steward, K. K., 1970. Nutrient removal potentials of various aquatic plants. Hyacinth Control J., 8: 34-35.

Stiff, M. J., 1971a. Copper/bicarbonate equilibria in solutions of bicarbonate at concentrations similar to those found in natural water. Water Res., 5: 171-176.

Stiff, M. J., 1971b. The chemical states of copper in polluted fresh water and a scheme of analysis to differentiate them. Water Res., 5: 585-599.

Stumm, W. and Morgan, J. J., 1970. Aquatic Chemistry. John Wiley and Sons, New York, 583 pp.

Surber, E. W. and Everhart, M. H., 1950. Biological effects of nigrosine used for control of weeds in hatchery ponds. Prog. Fish-Cult., 12: 135-140.

Sutton, D. L., Evrard, T. O., and Bingham, S. W., 1966. The effects of repeated treatments of simazine on certain aquatic plants and residue in water. Proc. Northwest Weed Control Conf., 20: 464-468.

Toth, S. J. and Riemer, D. N., 1968. Precise chemical control of algae in ponds. J. Amer. Water Works Assoc., 60: 367-371.

Tucker, C. S. and Boyd, C. E., 1978. Consequences of periodic applications of copper sulfate and simazine for phytoplankton control in catfish ponds. Trans. Amer. Fish. Soc., 107: 316-320.

Tucker, C. S. and Boyd, C. E., 1979. Effects of simazine treatment on channel catfish and bluegill production in ponds. Aquaculture, 15: 345-352.

Whitwell, T. and Bayne, D. R., undated. Weed control in lakes and farm ponds. Auburn University Agricultural Extension Service, Auburn, Alabama, Circular ANR-48, 6 pp.

Chapter 9

MISCELLANEOUS TREATMENTS

9.1   INTRODUCTION

Fertilization, liming, aeration, and weed control, which have already been
discussed, are the most commonly used water quality management tools. These procedures often have powerful effects upon the environment and can greatly improve
conditions for fish production. Effective procedures for removing turbidity,
reducing pH, removing chlorine, elevating salinity and hardness, and reducing
carbon dioxide concentrations are also available. Fish farmers often apply potassium permanganate and calcium hydroxide to ponds with the idea that these substances will improve water quality. However, these two treatments are not always
effective for the intended purposes. Water exchange and additions of salts for
reducing the effects of toxic metabolites on fish are practiced with varying degrees of success. The effectivenesses of therapeutants and piscicides used in
ponds are often affected by water quality.

In this chapter, I will discuss the use of these "miscellaneous treatments"
and attempt to establish which treatments are effective and which are not. It
should be understood that many of these miscellaneous procedures were obtained
from other disciplines and applied to fisheries. Often, it has been assumed that
a particular substance would affect a certain change in water quality, and treatment with the substance has been adopted as a management procedure without proper
evaluation.

9.2   POTASSIUM PERMANGANATE

Potassium permanganate ($KMnO_4$) is a strong oxidizing agent that reacts with
organic matter and reduced inorganic substances in water. The ions derived from
several valence states of manganese have been proposed as the active entities
responsible for oxidation by permanganate. Ladbury and Cullis (1958) reviewed
the mechanisms of oxidation by permanganate and showed the effect of pH on the
reactions. In alkaline, neutral, and weakly acidic solutions (natural waters
cover this pH range), the valence change of the manganese is from +7 to +4; permanganate (MnO_4^-) is reduced to manganese dioxide (MnO_2) in permanganate oxidations.

Because of its strong oxidation potential, potassium permanganate has many
applications. According to Lay (1971), this compound has had the following uses
in fisheries: disinfection, parasite and disease treatment of fish, algal control,
detoxification of piscicides, removal of reduced inorganic substances, and
alleviation of oxygen depletion in ponds. Each of these applications will be
discussed below.

It has been long been recognized that potassium permangante is toxic to bacteria

and especially to Gram-negative bacteria (Stearn and Stearn, 1930). The effect
on bacteria apparently involves gross oxidation of surfaces and membranes, thereby
disrupting normal physiological functions. Because the toxic mechanism involves
oxidation of living organic matter, competition of dissolved or particulate organic
matter in the environment for oxidation by potassium permanganate will reduce the
amount of potassium permanganate available to act on bacteria. Tucker and Boyd
(1977) found that potassium permanganate concentrations of 4 mg/l caused 100%
mortality of Gram-negative bacteria in cultures containing no organic matter other
than the bacteria themselves. The minimum concentration of potassium permanganate
causing 100% mortality in similar cultures of Gram-positive bacteria was 16 mg/l.
The influence of extraneous organic matter in the cultures on toxicity of potassium
permanganate was demonstrated by transferring cells of the bacterium Enterobacter
cloacae to either organic matter-free saline solution or to samples of sterile
pond water containing organic matter and then treating with potassium permanganate.
In these tests, the amounts of potassium permanganate required to oxidize the
extraneous organic matter in the solutions were determined by the method of
Engstrom-Heg (1971) and were termed the potassium permanganate demand. Results in
Table 9.1 demonstrate clearly that the amounts of potassium permanganate required
to produce a given percentage mortality of Enterobacter cloacae increased with
increasing organic matter levels — higher potassium permanganate demand.

Duncan (1974) lists a wide variety of fish parasite and disease organisms that
may be controlled with potassium permanganate. Some treatments involve exposure
of infected fish to high concentrations of potassium permangante for a short period.
For example, Bauer (1958) exposed carp infected with Trichodina to 100 mg/l of
potassium permanganate. Treatments of the type described above are often made to
remedy disease and parasite problems before fish are stocked into ponds. As will
be mentioned later, potassium permanganate is toxic to fish and high concentrations
cannot be used for pond treatments where fish will be exposed to the chemical for
extended periods. Management biologists frequently recommend applications of 2-4
mg/l of potassium permanganate to ponds to treat infected fish (Duncan, 1974).
Although this procedure is often effective in waters with low concentrations of
organic matter (Phelps et al., 1977), it is not likely to be effective in ponds
with dense algal blooms or high concentrations of other types of organic matter.
Jee (1979) showed that the effective concentration of potassium permanganate for
treating fish pathogens was 4 mg/l more than the potassium permanganate demand
of the water.

The potassium permanganate demand method of Engstrom-Heg (1974) requires
spectrophotometry, a tool often not available to fish farmers. Boyd (1979a)
reported a simple method for determining the potassium permanganate demand that
gives results comparable to spectrophotometry. Aliquots of a fresh, 1,000 mg/l
solution of potassium permanganate are used to prepare a series of potassium

TABLE 9.1

Percentage mortality of <u>Enterobacter cloacae</u> after 4-h contact with various concentrations of potassium permanganate in media with different $KMnO_4$ demand values
(Tucker and Boyd, 1977).

$KMnO_4$ (mg/1)	$KMnO_4$ demand (mg/1)				
	0	1	2	5	7
1	95.6	38.3	21.4	17.9	14.9
2	99.6	95.2	57.5	0.0	15.3
4	100.0	99.9	99.9	90.3	51.5
8		100.0	99.9	99.9	99.9
12			100.0	99.9	99.9

permanganate concentrations in 1,000-ml samples of the water of interest. A
suitable series of concentrations might be as follows: 0, 1, 2, 3, 4, 5, 6, 8,
10, and 12 mg/1. The potassium permanganate will initially impart a pink color
to the water, but this pink color will soon disappear if the oxidation of organic
matter converts all of the MnO_4^- to MnO_2. The highest potassium permanganate concentration in the series that loses its pink color is taken as the potassium
permanganate demand.

The toxicity of potassium permanganate to fish is also related to organic
matter concentrations in the water. The 24-h and 96-h LC50 values of potassium
permanganate for several species of fish ranged from 2 to 4 mg/1 in waters with
low concentrations of organic matter (Duncan, 1974). Tucker and Boyd (1977)
found that the toxic threshold for potassium permanganate to bluegill (<u>Lepomis
macrochirus</u>) and fathead minnows (<u>Pimephales promelas</u>) in pond waters increased
with increasing potassium permanganate demand (Table 9.2). Fish of neither species
were harmed when treated with potassium permanganate at the potassium permanganate
demand plus 4 mg/1. Fish ponds at Auburn University had potassium permanganate
demands of 0.5-7 mg/1. The high demands were for ponds with dense algal blooms.
Thus, potassium permanganate treatments of 8-10 mg/1 will be needed in some ponds
to effect control of fish diseases.

Since potassium permanganate oxidizes organic matter and kills bacteria, Lay
(1971) claimed that potassium permanganate would reduce the COD and BOD of pond
waters. Tucker and Boyd (1977) showed that potassium permanganate treatment
slightly reduced the COD of pond water samples. The reduction in COD for the
three samples averaged 0.75 mg/1 per 1 mg/1 of potassium permanganate. Potassium
permanganate treatment reduced the rate of oxygen depletion in pond waters that

TABLE 9.2

Percentage mortality of bluegill and fathead minnows after 48-h exposure to various concentrations of potassium permanganate. Each value based on 15 bluegill and 30 fathead minnows per treatment (Tucker and Boyd, 1977).

$KMnO_4$ (mg/l)	$KMnO_4$ demand of water (mg/l)				
	0.1	1	2	3	4
Bluegills					
0	0.0	0.0	0.0	0.0	0.0
2	0.0	0.0	0.0		
3	26.7	0.0	0.0		
4	100.0				
6		16.7	0.0	0.0	0.0
8		100.0	0.0	0.0	0.0
10			13.0	0.0	0.0
14			100.0	60.0	
Fathead Minnows					
0	3.3	3.3	0.0		3.3
4	0.0	3.3	0.0		0.0
6	100.0	6.7	0.0		0.0
8		13.3	0.0		0.0
10		83.3	0.0		0.0
12		100.0	33.3		0.0
14					0.0

were incubated in BOD bottles (Table 9.3), so potassium permanganate will reduce BOD — at least in samples of water incubated in the laboratory.

Treatment of ponds with potassium permanganate resulted in an increase rather than a decrease in the abundance of bacteria in the water (Table 9.4). The increase in bacteria was attributed to potassium permanganate killing algae and providing substrate for bacteria. The increase in bacterial abundance in the water does not cast doubt on the effectiveness of potassium permanganate in killing bacteria that cause fish diseases. The fish pathogens derive their nutriment from the fish rather from organic matter in the water.

Fitzgerald (1966) and Kemp et al. (1966) reported that potassium permanganate was an effective algicide. Tucker and Boyd (1977) showed that treatment of water in outdoor pools with potassium permanganate at 2-8 mg/l reduced rates of gross photosynthesis. Therefore, treatment of pond waters with potassium permanganate

TABLE 9.3

Dissolved oxygen remaining after 1 day in water samples treated with different concentrations of potassium permanganate and confined in BOD bottles (Tucker and Boyd, 1977).

Initial chemical oxygen demand of sample (mg/l)	Potassium permanganate (mg/l)			
	0	2	4	8
20	6.4	6.6	6.8	7.0
32	6.1	6.5	7.2	7.4
55	4.2	4.8	6.2	8.0
127	2.4	3.3	6.1	7.2

TABLE 9.4

Numbers of bacteria in waters of two ponds treated with potassium permanganate at a rate of 2 mg/l more than the potassium permanganate demand (Tucker and Boyd, 1977).

Date	Bacteria (log cells/ml)	
	Pond 1	Pond 2
5 Aug	2.9	3.6
9 Aug[a]	2.95	3.55
10 Aug	3.7	4.3
11 Aug	4.7	5.8
12 Aug	4.4	5.2
16 Aug	3.5	3.9
17 Aug[a]	2.6	2.9
18 Aug	2.8	3.5
19 Aug	3.9	4.5
20 Aug	4.0	4.55
23 Aug	3.0	3.2

[a]Potassium permanganate applied.

at 2-8 mg/l would be expected to increase the amount of dead organic matter in water by killing algae and to decrease the rate of oxygen production in photosynthesis.

Mathis et al. (1962) reported that potassium permanganate treatment added molecular oxygen to pond water according to the reaction:

$$2 \ KMnO_4 + H_2O \rightarrow 2 \ KOH + 2 \ MnO_2 + 1\tfrac{1}{2} \ O_2 \qquad (9.1)$$

Mathis and coworkers are not entirely wrong, for molecular oxygen is produced when potassium permanganate is added to waters containing organic matter. This results because the permanganate ion oxidizes organic matter and reduced inorganic substances to produce manganese dioxide:

$$MnO_4^- + 4 \ H^+ + 3 \ e^- \rightarrow MnO_2 + 2 \ H_2O \qquad (9.2)$$

The manganese dioxide then catalyzes the following reaction in which oxygen is evolved:

$$4 \ MnO_4^- + 2 \ H_2O \rightarrow 4 \ OH^- + 4 \ MnO_2 + 3 \ O_2 \qquad (9.3)$$

This equation is the same one reported by Mathis et al. (1962). The problem in the assumption that Equation 9.1 results in oxygen being released to pond water is: in pond water which is deficient in dissolved oxygen, much of the MnO_4^- is used immediately to oxidize organic matter and reduced inorganic substances. Since the oxidative reaction (Equation 9.2) produces MnO_2, the reaction releasing oxygen (Equation 9.3) will proceed. However, the reaction releasing oxygen will not continue to a measurable degree as long as any reduced substance remains to react with potassium permanganate. Thus, if more potassium permanganate is added to a pond than is needed to satisfy the potassium permanganate demand, the excess potassium permanganate will decompose to release oxygen. Assuming that all of the excess potassium permanganate decomposes to release oxygen, the amount of potassium permanganate needed to release 1 mg/l of dissolved oxygen may be calculated from stoichiometric relationships of Equation 9.3 as follows:

$$
\begin{array}{ll}
632.16 \ mg & 96 \ mg \\
4 \ KMnO_4 & = 3 \ O_2 \\
x & 1 \ mg/l \\
\end{array}
$$

$$x = 6.58 \ mg/l$$

Obviously, potassium permanganate treatment is not a suitable technique for supplying dissolved oxygen in fish ponds, because an amount equal to the potassium permanganate demand plus 6.58 mg/l would be needed to produce 1 mg/l of dissolved oxygen. Such a high application rate of this chemical would likely cause fish mortality.

Potassium permanganate is effective in removing reduced inorganic substances
such as hydrogen sulfide and ferrous iron from water (Welch, 1963; Willey et al.,
1964). The reactions are as follows:

$$3 \ Fe(HCO_3)_2 + KMnO_4 + 7 \ H_2O \rightarrow MnO_2 + 3 \ Fe(OH)_3 \downarrow + KHCO_3 + 5 \ H_2CO_3$$

$$3 \ H_2S + 4 \ KMnO_4 \rightarrow 2 \ K_2SO_4 + S + 3 \ MnO + MnO_2 + 3 \ H_2O$$

Using stoichiometric relationships depicted by the above equations, the amounts
of potassium permanganate theoretically needed to remove 1 mg/l each of ferrous
iron or hydrogen sulfide may be calculated as follows:

$$\frac{158.04 \ mg \ KMnO_4}{x} = \frac{167.55 \ mg \ 3 \ Fe^{2+}}{1 \ mg/l}$$

$$x = 0.94 \ mg/l$$

$$\frac{632.16 \ mg \ 4 \ KMnO_4}{x} = \frac{102.18 \ mg \ 3 \ H_2S}{1 \ mg/l}$$

$$x = 6.19 \ mg/l$$

When waters are depleted of oxygen, ferrous iron and hydrogen sulfide may be
present in measurable concentrations. These waters also contain reduced organic
matter. Thus, dosage rates calculated from ferrous iron and hydrogen sulfide
concentrations would not effect complete removal, for some of the potassium permanganate would be spent in oxidizing organic matter.

Orthophosphate is adsorbed by ferric hydroxide and removed from solution as an
insoluble precipitate (Einsele, 1936). Hence, when potassium permanganate is
applied to water containing ferrous iron, ferric hydroxide will precipitate and
orthophosphate will be removed from solution. Tucker and Boyd (1977) treated
an anerobic sample of pond water containing 11.8 mg/l of ferrous iron and 1.01
mg/l of filtrable orthophosphate (as P) with 8 mg/l of potassium permanganate.
A precipitate of ferrous hydroxide was observed to form and settle to the bottom
of the container. A few hours after application, the ferrous iron concentration
was 3.25 mg/l, and the filtrable orthophosphate concentration was 0.02 mg/l. No
changes in ferrous iron or filtrable orthophosphate concentrations occurred in
untreated samples of anaerobic pond water.

Thus, potassium permanganate treatment will kill bacteria, reduce COD and BOD,
remove reduced inorganic substances, and add small amounts of oxygen to the water.

TABLE 9.5

Dissolved oxygen concentrations (mg/l) in pools treated with potassium permanganate at 0600 h on 18 September. Each value represents the average of triplicate treatments (Tucker and Boyd, 1977).

Date	Time (h)	Potassium permanganate (mg/l)		
		0	4	8
15 Sep	1500	12.8	11.5	10.4
16 Sep	0600	6.2	6.0	6.0
	1500	12.4	11.6	11.3
17 Sep	0600	6.3	6.6	6.6
	1500	6.3	6.5	6.2
18 Sep	0600	0.2	0.6	0.2
	0630	0.2	0.6	0.2
	0700	0.3	0.7	0.2
	0730	2.0	2.0	0.6
	0800	5.2	4.6	1.6
	1000	10.5	9.5	3.6
	1500	15.0	14.0	10.2
19 Sep	0600	6.7	1.8	2.7
	1500	15.0	15.0	10.3

These effects suggest that potassium permanganate treatment would improve water quality in oxygen-depleted pond waters. However, the algicidal properties of potassium permanganate negate most of its beneficial influences on water quality. To illustrate, Tucker and Boyd (1977) treated oxygen-depleted water in outdoor pools with 0, 4, or 8 mg/l of potassium permanganate (Table 9.5). Dissolved oxygen concentrations did not increase immediately after potassium permanganate treatment at 0600 h, as one might expect, and concentrations of oxygen did not rise as high during hours following treatment in the pools treated with 8 mg/l of potassium permanganate as in pools of the other two treatments (0 and 4 mg/l). On the morning following treatment, dissolved oxygen concentrations were lower in pools that had been treated with potassium permanganate than in the untreated pools. The destruction of phytoplankton by potassium permanganate apparently caused the adverse effects on dissolved oxygen concentrations. In addition to killing phytoplankton, potassium permanganate treatment will remove phosphorus from oxygen-depleted water, thereby reducing photosynthetic rates by surviving phytoplankton. In summary, treatment of oxygen-depleted waters with potassium permanganate will actually hinder restoration of suitable oxygen concentrations.

Many fish farmers have determined through experience that potassium permanganate is not a suitable deterrent to dissolved oxygen problems. Therefore, the use of potassium permanganate in oxygen management is declining. Unfortunately, many biologists still recommend the application of potassium permanganate to oxygen-depleted waters.

Lawrence (1956) demonstrated that potassium permanganate oxidizes rotenone to nontoxic form. In tap water, 2.0 mg/l of potassium permanganate detoxified 0.05 mg/l of rotenone. In ponds and streams, concentrations of potassium permanganate ranging from 2.0 to 2.5 mg/l detoxified 0.05 mg/l of rotenone. In sampling fish populations in streams with rotenone, a seine may be placed across the stream at the downstream edge of the sampling area. This prevents the movement of fish into the toxic water of the sampling area, but rotenone still drifts downstream and kills fish outside of the sampling area. To counteract this undesirable aspect of sampling with rotenone, Lawrence (1956) dragged burlap bags containing potassium permanganate back and forth across streams just below the downstream barriers throughout the period that fish were dying in the sampling areas. Potassium permanganate was highly effective in preventing fish mortality downstream from the sampling area. Lawrence also successfully used potassium permanganate to reduce the kill of largemouth bass after partial poisoning of shallow water edges of ponds to reduce populations of small and intermediate bluegills as described by Swingle et al. (1953). Marking and Bills (1975) demonstrated that the small concentrations of antimycin used as a fish toxicant can also be detoxified with 1 mg/l of potassium permanganate. Engstrom-Heg (1971) emphasized that organic matter in water reduces the effectiveness of potassium permanganate in detoxifying piscicides and recommended use of the potassium permanganate demand test in establishing effective dosages. Engstrom-Heg found that potassium permanganate can be quickly reduced to a nontoxic residue in natural water by either tannic acid or sodium thiosulfate. The ratio for tannic acid is 2 parts of tannic acid to 3 parts of potassium permanganate. Sodium thiosulfate may be used in a 1:1 ratio to reduce potassium permanganate.

9.3 HYDROGEN PEROXIDE

There has been some interest in using hydrogen peroxide (H_2O_2) as an oxidizing agent in fisheries. Hydrogen peroxide will oxidize organic matter, so it would likely kill bacteria and reduce COD and BOD. Molecular oxygen is also released from hydrogen peroxide in water according to the reaction:

$$2 H_2O_2 \rightarrow 2 H_2O + O_2.$$

From stoichiometric relationships, the amount of hydrogen peroxide required to release 1 mg of oxygen is:

68 mg   32 mg
$$2\ H_2O_2 = O_2$$
x   1 mg/l
x = 2.12 mg/l

Presumably, the reaction of organic matter with hydrogen peroxide in oxygen-depleted waters would prevent the calculated amount of oxygen from being released. Hydrogen peroxide is not appreciably toxic to fish; 48 mg/l did not harm trout fingerlings in 48 h (McKee and Wolf, 1963). The toxicity of hydrogen peroxide to plants is not known. Research to determine if hydrogen peroxide could be used as a deterrent to oxygen depletion should be conducted.

Marathe et al. (1975) used hydrogen peroxide as a source of dissolved oxygen for fish transported in tanks to remote locations in India. They estimated that 0.05 ml (1 drop) of 6% hydrogen peroxide added to 1 l of water yielded approximately 1.5 mg of oxygen.

9.4   CALCIUM HYDROXIDE

Calcium hydroxide [$Ca(OH)_2$] may be used as a liming material in fish ponds and as a sterilant for bottom muds (see Chapter 3). Fish farmers in the southern United States use hydrated lime for a variety of other purposes. Many erroneously think that hydrated lime will oxidize organic matter and reduce COD and BOD, and they apply hydrated lime to oxygen-depleted pond waters. Hansell and Boyd (1980) treated samples of pond water with 0, 50, or 100 mg/l of hydrated lime. There was a statistically significant, though slight, reduction in COD of some samples. This reduction in COD did not result from oxidation of organic matter. The hydrated lime caused coagulation of plankton, some of the coagulated material settled to the bottom of the containers, and the COD was thereby reduced. Application of 100 mg/l of hydrated lime reduced BOD if the initial pH of the water was greater than 9. This reduction in BOD was apparently related to high pH after lime treatment (pH > 10.5) and subsequent death of microorganisms. Calabrese (1969) indicated that pH values >11 were lethal to fish, so the application of enough hydrated lime to reduce BOD would likely harm fish. Furthermore, the application of 100 mg/l of hydrated lime greatly reduced oxygen production by phytoplankton in all water samples, and 50 mg/l of lime adversely affected oxygen production in waters with an initial pH above 9. Again the unfavorable influence of hydrated lime was apparently related to the elevation of pH to toxic levels. Reduction in photosynthetic oxygen production is obviously undesirable in ponds with low dissolved oxygen concentrations.

High concentrations of carbon dioxide are frequently encountered in fish ponds when dissolved oxygen concentrations are low. Because high concentrations of carbon dioxide suppress oxygen absorption by fish, it is sometimes desirable to remove carbon dioxide when concentrations exceed 10-15 mg/l. Removal of carbon dioxide may be effected by calcium hydroxide treatment according to the following reactions:

$$Ca(OH)_2 + CO_2 \rightarrow CaCO_3 + H_2O$$

$$CaCO_3 + CO_2 + H_2O \rightarrow Ca(HCO_3)_2$$

These reactions may be combined to give:

$$Ca(OH)_2 + 2 CO_2 \rightarrow Ca(HCO_3)_2 \qquad (9.4)$$

The amount of calcium hydroxide theoretically required to remove 1 mg/l of carbon dioxide may be calculated from weight relationships shown in Equation 9.4:

$$\frac{74.08 \text{ mg}}{Ca(OH)_2} \quad \frac{88 \text{ mg}}{= 2 CO_2}$$
$$x \qquad 1 \text{ mg/l}$$
$$x = 0.84 \text{ mg/l}$$

Hansell and Boyd (1980) treated waters containing carbon dioxide at rates of 0, 0.84, 1.26, and 1.68 mg/l of calcium hydroxide for each milligram per liter of carbon dioxide. These rates corresponded to 0, 100, 150, and 200% of the amounts of hydrated lime theoretically required for complete carbon dioxide removal. The actual percentage removal of carbon dioxide was roughly 50% less than expected from calculations. The discrepancy was thought to result because calcium hydroxide did not dissolve well, and some of the material apparently settled to the bottom without reacting with carbon dioxide. Hansell and Boyd suggested that the amount of hydrated lime needed to remove all of the carbon dioxide from water be calculated from the equation:

Hydrated lime in mg/liter = $(1.68)(\text{mg/l of } CO_2)$.

Application of hydrated lime to remove carbon dioxide will not harm fish or other organisms, for the pH will not exceed 8.4 unless excess lime is added. Any beneficial influence of hydrated lime applications in oxygen-depleted waters no doubt results from carbon dioxide removal rather than from the reduction of COD and BOD.

Calcium hydroxide has occasionally been recommended as a fish eradicant. When

TABLE 9.6

Effects on pH of treating six samples of water from fish ponds with different concentrations of hydrated lime (Hansell and Boyd, 1980).

Hydrated lime (mg/l)	pH		
	Minimum	Average	Maximum
0	7.4	7.5	7.9
25	8.4	8.7	10.0
50	8.6	9.0	10.5
100	9.2	9.6	10.8
150	9.8	10.2	11.1
200	10.3	10.6	11.3
300	10.7	10.9	11.4
400	10.9	11.1	11.6
500	11.1	11.3	11.3

ponds are drained so that only a small volume of water remains, hydrated lime is applied to raise the pH and kill unwanted fish. Data from Hansell and Boyd (1980) illustrated the effect of hydrated lime on pH of waters from ponds (Table 9.6). Between 150 and 500 mg/l of hydrated lime were required to raise pH above 11, the lethal pH for pond fish. In general, the higher the initial pH, the less hydrated lime required to raise pH above 11. In a pond, more hydrated lime would probably be required to assure high pH, for it would not be possible to mix the lime as well as in the laboratory systems. Because of the high treatment rates necessary to raise pH to lethal levels, lime does not appear useful as a fish eradicant unless the volume to be treated is small or a large application of lime would be beneficial by increasing alkalinity. Studies should be conducted in ponds to determine the effectiveness of hydrated lime in killing fish.

Some fish farmers apply 25-75 kg/ha of hydrated lime to ponds where fish have absorbed substances causing off-flavor in their flesh. Although this treatment is widely acclaimed as effective, there is no reliable evidence to support the claims. In fact, there is no reason to suspect that the treatment would eliminate off-flavor substances from fish.

9.5   REDUCTION OF pH

The removal of carbon dioxide from water by aquatic plants increases the pH of natural waters. This results because carbonate concentrations increase as carbon dioxide is withdrawn and the carbonate hydrolyzes to yield hydroxyl ions. In most waters, alkalinity anions are associated with calcium and magnesium, and the increase in carbonate concentration resulting from carbon dioxide removal by plants finally exceeds the solubility product of calcium carbonate. The precipitation of calcium carbonate tends to limit the rise in pH because the hydrolysis of carbonate is the source of the hydroxyl ion that causes pH to rise. In other words, pH is directly proportional to the carbonate concentration. The precipitation of carbonate by calcium prevents the pH of most waters from rising above 9.5 or 10 in the afternoon, even when photosynthetic rates are high. However, in some waters calcium hardness is much less than total alkalinity, and alkalinity anions are associated with magnesium, sodium, or potassium (usually sodium). Magnesium carbonate is more soluble than calcium carbonate, and sodium and potassium carbonates are highly soluble. Thus, in waters with high alkalinity and low calcium hardness, carbonate resulting from carbon dioxide removal by plants accumulates and pH values may rise to 11 or 12.

Well waters of coastal plain areas often have high alkalinity and low calcium hardness. The geological materials in aquifers of such regions often contain high concentrations of sodium. Water that contains total hardness and total alkalinity values of similar magnitude infiltrates to the depth of the water table. When this water contacts the geological materials of the aquifer, the calcium and magnesium initially present are exchanged for sodium in the geological materials. This results in the natural softening of the ground water (Hem, 1970).

Certain ponds near the coast of South Carolina are filled with waters from artesian wells that have total alkalinity values of 200 to 500 mg/l and calcium hardness values below 20 mg/l (Boyd et al., 1978). Excellent phytoplankton growth occurs in these ponds, and pH occasionally increases to levels toxic to fish. Well water used to fill ponds at a fish hatchery in Meridian, Mississippi, has a total alkalinity of 150 mg/l and a calcium hardness of 12 mg/l. During periods of rapid plant growth, pH values in these ponds have reached 12 or more, and fish kills have resulted.

If phytoplankton blooms are dense, adequate light for rapid rates of photosynthesis is restricted to relatively shallow depths, and fish can seek haven from high pH in deeper waters. However, in ponds with abundant underwater weeds, pH may increase to excessive levels throughout the water volume.

Boyd (1979a) reported that pH of pond waters could be reduced by one of the following treatments: ammonium sulfate, which releases hydrogen ions upon nitrification; filter alum [$Al_2(SO_4)_3 \cdot 14H_2O$], which hydrolyzes to release hydrogen ions; agricultural gypsum ($CaSO_4 \cdot 2H_2O$), which increases calcium hardness resulting in precipitation of calcium carbonate. Mandal and Boyd (1980) established mud-water systems in outdoor pools where total alkalinities ranged from 130 to 170 mg/l and total hardness from 10 to 20 mg/l. Magnesium concentrations were low, hence total hardness was nearly equal to calcium hardness. Four pools were treated at the

TABLE 9.7

Average values for pH in control pools and in three series of pools treated for pH reduction. Each value is the average of measurements from four pools (Mandal and Boyd, 1980).

Treatment	Before treatment	Days after treatment					
		1	2	4	8	16	32
Control	9.2	9.2	9.3	9.4	9.9	9.3	9.4
Filter alum	9.1	9.0	9.0	9.2	8.8	8.3	9.1
Ammonium sulfate	9.0	8.7	8.9	9.2	9.1	8.8	8.5
Agricultural gypsum	9.0	8.6	8.6	8.4	8.5	8.6	8.2

rate of 4 mg/l of ammonium sulfate; enough agricultural gypsum was added to four pools to initially equalize total hardness and total alkalinity; filter alum was applied to four pools at the rate of 1 mg/l filter alum for each milligram per liter of phenolphthalein alkalinity; four pools served as untreated controls. Treatment with agricultural gypsum was clearly superior to the other treatments in reducing pH, for it was the only treatment for which average pH values were significantly lower than those of the controls on all subsequent sampling dates (Table 9.7). Values for pH were usually about 1 unit lower for the gypsum-treated than for the control ponds. None of the treatments produced a reduction in phytoplankton growth, as judged visually.

Of course, sulfuric acid, or some other strong mineral acid, could be applied to ponds to reduce pH. Concentrated acids are dangerous to handle, and this practice is not generally advisable.

Agricultural gypsum at concentrations up to those of a saturated solution (about 2,000 mg/l) apparently has no adverse affects on fish or other aquatic organisms (McKee and Wolf, 1963). For practical application of agricultural gypsum, I suggest an application rate of twice that used in the present study because some calcium added in the gypsum will be adsorbed by muds. Thus, enough gypsum should be applied to initially increase calcium hardness to twice the total alkalinity. The calculations are as follows:

$$\begin{array}{cc} 172.08 \text{ mg} & 100 \text{ mg} \\ CaSO_4 \cdot 2H_2O = Ca^{2+} = CaCO_3 \\ x & 1 \text{ mg/l} \end{array}$$

$$x = 1.72 \text{ mg/l}$$

Thus, 1.72 mg/l of gypsum will raise calcium hardness by 1 mg/l. However, agricultural gypsum is only 80% pure, and 1.72 mg/l ÷ 0.80 = 2.15 mg/l of agricultural gypsum will be required. Results of the calculations may be combined into an equation for estimating the application rate:

Agricultural gypsum in mg/l = (TA - CaH)(2.15)(2)

where TA = total alkalinity and CaH = calcium hardness.

The most popular method for reducing pH of waters has been the application of ammonium sulfate or some other acid forming fertilizer (Swingle, 1961). This practice is undesirable because concentrations of un-ionized ammonia will be high following the application of an ammonium salt to water. Furthermore, treatment with acid-forming fertilizers do nothing to change the cause of high pH. Gypsum treatment is safe and raises calcium hardness, hence there is a longer-lasting effect on pH. Further research on reducing pH in ponds is badly needed.

9.6   CONTROL OF TURBIDITY

Colloids may impart unwanted turbidity to pond water. Colloidal particles are minute (1-100 nm), and they remain suspended in water against gravitational forces. Colloidal particles in water are, as a rule, negatively charged and repel each other. Several procedures may be used to remove colloids from water, but the most effective technique is the introduction of electrolytes of opposite charge. The mechanism by which electrolytes cause coagulation of colloidal particles is too complicated to explain here. The interested reader may consult the treatment of this subject by Stumm and Morgan (1970). For our purposes, we may think of the positively charged electrolytes as combining with negatively charged colloids to neutralize part of the negative charge of the colloids as follows:

```
- - -      +        - -
Colloid + Cation  →  Colloid Cation
- - -      +        - -
```

Neutralization of the charge reduces the strength of repulsion between colloids and they agglomerate. The process of coming together of colloidal particles is termed flocculation, and when a floc of particles becomes heavy enough, it precipitates. The effectiveness of electrolytes in coagulating colloids increases with the charge on the electrolyte. For example, calcium ion is 30 times as effective in coagulating colloids as sodium ion, and aluminum and ferric ions are 1,000 times as effective as sodium ions. Therefore, trivalent ions, especially aluminum ions, are commonly used in flocculation (Sawyer and McCarty, 1967). Filter alum $[Al_2(SO_4)_3 \cdot 14H_2O]$ is probably the most widely used coagulating agent for clearing potable waters.

For years, electrolytes were not considered as coagulants for waters of fish ponds, and even today, most workers use organic matter to remove turbidity from pond waters. The widespread use of organic matter resulted primarily from the work of Irwin and Stevenson (1951). These investigators observed that ponds containing populations of underwater macrophytes usually had clear water, suggesting to them that metabolic and decomposition products from plants were an aid in maintaining clear water. This logic is questionable because underwater macrophytes will not grow in extremely turbid water because of light limitations. Nevertheless, these workers showed that applications of organic matter to ponds would clear waters of clay turbidity.

Irwin and Stevenson examined turbulence, mineral content, and watershed characteristics as possible factors associated with clay turbidity. They concluded that turbulence caused by the pond biota was seldom responsible for clay turbidity. However, wading of farm animals and wave action mix clay particles into pond waters. Livestock may be fenced out of ponds, and wind breaks often permit the development of shoreline vegetation which decreases erosion of edges by waves. There was no relationship between mineral content of water and clay turbidity in ponds. The most important factor influencing the clay turbidity in ponds was the watershed. Unprotected watersheds were particularly vulnerable to erosion, and runoff from such watersheds caused turbidity in ponds. However, if soils were composed of fine, dispersed clays, even grass cover did not preclude erosion. For example, spots of alkali soils on watersheds where the soil was dispersed and impermeable to water contributed to turbid runoff even when soils were covered with vegetation. Clay turbidity resulting from erosion of dispersed clay soils remained dispersed longer in pond water than turbidity resulting from the erosion of flocculated clay soils. In general, dispersed clay soils contain high concentrations of sodium, and flocculated clay soils contain appreciable calcium.

Waters from ponds with different concentrations of turbidity — Irwin and Stevenson used a Jackson turbidimeter to measure turbidity — were subjected to oxygen consumption analysis. The oxygen consumption analysis measured the oxygen equivalent of the potassium permanganate used in the oxidation of organic matter in a water sample. The oxygen consumption analysis was a precursor of the present day COD analysis. Ponds with turbidity values less than 50 mg/l usually had oxygen consumption values of 12-29 mg/l. Ponds with highly turbid waters (>100 mg/l) usually had oxygen consumption values of 5.6-10 mg/l. Thus, Irwin and Stevenson concluded that the turbidity of water was related to the quantity of oxidizable organic matter present.

In laboratory tests, applications of alfalfa hay or wheat straw caused carbon dioxide concentrations to increase, pH to decrease, and turbidity to precipitate. Because additions of acid reduced pH and also caused the precipitation of turbidity in laboratory systems, Irwin and Stevenson attributed the removal of turbidity

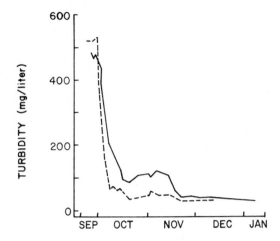

Fig. 9.1. Effects of applications of vegetation (hay) on the removal of clay turbidity from two ponds. Hay was applied to both ponds in September; the pond indicated by the solid line was treated again with hay in early November (Irwin and Stevenson, 1951).

TABLE 9.8

Quantities of dry vegetation (hay) required to reduce clay turbidity in pond waters (Irwin and Stevenson, 1951).

Turbidity[a] (mg/l)	Quantity of hay (g/m^3)
25	50
50	100
75	150
100	200
150	300
200	400

[a]Turbidity was measured with a Jackson Turbidimeter.

by organic matter to an increase in hydrogen ion concentration resulting from carbon dioxide released during decay of organic matter.

Results of two trials on turbidity removal from ponds with organic matter are presented in Fig. 9.1. As in the laboratory experiments, carbon dioxide increased and pH decreased following application of organic matter. Quantities of hay necessary to remove turbidity are given in Table 9.8.

Swingle and Smith (1947) also recommended the use of organic matter to remove clay turbidity. They found that two or three applications of barnyard manure at the rate of 2,240 kg/ha at 3-week intervals would normally clear water. Swingle and Smith also used applications of 84 kg/ha of cottonseed meal and 28 kg/ha of superphosphate at 2- to 3-week intervals to precipitate clay turbidity.

Organic matter for use in clearing turbidity is often difficult to obtain and to apply to ponds. It also decomposes and exerts an oxygen demand. The effects of organic matter on turbidity are not highly predictable, and several weeks often elapse before a treatment may be declared a success or a failure. Therefore it is surprising that so little emphasis has been given to the use of electrolytes for removing turbidity from pond waters.

Dillard (undated) recommended the use of agricultural gypsum at about 200 mg/l to remove clay turbidity. The gypsum was spread evenly over the water surface. Highly turbid waters often cleared in less than a week, while moderately turbid waters took 2-4 weeks to clear. Grizzell et al. (1975) recommended gypsum applications to moderately turbid ponds at 225 kg/ha and to heavily turbid ponds at 900 kg/ha. If the water did not clear in 7-10 days, additional gypsum application was suggested.

Boyd (1979b) tested the effectiveness of four coagulants, filter alum, hydrated lime, ferric sulfate, and agricultural gypsum, for precipitating clay turbidity from pond waters in settling columns. Three types of soil were used as sources of clay turbidity. Alum and ferric sulfate were much more effective than hydrated lime or gypsum in removing turbidity. Concentrations of the coagulating agents required to precipitate 50% of the clay turbidity from pond water in settling columns are given in Table 9.9. Filter alum was extremely effective, relatively inexpensive, and readily available in most localities, hence it was selected for further study.

Because alum is acidic, it has effects in addition to coagulation. Alum reacts in water as follows:

$$Al_2(SO_4)_3 \cdot 14H_2O + 6\ H_2O \rightarrow 2\ Al(OH)_3 + 6\ H^+ + 3\ SO_4^{2-} + 14\ H_2O$$

Some of the aluminum ions react with any colloidal clay particles present; the rest precipitate out as aluminum hydroxide. Below pH 6, an appreciable amount of the aluminum hydroxide is soluble. Some hydrogen ions also react with colloids, but most neutralize carbonate and biacarbonate to reduce total alkalinity and depress pH:

$$3\ Ca(HCO_3)_2 + 6\ H^+ \rightarrow 3\ Ca^{2+} + 6\ CO_2 + 4\ H_2O$$

The two equations may be combined to show the overall effect of alum:

TABLE 9.9

Concentrations of four coagulating agents (mg/1) necessary to remove 50% of the clay turbidity in 1 h from waters in settling columns. Turbid waters were prepared from three soils (Boyd 1979b).

Coagulating agent	Source of soil		
	Black belt prairie	Piedmont	Lower coastal plain
Alum	20	10	20
Ferric sulfate	20	20	20
Hydrated lime	100	1,000	250
Gypsum	250	1,000	1,000

$$Al_2(SO_4)_3 \cdot 14H_2O + 3\ Ca(HCO_3)_2 \rightarrow 2\ Al(OH)_3 + 3\ CaSO_4 + 6\ CO_2$$

The theoretical amount of alkalinity destroyed by 1 mg/1 of filter alum is:

594.14 mg   300 mg

$Al_2(SO_4)_3 \cdot 14H_2O = 6\ H^+ = 3\ CaCO_3$

1 mg/1   x

x = 0.5 mg/1

The pH reduction will depend upon the initial pH and alkalinity of the water. Alum treatment of pond water actually destroyed about 0.5 mg/1 of total alkalinity for each milligram per liter of alum. The effect of alum treatment on the pH of pond water is illustrated in Fig. 9.2.

Flocculation of colloids by alum is best at pH values of 5-6.5. Therefore, flocculation will be poor if enough alum is added to destroy all of the total alkalinity. Treatment of a water having 10 mg/1 total alkalinity with 25 mg/1 of alum would destroy all of the total alkalinity and depress pH below 5. Hydrated lime may be added to waters of low alkalinity at the time of alum treatment to improve conditions for turbidity removal. The amount of hydrated lime to neutralize the acidity of 1 mg/1 of filter alum is:

594.14 mg   222.24 mg

$Al_2(SO_4)_3 \cdot 14H_2O = 6\ H^+ = 3\ Ca(OH)_2$

1 mg/1   x

x = 0.37 mg/1

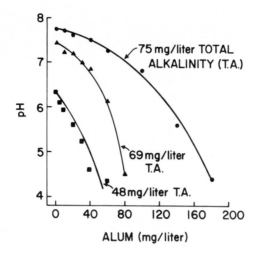

Fig. 9.2. Effects of different concentrations of alum on the pH of pond waters (Boyd, 1979b).

An alum requirement test was designed for measuring the amount of filter alum needed to remove clay turbidity from ponds. Water from a particular pond was used to fill eight, 1-liter settling cylinders (graduated cylinders will also suffice). Alum was added from a 2,000 mg/l stock solution to give concentrations of 0, 5, 10, 15, 20, 25, 30, and 40 mg/l. The contents of the cylinders were mixed by five vertical strokes of a plunger. The plunger was a plexiglass plate (0.5-cm thick X 5.7-cm diameter with four 1-cm diameter holes) attached at the center to a wooden rod. After 1 h, the lowest concentration of alum that produced a visible floc was taken as the alum requirement. Floc, if present, was readily visible against a white background in bright light.

Seven ponds were treated with alum and two served as untreated controls. For small ponds, commercial filter alum was dissolved in buckets of pond water and splashed over pond surfaces. Mixing was affected by a spray-type surface aerator operating for 10 min. In larger ponds, alum was dissolved in water and sprayed over pond surfaces with a boat-mounted, power sprayer. The propellor wake of the boat motor affected mixing.

Turbidity was measured with a nephelometer and reported in nephelometer turbidity units (NTU). Four of the ponds had light or moderate clay turbidity (19-40 NTU) and five had heavy clay turbidity (625-860 NTU). Alum requirements of ponds ranged from 15 to 25 mg/l. A floc began to form within 10 min after alum application was initiated, and within 1 h the floc was beginning to settle from the water. Alum treatment reduced turbidity values by 89-97% within 48 h (Table 9.10). Control ponds did not change appreciably in turbidity.

TABLE 9.10

Results of alum treatment to remove clay turbidity from fish ponds. Turbidity is reported as nephelometer turbidity units (Boyd, 1979b).

Pond	Area (ha)	Alum requirement (mg/l)	Alum applied (mg/l)	Turbidity (NTU)		Reduction in NTU (%)
				Initial	After 48 h	
M-17	0.07	15	0	33	24	
E-67	0.04	15	15	40	2	95
E-68	0.04	20	20	28	3	89
E-73	0.04	20	20	19	3	84
S-22	0.89	20	0	625	660	
S-23	0.89	25	25	840	72	91
S-25	0.40	20	20	860	58	93
S-26	0.40	15	15	665	51	92
S-27	0.40	20	20	830	24	97

Alum treatment reduced pH and alkalinity. The average decrease in total alkalinity was 0.44 mg/l for each milligram per liter of alum applied. The treated ponds had low alkalinities (5.6-17.8 mg/l) and pH dropped to 5 or less in four ponds. These four ponds were the ones with heavy turbidity. Better flocculation and turbidity removal would have probably been achieved if hydrated lime had been added to keep pH in the optimum range for flocculation. The alkalinity and pH of ponds gradually returned to initial levels over the next 2 months, and turbidity remained lower than before treatment.

Three other ponds were treated with alum at rates less than the alum requirement to determine if the test overestimated the alum treatment rate. Turbidity removal was incomplete (5-71% reduction) when 50% or 66% of the alum requirement was applied.

Data from McKee and Wolf (1963) indicate that alum is not appreciably toxic to fish. Goldfish (Carassius auratus), sunfish, and largemouth bass (Micropterus salmoides) were not harmed by 100 mg/l of alum in 7 days, but 250 mg/l killed fish of these species in 24 h or less. The 96-h LC50 for mosquito fish (Gambusia affinis) was 235 mg/l. Total alkalinity values were not reported.

The toxicity of alum to fathead minnows was related to total alkalinity of test waters. Apparently, fish will not die unless alum concentrations are somewhat higher than total alkalinity concentrations (Table 9.11). Although pH values declined to 4.41 in waters of some of the toxicity test, acidity probably did not

TABLE 9.11

Percentage mortality of fathead minnows after 96-h exposure to various concentrations of alum in waters with different total alkalinity. Test waters contained no clay turbidity. Each value is based on 20 fathead minnows per concentration (Boyd, 1979b).

Alum (mg/l)	Initial total alkalinity (mg/l)		
	64	33	14
0	0	2.5	0
5			0
10	0	0	0
20	0	0	0
30			5
40	0	0	97.5
60	0	20	100
80		100	
100	0		
140	0		
180	100		

cause fish mortality. Mount (1973) found that fathead minnows could survive pH 4.5 for long periods, and Swingle (1961) reported the acid death point of pond fish as 4.0. Death of fish in the toxicity tests (Table 9.11) was likely related to high concentrations of aluminum ion at low pH. At pH 4.4, the concentration of aluminum ion in equilibrium with $Al(OH)_3$ is approximately 1.4 mg/l.

In another series of toxicity tests, hydrated lime was applied at 0.37 mg/l per milligram per liter of alum, and it negated toxic effects in all trials. For example, in one test, 120 mg/l of alum killed 100% of the fish when hydrated lime was not applied and 0% when lime was applied. The floc formed when alum was applied to turbid waters in aquaria did not harm fish.

Bandow (1974) applied 92 mg/l of filter alum to a pond with an initial alkalinity of 150 mg/l. No fish mortality was observed and production was not adversely affected. Bandow also failed to observe adverse effects on invertebrate fish food organisms in three ponds treated with either 46, 62, or 92 mg/l of alum. Alum precipitates phosphorus as insoluble aluminum phosphate, but the species of aluminum responsible for phosphorus precipitation quickly disappear from solution if treated waters contain residual alkalinity (Stumm and Morgan, 1970). Thus, applications of alum to remove clay turbidity will not adversely affect the availability of phosphorus added in fertilizer later in the growing season.

Results reported by Boyd (1979b) indicate that alum is an effective coagulating agent for use in turbid ponds. The alum requirement test may be used to determine application rates. If this procedure cannot be conducted, the application of 25-30 mg/l of filter alum will likely remove the turbidity from most waters. An alum concentration of 25 mg/l caused flocculation in waters of 32 ponds representing turbidities of 32-744 NTU (Boyd, 1979b). If the alum requirement value is greater than the total alkalinity, hydrated lime should be applied to the pond at the rate of 0.40 mg/l for each milligram per liter of alum. Hydrated lime may be applied before or simultaneously with alum, but the hydrated lime and alum must not be mixed before they are applied over the pond surface. Alum should be dissolved in water and sprayed uniformly over the pond surface. Applications should be made during calm dry weather, for mixing by wind and rain will break up the floc and keep it from settling. The alum solution is highly acidic, so steps must be taken to prevent corrosion of equipment.

Ponds that are fertilized to promote fish growth should have waters with more than 20 mg/l of total alkalinity for optimum response to fertilizer nutrients. Therefore, for removing clay turbidity from most soft water ponds, it is most efficient to determine the lime requirement of muds and apply agricultural limestone to increase the total alkalinity. The large amounts of agricultural limestone needed to satisfy lime requirements often result in precipitation of clay turbidity. However, if clay turbidity persists, alum treatment may be implemented without danger of severe pH depression.

9.7 SALINITY, HARDNESS, AND CHLORIDE

At research stations, it is sometimes desired to culture certain species of fish at salinities or hardnesses greater than those naturally occuring in experimental ponds. Salinity may be increased with gypsum or rock salt (NaCl). Salinities greater than 1,500-2,000 mg/l require rock salt because of the limited solubility of gypsum. Neither chemical reacts appreciably with bottom muds or other constituents in the water, and application rates are easily computed from pond volume. For example, suppose the salinity of water in a pond containing $500 \ m^3$ is to be raised by 250 mg/l. Each cubic meter will require 250 g of rock salt, hence $0.25 \ kg/m^3 \ X \ 500 \ m^3 = 125$ kg of rock salt.

Total hardness values may be increased by gypsum application. Agricultural gypsum is 80% pure and contains about 18.6% calcium. Thus, each kilogram of agricultural gypsum equals 0.186 kg of calcium, or $0.186 \ X \ (100 \div 40) = 0.467$ kg of $CaCO_3$ (hardness is expressed as $CaCO_3$). To raise the total hardness of 1 m^3 of water by 1 mg/l would require: 1 mg/l $CaCO_3 \div 0.467$ kg of $CaCO_3$ per kilogram $= 2.14$ kg of agricultural gypsum. Gypsum applications will not increase total alkalinity.

Additions of sodium chloride and calcium chloride protect fish against nitrite toxicity. Crawford and Allen (1977) reported the 48-h LC50 of nitrite for Chinook salmon fingerlings (Oncorhynchus tschawytshn) as 19 mg/l in fresh water and >100 mg/l in sea water. Later, Perrone and Meade (1977) reported that the protective effect of sea water against nitrite toxicity resulted from chloride. Wedemeyer and Yasutake (1978) found that both calcium and chloride were involved in reducing nitrite toxicity to steelhead trout (Salmo gairdneri). Addition of 200 mg/l of sodium chloride reduced toxicity by a factor of three, but 200 mg/l of calcium chloride reduced toxicity by a factor of 50. Tomasso et al. (1979a) found that a chloride to nitrite ratio of 16:1 completely suppressed nitrite-induced methemo-globin formation in channel catfish (Ictalurus punctatus). Therefore, Tomasso et al. (1979b) suggested applying 25 mg/l of sodium chloride for each milligram per liter of nitrite to ponds to protect channel catfish from nitrite toxicity. Incidentally, calcium chloride was no more effective than sodium chloride in pro-tecting channel catfish from nitrite toxicity (Tomasso et al., 1980).

9.8 WATER EXCHANGE

The use of water exchange for the general improvement of water quality has already been discussed (Chapters 6 and 7). However, water exchange may be used as a specific means of reducing pH, ammonia, and nitrite levels. Tomasso et al. (1979b) indicated that the addition of fresh water to reduce nutrient loads and dilute ammonia and nitrite concentrations is one of the most effective management techniques available for protecting fish against ammonia and nitrite toxicity. More information on water exchange is presented in Chapter 10.

9.9 CHLORINE REMOVAL

Chlorine must occasionally be removed from water that is to be used for holding fish. The most effective method of chlorine removal is treatment with sodium thiosulfate which reacts with chlorine and chlorine residuals as illustrated below:

$$Cl_2 + 2\ Na_2S_2O_3 \cdot 5H_2O \rightarrow Na_2S_4O_6 + 2\ NaCl + 10\ H_2O$$

The number of milligrams per liter of sodium thiosulfate pentahydrate required to remove 1 mg/l of chlorine is:

$$\frac{496.2\ mg}{2\ Na_2S_2O_3 \cdot 5H_2O} = \frac{70.9\ mg}{Cl_2}$$

$$\frac{x}{x} = \frac{1\ mg/l}{}$$

x = 6.99 mg/l

White (1955) demonstrated that sodium thiosulfate was not toxic to bluegills, goldfish, or golden shiners (<u>Notemigonus</u> <u>chrysoleucus</u>) at concentrations of 180 mg/l at 22°C. Residual chlorine concentrations in municipal water supplies are normally between 0.5 and 2.0 mg/l. Hence, only 3.5-14.0 mg/l of sodium thiosulfate would be required for dechlorination.

9.10   ROTENONE

As indicated above, rotenone is widely used as a fish toxicant. In pond fish culture, rotenone is normally used to eradicate wildfish before stocking ponds (Clemens and Martin, 1952) and for partial poisoning in largemouth bass-sunfish ponds crowded with small and intermediate sunfish (Swingle et al., 1953). Rotenone is a complex organic compound ($C_{23}H_{22}O_6$) that occurs along with related compounds in roots of <u>Derris</u> <u>elliptica</u> and <u>Lonchocarpus</u> spp. and a few other leguminous plants (Shepard, 1951). Roots of these plants are dried, powdered, and used as a dust, or extracts of roots may be used to prepare liquid formulations. Three basic forms of rotenone are used as fish toxicants: 5% emulsifiable concentrate, 5% wettable powder, and 2.5% synergized emulsifiable concentrate.

Rotenone interferes with respiration and is extremely toxic to fish at low concentrations. Even under field conditions, 0.05-2.0 mg/l of commercial formulations will eradicate fish populations (Schnick, 1974). The actual concentration of rotenone following the application of 1.0 mg/l of a 5% formulation is only 0.05 mg/l.

A number of factors affect the toxicity of rotenone. It is more toxic at high temperatures than at low temperatures, and most workers agree that applications should be made when the water temperature is above 15°C (Schnick, 1974). Rotenone is more toxic in acidic or neutral waters than in alkaline waters. For example, the LC50 values for rotenone to goldfish increased from 0.10 to 0.12 μl/l of a 5% emulsifiable concentrate at pH 5 to 7 up to 0.33 μl/l at pH 10. More rotenone is required to kill fish in hard than in soft water (Foye, 1964). Effective eradication of fish in soft, acidic waters may result from applications of 0.25-0.5 mg/l of commercial formulations (Zilliox and Pfeiffer, 1960). However, Clemens and Martin (1952) found that concentrations of 1-2 mg/l were required for fish eradication in alkaline waters.

A number of methods have been used to apply rotenone for eradication of fish populations. These include surface application with mixing by a motor boat, spraying over the pond surface, discharging from low flying aircraft, and pumping through a weighted hose into deep water. Rotenone does not penetrate the thermocline readily (Clemens and Martin, 1952), and when pumped beneath the thermocline, rotenone does not disperse readily. However, for small, shallow ponds used in fish culture, uniform distribution of rotenone over pond surfaces is usually effective. Uniform surface coverage can best be achieved with a pressurized sprayer. Unfortunately, even when 1-2 mg/l of a commercial formulation of rotenone is applied to ponds, fish kills are not complete (Clemens and Martin, 1952; Turner, 1959).

Rotenone may be detoxified with potassium permanganate as mentioned earlier. However, its natural degradation to nontoxic form is fairly rapid. Rotenone loses its toxicity most rapidly when temperature and light intensity are high. Elevated alkalinity also favors degradation (Schnick, 1974). During spring and summer, rotenone will be detoxified within 1 to 2 weeks, but a much longer time is required in winter. Rotenone is extremely toxic to invertebrate fish food organisms, but invertebrate communities recover rapidly after detoxification of the rotenone.

9.11   FORMALIN AND MALACHITE GREEN

Formalin is widely used in fish culture for the control of fungi on fish eggs and external parasites on fish. It is relatively nontoxic to fish and is used at 1,000-2,000 µl/l (1,103-2,206 mg/l) for 15 min in constant flow baths, 167-250 µl/l (184-276 mg/l) in tanks or raceways for 1 h, and 15-25 µl/l (16.5-27.6 mg/l) for indefinite periods in ponds (Schnick, 1973). Unfortunately, formalin is highly toxic to plankton and pond treatments of 15 mg/l (13.6 µl/l) may cause dissolved oxygen depletion in ponds with heavy plankton blooms (Allison, 1962).

Malachite green has the chemical name 4-[p-(dimethylamino)-α-phenylbenzylidene]-2, 5-cyclohexadien-1-ylidene dimethylammonium chloride and is used to treat fungi on eggs and fish and certain external protozoan and bacterial infections on fish. It is usually applied to fish in tanks, troughs, raceways, etc., but malchite green is also used as a pond treatment. Malchite green is extremely toxic to fish, and pond treatments as low as 0.1 mg/l may kill fish. The chemical is apparently not harmful to plankton and higher aquatic plants at concentrations used in ponds (Nelson, 1974).

9.12   METHODS OF APPLYING CHEMICALS

Chemicals that are applied to ponds come in a variety of formulations: crystals, solutions, wettable powders, emulsifiable concentrates, and granules. Fish culture stations can afford rather elaborate equipment for applying chemicals to ponds. For example, chemicals may be dissolved in a tank of water or some other solvent and sprayed uniformly over the pond surface with a power sprayer. Liquids may be dispersed uniformly from a tank in a boat through a boom consisting of a pipe with a series of small diameter holes in its underside. A value is used to regulate the rate at which the solution is fed by gravity into the water; a pump may be employed to affect more uniform and forceful release. A similar device may be constructed to release the chemical below the pond surface by connecting small vertical tubes of the desired length to the holes in the boom. Dispensers similar to conventional fertilizers distributors have been mounted on boats and used to

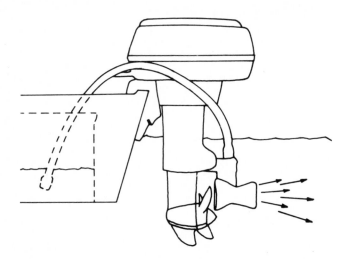

Fig. 9.3. A simple apparatus for mixing solutions of chemicals with pond waters. Available from the Carus Chemical Company, LaSalle, Illinois.

spread crystals and granules. These dispensers are usually hoppers with adjustable dispensing holes in the bottom. An auger is employed to prevent clogging of holes with coarse particles (Schoenecker and Rhodes, 1965). An even simpler device for applying solutions of chemicals to water is illustrated in Fig. 9.3. The outboard motor propeller mixes the chemical with the water as it is released from the siphon. Dispensers of this type are available commercially.

In many instances the owner of a single pond may need to apply a chemical. Usually, it is not practical to purchase or construct an elaborate dispenser. The chemical can be dissolved in a large container of water and applied to the pond surface. Application may be accomplished with a pressurized garden sprayer. However, if a sprayer is not available the chemical may be dissolved in water and splashed with a dipper over the pond surface from a boat. Care should be taken to dispense the solution as uniformly as possible. Granules may be broadcast by hand or with a "cyclone" seeder. Crystals may be placed in a burlap bag and towed behind a boat until they have completely dissolved. Only a little ingenuity is needed to develop a method for applying a chemical to a pond once the treatment rate has been established.

REFERENCES

Allison, R., 1962. The effects of formalin and other parasiticides upon oxygen concentrations in ponds. Proc. Annual Conf. Southeast. Assoc. Game and Fish Comm., 16: 446-449.
Bandow, F., 1974. Algae control in fish ponds through chemical control of

available nutrients. Minnesota Department of Natural Resources, Saint Paul, Minnesota, Investigational Report 326, 22 pp.

Bauer, O. N., 1958. Parasitic diseases of cultured fishes and methods of their prevention and treatment. In: V. A. Dogiel, G. K. Petrosheuski, and Y. I. Polyanski (Editors), Parasitology of Fishes, English Edition (1961). Oliver and Boyd, London, pp. 265-298.

Boyd, C. E., 1979a. Water Quality in Warmwater Fish Ponds. Auburn University Agricultural Experiment Station, Auburn, Alabama, 359 pp.

Boyd, C. E., 1979b. Aluminum sulfate (alum) for precipitating clay turbidity from fish ponds. Trans. Amer. Fish. Soc., 108: 307-313.

Boyd, C. E., Preacher, J. W., and Justice, L., 1978. Hardness, alkalinity, pH, and pond fertilization. Proc. Annual Conf. Southeast. Assoc. Fish and Wildl. Agencies, 32: 605-611.

Calabrese, A., 1969. Effects of acids and alkalies on survival of bluegills and largemouth bass. U. S. Fish and Wildlife Service, Washington, D. C., Technical Paper 42, 10 pp.

Clemens, H. P. and Martin, M., 1952. Effectiveness of rotenone in pond reclamation. Trans. Amer. Fish. Soc., 82: 166-177.

Crawford, R. E. and Allen, G. H., 1977. Seawater inhibition of nitrite toxicity to chinook salmon. Trans. Amer. Fish. Soc., 106: 105-109.

Dillard, J. G., undated. Missouri Pond Handbook. Missouri Department of Conservation, Jefferson City, 61 pp.

Duncan, T. O., 1974. A review of literature on the use of potassium permanganate ($KMnO_4$) in fisheries. U. S. Fish and Wildlife Service, Washington, D. C., Rep. FWS-LR-74-14, 61 pp.

Einsele, W., 1936. Uber die Beziehungen des Eisenderslaufs zum Photosphatkreislauf im Eutrophen Sec. Arch. Hydrobiol., 29: 644-686.

Engstrom-Heg, R., 1971. Direct measurement of potassium permangante demand and residual potassium permanganate. N. Y. Fish and Game J., 18: 117-122.

Fitzgerald, G. P., 1966. Use of potassium permanganate for control of problem algae. J. Amer. Water Works Assoc., 58: 609-614.

Foye, R. E., 1964. Chemical reclamation of forty-eight ponds in Maine. Prog. Fish-Cult., 26: 181-185.

Grizzell, R. A., Jr., Dillon, O. W., Jr., Sullivan, E. G., and Compton, L. V., 1975. Catfish farming. U. S. Department of Agriculture, Washington, D. C., Farmers' Bulletin No. 2260, 21 pp.

Hansell, D. A. and Boyd, C. E., 1980. Uses of hydrated lime in fish ponds. Proc. Annual Conf. Southeast. Assoc. Fish and Wildl. Agencies, 34: in press.

Hem, J. D., 1970. Study and Interpretation of the Chemical Characteristics of Natural Water. U. S. Geological Survey Water-Supply Paper 1473, U. S. Government Printing Office, Washington, D. C., 363 pp.

Irwin, W. H. and Stevenson, J. H., 1951. Physiochemical nature of clay turbidity with special reference to clarification and productivity of impounded waters. Bull. Oklahoma A. and M. College, Vol. 48, 54 pp.

Jee, L. K., 1979. The use of potassium permanganate in treating fathead minnows infected with Flexibacter columnaris. M. S. thesis, Auburn University, Auburn, Alabama, 37 pp.

Kemp, H. T., Fuller, R. G., and Davidson, R. S., 1966. Potassium permanganate as an algicide. J. Amer. Water Works Assoc., 58: 255-263.

Ladbury, J. W. and Cullis, C. F., 1958. Kinetics and mechanism of oxidation by permanganate. Chem. Rev., 58: 403-438.

Lawrence, J. M., 1956. Preliminary results on the use of potassium permanganate to counteract the effects of rotenone on fish. Prog. Fish-Cult., 18: 15-21.

Lay, B. A., 1971. Applications for potassium permanganate in fish culture. Trans. Amer. Fish. Soc., 100: 813-815.

Mandal, B. K. and Boyd, C. E., 1980. Reduction of pH in waters with high total alkalinity and low total hardness. Prog. Fish-Cult., 42: 183-185.

Marathe, V. B., Huilgol, N. V., and Patil, S. G., 1975. Hydrogen peroxide as a source of oxygen supply in the transport of fish fry. Prog. Fish-Cult., 37: 117.

Marking, L. L. and Bills, T. D., 1975. Toxicity of potassium permanganate to fish and its effectiveness for detoxifying antimycin. Trans. Amer. Fish. Soc., 104: 579-583.

Mathis, W. P., Brady, L. E., and Gilbreath, W. J., 1962. Preliminary report on the use of potassium permanganate to produce oxygen and counteract hydrogen sulfide gas in fish ponds. Proc. Annual Conf. Southeast. Assoc. Game and Fish Comm., 16: 357-359.

McKee, J. E. and Wolf, H. W. (Editors), 1963. Water Quality Criteria, 2nd edition. State of California, State Water Quality Control Board, Sacremento, Publication No. 3-A, 548 pp.

Mount, D. I., 1973. Chronic effect of low pH on fathead minnow survival, growth, and reproduction. Water Res., 7: 987-993.

Nelson, N. C., 1974. A review of the literature on the use of formalin-malachite green in fisheries. U. S. Fish and Wildlife Service, Washington, D. C., Report No. FWS-LR-74-12, 31 pp.

Perrone, S. J. and Meade, T. L., 1977. Protective effect of chloride on nitrite toxicity to coho salmon (Oncorhynchus kisutch). J. Fish. Res. Bd. Canada, 34: 486-492.

Phelps, R. P., Plumb, J. A., and Harris, C. W., 1977. Control of external bacterial infections of bluegills with potassium permanganate. Prog. Fish-Cult., 39: 142-143.

Sawyer, C. N. and McCarty, P. L., 1967. Chemistry for Sanitary Engineers. McGraw-Hill Book Co., New York, 518 pp.

Schnick, R. A., 1973. Formalin as a therapeutant in fish culture. U. S. Fish and Wildlife Service, Washington, D. C., Report No. FWS-LR-74-09, 131 pp.

Schnick, R. A., 1974. A review of the literature on the use of rotenone in fisheries. U. S. Fish and Wildlife Service, Washington, D. C., Report No. FWS-LR-74-15, 130 pp.

Schoenecker, W. and Rhodes, W., 1965. Potassium permanganate dispenser. Prog. Fish-Cult., 27: 55-56.

Shepard, H. H., 1951. The Chemistry and Action of Insecticides. McGraw-Hill Book Co., New York, 504 pp.

Stearn, E. W. and Stearn, A. E., 1930. Differential action of oxidizing agents on certain Gram-positive and Gram-negative organisms. J. Infect. Dis., 46: 500-513.

Stumm, W. and Morgan, J. J., 1970. Aquatic Chemistry. John Wiley and Sons, New York, 583 pp.

Swingle, H. S., 1961. Relationships of pH of pond waters to their suitability for fish culture. Proc. Pacific Sci. Congress 9 (1957), 10: 72-75.

Swingle, H. S. and Smith, E. V., 1947. Management of farm fish ponds. Alabama Polytechnic Institute Agricultural Experiment Station, Auburn, Alabama, Bull. 254, 32 pp.

Swingle, H. S., Prather, E. E., and Lawrence, J. M., 1953. Partial poisoning of overcrowded fish populations. Alabama Polytechnic Institute Agricultural Experiment Station, Auburn, Alabama, Circular 113, 16 pp.

Tomasso, J. R., Goudie, C. A., Simco, B. A., and Davis, K. B., 1980. Effects of environmental pH and calcium on ammonia toxicity in channel catfish. Trans. Amer. Fish. Soc., 109: 229-234.

Tomasso, J. R., Simco, B. A., and Davis, K. B., 1979a. Chloride inhibition of nitrite induced methemoglobinemia in channel catfish (Ictalurus punctatus). J. Fish. Res. Bd. Canada, 36: 1141-1144.

Tomasso, J. R., Simco, B. A., and Davis, K. B., 1979b. Inhibition of ammonia and nitrite toxicity to the channel catfish. Proc. Annual Conf. Southeast. Fish and Wildl. Comm., 33:

Tucker, C. S. and Boyd, C. E., 1977. Relationships between potassium permanganate treatment and water quality. Trans. Amer. Fish. Soc., 106: 481-488.

Turner, W. R., 1959. Effectiveness of various rotenone-containing preparations in eradicating farm pond fish populations. Kentucky Dept. Fish. and Wildl. Resources, Fish. Bull., 25: 1-22.

Wedemeyer, G. A. and Yasutake, W. T., 1978. Prevention and treatment of nitrite toxicity in juvenile steelhead trout (Salmo gairdneri). J. Fish. Res. Bd.

Canada, 35: 822-827.

Welch, W. A., 1963. Potassium permanganate in water treatment. J. Amer. Water Works Assoc., 55: 735-741.

White, C. E., Jr., 1955. Chlorine: its toxicity to goldfish, fathead minnows, golden shiners, and bluegills and its removal from water. M. S. thesis, Alabama Polytechnic Institute, Auburn, Alabama, 58 pp.

Willey, B. F., Jennings, H., and Muroski, F., 1964. Removal of hydrogen sulfide with potassium permanganate. J. Amer. Water Works Assoc., 56: 475-479.

Zilliox, R. G. and Pfeiffer, M., 1960. The use of rotenone for management of New York trout waters. Canadian Fish Cult., 28: 3-12.

Chapter 10

HYDROLOGY OF PONDS

10.1   INTRODUCTION

Familiarity with the water budgets of ponds is often an asset when one attempts to manipulate nutrient cycles, food webs, and water quality to favor fish production. The natural water budget is regulated by the local hydroclimate, geological features, and the manner of pond construction. However, the natural budget is sometimes altered by regulated inflow and outflow of water and consumptive use.

The water budget for a pond will include some or all of the following terms:

Gains	Losses
Precipitation	Evaporation and evapotranspiration
Direct runoff	Seepage
Inflow of streams	Spillway discharge
Ground water inflow	Consumptive use
Regulated inflow	Regulated discharge

Data on precipitation, direct runoff, and evaporation are available for most areas. Stream inflow, regulated inflow, spillway discharge, regulated discharge, and consumptive use can be easily measured or calculated. However, there have been few detailed studies of pond hydrology, and information on ground water inflow and seepage loss is meager.

In this chapter, I will discuss the individual terms in the water budget. These terms will then be used in calculating water balances for hypothetical ponds to illustrate the importance of hydrology in pond management. In my calculations, I will assume conditions that normally exist in Alabama, but the methods of calculating water balances are general and may be used for other conditions.

10.2   TYPES OF PONDS

From the standpoint of construction, there are two basic types of ponds: embankment ponds and excavated ponds (Anonymous, 1971). An embankment pond is made by building an embankment or dam across a stream or watershed. The land must slope, but the slope may range from gentle to steep. A variation of the embankment pond in level areas involves enclosing the pond on all sides by embankments. Of course, because there is no watershed, a water supply is mandatory. Excavated ponds are constructed by digging pits into nearly level areas. Because their capacity is obtained almost entirely by digging, excavated ponds are normally used where only a small volume of water is needed. Some excavated ponds are built in gentle to moderately sloping areas, and their capacity is obtained both by excavating and by building a dam.

Hydrologically, ponds are more varied than indicated above. Embankment ponds may be supplied by permanent streams, hence their water levels do not fluctuate and outflow occurs continuously. Embankment ponds that catch the flow of ephemeral streams or receive ground water seepage will usually have stable water levels during rainy months, but water levels may decline during dry months. Some embankment ponds may only store direct runoff (storm flow). Such ponds were called "terrace-water" ponds by Swingle and Smith (1939); they observed that water levels in these ponds often declined by 1 m or more during several weeks of dry weather. Watersheds for embankments ponds without permanent inflow must be large enough to fill ponds during the wet season, and ponds must be deep enough to store adequate water to carry them through the dry season. Pipe lines or other conduits supply water from wells, streams, or storage reservoirs to fill and maintain water levels in embankment ponds without watersheds. In some areas, the water table is near the surface of the land and excavated ponds fill from seepage. The water surface will always correspond to the water table level, and the water level may fall during dry weather. Some excavated ponds receive direct runoff to augment seepage, and other excavated ponds, which do not intercept the water table, depend entirely upon precipitation falling on the surface and direct runoff to supply water.

Ponds used for research in fish culture and for commercial fish production are usually embankment or excavated ponds without watersheds. They are usually filled and their water levels maintained by regulated additions of water. Sportfish ponds and ponds for small-scale fish culture include all of the types of ponds mentioned above.

10.3   SOURCES OF WATER
10.3.1   Precipitation

Annual precipitation totals vary from 25 to 250 cm in areas where fish are produced in ponds. Although precipitation may occur throughout the year at a given locality, more precipitation will normally occur during some months than others. Furthermore, both annual and monthly precipitation totals vary greatly among years. For example, the average annual rainfall (based on 40 years of data) at Auburn, Alabama, is 134 cm, but for individual years, rainfall totals have ranged between 100 and 200 cm. Likewise, the average rainfall at Auburn, Alabama, for July is 14 cm, but for different years, rainfall in July ranged from 7 to 48 cm. Data presented in Fig. 10.1 illustrate variations in rainfall totals at a given locality. Great variation in rainfall totals for months and years is common throughout the world (Miller, 1977).

Precipitation falling directly on a pond is seldom enough to greatly alter its water level. However, precipitation is the source of all water used in fish culture, so the fish culturist should be familiar with local rainfall patterns.

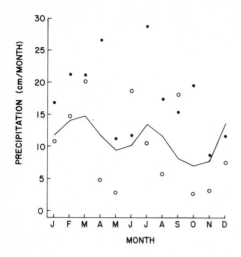

Fig. 10.1. The 40-year average rainfall (solid line) at Auburn, Alabama, and monthly rainfall for 1965 (open circles) and 1975 (dots). Data were supplied by the U. S. National Weather Service.

10.3.2   Direct runoff

Once the rate of rainfall exceeds the rate at which water can infiltrate watershed surfaces, water puddles on the ground surface and begins to flow down slope in response to gravity. Factors influencing the amount of direct runoff from a watershed are many: intensity and duration of precipitation, moisture content of soil, soil organic matter, soil type, soil texture, type and density of vegetation, land use, temperature, and watershed slope. Methods for calculating direct runoff are presented in many publications dealing with hydrology and will not be discussed here. Data presented by the United States Soil Conservation Service (Anonymous, 1971) and Schwab et al. (1971) are particularly useful for the United States. Obviously, the amount of runoff per hectare per centimeter of rainfall will vary greatly among storms, times, and localities, and average direct runoff data for a region may be misleading when one is interested in runoff affecting a given pond. Nevertheless, average direct runoff data are adequate to illustrate the usual magnitude of runoff. Hewlett and Nutter (1969) reported that the average percentage of the annual precipitation that becomes direct runoff in Georgia ranges from 3% on sandy, rolling soils to 18% on rugged terrain. Runoff data reported by many authorities, e.g., Swingle (1955) and Miller et al. (1963), were calculated by dividing stream discharge by the area of the drainage basin. Since streams receive both direct runoff and ground water seepage — inflow of ground water maintains stream flow during much of the year — runoff values based on stream flow are considerably larger than direct runoff values.

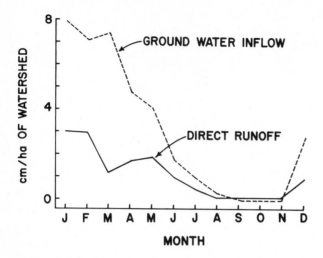

Fig. 10.2. Direct runoff and ground water inflow reaching a pond at Auburn, Alabama (Parsons, 1949).

Assuming that a watershed yields 15% of the rainfall as direct runoff, the volume of direct runoff per hectare resulting from a 5-cm rain is:

5 cm X 0.15 = 0.75 cm runoff
0.75 cm = 0.0075 m, and 1 ha = 10,000 m^2
0.0075 m X 10,000 m^2 = 75 m^3 of direct runoff

Runoff is often expressed in depth of water over a surface. Thus, 1 cm of runoff indicates that each unit of watershed surface yielded a volume of water equal to the area of the unit covered by 1 cm of water. The quantity of direct runoff reaching a pond will depend upon the size and runoff producing characteristics of the watershed.

The amount of direct runoff varies seasonally; Parsons (1949) reported that direct runoff from a watershed in Alabama was greatest in winter and lowest in fall (Fig. 10.2). As will be shown later, the seasonal distribution of runoff may be quite important in pond management.

10.3.3   Stream Inflow

The discharge of streams may be calculated by the equation:

$Q = Av$

where Q = discharge in m^3/sec; A = cross-sectional area in m^2; v = average velocity

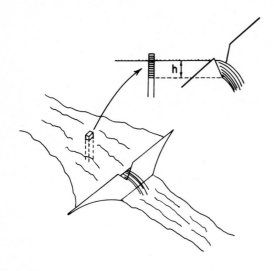

Fig. 10.3. A 90° triangular weir.

in m/sec. A current meter may be used to estimate average velocity; measurements
should be made at several different horizontal and vertical positions within the
cross section. Most streams that flow into ponds are too small to permit measurements of discharge by Equation 10.1. Weirs may be used to measure the discharges
of small streams. A weir is a barrier placed in a stream to constrict the flow
and cause it to fall over a crest (Fig. 10.3). The equation for calculating
the discharge of a 90° triangular weir, such as illustrated in Fig. 10.3, is:

$$Q = 1.37 \ h^{2.5}$$

where Q = discharge in m/sec and h = head in m. If small, the discharge may be
estimated from the time required to fill a container of known volume.

Stream flow varies seasonally as illustrated with data on the runoff per hectare
of drainage basin carried by streams in Alabama (Swingle, 1955):

Month	cm	Month	cm
Jan	8.6	Jul	3.0
Feb	9.7	Aug	2.3
Mar	10.7	Sep	1.5
Apr	7.4	Oct	1.0
May	4.1	Nov	3.6
Jun	2.5	Dec	4.6

10.3.4 Ground water inflow

Appreciable amounts of ground water may flow into ponds when the water table is high. Some ponds even have permanent or wet-weather springs discharging into them. Parsons (1949) presented data on ground water inflow for a 0.61-ha pond with a 10.9-ha watershed (Fig. 10.2). Values were greatest in winter, and no ground water inflow occurred during September, October, and November. Few data are available on ground water inflow, so the topic will not be pursued.

10.3.5 Regulated inflow

Water from pipe lines is frequently applied to ponds. Water flow in pipes may also be calculated by Equation 10.1. The cross-sectional area of a pipe is:

$$A = 3.1416 \ r^2$$

where r = the radius of the pipe. Thus, Equation 10.1 may be written as:

$$Q = 3.1416 \ r^2 \ \nu$$

At a constant velocity, discharge increases as the square of the radius. Hence, a 10-cm diameter pipe discharges four times as much water as a 5-cm diameter pipe, if water in both pipes flows at the same velocity. The calculations given below illustrate this point for 5-cm and 10-cm pipes in which water flows at 200 cm/sec:

$$Q \ (5 \ cm) = 3.1416 \ (2.5 \ cm)^2 (200 \ cm/sec)$$
$$Q \ (5 \ cm) = 3,927 \ cm^3/sec$$

$$Q \ (10 \ cm) = 3.1416 \ (5 \ cm)^2 (200 \ cm/sec)$$
$$Q \ (10 \ cm) = 15,708 \ cm^3/sec$$

In practice, it is usually not possible to measure ν. Small discharges from pipes may be estimated from the time required to fill a container of known volume. Larger discharges may be measured with water meters, piezometer tubes, orifice buckets, or from the dimensions of the streams flowing from open pipes (Anonymous, 1962, 1975). Instructions and nomographs for the use of the dimensions method are provided in many manuals and books on hydraulics, water flow in pipes, water wells, and hydrology. A particularly good discussion is provided in the book "Ground Water and Wells" (Anonymous, 1975) which is sold by the Johnson Well Screen Company, Minneapolis, Minnesota.

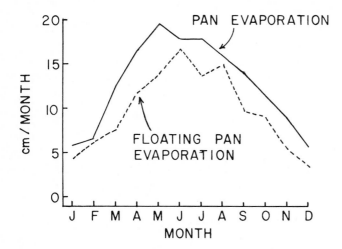

Fig. 10.4. Evaporation from a floating pan and from a pan located over soil at Auburn, Alabama. Both pans were Class A evaporation pans.

10.4   LOSSES OF WATER

10.4.1   Evaporation

Evaporation occurs at all air-water surfaces when the vapor pressure of the air is less than its saturation vapor pressure. Although a number of factors influence evaporation, the most important factors are temperature of air and water, relative humidity of the air, and wind velocity. In general, evaporation rates increase in warm months and decrease in cool months (Fig. 10.4).

Although the physics of evaporation is well understood, it is virtually impossible to obtain highly accurate estimates of evaporation from land or water surfaces. Equations based on energy relationships in evaporation (Satterlund, 1972) may be used to estimate potential evaporation. However, evaporation is often taken as the daily decrease in the depth of water in a metal pan. Class A evaporation pans are usually 121 cm in diameter and 22.5 cm deep; they are filled within 5.1 cm of the rim. Pans are mounted on an open wooden platform so that the pan base is 5-10 cm above the ground (Hounam, 1973). Changes in water depth may be accurately measured with a hook gauge. Annual evaporation from Class A pans varies greatly with climate: 49 cm/year at Minneapolis, Minnesota (Manson et al., 1968), 152 cm/year at Auburn, Alabama (Anonymous, 1968), and over 250 cm/year in some areas of the southwestern United States (Miller et al., 1963).

Water in a shallow, exposed pan heats more rapidly than water in a lake or pond, and evaporation from a pan usually exceeds evaporation from a lake or pond. For practical purposes, Hounam (1973) suggested using the following equation to convert pan evaporation to lake evaporation.

Lake evaporation = pan evaporation X 0.7

In the same locality, the temperature of water in a floating pan more nearly ap-
proaches the temperature of a lake surface than does the temperature of water in
a pan located over ground. Thus, floating pan evaporation should be a better
estimate of lake evaporation. However, Hounam (1973) pointed out that floating
pan evaporation is often unreliable because of inward and outward splashing of
water. In fish ponds, wave action is usually not as great as in lakes, and floating pans should be useful. Parsons (1949) encountered no difficulty in measuring
evaporation from a floating pan in a 0.57-ha pond; his findings are summarized
in Fig. 10.4. Studies are needed to correlate floating pan evaporation for ponds
with actual pond evaporation.

Ponds with dense phytoplankton blooms have higher surface water temperatures
than ponds with clear water. Idso and Foster (1974) reported an afternoon surface
water temperature of 31°C at the inception of a phytoplankton bloom, and a surface
water temperature of 35°C at the peak of the bloom. The higher surface water
temperature caused a 25% increase in the air to water vapor pressure difference
and probably had a significant influence on evaporation.

Aquatic macrophytes growing in ponds and trees and shrubs growing around the
edges of ponds may transpire considerable amounts of water. Evapotranspiration
rates per unit area by dense stands of aquatic plants may be 2-4 times greater
evaporation from a free water surface (Mitchell, 1974).

10.4.2   Seepage

Water may seep through the pond bottom or through the dam. It is difficult to
measure seepage directly, but it can be estimated from the following equation:

$$S = P + R - \Delta H - ET$$

where S = net seepage; P = precipitation; R = runoff; ΔH = change in storage;
ET = evapotranspiration. Using this method, Allred et al. (1971) found that the
seepage loss for 50 small bodies of water in Minnesota averaged 0.10 cm/day; the
maximum value was 0.15 cm/day. Parsons (1949) determined that the annual seepage
— primarily through the dam — from a pond near Auburn, Alabama, was 243 cm for one
year (0.67 cm/day). Parsons (unpublished) also measured seepage for 12 other
ponds on porous, Piedmont soils; rates ranged from 0.33 to 3.35 cm/day with an
average of 1.14 cm/day. Ponds with seepage rates above 0.50 cm/day were located
well up slope on watersheds and were relatively far above the water table. Ponds
on less porous soils of the Alabama Black Belt Prairie had seepage rates of 0.043-
0.46 cm/day; average = 0.16 cm/day. Parsons noted that, in general, larger ponds
had greater seepage rates than smaller ponds.

TABLE 10.1

Water requirements for farm uses (Schwab et al., 1971).

Use	liters/day	ha·m/season
Household (per person)	200-400	
Steer (per 500 kg)	35- 70	
Milk cow (per 500 kg; including barn sanitation)	70-150	
Horse (per 500 kg)	30- 45	
Turkeys (per 100 head)	40- 60	
Chickens (per 100 head)	20- 35	
Swine (per 50 kg)	4- 6	
Sheep (per 50 kg)	4- 6	
Irrigation (per hectare)		0.3-1.5

10.4.3   Outflow

Outflow may occur by spillway discharge or regulated drawdown through a valve or gate. Spillway discharge obviously depends upon the rate at which water is delivered in excess of storage:

Outflow = Inflow ± ΔStorage

This term is extremely variable for different ponds and hydrological conditions. Embankment ponds without permanent inflow often have large amounts of spillway discharge during rainy months and none during dry months. Regulated discharge is released according to the desires of the pond manager and will not be discussed.

10.4.4   Consumptive use

Ponds located on farms are often used for purposes in addition to fish production. Water requirements for various farm uses are given in Table 10.1.

10.5   APPLICATION OF HYDROLOGIC DATA

10.5.1   Water budgets of embankment ponds

Suppose that an embankment pond is built in the Piedmont area of Alabama. The pond has an area of 1 ha, an average depth of 1.5 m, and a watershed area of 10 ha. Reference to Figs. 10.1, 10.2, and 10.4, gives rainfall, direct runoff, ground water inflow, and floating pan evaporation. These data represent average conditions for specific localities, but for lack of better estimates, they will be used in the computations of water balance. To facilitate the solution of this

TABLE 10.2

Monthly values for precipitation, floating pan evaporation, direct runoff, and ground water inflow used in solving problems in the text.

Month	Precipitation[a] (cm)	Floating pan evaporation[b] (cm)	Direct runoff[c] (cm)	Ground water inflow (cm)
Jan	11.9	4.2	3.0	7.9
Feb	14.0	6.4	2.9	7.1
Mar	14.7	7.7	1.2	7.4
Apr	11.7	11.8	1.7	4.8
May	9.4	13.7	1.9	4.1
Jun	10.2	16.8	1.0	1.8
Jul	13.5	13.8	0.5	1.0
Aug	11.7	15.0	0.05	0.3
Sep	8.1	9.7	0.03	0
Oct	7.1	9.1	0.03	0
Nov	7.9	5.7	0.03	0
Dec	13.7	3.6	1.0	2.8

[a] 40 year average at Auburn, Alabama (Swingle, 1955).

[b] Auburn, Alabama (Parsons, 1949).

[c] For watershed with 6% average slope, sandy soils, and cover of horticultural crops and shrubs (Parsons, 1949). These values are for 1 ha of watershed; to change to depth of water in the pond receiving the runoff, the value must be adjusted for area of watershed and pond.

and the following problems, the data are given in tubular form (Table 10.2). The seepage loss for the hypothetical pond in the following problem will be taken as 0.5 cm/day. There will be no consumptive use or regulated inflow or outflow. The pond is deepened to 75 cm or more around edges, and it will yield spillway discharge anytime its volume exceeds 15,000 m^3. Assuming the pond is full and water is just trickling out the spillway on 30 June, water volumes at the last day of each month and monthly spillway discharges were calculated for 1 year (Fig. 10.5). Calculations were made as illustrated below:

ΔVolume = Rainfall + Direct runoff + Ground water inflow - Seepage - Evaporation

ΔVolume (July) = (13.5 cm)(1 ha) + (0.5 cm)(10 ha) + (1.0 cm)(10 ha) - (0.5 cm/day) (1 ha)(31 days) - (7.7 cm)(1 ha)

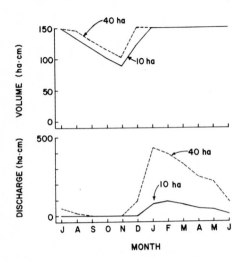

Fig. 10.5. Pond volume and monthly spillway discharge for two, 1-ha ponds with average depths of 1.5 m. One pond has a 10-ha watershed; the other has a 40-ha watershed.

ΔVolume (July) = - 0.8 ha·cm

ΔVolume (March) = (14.7 cm)(1 ha) + (1.2 cm)(10 ha) + (7.4 cm)(10 ha) - (0.5 cm/day)
    (1 ha)(31 days) - (7.7 cm)(1 ha)

ΔVolume (March) = 77.5 ha·cm

Pond volume declines during months with negative Δvolume values, and spillway discharge occurs if the Δvolume plus the volume at the beginning of the respective month exceeds 150 ha·cm.

During winter and spring, direct runoff and ground water inflow are appreciable and spillway discharge occurs. Pond volume decreases during summer and fall because of decreased inflow.

If another pond similar to the one described above has a 40-ha watershed instead of a 10-ha watershed, spillway discharge will be greater during winter and spring (Fig. 10.5). Likewise, pond volume will not decrease as much in summer and fall because of greater direct runoff from the larger watershed.

The annual loss of water through the spillway of the pond with a 40-ha watershed will be about 13 times the pond volume. Thus, applications of agricultural limestone would not be effective in increasing alkalinity and hardness because of rapid water exchange. Fertilizer nutrients applied to the pond in the spring would be lost in outflow before they could stimulate plankton growth. However, fertilization could be initiated in early June after spillway discharge has diminished. Clearly, the ratio of pond volume to watershed area is smaller than desirable for a sportfish pond.

Embankment ponds on highly porous soils may have drastic decreases in water levels during dry seasons. For example, consider a 1-ha pond with a 10-ha water-shed that has a seepage rate of 1.2 cm/day. Even if the pond was full of water on 30 June, it would lose water rapidly during the summer and fall:

Month	ΔVolume (ha·cm)
Jul	- 22.5
Aug	- 37.0
Sep	- 37.3
Oct	- 38.9
Nov	- 33.5
Total	-169.2

This loss in volume corresponds to a depth of 1.69 m for a 1-ha pond.

A 10-ha embankment pond without any natural inflow, other than rain, is con-structed on relatively impervious soil (seepage = 0.03 cm/day) in Alabama. The pond is filled with well water in the winter. How much regulated inflow will be required each month to keep the pond filled to the top of its drain pipe? The following equation is appropriate:

Required inflow = Seepage + Evaporation - Rainfall

Month	Required inflow ha·cm	m^3/min
Mar	0.0	0.0
Apr	10.0	0.023
May	52.3	0.12
Jun	75.0	0.18
Jul	12.3	0.028
Aug	42.3	0.095
Sep	25.0	0.058
Oct	29.3	0.066
Nov	0.0	0.0

10.5.2   Water budget of an excavated pond

A well that discharges 0.038 m^3/min is to be used to fill an excavated pond in Alabama. The pond is to be dug into relatively tight clay where seepage will be 0.05 cm/day. There will be no surface runoff or ground water inflow. How

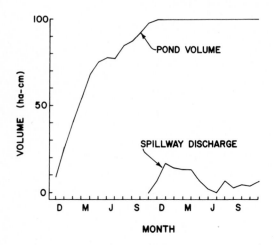

Fig. 10.6. Pond volume and monthly spillway discharge from a 2-ha excavated pond that receives 0.038 m³/min of inflow from a well. The pond is 1-m deep and has no watershed.

large could the pond be if it is to be kept at a constant depth of 1 m? Water in excess of that needed for 1 m of depth will overflow. To solve this problem, determine the month that gives a maximum value for the equation:

Seepage + Evaporation - Rainfall = ΔVolume

This month is June, for which ΔVolume = 8.1 cm (8.1 ha·cm or 810 m³). The well discharge for June is 0.038 m³/min X 1,440 min/day X 30 days = 1,642 m³. The desired area is 1,642 m³ ÷ 810 m³/ha = 2.03 ha, or for simplicity 2.0 ha. Assuming that the pond is completed on 31 October, projected depths and overflow volumes are given in Fig. 10.6.

10.5.3   Water budgets for channel catfish ponds

In the southeastern United States, channel catfish are often produced in embankment ponds without watersheds or ground water inflow. These ponds are either drained annually for fish harvest or fish are removed by seining without water drawdown. Obviously, water is conserved by removing fish without drawdown, but calculations will be for ponds that are drained annually. Assuming that ponds average 152 cm in depth and seep an average of 0.16 cm/day, I will use rainfall and evaporation data from Table 10.2 to estimate, on a hectare basis, the amount of well water needed to fill ponds during December, January, and February:

Pond depth - Available water = Well water required

Available water = Precipitation - Evaporation - Seepage

Month	Available water (cm)
Dec	5.14
Jan	2.74
Feb	2.64
Total	10.52

152 cm - 10.5 cm = 141.5 cm of well water required

This amounts to 1.42 ha·m or 14,200 m^3 of water. During the 90-day period, water would have to be introduced at 110 l/min per hectare to fill ponds. If ponds are full to the drain, the surplus precipitation in March will be lost as overflow. To maintain the water level in the ponds from 1 April until 31 October will require 52.6 cm of water, because there is a deficiency of available water during this period:

Month	Available water (cm)
Mar	2.04
Apr	- 4.9
May	- 9.26
Jun	- 11.4
Jul	- 5.26
Aug	- 8.26
Sep	- 6.56
Oct	- 6.96

The total requirement for water per hectare to initially fill ponds and to replace seepage and evaporation losses is 194.1 cm or 1.94 ha·m (19,400 m^3).

Ponds for commercial culture of channel catfish are often 4-10 ha and contain 6-12 ha·m. Approximately 1,100 l/min would be the minimum discharge needed to fill a 10-ha pond in 90 days. Thus, a 250-ha catfish farm would need enough wells to supply at least 27,500 l/min (27.5 m^3/min) in order to fill ponds during December, January, and February. Less water would be used to maintain water levels during the growing season. The average inflow to maintain water level during the period 1 April-31 October would be 17 l/min per ha, 170 l/min for 10 ha, and 4,250 l/min for 250 ha.

Although fish may be harvested by seining without draining ponds, fish farmers may find it necessary to drain ponds on a particular year. Thus, enough water must be available to quickly refill ponds or a year of production might be lost.

Many fish farmers flush well water through ponds in efforts to improve water quality. Water requirements calculated as above should be considered a minimum, whether ponds are drained for harvest or not. In fact, a water supply 1.5-2 times greater than the minimum would allow ponds to be filled more rapidly and provide a margin of safety for droughts.

Channel catfish farming is a water-intensive endeavor. Irrigation in the southeastern United States usually requires 0.30-0.45 ha·m of water per hectare of land (Schwab et al., 1971); catfish farming requires 4-6 times as much water. Assuming an annual production of 3,000 kg/ha, each kilogram of channel catfish produced requires about 6,470 l of water. In contrast, 42 l are needed for 1 kg of beef, and 54 l are required for 1 kg of pork (Schwab et al., 1971). Much of the water used in catfish farming is well water, so the impact of catfish farming on ground water — and vice versa — deserves more attention than it has received.

10.5.4 Water exchange to improve water quality

Fish farmers frequently drain water from near the bottoms of ponds and replace it with well water in efforts to improve water quality. This practice is thought to have two effects: supply oxygen-enriched water to ponds with low dissolved oxygen concentrations and flush water laden with nutrients and organic matter from ponds. Unfortunately, the effectiveness of water exchange in improving water quality has not been verified through research.

Water exchange is no doubt effective in improving water quality in small ponds. For example, suppose that 20 l/min are available to flush through a 0.1-ha pond with a depth of 1 m. If 20 l/min are supplied to the pond from 1 April through 31 October (214 days), the total inflow is 6,163 m^3. During this period, seepage and evaporation for the 0.1-ha pond would exceed precipitation by 52.6 cm or by 526 m^3. The preceding calculation is based on an average seepage rate of 0.16 cm/day and evaporation and precipitation data from Table 10.2. Hence, 5,637 m^3 (6,163 m^3 - 526 m^3) would serve to flush the pond. The pond has a volume of 1,000 m^3, so its volume would be exchanged 5.64 times (5,637 m^3 ÷ 1,000 m^3). Such a high water exchange rate would greatly improve water quality. However, for larger ponds exchange rates are usually smaller. Suppose that a 10-ha pond with an average depth of 1 m receives 500 l/min from 1 April through 31 October. The total inflow is 154,000 m^3; seepage plus evaporation will exceed precipitation by 5,600 m^3; 148,480 m^3 will be flushed through the pond. The pond contains 100,000 m^3, so its volume will be exchanged only 1.48 times.

In practice, well water is usually introduced into a pond when water quality problems arise. This technique will obviously not have an immediate effect on water quality. An inflow of 4,000 l/min in August would only exchange about 4 or 5% (value would vary with seepage and evaporation) of the total volume per day in a 10-ha pond of 1 m average depth.

Assuming that evaporation plus seepage equals 0.5 cm/day, the discharge rates necessary to exchange 1 ha·m (10,000 m^3) of pond water in different lengths of time are:

Days	Discharge (m^3/min)
1	6.78
2	3.51
5	1.42
10	0.73
15	0.50
20	0.38
30	0.27

Few wells discharge more than 8 m^3/min, and most discharge considerably less. Thus, the benefits of regulated inflow on water quality are often overestimated for large ponds. It is interesting to note that 1 cm of rain falling on 1 ha = 1 ha·cm = 100 m^3 or the equivalent of 0.069 m^3/min for 1 day.

Well water normally contains no dissolved oxygen, but it can be aerated by gravity flow over cascade aerators. The benefit of aeration by inflowing water also varies with pond size and inflow rate (see Chapter 7).

REFERENCES

Allred, E. R., Manson, P. W., Schwartz, G. M., Golany, P., and Reinke, J. W., 1971. Hydrology of ponds and small lakes. University of Minnesota Agricultural Experiment Station, Minneapolis, Minnesota, 62. pp.

Anonymous, 1962. Measurement of irrigation water. In: U. S. Soil Conservation Service National Engineering Handbook, Section 15. U. S. Soil Conservation Service, Washington, D. C., 72 pp.

Anonymous, 1968. Auburn University 1967 local climatological data. Auburn University Agricultural Experiment Station, Auburn, Alabama, 46 pp.

Anonymous, 1971. Ponds for water supply and recreation. U. S. Soil Conservation Service, Washington, D. C., Agricultural Handbook No. 387, 55 pp.

Anonymous, 1975. Ground Water and Wells. Johnson Division, VOP, Inc., Saint Paul, Minnesota, 440 pp.

Hewlett, J. D. and Nutter, W. L., 1969. An Outline of Forest Hydrology. University of Georgia Press, Athens, Georgia, 137 pp.

Houman, C. E., 1973. Comparison between pan and lake evaporation. World Meteorological Organization, Geneva, Switzerland, 52 pp.

Idso, S. B. and Foster, J. M., 1974. Light and temperature relations in a small desert pond as influenced by phytoplanktonic density variations. Water Resources Res., 10: 129-132.

Manson, P. W., Schwartz, G. M., and Allred, E. R., 1968. Some aspects of the hydrology of ponds and small lakes. University of Minnesota Agricultural Experiment Station, Minneapolis, Minnesota, 88 pp.

Miller, D. H., 1977. Water at the Surface of the Earth. Academic Press, New York, 557 pp.

Miller, D. W., Geraghty, J. J., and Collins, R. S., 1963. Water Atlas of the

United States. Water Information Center, Inc., Port Washington, New York, 81 pp.

Mitchell, D. S., 1974. The effects of excessive aquatic plant populations. In: D. S. Mitchell (Editor), Aquatic Vegetation and Its Use and Control. Unesco, Paris, pp. 50-56.

Parsons, D. A., 1949. The hydrology of a small area near Auburn, Alabama. U. S. Soil Conservation Service, Washington, D. C., 40 pp.

Satterlund, D. R., 1972. Wildland Watershed Management. Roland Press, New York, 370 pp.

Schwab, G. O., Frevert, R. K., Barnes, K. K., and Edminster, T. W., 1971. Elementary Soil and Water Engineering. John Wiley and Sons, New York, 316 pp.

Swingle, H. S., 1955. Storing water for use in irrigation. In: Proc. Water Resources and Suppl. Irrigation Workshop. Alabama Polytechnic Institute Agricultural Experiment Station, Auburn, Alabama, pp. 1-6.

Swingle, H. S. and Smith, E. V., 1939. Fish production in terrace-water ponds in Alabama. Trans. Amer. Fish. Soc., 69: 101-105.

306

310